AGATHA CHRISTIE'S GOLDEN AGE

AN ANALYSIS OF
POIROT'S GOLDEN AGE PUZZLES

JOHN GODDARD

With an Introduction by Dr John Curran

STYLISH EYE PRESS
23 Parkside Gardens
London SW19 5EU

www.stylisheyepress.com

First published 2018
Second impression 2018

Hardback ISBN - 978-1-9996120-0-9
Paperback ISBN - 978-1-9996120-1-6
mobi ISBN - 978-1-9996120-2-3
epub ISBN - 978-1-9996120-3-0

Printed and bound in the United Kingdom by
www.spiffingcovers.com

Typeset in Minion Pro 12pt

Cover design and layout by www.spiffingcovers.com

To my wife Linda
for her wise counsel and support

ACKNOWLEDGEMENTS

This is not an 'official' Agatha Christie publication in the sense of one sponsored by her estate but an independent project on which I have been working since 2005. Although I have worked on it very largely on my own, some people have provided important support to me for which I am very grateful.

Dawn Hudson and Christopher Blain, both from the law firm Freshfields Bruckhaus Deringer, for whom I worked for over 25 years, did invaluable jobs in relation to, respectively, the initial typing of the manuscript and legal research for the commentaries.

My old school friend, the biographer Peter Parker, and my old Cambridge friend, Ben Staveley, gave me helpful insights into the world of writing and publishing; and Peter Wienand and Owen O'Rorke of Farrer & Co provided expert advice on publishing law.

Liz Bourne did a thorough job of editing and I was greatly assisted by the self-publishing company Spiffing Covers, especially James Willis, its Creative Director, and his colleague Richard Chalkley, who have been enthusiastic, inventive and reassuring advisers in relation to all aspects of publication including the creation of the book's very stylish cover design.

But, most of all, I am particularly grateful to the leading Agatha Christie expert, Dr John Curran, author of *Agatha Christie's Secret Notebooks* and *Agatha Christie's Murder in the Making*. When I first contacted John about my book in July 2017, he seemed genuinely interested in it because no such analysis had been published before. He was therefore happy for me to go over to Dublin and spend two days with him discussing the whole book in detail. He made a large number of helpful suggestions, both on the introductory sections and the commentaries, particularly stressing the need for examples in the former and for reducing the length of the latter. The book is better for his advice and I much appreciated having the opportunity to discuss it with him at such length.

John Goddard   Wimbledon, May 2018

CONTENTS

INTRODUCTION

In the 42 years since the death of Agatha Christie every aspect of her existence has come under scrutiny, resulting in book-length studies of her life, her disappearance, her travels, her archaeological work, her Notebooks, her homes, her novels and short stories, her poisons, her contribution to theatre and screen; there have been biographies of Poirot and Miss Marple, quiz and crossword books, travel guides, studies of her jacket designs, recipes culled from her work, guides for book-collectors. In fact, every conceivable angle; or so I thought…

But when, in July 2017, I received an email from John Goddard describing his approach to a study of the Queen of Crime, I was convinced that he had found a new angle – and so it proved.

Agatha Christie's Golden Age analyses, in forensic detail, the puzzle element of the Poirot novels between the little Belgian's first investigation, *The Mysterious Affair at Styles*, and *Five Little Pigs*. It is, after all, the ingenious puzzles which Agatha Christie devised over her half-century of creativity that set her apart from all other detective novelists. She teased and tantalised generations of readers – and continues to do so – and they were happy to acknowledge her superiority.

John's structure for analysing these puzzles by reference to the three criteria of Solution, Plot and Clues is cogently argued and highly original, showing how well – or, sometimes, otherwise! – the plots are structured. This approach also provides an accessible way for readers – not just Christie scholars but her general readership – to understand how the novels work as puzzles. And you will never look on the clue of, for example, the 'buckled shoes' (*One, Two, Buckle My Shoe*) and the 'wiped bottle' (*Five Little Pigs*) in the same way again.

I am delighted to write this Introduction to an innovative and thought-provoking examination of the work of Agatha Christie.

Dr John Curran   Dublin, May 2018

PREFACE

This book makes two assumptions. The first is that Agatha Christie, who is the best-selling novelist of all time, is still as popular as ever. This is supported partly by the enormous continuing attraction of her books and plays and partly by the adaptation of her work for television and film.[1] But it is also evidenced, perhaps more clearly than ever nowadays, by the websites to which her fans flock in order to express their opinions, to list their favourite novels or to participate in threads about why one book is better than another. There seems to be a tireless interest in the author's works.

The second assumption is that, since she is renowned above all for the brilliance of her puzzles, her numerous fans will welcome the idea of looking again at her novels from the perspective of how well the puzzles work.

That then is the purpose of this book: to produce analytical commentaries assessing the quality of the puzzle elements in certain of Agatha Christie's novels.

This is a largely unexplored field because, although there have been various books about Agatha Christie's life and works, none purports to attempt a comprehensive analysis of the three puzzle elements of Solution, Plot and Clues, which are clearly explained in The Puzzle Element chapter.[2] This book aims to remedy that omission, albeit conservatively at this stage with the Poirot Golden Age novels.

In assessing the novels against those three elements, the commentaries do not simply recite the explanations given by Poirot at the end of each novel. Rather, they reconstruct the murder plans and assess the validity of the clues in a more organised and complete way than happens during the stories where, for dramatic reasons, the author fits different pieces of the jigsaw together at different points in the novel or where Poirot, in his interpretation of them, is sometimes not as clear as he might be.

This carefully organised approach, supplemented by numerous previously unmade points about the puzzle elements in the stories, is intended to enhance understanding and appreciation of the puzzles and to give readers the chance to enjoy again, at a readable length, the intrigue or cosiness of a favourite novel from a new perspective. Indeed, I hope that they will be enthused to re-read that novel as well as other Agatha Christie detective stories.

As for my credentials for writing this book, I have, first and foremost, been a committed Agatha Christie fan since 1967 when I started reading her books at the age of 11, probably having been attracted by Tom Adams' brilliant paperback covers. I still have my Odhams Books Certificate of Membership of the Agatha Christie Crime Collection from 1969. Since then I have read all her books many times and, because I was fascinated from the outset by the forensic analysis and assessment of clues that her puzzles required, my approach was always that of an actively detecting reader.

Secondly, I have also read whatever books I could find commenting on her novels. One of the first was Professor Robert Barnard's *A Talent to Deceive*, which includes an Annotated List with a brief commentary (usually about 50–100 words) on each of the author's detective works. His comment about *The Man in the Brown Suit* included "the plot would probably not bear close examination, if anyone were to take the trouble". I remember treating that as a sort of challenge and deciding to "take the trouble" by writing an analysis of the plot.

As I did so, it occurred to me that plot analysis could be applied to her other novels but that a carefully constructed and consistent approach would be needed. In trying to identify such an approach, I read what I could find on the subject. I was left in no doubt that the puzzle element is at the heart of detective fiction. But I also realised that, although there was guidance on what should or should not be in a detective story, no one seemed to have established and defined the elements that make a detective story work successfully as a puzzle.

My reading also revealed that some writers would assert that certain of Agatha Christie's novels were in, or not in, their 'top ten' (or some similar category). But none of those writers would list all the other novels falling within their top ten. Of course, I could tell from the generalised language they used – for example, that a novel had a "brilliant solution" or was "superbly plotted" or "magnificently clued" – which novels were probably in their top five or top 20 but not where they drew the line at number ten. Indeed, I often got the impression that about 15 novels fell within their top ten.

This reinforced my view that a more disciplined, precise and objective approach was needed for assessing the novels, not for the purpose of producing a definitive top ten or 20, but in order to enhance reader understanding and appreciation of the strengths and weaknesses of the novels as puzzles. Although no such approach appeared to exist in any of the books I had read, my reading had helped me to identify the puzzle elements of Solution, Plot and Clues. Having done that, I then had to read the novels again many more times from an even more analytical perspective.

My final credential is that, although I am not a qualified academic in English Literature, my degree from Cambridge University was in Law, following which I spent a legal career of over 25 years as a litigation lawyer in a large City of London law firm carrying out many similar analytical exercises to those which

I have carried out in undertaking this project. As a litigator in such a firm, one is constantly using forensic skills: analysing complex series of facts and voluminous documents in a disciplined, inquisitive and detailed manner; extracting the key information from them whilst identifying and trying to resolve gaps, problems and inconsistencies; and then presenting the results in a clear, coherent and organised way. Essentially this is precisely my approach in producing these analytical commentaries.

I was also helped, as I re-read and analysed the novels, by comments made in the books listed in the Bibliography; my thanks are due to the authors of all of them. However, my commentaries, based on my longstanding enthusiasm for the novels and my professional analytical experience, are ultimately my own work and I take responsibility for any mistakes and omissions.

Finally, a word about revealing the names of the murderers. It used to be the case that books on the author's work made a virtue out of not revealing the names of murderers for fear of spoiling the reader's enjoyment of novels as yet unread. This practice was largely replaced in later books by the adoption of an apologetic tone for revealing murderers' names, justified on the ground that the book would not serve its purpose unless they were divulged. We have for some time been at the stage where murderers are freely identified on that ground but without an apology. This is unsurprising today when many murderers will be known to members of the public because of film and television dramatisations. In my commentaries, the criminals are always named because otherwise it would not be feasible to analyse the puzzles properly.

CHAPTER 1

Agatha Christie's Crime Novels

This book analyses Hercule Poirot's 21 Golden Age novels. However, since Agatha Christie wrote 66 crime novels altogether, readers may appreciate an overview of those novels.

Historical Perspective

The history of her crime novels has been well traversed, to very much the same effect, by other commentators. So a short summary should suffice. She made her debut (aged 30) in 1920 with *The Mysterious Affair at Styles*, which introduced Hercule Poirot. For about the next decade, she divided her novels between detective stories and thrillers. It was during that period that in 1926 she produced her first masterpiece, a detective novel, *The Murder of Roger Ackroyd*, which, as we shall see in the next chapter, was controversial because of its solution.

In 1930 she produced the first Miss Marple novel, *The Murder at the Vicarage*, but a dozen years were to pass before publication of the next Miss Marple novel, *The Body in the Library*, in 1942. Instead her principal focus was on Poirot and, in a largely glorious golden decade in the 1930s, she produced some very fine Poirot novels with particularly ingenious solutions or murder plans – *Peril at End House, Lord Edgware Dies, Murder on the Orient Express, The ABC Murders, Death on the Nile* and *Hercule Poirot's Christmas*. At the end of the decade she also produced her second masterpiece, *And Then there were None*, in which neither Poirot nor Miss Marple appears.

At the start of the 1940s she continued to produce high-quality Poirot novels – *One, Two, Buckle My Shoe, Evil under the Sun* and *Five Little Pigs*. During that period she also wrote, but held in reserve, what was to become Poirot's final novel, *Curtain*, published in 1975. During the 1940s she also wrote some other fine detective novels. In addition to Miss Marple's *The Body in the Library*, two such novels were *Towards Zero* and *Crooked House*, in which neither Poirot nor Miss Marple is the detective. But there was also greater inconsistency in quality than in the previous decade, with novels such as *Sparkling Cyanide* and *The Hollow*.

1950 saw the publication of a Miss Marple novel, *A Murder is Announced*, the first two-thirds of which Professor Barnard (chapter 7) regards as "as good as Agatha Christie ever wrote". But he regards the last 50 pages as "a damaging collapse into something approaching absurdity"; for him that collapse is "symbolic", with the book seeming to mark the end of Christie's classic period. There was then a slow decline in the 1950s which, with exceptions (most notably *Endless Night* in 1967), continued generally downwards until 1973 with the novels having less ingenuity and being less tightly plotted.[1] Her final published novels were *Curtain* and *Sleeping Murder*, the latter being a Miss Marple novel which, like *Curtain*, was written many years before but also held in reserve. It was published in 1976, the year of her death.

Hercule Poirot

Hercule Poirot appears in precisely half (33) of Agatha Christie's crime novels. He had been one of the most celebrated members of the Belgian police but in his opening novel he is retired and living as a First World War refugee in the English village of Styles St Mary. There he is asked to investigate the murder of Emily Inglethorp by an old friend, Hastings, who narrates the story of that investigation, *The Mysterious Affair at Styles*, as well as seven later novels. Poirot's first words in detective fiction are "*Mon ami* Hastings!".

Poirot's career as a professional but unofficial sleuth then continues for 55 years until *Curtain*, in which his last words, "*Cher ami!*", are also to Hastings. During that career he becomes the most famous fictional detective of his time. So, how does he do this? What are his methods? Although he becomes somewhat intuitional in his later cases, sensing clues in the way that Miss Marple does, the vast majority of his career is spent arranging facts and clues with 'order and method' and producing a logical solution by applying his 'little grey cells'.

He starts with the facts he is given. Then, in cases where an inspection of the murder scene is appropriate, he conducts a careful examination. Despite scoffing at physical detection (and claiming to rely rather on logic and psychology), he does examine clues minutely in his first three novels, going down on his knees to smell a stain in *The Mysterious Affair at Styles*, looking under the mats in *The Murder on the Links* and crawling about in the summer house in *The Murder of Roger Ackroyd*. On a later occasion he even recreates the main clue in *Murder on the Orient Express*, which is in the form of a charred fragment of paper, by placing it between two flattened humps of wire and then holding the humps together with some curling tongs over the flame of a spirit lamp, so as to make the words on the fragment appear.

He says in later Golden Age novels that "The Hercule Poirots, my friend, need only to sit back in a chair and think" (*Dumb Witness*) and, very similarly, "It is enough for me to sit back in my chair and *think*" (*Five Little Pigs*). But the fact is that in the first of those he is immediately challenged by Hastings, who wants to know why they are therefore walking along an exceedingly hot street on an exceedingly hot morning, and in the second he helps

Meredith Blake row a boat from Handcross Manor to Alderbury (and back) and he visits his laboratory.

Poirot's next stage in gathering evidence is to question the suspects – sometimes in a pleasantly disarming manner, sometimes threateningly – knowing that they are bound to speak the truth at some point because that is easier than telling lies. He believes that "no one, in the course of conversation, can fail to give themselves away sooner or later" (*Death in the Clouds*) and that "there is nothing so dangerous *for anyone who has something to hide* as conversation!" (*The ABC Murders*). The result is that suspects react by providing more evidence – changing their stories, contradicting one another – and that more clues come to light. Sometimes there are even consequential murders which are committed in haste without the same ingenious planning as the original crimes (*Lord Edgware Dies*; *Death on the Nile*).

Having gathered the facts and then used order and method to arrange them with neatness and precision, he considers the psychology of the crime by reference to the murder method, the victim and the other people involved in the case. "It is not the mere act of killing, it is what lies behind it that appeals to the expert" (*Lord Edgware Dies*) and, more specifically, he goes on to say about murderer and victim, for example, "*When I know what the murderer is like, I shall be able to find out who he is*" (*The ABC Murders*) and that "*Because* the victim was the kind of person he or she was, *therefore* was he or she murdered!" (*Evil under the Sun*).

After he has assessed the likely personality of the murderer, the character of the victim and the true relationship between the two, suspects are gradually eliminated from suspicion. However, where the solution is still unclear, or where his solution now looks to be in doubt, he can berate himself mercilessly for his stupidity.

But then, by applying his little grey cells to the final pieces of the puzzle, rejecting the false clues and interpreting the real ones, and dismissing solutions which do not fit all the facts, he identifies the only solution which explains every clue. He says in *Evil under the Sun* that "every strange-shaped little piece must be fitted into its own place." If it does not, then that solution cannot be the correct one: "If the fact will not fit the theory – let the theory go" (*The Mysterious Affair at Styles*).

However, when every fact does fit and he is certain who the murderer is, he can still avoid communicating his thinking clearly to colleagues or readers. Indeed, any hints which he gives usually mystify, rather than clarify, like his comment in *Lord Edgware Dies* that "*The page had to be torn*" or his comment in *The ABC Murders* that Hastings has "a genius for stating the obvious" while managing not to say what his 'obvious' statement is.

It is not usually until the denouement that Poirot identifies the murderer. On such occasions he may accuse a number of the assembled suspects in turn before identifying the murderer and from time to time he lays a trap (*The Murder on the Links*; *Cards on the Table*) when the clues support but do not actually prove his solution.

Sometimes, admittedly, his solutions can include elements that are based on guesswork (*The Mysterious Affair at Styles* and *Murder on the Orient Express*) or a feeling (*Three Act Tragedy*) or assumptions (*Dumb Witness*) or intelligent supposition (*Appointment with Death*). But, generally speaking, his solutions are very soundly based on a careful and logical, sometimes brilliant, analysis of the clues with which he is presented.

Occasionally, that analysis is prompted by his obsession with neatness and symmetry. In *The ABC Murders*, Hastings accuses him of choosing to live in a particular building entirely on account of its strictly geometrical appearance and proportions. In *The Mysterious Affair at Styles*, Hastings suggests that a speck of dust would cause Poirot more pain than a bullet wound. In that story Poirot straightens a vase on the mantelpiece on two separate occasions; he suddenly realises that, since he had straightened the vase on one occasion, he would not have needed to do so on the second unless in the meantime someone had moved it; so he looks inside it and the key document is there, torn into strips. And as for his mystifying comment about the page that 'had to be torn' in *Lord Edgware Dies*, he makes what appears to be the key deduction from the torn page but he can't leave it at that because he can't understand why someone would tear a page instead of cutting it neatly; and his perseverance pays off because hc then makes an unexpected second and even cleverer deduction from the torn page.

Poirot's obsession with neatness and symmetry is not the only characteristic that helps him. He seems to go out of his way to look rather ridiculous, except when being very serious at the denouement, in order to be underestimated by murderers and suspects. He does this in various ways.

One way is with his appearance. He is a plump little man who is inordinately proud of his luxuriant moustaches and who overdresses with great sartorial elegance. As Hastings writes in *The ABC Murders* "It was an unfortunate circumstance that the first time people saw my friend they were always disposed to consider him a joke of the first water." Amy Leatheran, the narrator in *Murder in Mesopotamia*, writes "When you saw him you just wanted to laugh!" while Meredith Blake in *Five Little Pigs* thinks, "Really a most impossible person – the wrong clothes – button boots! – an incredible moustache!"

A second way is to emphasise that he is a foreigner. When he visits Meredith, "It was no moment for trying to seem English. No, one must be a foreigner – frankly a foreigner – and be magnanimously forgiven for the fact" and in *Peril at End House* Nick Buckley was "afraid that this queer little foreigner was going to be a nuisance." Poirot's most effective foreigner element is his comic use of the English language. He creates the impression that, because he can't speak English properly, he must be foolish. As he himself explains in *Three Act Tragedy*, "to speak the broken English is an enormous asset. It leads people to despise you. They say – a foreigner – he can't even speak English properly."

A third way is boasting. Thus, in *The Mystery of the Blue Train* he says "My name is Hercule Poirot and I am probably the greatest detective in the world" and in *The ABC Murders* he says "I am better than the police." He explains the purpose of boasting in *Three Act Tragedy*, straight after his remarks about speaking broken English: "Also I boast! An Englishman he says often 'A fellow who thinks as much of himself as that cannot be worth much'. That is the English point of view. It is not at all true. And so, you see, I put people off their guard."

The effect of putting people off their guard in these ways is reflected in thoughts by, for example, Jane Wilkinson, the murderer in *Lord Edgware Dies*, "I never thought you'd be so horribly clever. You don't look clever"; and Mary Debenham, one of the murderers in *Murder on the Orient Express* who thought he was "A ridiculous-looking little man … The sort of little man one could never take seriously."

Causing people to underestimate him is not Poirot's only technique with murderers. He can trick them into doing things which, although they don't realise this, will confirm their guilt for him, such as getting Cartwright to pretend to collapse in *Three Act Tragedy* or Gale to disguise himself in *Death in the Clouds* or Christine to go on a picnic in *Evil under the Sun*. He is also adept at tricking characters into misleading themselves about his thinking, for example, by allowing them to believe in *The Murder of Roger Ackroyd* that he is referring to Ralph when he is referring to Sheppard or that he is referring to Miss Russell when he is referring to the steward; or allowing them to believe in *Death on the Nile* that he thinks that the murderer of the third victim had swung onto the deck below rather than gone into a cabin.

A final feature of Poirot's detection, albeit in only one-third of the Golden Age novels, is his relationship with Hastings. Reliance on Hastings may seem surprising because Hastings has little, if any, capacity for intellectual application or logical deduction of the sort that Poirot values and he is slow at spotting and interpreting clues. Thus, as early as *The Mysterious Affair at Styles*, Poirot says to him "We must be so intelligent that [the murderer] does not suspect us of being intelligent at all. There, *mon ami*, you will be of great assistance to me" – a comment which Hastings plainly does not interpret correctly since he is "pleased with the compliment".

However, Poirot recognises that Hastings may unwittingly say something helpful. For example, towards the end of *The Murder of Roger Ackroyd* (in which Hastings does not appear) Poirot longs for him, with his knack of "stumbling over the truth unawares" and, as we have seen in *The ABC Murders* (in which he does appear), Poirot appreciates Hastings' "genius for stating the obvious".

Thus, in *The Mysterious Affair at Styles* it is Hastings who remarks that he had only previously seen Poirot's hand shake when he was twiddling with the things on the mantelpiece; in *Peril at End House* it is Hastings who first suggests that Nick Buckley had left something unsaid (that she had *already* asked Maggie to come); and in *The ABC Murders* it is Hastings who suggests correctly that the third letter was sent to the wrong address on purpose. So, although contributions of this sort are rare, Hastings is a helpful companion and friend to Poirot.

Jane Marple

Miss Jane Marple appears in 12 novels. A short section on her follows, simply in order to compare her detection methods with Poirot's, with the examples coming from her two novels in the Golden Age period covered by this volume.

Like Poirot, Miss Marple starts by collecting the facts. Poirot then works from those facts to produce a theory using order and method and his 'little grey cells'. Miss Marple produces a theory and then works back to the facts to check that they fit and, if they do, the theory has to be the right one. That is the real difference between Poirot and Miss Marple.

But how does she produce her theory in the first place? Sometimes she uses logic or at least presents her ideas in a way that sounds logical. For example, she produces a genuinely good logical analysis in relation to the timing of the note supposed to have been written by Protheroe at 6.20 pm in *The Murder at the Vicarage*. Mainly, however, the answer lies in two special talents which she has.

First is an instinct for recognising evil, honed by a mistrust of almost everyone. Thus, in *The Murder at the Vicarage* the Vicar says that she "systematically thinks the worst of everyone" and she herself says "I always find it prudent to suspect everybody just a little." In *The Body in the Library* she says "everybody has been much too *credulous* and *believing*. You simply cannot *afford* to believe everything that people tell you. When there's anything fishy about, I never believe anyone at all!"

Second is a thorough appreciation of human nature, honed by careful observation (her cottage is next door to the Vicarage in *The Murder at the Vicarage*) and by an impressive recollection of village gossip enabling her, as she says in that novel, "to compare people with other people you have known or come across."

With these two special talents, she is able to draw parallels between village life and the more significant crimes she is detecting and so to solve murders by using village analogies. These analogies may derive from the appearance or character traits of the villagers (Edie Chetty's fingernails in *The Body in the Library*) or from acts of minor wrongdoing committed by them (Tommy Bond putting a frog in a school clock as a prank, just as Blake puts the body in the library).

As well as using her two special talents, she also jumps to correct conclusions. This can only be put down to intuition, which, as she says in *The Murder at the Vicarage*, is "a very sound way of arriving at the truth". The problem is that the reader does not necessarily have Miss Marple's instinct for evil or her knowledge of village life or her intuition.[2]

So what she tends to do, in order to keep readers engaged in trying to solve the puzzle, is to provide them with clues by way of observations which *she* makes to other characters (such as the Tommy Bond anecdote in *The Body in the Library*). The result of her style of detection is that she usually has a very plausible theory rather than any proper evidence of the murderer's guilt.

Other Novels

That leaves 21 other crime novels, not all of which are detective stories. Indeed, what is perhaps her most popular masterpiece, *And Then There Were None*, is really a murder mystery rather than a detective story. It falls about halfway along a spectrum which has detective novels at one end (e.g. *The Sittaford Mystery*; *Towards Zero*), with thrillers towards the other (e.g. *The Man in the Brown Suit*; *The Seven Dials Mystery*) and ending with adventure mysteries involving Tuppence and Tommy Beresford (e.g. *By the Pricking of My Thumbs*; *Postern of Fate*).

Short Stories

In addition to the 66 novels, the author published some volumes of short stories. These are not addressed in the analytical commentaries. In a short story the solution occurs so relatively soon after the problem is posed that this doesn't allow sufficient space or time for the murder plan or solution to reach the same level of ingenuity or complexity; or for there to be the same level of mystification or misdirection as is permitted by having several suspects with varying motives and alibis or imaginative clues; or for us to see the detective at work and participate in the detection process.

Of course, short stories can be ingenious or mystifying and enjoyable (particularly those in the 1947 collection, *The Labours of Hercules*). But, if one were to subject them to the same level of analysis as the novels, they would perform so relatively poorly that the exercise would not be fair. It would be like assessing the quality of a normal crossword puzzle against one which is simpler and a fraction of the size. As Professor Barnard says (chapter 3), "If one read only Conan Doyle one would think the detective formula unsuited to the longer length. If one read only Agatha Christie, on the other hand, one would think it unsuited to the short story."

Qualities as a Writer

Commentators who have assessed the author as a novelist have sometimes been critical of her characterisation (rudimentary, stereotyped, cardboard, even schoolgirlish), her settings (myopic and lacking feel and vividness) and her style (journeyman, simple and pedestrian).[3]

However, the criticisms are simply not fair in relation to a number of her characters. She is very good at painting characters so that readers dislike them (Alfred Inglethorp in *The Mysterious Affair at Styles*; Louise Leidner in *Murder in Mesopotamia*; Mrs Boynton in *Appointment with Death*; Simeon Lee in *Hercule Poirot's Christmas*). She is also very good at painting characters so that readers take their side (Nick Buckley in *Peril at End House*; Sir Charles Cartwright in *Three Act Tragedy*; Norman Gale in *Death in the Clouds*; Jackie de Bellefort in *Death on the Nile*). A cleverness with that second category is that they all turn out to be murderers. She also paints strong characters which makes readers rather uncertain about whether to like them or not (Jane Wilkinson in *Lord Edgware Dies*; Patrick Redfern in *Evil under the Sun*; Amyas Crale in *Five Little Pigs*).

All of those examples are in fact murderers or victims and, beyond her detectives, that is really where she focuses her skills of characterisation. It is with the other characters that the criticisms can have merit, although there are notable exceptions where the characters are, for example, given convincing dialogue (the gossipy Caroline Sheppard in *The Murder of Roger Ackroyd*; the talkative Carrie Gardener in *Evil under the Sun*) or have a notable trait (Mr Goby who looks at objects rather than at the person he is addressing in *The Mystery of the Blue Train* and later novels).

As for her settings, although she rarely describes the interior or exterior of country mansions or town houses fully, or gardens or scenery in detail, her descriptions of the relevant rooms – library, study or drawing room – or other murder venues – train, boat or plane – are usually detailed enough and sometimes supported by a helpful map or plan. Her more general landscapes – in the village or by the seaside – are always described sufficiently for the atmosphere of the story, often also conjuring up an enjoyable, cosy familiarity for the reader.

Some of her settings would also have been regarded as enticingly exotic during the Golden Age (the Blue Train and the south of France; the Orient Express; the *Prometheus* airliner; the Nile steamer S.S. *Karnak*). But it is interesting that, despite her popularity in the United States and being half-American herself, she never used an American mainland location as the main setting in any of her novels, perhaps because, unlike France and the areas to which she travelled on archaeological expeditions, she was not very familiar with that part of the world.

As to her style, her short simple paragraphs and sentences and her uncomplicated vocabulary encourage quick, easy and enjoyable reading. She can have a light touch and be rather humorous, though perhaps causing readers to smile rather than laugh, but she is also able to create a tense or sinister atmosphere. She can also, aided by the length of time over which she wrote, make quite sharp observations about changes in lifestyle at different levels of society. Her books following the end of the Second World War illustrate this best. But she also made a real effort to reflect more modern times in her later years, despite being in her seventies.

So, an Agatha Christie novel is more than just a puzzle.[4] And, of course, where she succeeds with qualities of characterisation, setting, humour, atmosphere, observation or social commentary, and where she entertains with her skills as a readable storyteller, this enhances the puzzle's chances of engaging and maintaining the interest of readers in the story, helping them to recall its original impact years later.

However, it is the puzzle which is at the heart of the detective story and even those commentators who have criticised the author as a novelist have simultaneously accepted, even argued, that her lack of literary depth (as they see it) and use of characters with little more personality than jigsaw pieces have actually allowed her to concentrate on her real strength, the puzzle. In doing so, she was able to give her readers precisely what they wanted.

CHAPTER 2

THE PUZZLE ELEMENT

Puzzles

As Professors Maida and Spornick (chapter III) say, "The heart of the classical detective story is the puzzle – that complex structure which offers the reader intrigue and intellectual stimulation." Readers of Agatha Christie's detective novels fall within a wide range – from those at one end who actively try to detect the solution, through those in the middle who approach the puzzle with different levels of intellectual application, to those at the other end who enjoy the puzzle element but are content for it to unfold on the understanding that they will be provided at the denouement with a satisfying solution which, had they wished to apply themselves more intellectually, is one which they see they could have detected for themselves.

Wherever readers fall within that range, the prospect of reading an Agatha Christie puzzle will give them the same enjoyable anticipation of intellectual stimulation that they might get when embarking on a board game or a crossword puzzle. The irony is that readers who like to try to detect the solution can be disappointed when they succeed because, although they want the game played by the 'rules' of detective fiction, they may actually enjoy it more when they are successfully deceived by the author.

Even though a detective novel might be seen as creating a game between players (the creator of the novel and the reader who is trying to solve it), the board games analogy is not an entirely apposite one. This is partly because games have strict rules whereas the 'rules' of detective fiction are, as we shall see later, not really 'rules' at all.

But it is more because games are played against opponents who 'react' to one's own moves. The author cannot react to a reader's developing thinking because the author's moves were all played when writing the story. The author is, rather, in the position of a crossword compiler who has created a puzzle and can do nothing more than challenge the reader to solve it.

A detective story, in which the author similarly lays down a challenge to the reader, is therefore much more like a crossword puzzle than a game:

- Detective stories and crossword puzzles both have solutions, which are the result of combining a number of interconnecting items;
- They both have clues from which the solution can be ascertained;
- And they both need to be plotted – although this happens in rather different ways.

A crossword puzzle is plotted by the carefully constructed interweaving of vertical and horizontal squares into which proper words can be placed so as to provide the solution in the form of a completed grid.

Plotting a murder puzzle, however, starts with the solution. As indicated by Howard Haycraft and Julian Symons, a detective novel is constructed backwards from a deception or central idea. As Agatha Christie herself indicated, "You start with the wish to deceive, and then work backwards."[1]

What this means, generally speaking, is that an author will start by settling on one or more of three things – the identity of the unexpected murderer (the *whodunnit*), the murder plan by which the murder is to be committed (the *howdunnit*) and the motive for committing it (the *whydunnit*). Those three things provide the solution to the puzzle, which will not be revealed to the reader until the denouement. In other words, the solution is the first stage for the author whereas the crossword compiler needs a grid into which he can fit a solution.

Marie Rodell (chapter 8) describes the author's first stage as the "first conflict" – the conflict between murderer and victim, culminating in the murder. Armed with that solution, the author moves to the second stage – the "second conflict", that between murderer and detective or, as suggested earlier, between author and reader.

At that second stage the author works out a plot by which the solution is to be revealed to the reader. The plot is constructed partly backwards from the murder, as the author creates other suspects, decides how the body is to be found and manufactures clues, and partly forwards from the murder, as the author decides how the detection is to unfold so that the clues will mystify and misdirect the reader before ultimately providing the solution. The actual telling of the story is the description of the "second conflict".

The Three Elements of the Puzzle

As Panek says (chapter 1), "Puzzles are created in order to be solved." What this means in relation to an Agatha Christie murder puzzle is that the purpose of the two-stage construction is to create a fictional *murder* solely for the purpose of telling a *story* in which that murder can be *detected*.

The three key words are the ones I have italicised – 'murder', 'story' and 'detected'. In a good puzzle (1) the murder will have an ingenious solution, (2) the story will be well plotted and (3) the detection will be well clued. Thus we have the three puzzle elements – Solution, Plot and Clues, which I have defined as follows:

1. Solution: Creation of an ingenious and satisfying solution involving a clever and convincing murder plan and a credibly motivated but unexpected murderer.
2. Plot: Presentation of the murder and its suspects, clues, detection and solution in a well-paced, tightly-constructed plot, which engages, mystifies and deceives the reader until the denouement.
3. Clues: Detection of the solution through an assessment of fairly presented but imaginative clues which intrigue or deceive the reader.

I have not seen puzzles deconstructed into these three puzzle elements in any of the books that I have read. Nor have I seen any comprehensive generalised definition of the three puzzle elements of the sort that I have ventured here. However, I believe that my approach is the logical analytical culmination of the numerous comments on the puzzles which I have seen in those books.

A good example is Haycraft's dictum in *Murder for Pleasure* (chapter XI – *The Rules of the Game*), which Symons quotes in *Bloody Murder* (chapter 1), that "the *crime* in a detective *story* is only the means to an end which is – *detection*." Haycraft does not deconstruct his sentence into elements and so I have italicised the words 'crime', 'story' and 'detection' in order to demonstrate my deconstruction into the three puzzle elements of Solution, Plot and Clues.

The quality of the puzzles will be assessed in the commentaries by reference to those three puzzle elements, which will shortly be considered at a little more length. Before doing that, however, it is worth saying a little about the 'rules' of detective fiction.

The 'Rules' of Detective Fiction

Not all detective novels are centred on a murder – *The Moonstone* (1868) by Wilkie Collins and *Gaudy Night* (1935) by Dorothy L.

Sayers, for example, are not. But where the detective novel is a murder puzzle, as Agatha Christie's are, then (1) the story plainly needs to be plotted around a murder, for which there are various suspects including the murderer, (2) there should be a reasonable number of clues which are presented to the reader in a way which is fair and timely (but which also may conceal their true significance) and from which the reader could, if analysing the clues correctly, detect the solution, and (3) a coherent explanation of the solution should be provided.

But, beyond that, the truth is that there aren't really any 'rules' of detective fiction in a strict sense – just strong, reasonably authoritative suggestions, principally consolidated in two lists in 1928 (see below), for authors who want to be considered as having played fair with readers.

By the 1920s, based on the age and popularity of detective stories, readers had a good idea about what to expect from them. But, as Haycraft points out in *Murder for Pleasure*, little of note about the genre had appeared in print by then. Exceptions were G.K. Chesterton's 1902 essay "A Defence of Detective Stories" and Carolyn Wells' 1913 *Technique of the Mystery Story* (revised in 1929).

However, by the middle of the 1920s intelligent criticism about what one should and should not expect in detective stories started to emerge (in R. Austin Freeman's 1924 "The Art of the Detective Story"; A. A. Milne's 1926 Introduction to his 1922 *The Red House Mystery*; E. M. Wrong's 1926 *Crime and Detection*; W. H. Wright's 1927 Introduction to *The Great Detective Stories*; and Dorothy L. Sayers' 1928 Introduction to *Great Short Stories of Detection, Mystery and Horror*).

In 1928 S. S. Van Dine (a pseudonym for W. H. Wright) wrote that there were "very definite laws – unwritten, perhaps, but none the less binding" and that year the 'rules' of detective fiction were consolidated in two lists: Van Dine's own "Twenty Rules for Writing

Detective Stories" and Ronald A. Knox's "Ten Commandments of Detection" in his Introduction to *The Best Detective Stories of 1928*.

I am not going to set out these 30 'rules' here since both lists are reproduced in Haycraft's *The Art of the Mystery Story* and they are discussed in Dr Curran's *Murder in the Making*. They can, of course, also be found by an internet search. Suffice it to say here, therefore, that having an investigating officer as the murderer (Superintendent Sugden in *Hercule Poirot's Christmas*) or having two culprits rather than one (*The Mysterious Affair at Styles*; *Death on the Nile*; *One, Two Buckle My Shoe*; *Evil under the Sun*) would constitute a breach of the 'rules'. However, many of the 'rules' have been regularly ignored or broken by authors in their attempts to create more mystifying puzzles.

Roger Ackroyd

The most controversial of Agatha Christie's novels in the context of the 'rules' was published early in her career with *The Murder of Roger Ackroyd* (1926) in which the murderer was the 'Dr Watson' figure – the narrator of the story, Dr James Sheppard, who acted as Poirot's assistant. Although the publication of *Ackroyd* preceded the publication of the two lists of 'rules' by two years, it seems fair to say that those lists were consolidating (rather than creating) 'rules' which would have reflected reader expectations in 1926, making it reasonable to assess any breach by *Ackroyd* against those 'rules'.

Whether or not the author cheated in *Ackroyd* is considered in some detail in the *Ackroyd* commentary. But it is worth making two preliminary points at this stage. First, one would certainly not think she had cheated on looking at the initial critical reaction in two of the most prestigious literary publications in London and New York. *The Times Literary Supplement* regarded it as a "well-written" and "very puzzling" detective story of which "the only criticism" was that there were too many sub-plots (10 June 1926).

The New York Times Book Review thought that it was "inferior" to the best detective stories and "conventional" and that the identity of the murderer was a "perfectly fair procedure" (18 July 1926).

Secondly, in contrast, some critics and readers did feel let down. One of the most authoritative voices at the time was W. H. Wright. In his Introduction to *The Great Detective Stories* (1927), he wrote "The trick played on the reader in *The Murder of Roger Ackroyd* is hardly a legitimate device of the detective-story writer; and while Poirot's work in this book is at times capable, the effect is nullified by the dénouement."

But Wright was not alone. The *News Chronicle* thought it a 'tasteless and unforgivable let-down by a writer we had grown to admire'; one reader wrote to *The Times* to say that he was so shocked by the denouement that he was not going to buy any more of the author's books; another complained that it had "spoilt her books for me ever afterwards"; and another (a doctor) exclaimed that it was "awful … so unfair. And making him a doctor, too!".[2]

Dorothy L. Sayers, however, came to the author's defence. In her Introduction to *Great Short Stories of Detection, Mystery and Horror* (1928), she thought *Ackroyd* a "*tour de force*" (p.98) and said that Wright's opinion merely represented "a natural resentment at having been ingeniously bamboozled", adding that "It is, after all, the reader's job to keep his wits about him, and, like the perfect detective, to suspect *everybody*." In my view, as is explained in the commentary on *Ackroyd*, there was no improper breach of the 'rules'.

Solution

Turning, then, to the three puzzle elements, I am going to limit my examples to the Poirot Golden Age novels (with some irresistible exceptions) since the three sections might otherwise comprise a series of long lists.

As we have seen, a good puzzle needs an ingenious and satisfying solution involving a clever and convincing murder plan and a credibly motivated but unexpected murderer. *Ackroyd* is a prime example of a novel that would score just about top marks in the Solution category.

But the author created a number of other memorable solutions where the murderer does not even appear to be a suspect or carries out a murder plan which it seems he could not possibly have executed.

The most memorable solutions tend to be those where the deception can be described in a few words. The reader may over time have forgotten the names of the characters or even the title of the novel but he can still remember its original impact well enough to say that the murderer was 'All of them' (*Murder on the Orient Express*) or 'The one who appeared to be the intended victim' (*Peril at End House*) or 'The policeman' (*Hercule Poirot's Christmas*). Or he could say – taking advantage of the irresistible exceptions – 'One of the people we thought was dead' (*And Then There Were None*) or 'The child' (*Crooked House*) or even 'Poirot' (*Curtain*).

However, brevity is not everything. One of Agatha Christie's best novels requires a few more descriptive words 'The murderer concealed the main murder in a series of murders' (*The ABC Murders*). A similar number of words can be used for other novels such as 'The murderer's first murder was just a dress rehearsal for the main murder' (*Three Act Tragedy*) or 'The murderer was the most obvious suspect after all, even though he had an alibi' (*The Mysterious Affair at Styles*).

With some very good stories, it is hard to do justice to them in so few words because their cleverness is not just in the identity of the murderer but in the impressive ingenuity of the murder plan (*Lord Edgware Dies*; *Death on the Nile*; *One, Two, Buckle My Shoe*; *Evil under the Sun*). Even though the murder plans in novels like those may be highly unlikely to happen in real life, they can still be convincing at the puzzle level, which is what Agatha Christie intended. As Laura Thompson points out in *Agatha Christie* (in the chapter *English Murder*), the murder in the puzzle is there to be solved, not to be compared with reality.

Unexpectedness and ingenuity are not the only important qualities. Some murder plans are simple, even opportunistic (*Cards on the Table*; *Five Little Pigs*) but the solution can still leave readers with a sense of satisfaction because the character clues make it so convincing, almost as if the novels work so well because the murderer is not the product of a trick.

Finally, the murderer needs to have a credible motive. Generally speaking, they do, although there are occasions where the motive is a weakness (*Murder in Mesopotamia*; *Hercule Poirot's Christmas*; *Evil under the Sun*). However, motive can also be a strength in novels, either when its originality alone makes the novel memorable (the dress rehearsal motive in *Three Act Tragedy*) or when it comes as such a surprise that it makes an unexpected murderer really quite obvious if only we had spotted it (*The ABC Murders*; *One, Two, Buckle My Shoe*).

Plot

Although a good puzzle ends with an ingenious solution, the majority of the puzzle, which is worked out at the second stage of construction, precedes the denouement and presents readers with the murder, the suspects, the clues, the detection and finally the solution. In a good puzzle this presentation should aim to engage, mystify and deceive the reader in a well-paced, tightly constructed plot.

A good plot is vital for a good puzzle – particularly to readers who might want some mental stimulation but are content not to participate actively themselves in trying to complete the jigsaw of clues.

What then makes a good plot? A good plot will engage the interest of the reader. This may be achieved initially by non-puzzle elements such as a dramatic or memorable opening ("You do see, don't you, that she's got to be killed?" in *Appointment with Death*); a familiar setting (*Evil under the Sun*) or a novel one (*Death in the Clouds*); or an intriguing or likeable character (Nick Buckley in *Peril at End House*).

A good pace is then important to maintain the reader's interest and, if the story seems to start quite slowly, it needs to acquire pace reasonably promptly (as *Death on the Nile* does) and to absorb the reader with puzzle elements which may include suspicious facts concerning the suspects (past histories, true identities, inter-relationships), evidence affecting their means, motive and opportunity or even further murders, leading in turn to further issues of means, motive and opportunity.

In presenting these puzzle elements to readers, a good plot will ensure that all the pieces of the jigsaw fit together tightly to make a complete and coherent puzzle, which unfolds in an intelligently constructed order. As will be seen in the commentary on *Murder on the Orient Express*, the plot involves the interweaving of five different versions of events and is a particularly brilliant example of plotting. So too is the mystery of Miss Sainsbury Seale's true identity and role in *One, Two, Buckle My Shoe*, while the structural device in *Five Little Pigs* of looking retrospectively at a murder committed 16 years earlier provides a most satisfying way of revealing the narrative.

However, a plot should not only be tightly constructed. As Professor Cawelti says (chapter 5), a successful detective tale must not only be solved, it must mystify; and, as we have already seen, it must deceive. So, as it unfolds, the plot should, crucially, make the reader doubt views he may have formed about the likely guilt or innocence of certain suspects or about the implementation of the murder plan or about the significance of particular clues and cause him to make incorrect assumptions or to divert his attention from items of significance by directing it to items which are in fact irrelevant.

These deceptions can, provided they are tightly constructed, work wonderfully well for different reasons – for example, because the murderer never seems to be a suspect (*The Murder of Roger Ackroyd*) or because the murder plan and alibi are so intricately worked out (*Lord Edgware Dies*) or because the plot looks very simple when in fact it conceals a complex incrimination (*The ABC Murders*).

To achieve all this, while also trying to provide an ingenious solution and to describe a process of detection, is an exercise requiring great skill and delicacy. Taking Agatha Christie's crime fiction as a body of work, one can confidently say that that exercise – plot construction in detective novels – was one at which, when at her best, she has never been surpassed.[3]

Clues

We already know from Haycraft and Panek that a fictional murderer is only created so that he can be detected. As Rodell says (chapter 3), "It is the detection, then, which is of prime importance in a detective story: the unravelling of the puzzle." Readers must therefore enjoy the intellectual stimulation provided by the element of detection – even if only a very small number actually hope or try to detect the solution – because otherwise they would read a different type of novel.

A good puzzle provides that stimulation by offering clues to aid the detection of the solution and it therefore needs to be well clued. There are so many clues in Agatha Christie's novels that a summary of good clueing faces the danger of being overloaded with even a relatively small number of examples.

I have tried to avoid that but, since quite a lot of clues still appear in the summary, I have usually abbreviated the title of the novel to one word where it has already been referred to in this chapter; and I have only mentioned a clue once, even when it could act as an example on two or three occasions.

Clues may be revealed in various ways – for example, through forensic investigation or the questioning of suspects or observations by the detective or even by chance. A simple clue may take the form of factual evidence or information. This could be about what someone did or saw or knew or heard; or about timing, location, distance, even the weather; or about the murder weapon; or about human traces such as fingerprints or footprints (or the absence of them) at the scene of a crime. But in Agatha Christie's detective novels simple clues can overlap with many other types of clue.

Those clues may be tangible, ranging from everyday items (the 'crushed coffee cup' clue, Poirot's first clue in *Styles*) to the mechanical (the 'dictaphone' clue in *Ackroyd*) or the chemical (the 'hydrochlor scrap' clue in *Sad Cypress*). Like those examples, clues may be in the form of movable tangible objects (the 'lead-piping' clue in *The Murder on the Links*) but they may also be immovable physical fixtures or markings (the 'creaking stairs' and 'bunker' clues in that novel). Or a clue may be sensory, such as smell (the 'jasmine' clue in *Pigs*) or sound (the 'Bob barking' clue in *Witness*), perhaps overlapping with a tangible clue such as a bottle (the smell from the 'nail polish' clue in *Nile*).

Clues may take the form of personal characteristics, whether of appearance (the 'sun-tanned bodies' clue about Arlena and Christine in *Evil*) or of profession (the 'actor' clue about Cartwright in *Three Act Tragedy*) or of knowledge (the 'chemistry professor' clue about Bella in *Witness*) or of behaviour (the 'wiped bottle' clue about Caroline in *Pigs*) or of personality (the 'over-calling' clue about Roberts in *Cards*) or – as Poirot might have said – of psychology (the 'weak as water' clue about Sheppard in *Ackroyd*). Or the clues may come from the use of language, whether verbal (the 'wife's friend' clue in *Buckle*) or written (the 'Eliza letter' clue in *Cypress*) or textual (as in *Ackroyd* where, as we shall see in the commentary, Sheppard uses ingenious words in order, so he puts it, "to mask the ugliness of naked facts").

Good clues will catch the imagination of the reader. With the very best ones, this may be because, as readers learn at the denouement, they have been very cleverly constructed (the 'Paris' and 'Carlotta letter' clues in *Edgware*; the 'church clock' clue in *Ackroyd*; the 'scorching' clue in *Nile*; the 'grand slam' clue in *Cards*; and two which comprise a combination of clues, the 'resemblance' clue in *Christmas* and the various 'buckled shoes' clues in *Buckle*). Or clues may catch the imagination of the reader simply because for some indefinable reason they have the capacity to remain highly memorable (the 'ornaments' clue in *Styles*; the 'kimono' clue in *Orient*; the 'brooch' clue in *Witness*; the 'thornless rose' clue in *Cypress*).

Some clues will intrigue the reader as soon as he spots them, either because he just cannot work out what they mean (the 'damaged face' clue in *Buckle* or the 'in from outside' clue in *Mesopotamia*) or because, even though he thinks he has an idea about what they mean, he knows that there is every chance that, through misdirecting emphasis, he will be skilfully deceived as to their true significance.

As Rodell says in her classic general introduction to types of clues and how to conceal them (chapter 7), a good clue is one which does in fact point in the right direction, but which seems at first to point in another direction (the 'stolen dagger' clue in *Links* or the 'calendar' clue in *Christmas*) or to mean something other than it does (the 'dictation' clue in *Ackroyd* or the 'wasp' clue in *Clouds*) or to point nowhere at all (the 'telephone call' clue in *Ackroyd* or the 'misaddressed letter' clue in *ABC* or '*The Moon and Sixpence*' clue in *Pigs*).

However, there will be other imaginative clues which the reader does not spot at all because, even though they appear openly without concealment, they are presented with such sleight of hand that the reader is deceived into not realising until the denouement that they are clues at all (the 'letter greeting' clue in *Peril* or the 'jury' clue in *Orient*).

But good clueing can also involve deceiving the reader by concealing clues. Such a concealed clue might be hidden in casual conversation (the 'limp' clue in *The Mystery of the Blue Train* or the 'dress rehearsal' clue in *Tragedy*); or hidden in an apparently unimportant sentence or paragraph (the 'heavy quern' clue in *Mesopotamia* or the 'strolling' clue in *Appointment with Death*); or hidden among other facts which appear to be more relevant (the 'last dose' clue in *Styles* or the 'steward' clue in *Ackroyd* or the 'sponge bag' clue in *Orient* or the 'white coat' clue in *Clouds*); or it might be hidden by being made up of different pieces of information which are only revealed pages apart (the 'overcoat' clue in *Links* or the 'London' clue in *Cypress*).

Imagination, intrigue and deception make for the best clues but all clues must satisfy two important requirements. First, they should be presented fairly. This does not mean that a clue should be presented in a way that makes its significance clear to the reader. Quite the reverse, since, as we have just seen in the examples, good clueing will include presenting clues in a way that conceals their true significance. However, for a clue to be fairly presented, its significance should be capable, theoretically at least, of being spotted by the careful reading of the most astute reader.

What in practice this means is that the clue should not be beyond the reader's comprehension or hidden in incomprehensible language; that any clue which is presented simply to mislead (a red herring) should have some reasonably credible explanation for its introduction; and the narrative must not lie – as Rodell says (chapter 11), "Characters in the book may lie, and the viewpoint character may be mistaken, but any categorical statement by the author must be true."

Secondly, the clues should be the means by which the solution can be and is detected. Even if the reader is not actually trying to complete the mental jigsaw of clues himself, he needs to know that he had the chance to participate in solving the puzzle and so it is important to him to see the solution being detected through the clues, whether they are ones which are explained during the story (the 'footprints' clue in *Links* or the 'charred fragment' clue in *Orient*) or whether they are ones whose explanation must await the denouement (the 'window' clue in *Mesopotamia*, the 'pink balloon' clue in *Christmas* or the 'pince-nez' clue in *Edgware*). As Van Dine's Rule 6 says, if the detective does not reach his conclusions through an analysis of clues, he has no more solved the problem than "the schoolboy who gets his answer out of the back of the arithmetic".

It is by reference to the three criteria of Solution, Plot and Clues that the commentaries analysing the author's puzzles have been prepared.

CHAPTER 3

Poirot's Golden Age Puzzles

Since it would not be practicable to produce commentaries for all of the author's 66 crime novels in one volume, I considered carefully how best to make this task more manageable.

I decided that I should focus on the period known as the 'Golden Age' of detective fiction.[1] This can fairly be regarded in the United Kingdom as being roughly the period between the end of the First World War (1918) and that of the Second (1945), though beginning in Agatha Christie's case in 1920 when her first novel was published (October 1920 in the United States; January 1921 in the UK).[2]

The author published 36 crime novels until the end of 1945, which again struck me as too many for one volume. So, reducing the number further, I decided to focus on the author's great detective of that period, Hercule Poirot.

In fact, that choice worked well because the author came to a natural break with Poirot in 1942 after 21 novels.[3] Having earlier given him a four-year break after *The Mystery of the Blue Train* (1928), she then published 16 Poirot novels between 1932 and 1942 before giving him another four-year break until *The Hollow* (1946). So I decided that my cut-off date should be 1942. If I had gone beyond that, there would have been no natural break until Poirot's final novel, his 33rd, which again struck me as too many for one volume. Staying in the Golden Age was not only logical numerically but it would also allow readers to assess a coherent body of work.

I am conscious that my focus on Poirot results in omitting my commentary on *And Then There Were None* (1939), despite it being the author's most popular book. However, there are no plausible thematic grounds for including it on this occasion.

Nevertheless that novel could be included in a second volume of *Agatha Christie's Golden Age* covering her 11 non-Poirot novels published up to 1942 (in each of which, interestingly, the principal protagonist, or one of the principal protagonists, opposing the murderer, is a woman[4]).

The novels which have been chosen for this volume are listed in chronological order on the Contents page, with the year of publication in the UK and, where a novel has a different title in the United States, with that title appearing in brackets.

Finally, I should say that I have very largely treated each novel entirely separately. There are numerous occasions where I could have cross-referred to other novels with the same or similar puzzle elements. However, with a very few occasional exceptions, I have deliberately avoided lengthening the commentaries with a 'compare and contrast' approach because I believe that each novel should be considered individually.

Indeed, this introduction is already long enough. So, let us get to the puzzles.

1

The Mysterious Affair At Styles

Solution

Poirot investigates the murder at Styles Court in Essex of wealthy, elderly Emily Inglethorp, who dies of strychnine poisoning on Wednesday 18 July.

The story, set during the First World War, is narrated by Hastings, who is home on sick leave from the Front when invited to stay at Styles by Emily's stepson, John Cavendish. Oddly, we are not told Hastings' Christian name or military rank but we know that he is nearly 30 since John, aged 45, is his senior by a good 15 years.

When Hastings arrives at Styles on 5 July, the occupants, in addition to Emily and the servants, are John and his brother Lawrence, neither of whom work, although they are qualified as a barrister and doctor respectively; John's wife, Mary, who works "on the land"; Cynthia Murdoch, Emily's protégée who works in a hospital dispensary; Evelyn Howard, a hearty lady of about 40, who is Emily's companion; and Evelyn's cousin, the black-bearded Alfred Inglethorp, who had become Emily's secretary and then her second husband after their engagement three months ago. John regards Alfred, who is at least 20 years younger than Emily, as a "Rotten little bounder".

Just before 5 am on Wednesday 18 July Emily has a fit in her bedroom. Hastings and Lawrence are joined by John in the passage outside but the door is locked or bolted from the inside, as appears to be the case with the two other doors into her room – one from Cynthia's room and the other from Alfred's, which they break down. They are then joined by Cynthia and Mary and by Dr Bauerstein, who had been at Styles earlier that evening. Emily cries out "Alfred – Alfred –" before falling back dead on the pillows. Hastings, who suspects poison, suggests to John that Poirot, who is an old friend of his living in the local village of Styles St Mary, should investigate.

At the inquest strychnine is confirmed as the cause of death by Bauerstein, a poisons expert and thus a fourth person who knows about poisons – along with Lawrence, a qualified doctor, Cynthia, a hospital dispenser, and Evelyn, who works as a nurse after leaving Styles on 6 July following a row about Alfred.

Readers may well think that the strychnine had been administered in Emily's after-supper coffee because Hastings points out that, when she went up to bed, there were three witnesses (Cynthia, John and himself) who "could swear that Mrs Inglethorp was carrying her coffee, as yet untasted, in her hand". But this is misdirection because, as we learn, the effects of strychnine would be felt fairly rapidly. Although they might be retarded by a heavy meal, Emily had not eaten much at supper and yet her symptoms did not appear until 5 am.

Another possibility is that the strychnine was in the cocoa which Emily would warm up in a saucepan in her room at night with a spirit lamp. The cocoa tray had been outside her room from about 7.15 pm until Annie, the housemaid, who noticed "salt" on the tray, brought it in at about 8 pm. Hastings thinks that the "salt" was strychnine but at the inquest Bauerstein says that strychnine has a bitter taste which cocoa (unlike coffee) would not have masked.

So, how was it administered? We learn at the inquest that Emily was taking a "tonic" or "medicine" containing strychnine, which was used as a stimulant in those days.[1] But it seems that the tonic was not the cause because she had been taking it without ill effects, even being down to the last dose in the bottle.

However, Poirot reminds us at the denouement that she had an empty box of bromide sleeping powders. He describes the effect of bromide on a solution containing strychnine by reading an extract from a book on dispensing and says that the introduction of bromide powders into the bottle would result in the greater part of the strychnine being precipitated to the bottom, causing the last dose to be lethal. Although we are not told this, the book is *The Art of Dispensing* by Peter MacEwan, F.C.S., first published in 1888.

The addition of bromide to create a lethal sediment is a cleverly original murder method (although the extract does say that a lady died taking a similar mixture, presumably inadvertently) and it explains how Emily was killed by taking only one dose on the evening of 17 July. Her symptoms were delayed because, in a sub-plot which was not part of the murder plan, a narcotic (the "salt") was added to her cocoa, retarding the effects of the strychnine.

The murder was planned by Alfred and Evelyn, who were after Emily's fortune. In fact, the murder should have happened the night before but Emily forgot to take her tonic. Thus the fatal dose was taken 24 hours later "than had been anticipated by the murderer", Alfred, who feared that his accomplice, Evelyn, might panic at not hearing of their success, and so began to write a letter to reassure her, which he left unfinished in his desk. At the denouement Poirot produces this letter in "the murderer's own handwriting" and introduces us to "the murderer, Mr Alfred Inglethorp".

Notably, Poirot calls Alfred "the murderer" three times, so treating him as the principal offender and Evelyn as an "accomplice" (as he calls her twice) – that is, a person who aids, abets, counsels or procures an offence. Alfred is indeed a more memorable murderer but the bromide idea was Evelyn's, as seen from his letter ("That idea of yours about the bromides was a stroke of genius"), and she may even have added the bromide to the tonic (we are not told who took this key step) before leaving Styles on 6 July, after staging her row, because Poirot says "The tragedy will not take place until nearly a fortnight later".

However, Alfred must have been the person who, when pouring Emily's tonic after Evelyn had left Styles, was "always extremely careful not to shake the bottle but to leave the sediment at the bottom of it undisturbed". Interestingly, the sixth edition of *The Art of Dispensing* (1900) says that the lady who died "carefully refrained from shaking the bottle" (page 368) but the ninth edition (1912), which is the same as the author's extract, omits this (page 376).

Another "exceedingly clever" element of the murder plan is that Alfred prepares "a lot of manufactured evidence against himself" so that he will be arrested before then producing an "irreproachable alibi". As Poirot explains, under English law at the time, "a man once acquitted can never be tried again for the same offence" – the *double jeopardy* rule.[2]

When Poirot refers to "manufactured evidence", he must have mainly in mind the occasion on 16 July when Evelyn, disguised as Alfred with pince-nez and a false beard, purchases a phial of strychnine at the village chemist, signing the register in Alfred's name, while he is in fact, we later learn, seen by five witnesses escorting Farmer Raikes' wife over two miles away.

But there is also other manufactured evidence – Evelyn's row; her vehement comments about Alfred being after Emily's money and being likely to murder her; Evelyn's story about his time with Farmer Raikes' wife; his pouring of Emily's coffee; and his absence on the fatal night. In addition, there is evidence which he did not manufacture – an apparent quarrel with Emily the afternoon before the murder (though in fact her quarrel was with John); and her dying words "Alfred – Alfred –" which were, as Poirot says, an accusation.

The final element of the murder plan is to incriminate John. So, when Evelyn signs for the strychnine as Alfred, she does so in John's handwriting; she hides the pince-nez and strychnine phial in his room; and she hides the false beard in the attic where it is found by Poirot and Hastings to whom she presents the packaging, saying it was on top of a wardrobe, which turns out to belong to John, who is sent to trial for the murder.

All the while, however, the real murderer is the product of a clever double bluff: the black-bearded Alfred, whom we all suspect, turns out to have an alibi and, while we then focus on the other suspects, he turns out to be guilty after all. That sounds very satisfactory but, unfortunately, there are problems.

First is the double jeopardy plan. Poirot is right that under English law at the time "a man once acquitted can never be tried again for the same offence" but the key words are "acquitted" and "tried again". He must be tried and acquitted. It is not enough to be *arrested*. However, this is not how the story is written. In the same paragraph Poirot says "He wished to be arrested. He would then produce his irreproachable alibi – and hey presto, he was safe for life!". And that reference to "arrested" was not just a slip of the pen because Poirot refers a number of times to "arrest" in chapters 5, 7 and 13.

This distinction between *arrest* and *acquittal* is fundamental to the viability of the murder plan. It was *possible*, though risky to assume, that Alfred's alibi might remain hidden until after his *arrest* without Mrs Raikes or any of the five witnesses coming forward, although in fact they do so. However, it seems *impossible* to believe that, with the publicity of a *trial* and no reason for the witnesses to remain silent, his alibi could have remained hidden until then. And, even if it was hidden until deployed at the trial so as to lead to his acquittal, that would not have helped *Evelyn* if the truth was later discovered since, under section 8 of the Accessories and Abettors Act 1861, accomplices were liable to be tried and punished as principal offenders.

Next is the problem of the will. In chapter 13 Poirot explains the criminals' plan: "They had already arranged their infamous plot – that he should marry this rich, but rather foolish old lady, induce her to make a will leaving her money to him, and then gain their ends by a very cleverly concealed crime".

However, Alfred did not need to "induce" Emily to make a will after marrying her since the marriage had automatically revoked any previous will[3], making her intestate, and meaning that Alfred as her husband would inherit her personal estate anyway.[4] But, if he thought it *was* necessary, why would he and Evelyn plan for Emily to take the last dose on 16 July before she had even made a post-marriage will in Alfred's favour? So the murderers' thinking, as explained by Poirot, does not work as a matter of law or planning.

Finally, the extent of the criminals' intentions, when Evelyn buys strychnine at the chemist, is confused by Poirot's explanation in the final chapter where he describes this as "a plan to throw suspicion on John Cavendish", even going on to refer to "the strychnine, which, after all, is only wanted as a blind to throw suspicion on John Cavendish". But surely purchasing the strychnine was a key part of the double jeopardy plan, being intended – whether Evelyn pretended to be John or not – to create the main element of the manufactured evidence and allowing Alfred then to produce his "irreproachable alibi".

Plot

This story is significant because it is the first detective novel of the author (out of 66) and so of Poirot (out of 33) and Hastings (out of 8). Hastings, who had met Poirot in Belgium, is sorry that he now "limped badly", an odd statement since next morning he darts about "with the agility of a grasshopper" and later rushes, runs, leaps, gambols, dashes, tears and skips. It also seems odd that the crime should attract, as Hastings says in the first paragraph, "world-wide notoriety" and "sensational rumours".

Nevertheless, his narrative is generally most engaging – partly because of the charm with which he reveals his slowness in spotting and interpreting clues and partly because his self-flattery suggests rather humorously that he thinks he is more accomplished than he is. But, in fairness to him, when he says "I flatter myself that my first judgments are usually fairly shrewd", he is talking about his dislike of Alfred. He also has a shrewd premonition of approaching evil and his ransacking of the library for a book on strychnine is inspired since there has been no mention of strychnine before then.

He also provides two plans and three facsimiles. He does not describe Styles beyond the plans (which are of the first floor and Emily's bedroom) but he does describe the grounds and says that there is a park which his bedroom overlooked. In fact, as the first-floor plan shows, the only window of his bedroom, which was in the left wing, looked out over the courtyard.

The plan also shows Emily's bedroom with only one window whereas on the plan of her bedroom there are two and the text refers to "the left-hand window"; in some editions the letter "B", showing the door to the servants' rooms, is missing; and in most editions Cynthia's name is wrongly spelled "Murdock" with a 'k'. Her room was in the right wing and, when Hastings says in chapter 8 that, apart from her room, every room was in the left wing, this is wrong since Alfred's and Emily's rooms were also in the right wing.

The exposition – the provision of background information – in the first chapter is rather cluttered, introducing the suspects so fast that we get little sense of them except for Alfred as a fortune hunter. We get a better sense as the story develops and directs us to various male-female relationships including Emily/Alfred, Alfred/Mrs Raikes, Mary/Bauerstein and John/Mary. These divert us from Alfred/Evelyn's relationship to which we are never directed save in the context of her vehemence against him.

On the whole, the story, which has 13 chapters, moves at a reasonable pace. But the most noticeable feature of the plotting is the sheer volume of clues. A reader simply could not absorb them all, let alone explain their significance, as Poirot brilliantly manages to do.

There are four sub-plots. Two flow from Emily's quarrel with John at 4 pm on 17 July while the other two concern Lawrence's attempt to shield Cynthia and the role of Dr Bauerstein. The plotting of the two sub-plots arising from the quarrel (Emily making and then destroying a new will in favour of Alfred; and Mary drugging Emily's cocoa and entering her room) is complicated, so it is helpful to understand it before looking at the clues.

The quarrel concerns John's relationship with Mrs Raikes. Emily refers to a "scandal between husband and wife" (meaning John and Mary). They also discuss wills being revoked by marriage and Emily, thus realising that she has no valid will after her marriage and presumably thinking (incorrectly) that her fortune will go to John with whom she has just quarrelled, makes a new will in Alfred's favour, witnessed by the gardeners at 4.30 pm. However, while then looking for stamps in Alfred's desk, she finds his unfinished letter to Evelyn. Staring at the document in disbelief, she asks Dorcas, the parlourmaid, to make up a fire (in which she burns the new will) and at 5 pm she refers again to a "scandal between husband and wife" (but this time meaning Alfred and herself).

Then Mary, who had overheard the quarrel, sees Emily holding the document, which she (wrongly) believes will provide proof of John's infidelity, and demands to see it. Emily refuses, assuring her (truthfully) that it has nothing to do with her. As a result Mary drugs Emily and Cynthia's drinks so that at about

5 am she can enter Emily's bedroom, passing through Cynthia's, and find the document in Emily's despatch case. But before she can open it, Emily wakes, seized with a paroxysm (caused by the strychnine), and so she retreats to Cynthia's room. Next morning, after discovery of the body, Alfred forces the lock on the despatch case, finds the letter and tears it into strips which he puts in a spill vase on the mantelpiece.

The way these sub-plots are interwoven together and into the main (murder, alibi and incrimination) plot is impressive, mystifying and, for readers happy to face its complexity, engrossing. But an oddity about the will which Emily burns is that at John's trial Mr Phillips K.C. cannot understand why she made a fresh one "with the old one still extant". He says that she may have had "an idea that it was revoked by her marriage" and is plainly indicating that she was wrong. But readers know (and Mr Phillips should have known) that Emily was right, Poirot and the lawyer, Mr Wells, having said so in chapter 5.

However, the biggest criticism of John's trial is that Poirot allows it to proceed at all when he knows the solution. He claims that clearing John "might have meant a failure to convict the real criminals" and even says that the criminals being in the dark as to his real attitude "partly accounts for my success". But putting John on trial didn't cause the criminals to do, or not do, anything to lead Poirot to the "last link in my chain". Less compelling still is allowing the trial to proceed because only its "great danger" could restore the conjugal happiness of John and Mary, which is a pretty incredible reason for Poirot allowing an innocent man to be tried for murder, even though he is released.

Clues

In chapter 4 Poirot lists "six points of interest" found in Emily's bedroom as: one, a coffee cup that had been ground into powder; two, a despatch case with a key in the lock; three, a damp stain on the floor smelling of coffee; four, a fragment of dark green fabric; five, a splash of candle grease on the floor; and six, a cardboard box such as chemists use for powders. So, it is a surprise that, when revealing the solution, he starts by listing only three of those clues – Numbers Four, Three and Six in that order.

Much more surprising is that the bottle of tonic is not only omitted from his list but is not even mentioned as an item in the bedroom. Since he conducts a "minute inspection" of it, the failure to mention the 'tonic' clue until the inquest (or send it for analysis) is extraordinary, making it almost impossible to deduce what his "probably utterly impossible idea" in chapter 5 is.

In fact we are not told what it is. But just beforehand Cynthia had said that Emily's sleeping powders, which she had made up (as clued by Number Six, the box with no chemist's name because Cynthia worked in a dispensary), were bromide – the 'bromide' clue. So one assumes in retrospect that his idea was that Emily had been killed by bromide being added to her tonic.

After all, he knows that Emily had not drunk her coffee, as clued by Number Three, the damp, coffee-smelling stain. He explains that, when he put his case on her table, it tilted, throwing the case to the floor. When he saw the 'coffee stain' clue, he realised that the table had done the same to her coffee cup.

Despite the extraordinary omission, readers do learn about the 'tonic' clue and the strychnine at the inquest. Of course, they still need a chemist's knowledge to interpret the 'bromide' clue by knowing its effect on a tonic containing strychnine. But, for such readers, there is a better clue still – indeed the main challenger for best clue in the book. It comes at the inquest when Dorcas dispels the idea that the chemist had mistakenly included too much strychnine in the tonic. She says: "The medicine had not been newly made up. On the contrary Mrs Inglethorp had taken the last dose on the day of her death".

The beauty of this well-hidden clue is that she is saying that, since Emily had taken the medicine various times, there could not have been a mistake. So we focus not on the "last dose", which provides the key clue, but on the absence of a mistake. Although Poirot does not mention the 'last dose' clue in his revelations, readers would not have known that Emily had taken the last dose if Dorcas had not said so.

Next, Poirot still has the problem that the strychnine's effects would probably be felt within an hour. This is resolved with the 'missing coffee cup' clue. In chapter 5 he had examined five coffee cups, which had remained in the drawing room overnight because Annie had not cleared them away. Hastings had identified these as belonging to Mary, Cynthia, Lawrence, John and himself. With there being no cup for Alfred (because he did not drink coffee) and with Emily having taken her cup to her room (the one that was crushed), Poirot assumed that all the cups were accounted for. He tasted the grounds in the five cups and was half puzzled, half relieved. Perhaps this was because, knowing that Cynthia had slept so soundly that she had to be shaken awake, he had previously assumed from this 'sound sleeper' clue that she had been drugged and he was puzzled, but relieved, to find that she had not been.

He then learns in chapter 8 that Bauerstein had been there that evening and he goes into an "absolute frenzy", twice saying "That alters everything – everything!". He later explains that Annie *had* brought in a cup for Alfred, not knowing (surprisingly) that he never drank coffee, and Bauerstein had used his cup. So six cups (plus Emily's) had been used. But, he says, when Dorcas "cleared them away" next morning, she only found five – though in fact she did *not* clear them away; if she had, he could not have conducted his tasting.

Bauerstein's presence "changed the face of the whole affair, for there was now one cup missing". Poirot was sure that the missing (sixth) cup was Cynthia's because the five cups all contained sugar, which she never took, as he learned after the tasting exercise. However, there are oddities about the significance attached by Poirot to the 'Bauerstein presence' clue,

The first is that he is not aware of it until chapter 8. This is extraordinary because in chapter 4 Hastings had told him the whole story "keeping back nothing, and omitting no circumstance, however insignificant" and in chapter 5 had "recapitulated the scene of the night before" and yet had omitted Bauerstein, who had arrived plastered with mud. Secondly, Hastings does not say that Bauerstein had a cup of coffee. Thirdly, since Poirot knew that the five cups contained sugar, he could have deduced that Cynthia's cup was missing anyway on learning in chapter 5 that she never took sugar.

Nevertheless Cynthia's 'missing coffee cup' clue leads Poirot to say that his attention had been attracted by Annie having seen "salt" on Emily's cocoa tray – the 'salt' clue – and he adds that he had "accordingly" secured a sample of the cocoa, which he sent for analysis. In fact he secured his sample *before* hearing Annie's story but, more importantly, he does not explain his reasoning for *linking* Cynthia's 'missing coffee cup' clue with Emily's 'salt' clue.

Nor does he ever actually tell us that he sent Cynthia's coffee cup (once found) to be analysed. Presumably he must have done because he goes on to say "Here is the analyst's report. Mrs Cavendish [Mary] administered a safe, but effectual, narcotic to both Mrs Inglethorp [Emily] and Mademoiselle Cynthia". The fact that Emily (and Cynthia) had been drugged by Mary is coincidental to the murder plan and her purpose in doing so, and in removing Cynthia's cup, will be referred to in the context of the clueing of that sub-plot. Its relevance in the present context (of the clueing of the murder plan) is that the drugging of Emily's cocoa explains her retarded strychnine symptoms.

As for Alfred, there is so much evidence against him that Poirot is mystified that he does not deploy his alibi. At the inquest he murmurs "*Sacré*! Does this imbecile of a man *want* to be arrested?" and after it he describes Alfred's refusal to say anything as "the policy of an imbecile" and act of a "lunatic". So he deduces from this 'lunatic policy' clue that Alfred, in not revealing the alibi, *wants* to be arrested. That is a good deduction. However, the timing of his thinking does not work.

When explaining the deduction, he claims that "at the beginning" he had said "several times" that he did not want Alfred "arrested *now*" (with emphasis on the italicised "*now*"). In fact he had said just once that Emily "would never forgive me if I let Alfred, her husband, be arrested *now* – when a word from me could save him!". But, if he said that because he realised *then* that Alfred *wanted* to be arrested, why would he have murmured "*Sacré*! Does this imbecile of a man *want* to be arrested?" and go on to say "I tell you, *mon ami*, it puzzles me. Me – Hercule Poirot!". Moreover, he had not by then acquired the evidence of the five witnesses which would have enabled him to save Alfred. So, Poirot's 'arrested *now*' clue is in the wrong chronological place in the puzzle, which is a shame because, if it had been placed after Alfred's refusal to deploy his alibi, it could have been a very imaginative one.

As for Evelyn, Poirot suspects her because she had lied at the inquest about a letter dated 17 July sent to her by Emily. He says that the words were written by Emily but that the date was different, the "1" having been written in before the "7" by Evelyn, so turning a letter written on 7 July to 17 July.

The '17 July letter' clue is a fairly good one to Evelyn lying but the question it raises, which Poirot even asks himself, is why she wanted to conceal the *actual* letter of 17 July, which Annie told us Emily wrote. Strangely, Poirot never answers his question and we never learn the contents of that letter.

There are other clues against Evelyn – the 'nursing' clue, with her work as a hospital nurse, her father having been a doctor; the 'Alfred hatred' clue, where her overvehemence was "too violent to be natural"; and the 'cousins' clue, which was a clue to her complicity with her cousin and to her impersonation of him, as to which Poirot refers to a distinct resemblance, especially in their gait and bearing. However, we had been told that he was a "rotten little bounder" while she had "a large sensible square body".

It is *after* the inquest in chapter 6, at which Alfred explains away the "Alfred – Alfred –" dying words clue by suggesting that Emily may have mistaken Bauerstein for him, that Poirot suggests that Alfred had been impersonated. When doing so, he refers back to the second of "two facts of significance", mentioned in chapter 5, namely that Alfred "wears very peculiar clothes, has a black beard, and uses glasses". But it is odd that he should regard this as significant then because he has not yet been told of any occasion when Alfred might have been impersonated; Mr Mace from the chemist did not even mention Alfred to him.

The "last link" in Poirot's chain is Alfred's 'unfinished letter' clue, which is only revealed to readers when Poirot reveals the solution. Without it, there was, he says, "absolutely nothing" to connect Alfred with the crime. It had originally been planned for the Monday night, as clued by the 'bell wire' clue, with the wire of Emily's room bell having been cut to shut her off from help. With her forgetting to take her tonic, one can understand Alfred writing reassuringly to Evelyn. But it seems most unlikely that he would add "There's a good time coming once the old woman is dead and out of the way. No one can possibly bring home the crime to me".

As noted earlier, Emily finds the letter while looking for stamps in Alfred's desk. Poirot guesses (the first of three guesses) that, having no stamps herself (because later she asks Dorcas to fetch some – the 'stamps' clue), she tried her own keys in his desk. Poirot had unlocked it in chapter 4, using one of Emily's keys, which he therefore knew fitted, and had remarked "There were no stamps in the desk, but there might have been, eh, *mon ami*?", suggesting that he had, impressively, already thought of Emily looking in Alfred's desk.

After finding the letter, she puts it in her despatch case. When Poirot inspects her bedroom, the despatch case with a key in the lock "engaged his attention for some time", even though he doesn't look inside. Instead, an hour later, when he sees that the lock has been forced, he knows from the 'forced lock' clue that the despatch case must have contained "enough of a clue to connect the murderer with the crime".

One would have thought that, having retrieved the letter, Alfred would destroy it (it was only eight lines of text, so he could have put it in his mouth and eaten it) but Poirot "reasoned" that, since he dared not keep it on him, he had hidden it in the room. So, it is very surprising that Poirot does not search for it more thoroughly. But he does eventually find it as a result of the 'ornaments' clue.

The first element of the 'ornaments' clue comes when, during his inspection of Emily's bedroom, he straightens the ornaments on the mantelpiece (chapter 4). The second comes when, finding the lock forced, his hands shake as he straightens the spill vases on the mantelpiece (chapter 5). The third comes two months later when, as he is building a card house, Hastings remarks that he had only seen his hand shake once, which was when he found the forced lock and was twiddling the things on the mantelpiece (chapter 11).

On being told this, Poirot has "an idea gigantic!". He later explains that, if he had straightened the objects when first in the room, he would not have needed to straighten them an hour later unless in the meantime someone had touched them. So he rushes to Styles where he finds the letter in strips in a spill vase.

This 'ornaments' clue is excellently constructed and probably beats the 'last dose' clue to being the best in the book. Its operative parts are the first and second elements, with the third element prompting readers to look back to the second. Those operative parts are brilliantly concealed, not just by being in different chapters but by the language deploying them. Thus, on the first occasion straightening the ornaments seems unimportant compared with the concern about the crushed coffee cup while on the second straightening the spill vases seems unimportant compared with Poirot's shaking hands. The only weakness is that Alfred would surely have retrieved this damning evidence later, as to which Poirot says unpersuasively that, since no one had looked in the spill vase in the first week, they were unlikely to do so later.

What will have surprised readers is that Poirot's apparent starting point – his "six points of interest" – has been of little help in identifying the criminals. Number Six turns out, once we know that the powders are bromide, to be crucial to the murder plan while Number Three, the stain, tells Poirot that Emily had not drunk her coffee.

However, Numbers One, Two, Four and Five relate only to sub-plots. Although Number Two, the despatch case with a key in the lock, looks in retrospect as if it is also a clue in the murder plot because of the forced lock, it had not yet been forced when Poirot listed it. So it was just intended as a clue to Mary's attempt to find the document which Emily had refused to show her.

Mary's attempt flowed from overhearing Emily's quarrel, which Poirot knows was with John because Mary's "lack of frankness" at the inquest was a clue which could "only be explained" if the quarrel had been with him. The quarrel leads, first, to Emily making a new will. But, since she then burns it, what clues tell Poirot that she had made a will and then destroyed it?

First are the 'will and testament' and 'possessed' clues (of which we see facsimiles) showing that Emily made a will. In her grate was a fragment of charred, thick paper with the letters "… ll and …" (as in 'will and testament') and in her wastepaper basket was a crumpled envelope on which she had tried out spellings of the word "possessed", a word almost certain to be in a will.

Second is the 'begonia' clue, showing she made the will that afternoon. Poirot sees traces of brown mould near her desk similar to that in the begonia beds and deduces that she must have called in the two gardeners, who were planting begonias that afternoon, to witness the will. That is a good deduction. Less good is his lack of interest in the blotting paper which concealed the contents of the will. In fact, the police (not Poirot) find the blotting paper which, when reversed in a mirror, shows that it left everything to Alfred.

Third is the 'hot weather' clue, which shows that Emily destroyed the will. This clue works very well because it combines three pieces of information provided at different points – that Styles was "quite a war household" where every scrap of waste paper was saved (chapter 1); that Emily told Dorcas to light the fire in her bedroom (chapter 2); and that it was 80° that day (the first of Poirot's "two facts of significance" in chapter 5). At the denouement he says that, when he heard of Emily wanting a fire lit on such a hot day, he deduced that it was so she could destroy a document because, with Styles being a war household, there was no other way of doing so.

Poirot had assumed for a time that Emily *destroyed* the will because of the quarrel. In fact it caused her to *make* the will. But having made it, she then decided to destroy it. It is that decision which causes Poirot to describe the hot weather as "the key to the whole riddle!" since it indicates that she must have become aware of something (the 'unfinished letter' clue) which had made her as anxious to destroy the will as she had earlier been to make it.

The quarrel leads, secondly, to Mary's attempt to obtain that document. The clueing of that sub-plot is where Poirot starts at the denouement with Number Four, the fragment of dark green fabric caught in the bolt of the door between Emily's and Cynthia's rooms. He says that it was torn from a green land armlet belonging to Mary, the only person at Styles working "on the land". That deduction depends upon knowing that the land uniform includes a green armlet, so modern readers, only told that Mary was wearing her *white* land smock, could hardly interpret this 'dark green fabric' clue.

However, Poirot is convinced that Mary had entered Emily's room through Cynthia's. His response to the argument that the door was bolted on the inside (i.e. Emily's side) is that "we have only her [Mary's] word for it". Mary did indeed say that the door was bolted in chapter 9 (adding "I said so at the inquest" – though in fact she did not say so then) but we don't only have her "word for it". Annie says that the door was bolted when she entered Emily's room at about 8 pm and that, before she left (presumably with the door still bolted), Emily had come up to bed. So, despite Poirot's assertion that Mary had unbolted the door "some time in the evening", there was never an opportunity, except when Emily was there, for her to have done so.

However, Poirot also believes that Mary had been in Emily's room for other reasons. One is the 'falling table' clue. Mary claims at the inquest that she went to Emily's room after hearing the table fall. Yet, as Poirot proves by knocking it over, unheard by Hastings in the left wing, she could not have heard this from her room. Another is the white candle grease on Emily's floor (Number Five). Emily had no candlestick and since the only candle known to have been brought in was Lawrence's pink one, Poirot deduces from the 'candle grease' clue that Mary, startled by Emily waking, dropped her candle before retreating to Cynthia's room without the document.

But how does Poirot deduce that that document is unrelated to John's intrigue? The clear implication for readers was that, when Emily used the words "scandal between husband and wife" in her quarrel and again an hour later, she was still upset by *that* scandal. However, by looking at the matter psychologically, Poirot deduces that the second scandal was not the same as the first one concerning Mrs Raikes but a scandal concerning Emily herself.

He says that at 4 pm she had been angry but was "completely mistress of herself" whereas an hour later she was "in violent distress". However, she hardly sounds like she was "completely mistress of herself", saying to John "How dare you? I have kept you and clothed you and fed you! You owe everything to me! And this is how you repay me! By bringing disgrace upon our name!". And on the second occasion, when she says to Dorcas "I'd rather hush it up if I could", that might be suitable for John's intrigue but it is a very odd reaction to Alfred's letter, which refers to her being out of the way. Indeed "scandal between husband and wife" is an odd description of it.

Nevertheless, Emily locks it in her despatch case. But it is not the case which is the crucial element of Number Two but the key in the lock, with a bit of twisted wire through the handle (the 'twisted wire' clue). In addition, Poirot finds a bunch of keys, one of which, the 'shining key' clue, also unlocks the case and he later learns from Dorcas that Emily had lost the original key (the one in the lock) but had a duplicate (the shining one on the bunch).

As a result of this rather confusing mixture of clues and evidence, Poirot guesses (the second of his three guesses) that the original key went missing because the 'twisted wire' clue suggested that it had been wrenched off a key ring; and that, if it had been found, Emily would have replaced it on her bunch; but that, since the "shining key" was on the bunch (presumably put there by Emily), *somebody else* had the *original* key and inserted it in the lock.

That deduction, made in chapter 5, is a good one. What he is saying is that somebody wrenched the original key from the bunch in order to open the case. But that is not what he says at the denouement. There, seemingly having forgotten the wrenching, he says that Mary "happened" to pick up the key, which is far less convincing.

Mary could enter Emily's room through Cynthia's without waking them because she had drugged them both. We saw with the clueing of the murder plot that Poirot, referring to the analyst's report, said that Mary had administered a safe, but effectual, narcotic to both Emily and Cynthia.

Poirot guesses (the last of his three guesses) that Emily drank her drugged cocoa after picking up the pieces of her broken coffee cup which had been thrown to the floor by the tilting table. Later Mary, fearing that the drugged cocoa had been the cause of Emily's poisoning, dared not touch its remains because too many eyes were on her but she drops *Cynthia's* drugged coffee cup (the missing one) into a vase where it is later discovered by Lawrence.

As for *Emily's* coffee cup, which had been crushed into fragments (Number One), Poirot gets a clue who did this in chapter 4 when Hastings says that Lawrence had seen something that "absolutely paralysed him" in Emily's room – the 'paralysed' clue having been omitted when Hastings told Poirot "the whole story". Poirot later suggests that, despite Lawrence's claim in chapter 9 that the door into Cynthia's room was bolted, he had seen over Hastings' shoulder that it was unbolted (before Mary shot the bolt across after Emily's death). So the door had a bolt high enough for Lawrence to see it over Hastings' shoulder but low enough to catch Mary's armlet.

After seeing the door unbolted, Lawrence believes Cynthia is guilty and so crushes the coffee cup to prevent its contents being tested. He tries to shield her because, in the sub-plot of his attempt to protect her, he is in love with her, as clued by the sour face he makes "every time" she speaks and laughs with John – though in fact this only happens twice (in chapters 1 and 8).

There are various clues against Lawrence himself, beyond the 'paralysed' clue, including his medical qualification, his lack of funds, his inheritance of Styles if something were to happen to John (as the nearest lineal ancestor under section 6 of the Inheritance Act 1833), his resistance to using Poirot, his insistence that Emily died of natural causes, the false beard ordered in his name, his idea of visiting Cynthia's dispensary and his inspection there of a bottle of strychnine in the poison cupboard.

Poirot knows that Lawrence inspected the poison cupboard because he had asked Hastings in chapter 9 whether it was near "the window" and was told that it was not. Since Cynthia had had to call Lawrence to join the others on "the balcony" (chapter 2), he could not have been with them, but still inside looking at the cupboard. This 'balcony' clue is well interpreted by Poirot, though his use of "window" in chapter 9, when "balcony" had been used in chapter 2, makes it hard for readers to spot.

The final sub-plot concerns Bauerstein. He has a beard (like Alfred and the strychnine purchaser). He arrives at Styles on the fateful evening plastered in mud and could have dropped something into Emily's coffee. And later he returns to the house as Emily is dying, even though it is about 5 am.

In fact Bauerstein is arrested for espionage, not murder. Poirot is not surprised – though Bauerstein is acquitted – so, what were the clues? One, that Styles was only four miles from the coast (not that readers had been told this). Two, that it was odd that a famous London doctor should bury himself in Styles St Mary and walk about at night. And three, that he was German (not that we had been told this either; indeed in chapter 9 we were told he was Polish).

Finally, the first edition's dust jacket reads "This novel was originally written as the result of a bet, that the author, who had previously never written a book could not compose a detective novel in which the reader would not be able to "spot" the murderer, though having access to the same clues as the detective. The author has certainly won her bet". That is a brave assertion because, even though we get the 'tonic', 'bromide' and 'last dose' clues, only a reader with a chemist's knowledge would have been able to spot the murder method before Poirot quotes from *The Art of Dispensing* at the denouement. Similarly, as to the criminals, despite the excellent 'ornaments' clue, we did not actually get the 'unfinished letter' clue, or know that it implicated Alfred and Evelyn, until the denouement.

Poirot also sends readers on a false investigative trail by telling Hastings in chapter 7 that "at most, two persons were speaking the truth at the inquest without reservation or subterfuge". We later learn that he means John and Cynthia. However, although Alfred, Mary, Evelyn, Lawrence and Bauerstein may have lied, that still leaves six other witnesses. Some of those may have been mistaken but it is not right that all of them (even Amy Hill who sold the will form) were guilty of reservation or subterfuge.

However, where Poirot really goes wrong is in not looking inside Emily's despatch case. He says "I have no authority to go through these papers" and yet he questions Dorcas "with Mr Cavendish's full approval". Had he looked inside, his "last link" would have been almost his first – but then there would have been no mysterious affair at Styles.

The Murder On The Links

Solution

This story is narrated by Captain Arthur Hastings whose Christian name and military rank were not given in his first novel.[1]

Poirot investigates the murder of millionaire Paul Renauld, who is found stabbed in the back at 9 am on Wednesday 8 June, lying face down in a freshly dug open grave on the links course adjoining his house, Villa Geneviève, at Merlinville in northern France. Poirot, who had received a letter from Renauld, written the day before, arrives there later on 8 June.

Renauld's wife, Eloise, says that, after they had gone to bed on 7 June, she was woken at about 2 am by two masked, bearded assassins. One bound and gagged her while the other held her dagger paper knife over Renauld's heart. The men, presumed to be Chileans, demanded "the secret" from him in South American Spanish, rifled the safe and hustled him out of the door half dressed, at which she fainted.

Other than the three servants, who heard nothing, no one else was in the house because on 7 June Renauld had asked his son Jack, who had been in Paris since 23 May, to go to Santiago and sent the chauffeur Masters on holiday.

We learn that Renauld bought the villa only six weeks before; that he had changed of late; that Madame Daubreuil, who lived nearby with her daughter Marthe, had recently had money to spend; that his secretary, Gabriel Stonor, thought she was blackmailing him; that Renauld quarrelled with Jack before his departure to Paris about his wish to marry Marthe; that next day he made a will leaving his fortune to Eloise, superseding one which would have given Jack half; that on the fatal night he was visited by an unknown lady who left at about 10.25 pm and whose name might be "Duveen" (because this was on a cheque fragment found in his study); and that in the overcoat he was wearing was a letter from "Bella" saying "I'd as soon kill you as let her have you!".

The dagger paper knife with which he had been stabbed was a First World War souvenir, produced by Jack who had served in the Air Force (or Flying Corps). It is put in a jar in a small shed leaning against the house to which the body is moved from the grave. Next morning (9 June) it is stolen by a young woman known only as Cinderella, who is let into the shed by Hastings

The day after that a second body is found in a ramshackle shed (not the small shed) near the links, stabbed with what looks like the same dagger. The body – a man aged about 50, like Renauld – is well dressed but his nails are broken and discoloured and a ragged coat and trousers are nearby. After breakfast on 10 June the doctor says that he died at least 48 hours ago and probably longer, which takes us back to at least the morning of 8 June when Renauld was found – and yet he seems to have been stabbed with a dagger stolen on 9 June.

As early as chapter 17 (out of 28) Poirot knows "one murderer", having solved the "crime" relating to the man in the shed, who was not in fact stabbed to death. He was an abusive tramp who got into the Renaulds' garden on 7 June and died of an epileptic fit. The Renaulds decided to pretend that the body was Renauld himself, who had been killed by Chilean abductors. But why?

About 20 years before, there was a famous murder case – the Beroldy case. Madame Beroldy was found bound and gagged in her bedroom with her husband stabbed dead on the bed. She claimed that the crime had been committed by two masked, bearded Russians, who had demanded the "secret"; that her husband had refused and been stabbed; and that the men had stolen papers from the safe. It was alleged that she had invented the Russians and committed the murder with her lover, Georges Conneau. He had vanished and she was acquitted at trial after claiming that he alone was guilty.

Conneau had fled to Canada and become Paul Renauld. He married under that name and built a fortune in South America. After 20 years he bought Villa Geneviève, only to find that his neighbour, Madame Daubreuil, was Madame Beroldy. She began to blackmail him and, to make matters worse, Jack fell for Marthe, who believed that he would inherit half the fortune. Renauld refused to let Jack marry her, resulting in the quarrel on 23 May. If she were to do so, the Daubreuils would have two ways into Renauld's money – blackmail and marriage. Renauld saw "only one way of escape – death" (chapter 21).

So a plan was concocted, reminiscent of the invented Russians in the Beroldy case, to make it appear that he was abducted at 2 am on 8 June by two Chileans and murdered on the links. The body, which would be falsely identified as Renauld by Eloise, would be provided by the tramp.

Since the Renaulds could not risk the identification being contradicted, the chauffeur Masters was sent on holiday and a telegram was sent to Jack in Paris, asking him to go straight to Cherbourg and sail to Buenos Aires for Santiago on an important matter. Then, to reinforce the danger to Renauld, he wrote to Poirot. After that, he and Eloise removed the dead tramp's clothes, put him in Renauld's clothes and "they" (says Poirot) drove the dagger through his heart before leaving him in the ramshackle shed.

That night (7 June) Renauld would bind and gag Eloise in the bedroom; slip on a coat over his underclothes; leave by the bedroom window, climbing down a tree; smooth out his footprints on the flowerbed; go to the links; dig a grave for the tramp's body (but where it would be found by men digging a bunker); move the tramp there from the shed; batter his face with a piece of lead-piping to make it unrecognisable; put the coat in the grave; don the tramp's clothes; and go to the station, leaving unnoticed on the train just after midnight.[2] He would then escape abroad, restarting under a new name.

Once the body was found by those digging the bunker, Eloise would falsely identify it. The abduction time would be confirmed by a wristwatch dashed to the ground after its hands had been moved forward to 2 am. With the crime presumed to have happened then, no one leaving on a train two hours earlier would be suspected. Later she would join him abroad, with control of the fortune under his new will.

That, then, is the first "crime". The unnamed tramp dies of an epileptic fit. Since it is pure luck that he walks into the Renaulds' garden, there is no clever murder plan, although one credits the Renaulds for their opportunistic use of the body and for the careful abduction planning. But what would they have done without an epileptic trespasser? Poirot says "How they meant to manage the body business, I do not know – possibly an art student's skeleton and a fire – or something of the kind" (chapter 21). That does not sound convincing.

The main crime – Renauld's stabbing – occurs while he is digging the grave for the tramp who is still in the shed.

As for suspects, Eloise seems most unlikely because of her genuine grief on learning that the body in the grave is Renauld's, not the tramp's. So do Madame Daubreuil (who would lose her blackmail victim) and Stonor (who does not arrive until 9 June). Therefore, ignoring Masters and the servants, the realistic suspects appear to be Marthe; Cinderella (who stole the dagger); and the lady evening visitor, who turns out to be Jack's previous girlfriend,

Bella Duveen, who had come to Merlinville to see Jack; since he was not there, she saw Renauld, who tried to buy her off with a cheque before she left at 10.25 pm.

But Jack himself, who did not sail from Cherbourg, becomes the main suspect when he returns to Merlinville on 9 June after reading of his father's death. He admits that before going to Paris on 23 May he had argued with his father, wishing he were dead, and he is arrested for murder by Monsieur Giraud, the famous detective from the Paris Sûreté, when it is realised that he had come to Merlinville on the fatal night to see Marthe.

In fact, after his train arrived at 11.40 pm, he heard a cry as he walked across the links. He then saw the grave and a body lying face down with a dagger in its back (Renauld). And then he saw Bella. It is not clear what she did between 10.25 pm and then but each of them (wrongly) took the other to be the perpetrator. She ran and he returned to Cherbourg instead of seeing Marthe.

After his arrest, Jack, despite believing Bella guilty, says nothing about having seen her because he once loved her. However, in order to exonerate him, she then gives herself up and he is released. At that point readers are supposed to believe (as Jack and Hastings do) that Bella is the murderer.

However, the murderer is Marthe. She did not care for Jack but he was, she believed, the heir to half the fortune. If she killed Renauld, who stood in the way of her marrying Jack, the marriage could proceed and she would be wealthy – a credible motive, but flawed because Renauld had changed his will.

Just as the tramp's death gave the Renaulds a stroke of luck, so Marthe got one when overhearing the Renaulds concocting their abduction plan. She only had to stab Renauld as he dug the grave. So the murder is no more ingenious than the first "crime" and founded, as they both are, on strokes of luck, neither is very satisfying. There is a cleverness in the "crimes" being committed by different people, particularly with the second body being stabbed by the person who was found dead first. However, that cleverness is too complicated to be enjoyable or memorable and sold too cheaply by being revealed so long before the denouement (chapter 21).

Beyond this, there is still the mystery of how both Renauld and the tramp were stabbed with what looks like the same dagger. Until chapter 24 we believe that there may be two daggers (the one used to kill Renauld, stolen by Cinderella and the one used on the tramp) but the situation is more complex.

Jack had *three* dagger paper knives made. He gave one to his mother – the one with which she said Renauld was threatened but which was plunged into the tramp. He gave the second to Bella and we assume (after she gives herself up) that she used it to kill Renauld. He gave the third to Marthe and this was the dagger in fact used to stab Renauld and then stolen by Cinderella.

Cinderella was really Bella's twin sister, Dulcie. Dulcie wrongly thought that the dagger used to stab Renauld (the third dagger) was Bella's and assumed that Bella had murdered Renauld, mistaking him for Jack who had rebuffed her. So she stole the third dagger (whereas Bella's was in fact the second) in order to eliminate evidence against her sister and threw it into the sea.

The tale of the daggers helps Poirot identify Marthe as the murderer. He reasons that, if Bella's dagger (the second) can be found among her effects (as it is), then the dagger which Dulcie threw into the sea after it was used to kill Renauld cannot be Bella's but must be the third – so supporting her innocence and Marthe's guilt. This provides quite a good outcome to the dagger mystery but at the expense of some convoluted reasoning; and we only learn that Bella's dagger was found among her effects *after* Poirot has exposed Marthe.

Plot

After the two "crimes" and the dagger mystery, Cinderella's true identity is the last main plotting issue. It is quite a good, if unclued, twist when she turns out to be Dulcie Duveen rather than Bella.

However, the reaction in chapter 11 to her theft of the dagger is astonishing. Although Hastings committed a "grave fault" in letting her into the shed, no one asks him any more about her after he says she is "an English lady who happens to be staying in Merlinville". Not even Giraud, who calls her "the assassin, or an accomplice of the assassin".

While Hastings falls for Cinderella, Poirot and Giraud become enemies, even betting 500 francs on who will find the murderer first. Giraud's low point is not the wrongful arrest of Jack but his failure to look in the ramshackle shed on 8 June, even though the tramp's body is there.

Pretty much from the outset the story is an engaging one.[3] It moves at a fair pace and the author plots the interweaving of the Beroldy case and the two present-day "crimes" quite mystifyingly and with great skill. Until about chapter 20. There the narrative gets so tortuous, with theories and clues and being knocked about by Poirot and Hastings, that it becomes hard to follow the thinking and harder still to work out what really matters. Hastings' admission that he is "hopelessly fogged" is entirely justified.

Poirot is again hard to follow in chapter 21 in which he refers back to his opaque remark in chapter 17: "One may have a crime without a murderer, but for two crimes it is essential to have two bodies". Hastings thought the remark "so peculiarly lacking in lucidity that I looked at him in some anxiety".

At the end of chapter 21 Poirot produces a photograph of Bella. Hastings thinks she is Cinderella. He loves her but she stole the dagger, a conflict that causes him to spend too much time in the next chapter on confusing and wrong theories before pinioning Poirot's arms to his side so that Cinderella can escape. This extraordinary episode ends when Hastings realises that Cinderella is not Bella but Dulcie. There is even a happy ending with, it seems, her agreeing to marry him.

By then readers have also been treated to Eloise's obviously false threat to make a will excluding Jack – and so in effect Marthe – from the fortune and to Marthe's attempt to kill her before she can do so. Before her unmasking, upstairs at Villa Geneviève, Hastings records: "Then rushing to the tree in the flowerbed, he swarmed up it with the agility of a cat. I followed him, as with a bound he sprang in through the open window". He is talking about Poirot, which hardly seems credible.

By that stage, having had to face so much complicated reasoning and so many clues, readers may well feel that the mystification generated by the first half of the story has been largely dissipated. They will probably have no interest in unexplained loose ends such as Poirot's "meaningless" question about Stonor in chapter 27 (which he does not explain); and, deprived as they even are of a scene describing Poirot's triumph over Giraud, they will do well to remember much of the plot beyond there having been a murder on the links.

Clues

The most noticeable clueing feature is the distinction between tangible clues and Poirot's 'psychological' ones. He accepts that studying fingerprints and footprints and cigarette ash is vital but he does not want to make himself "ridiculous" by studying such clues – a surprising remark since he showed a real appetite for tangible clues in his first novel, which he repeats in this one.

The distinction appears most sharply in his hostility with Giraud, the "human foxhound", the expert on tangible clues. As Poirot says (chapter 9) "You may know all about cigarettes and match ends, Monsieur Giraud, but I, Hercule Poirot, know the mind of man". What matters for him is "above all, the true psychology of the case" (chapter 2).

Thus, he says that the same brain lies behind Renauld's abduction and a similar crime – "a true clue – a psychological clue" (chapter 9); that Hastings mistakes Madame Daubreuil's "character" (chapter 17); that three times Renauld displayed a change of view and action – "three psychological points therefore" (chapter 20)[4]; that the worst point against Jack is "psychological – heredity, *mon ami*, heredity!" (chapter 21); and, similarly, that Marthe's mother is the notorious Madame Beroldy (chapter 28).

In analysing the particularly complex intermixture of clues in this story, caused by the different "crimes" being committed by different people, it makes sense to start with the "crime" that Poirot solves first. Here he is ahead of readers because he knows of an "almost precisely similar" crime, albeit with mythical Russian villains rather than Chileans. Because of this 'Beroldy similarity' clue, he suspects Eloise's involvement and looks at her wrists, knowing that loose cords in the Beroldy case had caused suspicion.

In fact the cords had bitten into Eloise's flesh but, since an accomplice could have tied them, we get two other clues that she was not involved in the murder. One is that she was much more grief-stricken when she *saw* that the body was her husband (not the tramp) than when *hearing* of his death. This 'grief-stricken' clue is rather clever but, because she might be acting, Poirot prefers the 'fainting' clue: that she genuinely swooned on seeing his body. So, realising that she was not involved in Renauld's murder, he starts again but he still disbelieves her abduction story because of various other clues.

First is the 'open door' clue, the front door having been found ajar. He thinks it "an unparalleled piece of good fortune" that the assassins *found* the door ajar and does not understand why they would have *left* it open. There was a tree up to the bedroom window which he thinks they would have forced.

Second is the 'creaking stairs' clue. Eloise says that the assassins hustled her husband out of the door (not the window) but Poirot thinks that the creaking stairs, with *three* people descending, "would awaken the dead" and yet the servants heard nothing, meaning that the stairs were not used.

Third is the 'footprints' clue revealing that, although Renauld left the door open to suggest that the assassins left that way, he went out of the window, down the tree. Its roots were in a flower bed in which one had to step in order to get from the tree to the path. Yet the mould was smooth. But the footprints of the gardener, who had planted geraniums in *two* flower beds on 7 June, were in the other one and Poirot twice describes those footprints as "the most important" things they have seen (chapters 6 and 7).

His point becomes clearer in chapter 9 when he emulates Sherlock Holmes' reference to the curious incident of the dog in the night-time in *Silver Blaze*. Holmes was told that the dog did nothing. "That was the curious incident", he replied. The fact that it did not bark meant that the midnight visitor was someone it knew well. Poirot says "Then there is the matter of the footprints in the flower-bed". "But I see no footprints?" says Giraud. "No", says Poirot. "There are none". He explains in chapter 12 that the gardener's footprints should have been in *both* flower beds and so someone must have smoothed over the bed in order to obliterate his own footprints after using the window and the tree.

He adds that Renauld thereby furnished "the most positive evidence against himself" (chapter 21). But why is that? Of course, it means that the window was used but why not by Chilean abductors (as Poirot actually assumes in chapter 12)? Is his point that they would not have smoothed over a flower bed? He does not say. So, although the 'footprints' clue is quite clever, one thinks that the author contrived it to have her own *Silver Blaze* clue.

Fourth is the 'smashed wristwatch' clue. Although the glass is broken, the watch itself still works, with the hands pointing to 7 pm even though it is just after 5 pm when Poirot sees it. He reckons that the hands were moved on to 2 am at about midnight and that the watch was then smashed so that anyone leaving by the 12.17 am train would have an alibi. That is a good deduction but which of the Renaulds smashed it? Since Renauld had to get to the links, dig a grave, move the tramp, disfigure his face, bury him, don his clothes and get to the station by 12.17 am, he cannot have been smashing it at midnight. So, Eloise must have done so with her tightly bound hands.

Fifth is the 'assassins' items' clue. The spade was Renauld's; the gloves were his gardener's; and the dagger seems to have been Eloise's. As Poirot says: "You do not think it odd that these strangers should come unprovided with a weapon, with gloves, with a spade, and that that they should so conveniently find all these things?". Although a South American cigarette stub and match are by the body, Poirot reckons they were planted. For him, "the word Santiago, to my mind, is a red herring dragged continually across the track to put us off the scent".

So, disbelieving the abduction story, Poirot reviews the Beroldy case in Paris. He returns with a theory, which he is sure is right, but then hears of the second body. He is "flabbergasted" – a new murder is "impossible". But almost immediately he fits the second body into his theory. So his theory must work (i) before that body is found and (ii) afterwards. In analysing the clueing of this most unusual position in a disciplined way, one needs to look at the two situations separately, starting with the first.

When Poirot returns, he has a photograph showing that Madame Daubreuil is Madame Beroldy. However, it was "very unlikely" that she, as Renauld's blackmailer, would have inspired Eloise's "almost precisely similar" story. So who – Poirot's logic runs in chapter 20 – could have done so other than Georges Conneau, for whom Eloise must have lied? She would only have lied – Poirot's logic runs in chapter 21 – for herself or the man she loved or her child; since neither the first of those (herself) or the third (Jack) could be Conneau, the person for whom she had lied must be the second (the man she loved, Paul Renauld); and so he must be Georges Conneau.

Although one has to read Poirot's logic a few times, it does work – subject to one point, namely the assumption that only Conneau or Madame Beroldy could have copied the Beroldy case. That was his key deduction from the 'Beroldy similarity' clue in chapter 9: "That, when you have two crimes precisely similar in design and execution, you find the same brain behind them both". But in chapter 12 he identified two options: "either the brain that planned the first crime also planned this one, or else an account read of a *cause célèbre* unconsciously remained in our assassin's memory and prompted the details". His English for the second option is not very clear but it seems that *anyone* remembering the Beroldy case, which was a *cause célèbre* and fully reported, could have copied it and, if so, that undermines his logic.

Nevertheless, having deduced that Conneau is Renauld, various clues fall into place supporting Poirot's theory about the abduction before he knows of the second body: (a) that Renauld changed after coming to Merlinville; (b) that he made payments to Madame Daubreuil (and Stonor suspected blackmail); (c) that on 23 May he quarrelled with Jack about marrying Marthe; (d) that on 24 May he left his fortune to Eloise; (e) that on 7 June he wrote to Poirot; (f) that on 7 June he sent Masters away despite saying that a car would meet Poirot at Calais; and (g) that on 7 June he ordered Jack to Santiago.

It is in connection with Jack being sent away that Poirot says in chapter 21 that Eloise "only made one slip". When Jack comes to Merlinville on 9 June, she notes that he had not sailed and says "After all, it does not matter – now". Poirot emphasises "*now*", presumably meaning that, with the Renaulds' plan having failed, there was *now* no need for Jack to be abroad. But the 'not matter – *now*' clue is pretty opaque and an odd selection as the "one slip" since she could just have meant that, after Renauld's death, Jack now had no need to perform a genuine task in Chile.

A final clue for Poirot's theory before hearing of the second body is Renauld's remark to his lady evening visitor: "Yes – yes – but for God's sake go now". Although he could just have wanted her to go because the meeting was unpleasant, the 'Go now' clue is more subtle because it reveals, says Poirot, that time was slipping by if Renauld was to get the 12.17 am train.

Then Poirot learns of the second body. It is odd in retrospect that he did not expect it since it is no real leap from expecting a fake body (his suggestion of a skeleton) to producing a real one. But his expectation does explain how, moments after saying that a new murder is "impossible", he can indicate precisely how it is possible – with the Renaulds using a real body instead.

In that second situation with the new body, other clues also fall into place. First is the 'lead-piping' clue – a short piece of lead-piping lying by the spade. Although Poirot saw it before learning of the tramp's body, it would have made no sense as a clue until then because it was to be used to make the tramp's face unrecognisable.[5] In chapter 21 he says that the lead-piping "first set me on the right track" – but how can that be when he had a theory *before* knowing that a body was to be disfigured and when no disfiguring would be required for a skeleton?

Second is the 'man's work' clue. In chapter 4 Poirot had described digging the grave as "laborious work", which was "a man's doing". But he did not think that Jack would have dug a grave for Renauld because he would have wanted the body found in order to claim his inheritance. The answer to the 'man's work' clue is that the second body, not Renauld, was to be buried and that Renauld himself was digging the grave.

Third is the 'bunker' clue, the whitewashed line around the grave, showing that a bunker was to be made there. Poirot thought this an odd place to bury the body because, when the bunker was dug, it would be found. So the grave was dug by someone who, like Jack, wanted the body found, in which case

81

why dig a grave at all? A good question, answered by the second body, which was to be found when the bunker was dug (so that Madame Daubreuil would accept Renauld's death) but not before because a delay in finding it would reduce the chances of realising that it was not Renauld.

Fourth is the 'underclothes' clue – that Renauld was curiously wearing only underclothes under his overcoat, presumably because after digging the grave he proposed to put on the tramp's clothes.

As well as those clues, which Poirot had before seeing the tramp's body, he gets more clues on seeing it. The swarthy body did not have a gentleman's hands but hard skin and dirty, broken fingernails (suggesting it was the tramp seen arguing with Renauld by Marthe); that it was nevertheless well dressed, although a ragged coat and trousers were nearby (indicating that Renauld had dressed him in his neat clothes and would be donning his rags); that the wound had not bled and the dagger was hardly discoloured (indicating that he was stabbed after death); that there was foam on his lips (indicating that he had died of an epileptic fit); and that there were marks on the dirt (indicating that he had been dragged into the shed by two people, one of whom, as indicated by the shoe prints, was a woman).

There is also a woman's hair coiled round the dagger handle. This is actually the 'second woman's hair' clue because, when Poirot inspected Renauld's study, he found a long black hair on the chair, which he assumed belonged to his lady evening visitor (the 'first woman's hair' clue). When Hastings sees the 'second woman's hair' clue on the dagger, he describes it as "a woman's long black hair, similar to the one Poirot had taken from the armchair in the library" (he means study). There are two significant points about Hastings' description of the 'second woman's hair' clue.

One is that it is "similar" to the 'first woman's hair' clue, making readers very likely to assume that the hairs belonged to the same person and that the lady evening visitor (not yet known but clearly not Eloise) had used the dagger on the second body. So, Poirot should not really assert, as if it were obvious, that the second woman's hair was "Madame Renauld's, of course" (chapter 21).

The other, which makes it even more difficult to deduce that Eloise's dagger had stabbed the tramp, is that the second woman's hair was black and yet Hastings had said in chapter 5 that Eloise's "once dark hair was now almost entirely silvered". This 'silvered' clue is presented very cleverly, with the key words being "once dark" and "almost", perhaps letting the most astute reader deduce that, if Eloise wasn't *entirely* silvered, she still had some dark hair.

However, he would need to be very astute because her silvered (rather than dark) hair is emphasised when she steps out of the shed with "the sun flashing on the silver threads in her hair". This is so closely juxtaposed to the 'second woman's hair' clue that it cleverly misdirects readers away from thinking that the black hair could be hers.

The final clue about the first "crime" concerns the time of the tramp's death. The body is found on 10 June but Poirot's theory has the tramp dying on 7 June, which works if, as he says in chapter 20, the doctor had said that the tramp had been dead at least 48 hours "with a possible margin of twenty-four hours more". But the doctor had not said that. What he had said in chapter 14 was that he had been dead at least 48 hours "and probably longer". Thus he could have died *after* Renauld. So Poirot cheats with the 'tramp timing' clue.

Having solved the first "crime", Poirot still has to solve Renauld's murder. There are various 'Jack' clues: his father's refusal to let him marry Marthe; the violent quarrel; his belief that he would inherit half the fortune; and his presence in Merlinville on the fatal night. But, for Poirot, the worst clue is psychological – the 'Jack heredity' clue: he is the son of Georges Conneau.

The best clue relating to Jack, however, concerns his claim that, after arriving in Merlinville on the 11.40 pm train, he saw Marthe. In chapter 18 Poirot checks with her that he was in Merlinville and she says "Yes. He told me". Readers would do well to spot this satisfying 'He told me' clue, which reveals that, if Jack had only "told" her, she had not actually *seen* him.

However, readers also know that Poirot regards a stab in the back as distinctly a woman's crime. With the 'woman's crime' clue in mind, the obvious suspect is the woman who stole the dagger. But the 'stolen dagger' clue implicates Cinderella whose real name is unknown until, it seems, chapter 21 when Hastings sees the photograph of Bella Duveen, found by Poirot in Jack's drawer (the 'Bella photograph' clue), and thinks she is Cinderella.

So the 'stolen dagger' clue seems to implicate Bella Duveen, which makes sense because of other clues against her in chapter 4. One is the threatening 'Bella letter' clue found in the overcoat worn by Renauld, which readers assume was sent to him, although it merely starts "My Dearest One". Another is the 'Duveen cheque' clue, the fragment found in Renauld's study, with the word "Duveen" on it, making Poirot think that she might be the lady evening visitor who had left the 'first woman's hair' clue.

But the way that Poirot matches 'Bella' with 'Duveen' is rather unpersuasive. In chapter 10 Stonor is asked if he has heard the name 'Duveen' in connection with Renauld. He doesn't think so but it sounds familiar. He is then asked whether he knows a friend of Renauld's called 'Bella'. He shakes his head. Then he says "Bella Duveen? Is that the full name? It's curious. I am sure I know it". But no one had said that it was the full name.

However, that does not stop Poirot saying in chapter 20 that, since 'Bella Duveen' was "faintly familiar" to Stonor, they can "take it for granted that Bella Duveen is the full name". And on that basis, the name is assumed, with Poirot even adding in chapter 21 that, since it was "faintly familiar to Monsieur Stonor, though evidently not in connection with the Renauld family, it is probable that she is on the stage". But how does that follow? Poirot says: "Jack Renauld was a young man with plenty of money, and twenty years of age. The stage is sure to have been the home of his first love". But how can one be "sure" of that?

Despite those uncompelling deductions, Poirot locates Bella, performing with her sister, on stage in Coventry, after which Hastings is visited by Cinderella (Dulcie, though he thinks it is Bella). During the visit he leaps to "the truth": if Bella, who had scrawled her love for Jack on the 'Bella photograph' clue, had written the threatening 'Bella letter' clue *to Jack* (not Renauld), she could have killed Renauld, mistaking him for Jack and later stolen back the dagger.

Hastings' idea of Bella mistaking Renauld for Jack is supported by two clues. One is the 'amazing likeness' clue, which had made Hastings feel, on first seeing Jack, that Renauld had come to life again. The other is that Renauld was wearing *Jack's* overcoat while digging the grave – the 'overcoat' clue. In chapter 4 we learned that Renauld was of medium height and Poirot noted that he wore his overcoat "very long". In chapter 11 we learned that Jack was tall and Poirot measured an overcoat in the hall, which Hastings guessed belonged to Stonor (also tall) or to Jack. Then in chapter 20 Poirot revealed that he had measured Jack's overcoat, which he wore "very short".

When combining those elements of the 'overcoat' clue with another element from chapter 11 – Jack realising during the quarrel with his father that he needed to run for his Paris train – Hastings deduces that he hastily took the wrong coat, which is why Renauld had worn Jack's coat containing the 'Bella letter' clue while digging the grave. His deduction about *Renauld* is a good one but his overall idea about *Bella* is not only wrong but also applied, as he spots in chapter 25, to the wrong person because, although "like her as two peas", Bella, the girl in the photograph, is *not* Cinderella, who turns out to be her twin sister, Dulcie.

Poirot says that the 'Bella photograph' clue should have told Hastings this because, although the sisters were very alike, they were not indistinguishable. And, says Poirot, he should not have been mistaken because one girl was fair and the other dark on stage in Coventry. The fair hair was a wig, worn for contrast, as Poirot explains when asking whether it was conceivable with twins that one should be fair and one dark. However, he rather cheats when relying on this 'twins' clue since he had not yet read Dulcie's letter revealing that they were twins; they could just have been sisters who were very alike.

Nevertheless, it was Dulcie who, having seen a dagger identical to Bella's in the shed, had stolen it, thinking that Bella had murdered Renauld, mistaking him for Jack in the dark due to the 'amazing likeness' and 'overcoat' clues.

It is a pity that Dulcie and Hastings, in having the same (wrong) idea about Bella, both overdo the 'overcoat' clue by referring to it as "fancy" and to its "pattern" – words which had not been in the text. But the 'overcoat' clue is still a good one, partly because it is constructed over 16 chapters but also because it acts as a red herring by making us think that the murderer may have got the wrong victim whereas Marthe knows full well who she is stabbing.

In exposing Marthe as the murderer, Poirot enumerates "four points of note". Point (1) is that she could have overheard Renauld's plans. In chapters 13 and 18 Hastings and Marthe overhear conversations in adjoining gardens, and so, says Poirot, "there is no reason why she should not have overheard everything else, especially if Mr and Madame Renauld were imprudent enough to discuss their plan sitting on the bench". That is right; she *could* have overheard it *if* they had discussed the plan there. But that does not mean that she (or they) did, which makes the 'overheard conversation' clue an unconvincing starting point for Poirot's solution.

Point (2) is that she had a direct interest in causing Renauld's death. In other words, she had a motive – money, which Poirot tells us in chapter 17 is one of the three motives for murder, the others being *crime passionnel* (by which he seems to mean not only murders committed for love or in the heat of the moment but any murder committed for an emotional reason); and murder for an idea, implying some form of mental derangement.

Point (3) is that she was the daughter of the notorious Madame Beroldy. This is one of Poirot's psychological clues – the 'Marthe heredity' clue: murder would not horrify the daughter of Madame Beroldy who in his opinion was morally and virtually the murderer in the Beroldy saga.

Point (4) is that she was the only person, besides Jack, likely to have the third dagger. No reason is given for this, even though it led Poirot "infallibly" to her. He simply says "One he gave to his mother, one to Bella Duveen – was it not highly probable that he had given the third one to Marthe Daubreuil?". Even though Jack loved Marthe, this is not entirely satisfactory, particularly since Poirot had said in chapter 24 that Jack had "doubtless" retained it for his *own* use. And, even if he had not, might he not have given it away before meeting Marthe?

The "four points of note" against Marthe are therefore unpersuasive and make her guilt possible – as the 'woman's crime' clue does – which may be why Poirot describes them as "points of note" rather than clues.

Perhaps more persuasive is the 'anxious eyes' clue referred to by Poirot in explaining when he first suspected her. She had "anxious eyes" in chapters 2, 7 and 13 (chapter 13 is even entitled "The Girl with the Anxious Eyes") and she is or looks anxious, afraid, apprehensive, frightened and troubled during the story. Although Hastings and Marthe misdirect us (chapters 15 and 24) towards her anxiety about Jack, Poirot correctly points out that, when they first saw her anxious eyes (chapter 2), she did not then know that Jack had been in Merlinville on the fatal night.

Although the clueing of the murderer may be disappointing, there are among the many other clues (too many really) some which are quite clever. The 'silvered' clue, showing that Eloise's dagger was used to stab the tramp, probably beats the 'overcoat' clue to being the best while the 'footprints' clue is the most memorable because of its resonance with Sherlock Holmes.

Finally, one irony will not be lost on readers. Try as Poirot might to emphasise the psychological clue, he does regard the footprints as "the most important" things they have seen; he says that it was the 'lead-piping' clue which "first set me on the right track"; he searches Jack's effects (and finds the 'Bella photograph' clue); he arranges for Dulcie to search Bella's effects (and so produce the second dagger); and, after finding the 'Duveen cheque' clue, he advises that "The moral of that is, always look under the mats!".

The Murder Of Roger Ackroyd

Solution

Poirot investigates the murder of Roger Ackroyd, who is stabbed in the neck with a Tunisian dagger in his study at Fernly Park in King's Abbot on Friday 17 September. Ackroyd, aged 43, is a widower, with a stepson, Ralph Paton, aged 25, who is due to inherit his fortune.

Ackroyd is the most famous victim in detective literature. Rightly so because, in a stunning solution, the murderer is the Dr Watson figure – the middle-aged village doctor, James Sheppard, who acts as Poirot's assistant and is the story's narrator. By Saturday lunchtime Poirot says "You must have indeed been sent from the good God to replace my friend Hastings" and "You and I, M. le docteur, we investigate this affair side by side".

In addition to Ralph, the suspects are Mrs Cecil Ackroyd (Ackroyd's widowed sister-in-law); Flora, her daughter; Ackroyd's friend, Major Hector Blunt; Ackroyd's secretary, Geoffrey Raymond; the butler, Parker; the parlourmaid, Ursula; the housekeeper, Mrs Russell; and a stranger, Charles Kent. Like Sheppard, his gossipy sister Caroline, who lives with him, never seems to be a suspect.

Sheppard knows, as the doctor who had attended Mr Ashley Ferrars, that he was poisoned by his wife. So he blackmails her for a year, during which she becomes secretly engaged to Ackroyd. Then on 16 September Sheppard sees her talking with Ralph. This strikes him "disagreeably" because he thinks she is confiding in him, though in fact she is not.

However, she does tell Ackroyd that afternoon about poisoning her husband and, after seeing his horrified expression, she commits suicide that night with an overdose of veronal. Sheppard is sure that she would have told Ackroyd about the blackmail. If so, Ackroyd would ruin him.

On his round next morning Sheppard bumps into Ackroyd, who insists that he comes to dinner that evening. So Sheppard starts to formulate a very clever murder plan to be implemented after dinner. Most impressively, despite seeing three more patients on his round and conducting his midday surgery, he formulates it by the time he sees his fourth surgery patient, an American steward from the liner, *Orion*, who is to play a key but unwitting role.

During the afternoon he also identifies a scapegoat after being told by Caroline that she had overheard Ralph saying to an unknown girl in the wood that Ackroyd would cut him off with a shilling and that he does not want him altering his will. Sheppard goes to the Three Boars to see Ralph, who is in "the devil of a mess" but cannot – according to Sheppard – let him in on it.

In fact Ralph does let him in on it, revealing that six months ago he had secretly married Ursula, the parlourmaid; that she (the unknown girl) was going to tell Ackroyd; and that because of his inheritance he had begged her not to. We do not know this then and so, when Sheppard cleverly asks himself "Could I do anything with the boy? I thought I could", we think he plans to help him whereas in fact he incriminates him by taking a pair of his shoes and leaving its prints on the windowsill of Ackroyd's study after the murder.

Before dinner, Sheppard puts the shoes into his doctor's black bag along with a dictaphone recently bought by Ackroyd. It had gone wrong and Sheppard, with his love of machinery, had persuaded Ackroyd to let him mend it. Instead, having ample time before dinner, Sheppard adds to it a little device, based on the principle of a simple alarm clock, so that it can be activated to play back a recording of Ackroyd's dictated words at a predetermined time.

Armed with his black bag, Sheppard gets to Fernly Park just before 7.30 pm. In the drawing room he sees the Tunisian dagger in a silver table. Since this cannot be traced to him, he pockets it to use instead of the "very handy little weapon" (we are not told what) which he has brought with him.

After dinner Ackroyd leads Sheppard to the study. His black bag is brought in because it also contains Ackroyd's tablets. Ackroyd asks him to check that the window behind the curtain is closed, which Sheppard says it is. Then Ackroyd tells him about Mrs Ferrars killing her husband and being blackmailed. Sheppard asks the blackmailer's name. Ackroyd says that she had refused to say but had added that he would hear from her within 24 hours.

Ackroyd says that, if no word comes, he will let the matter drop but at 8.40 pm Parker brings in the evening post including a blue envelope, which Ackroyd says she must have posted last night. He opens it and reads aloud: "I leave to you [the words "to you" making plain that she had not told the police] the punishment of the person who has made my life a hell upon earth … I would not tell you the name this afternoon, but I propose to write it to you now". Ackroyd, in his armchair, pauses, saying he must read the rest alone.

Sheppard, standing, urges him to read on but Ackroyd refuses. Sheppard later explains that urging Ackroyd to read on was his best chance of getting him *not* to read. Perhaps Sheppard thought that, if Ackroyd read the name, he might react by rising immediately from his chair whereas, not knowing it, he would remain in it, enabling Sheppard to stab him from behind, as he does, with the Tunisian dagger before closing Ackroyd's hand around the handle.

Sheppard then takes out the dictaphone and sets it on the table by the window, timed to go off, with a recording of Ackroyd's voice, at 9.30 pm when Sheppard will have an alibi. He then moves the grandfather chair by two feet so as to conceal the dictaphone from those later coming into the room. He must also take or burn the letter and envelope which we later learn have disappeared.

At 8.50 pm, he leaves the study, telling Parker that Ackroyd does not want to be disturbed. He steps out of the front door, runs to the summer house, takes out Ralph's shoes, slips them on, walks in the mud, leaves prints on the sill as he climbs in through the study window, which he had left unlatched, locks the door on the inside, goes back out of the window, runs to the summer house, changes back into his shoes and races down to the gates, passing through them as the church clock chimes 9 pm. The timing sounds tight but Poirot, who checks it, says that it took "ten minutes exactly". Sheppard arrives home at 9.10 pm.

At 9.30 pm the dictaphone starts and Ackroyd is heard by his secretary, Raymond (talking, he thinks, to Sheppard) and by his friend Blunt (talking, he thinks, to Raymond). At 10.15 pm Sheppard's telephone rings. He answers and then tells Caroline that it was Parker ringing to say that Ackroyd had been murdered.

In fact it was not Parker – but the steward from the American liner, *Orion*, ringing from King's Abbot station, just before taking the 10.23 pm night train to Liverpool. As agreed with Sheppard earlier, he had delivered a note to a patient and was innocently telephoning with the patient's reply.

The purpose of this ploy is to allow Sheppard to return to Fernly Park, which he then does, and so be present when the body is found, as he and Parker break in through the locked study door. He has to be present then in order to remove the dictaphone on which his alibi depends, putting it in the black bag which he has again brought, and to push back the grandfather chair, which he does while Parker is sent to telephone the police and fetch

Raymond and Blunt. Of course, Parker denies having made the call, which is later traced to the railway station. But by this time the steward is on his way to the high seas.

Although the real brilliance of the book is in the identity of the murderer, the murder plan itself is very clever, its key being the alibi based on the novel use of a dictaphone and timer. But it is lucky that the dictation was overheard. And the plan has a weakness – the telephone call. Poirot astutely manages to match the call from the station with the steward who had been a patient that day and taken the train to Liverpool eight minutes after the call (not three, as in chapter 12) from where he sailed on the *Orion* on Saturday. Once located on the *Orion*, he reveals the true content of the call from there by wireless message. Sheppard would have done better to pretend that he was returning to Fernly Park after leaving something there which he needed early next day.

Sheppard is also lucky that the post is not brought in later because he is not the only one using the summer house. At 9.10 pm Ackroyd's housekeeper, Miss Russell meets Charles Kent, a drug addict who turns out to be her illegitimate son, until about 9.25 pm. At 9.25 pm Ralph passes the gates and just after 9.30 pm meets Ursula who returns to the house by 9.45 pm. If Sheppard had murdered Ackroyd a little later, those meetings may have stopped his plan from working.

As well as murdering Ackroyd, Sheppard incriminates Ralph in three ways. First, with the shoeprints, but we are not told how he took the shoes from Ralph's room (hardly a pocketable item) – perhaps in his black bag when Ralph wasn't looking?

Secondly, by suggesting a motive, which Poirot describes in chapter 13 as a "scrape" which Ralph feared might get to Ackroyd's ears (marrying Ursula). In fact he also had a more simple inheritance motive as Ackroyd's beneficiary – though Sheppard says "truthfully" (chapter 9) that this did not occur to him.

Thirdly, by helping Ralph to vanish, so suggesting he has guilty knowledge. Sheppard meets him after the murder, tells him that suspicion will fall on him or Ursula and takes him to a nearby home for the mentally unfit to hide as a patient, although we are never told how Sheppard intended to bring Ralph out of hiding and get him convicted.

Plot

Narrated in an amusing laconic style, with a marvellous characterisation of the inquisitive and gossipy Caroline[1], and supplemented with plans of the right wing of Fernly Park and the study, this is a very tightly plotted story in which the sub-plots dovetail beautifully with the murder and incrimination plans.

The meetings in the summer house relate to the main sub-plot (Ralph/Ursula) and the second sub-plot (Kent/Miss Russell). Ursula, dismissed that afternoon by Ackroyd after revealing her secret marriage, has a reproachful meeting with Ralph and at some point throws her wedding ring into the goldfish pond. Kent, who is given money by his mother, Miss Russell, is later detained in Liverpool (where the *Orion* steward went on the train).

The other sub-plots are less extensive. One involves Parker, who may be the blackmailer, having blackmailed a previous employer. The other four suspects are (along with Sheppard) accused by Poirot in chapter 12 of hiding something and he gradually exposes the secrets of Flora, who claims she saw Ackroyd at 9.45 pm (her secret is the theft of £40); Raymond (he is badly in debt); Blunt, who received a legacy of the amount paid by Mrs Ferrars to the blackmailer (he loves Flora); and Mrs Ackroyd (she looks for Ackroyd's will and takes a valuable piece from the silver table in which the Tunisian dagger was kept).

To construct a plot in which the narrator is the murderer, without revealing that until the appointed time and without cheating in the plotting or clueing, is a mark of genius which would have required considerable care and skill on the author's part.[2] The only real plotting issue is whether she does cheat.

As indicated in The Puzzle Element chapter, some people felt let down. But, for most of them, the feeling seems to have arisen just from an instinctive sense of having been tricked. If they tried to explain why, they would say that the murderer should not be the narrator because he could not be completely honest about his thoughts or deeds, either generally or in the ten minutes either side of 8.50 pm. A smaller, second category would have felt that the 'rules' of detective fiction discussed in The Puzzle Element chapter had been broken.

As to the first category, they have just been outwitted, knowing full well that the purpose of a detective novel is to create a puzzle which will, they hope, be so mystifying that they will do excellently to solve it. Their failure to spot that the murderer might be the detective's assistant, or the village doctor, or even the narrator, does not mean that there has been illegitimacy in this brilliant development of the mystification found in detective stories from the outset.

Indeed, the author has played fairer than she needed. In chapter 13 Poirot tells Sheppard that "the person who speaks may be lying". How, he asks, does he know that Sheppard left at 8.50 pm? "Because I told you so", replies Sheppard, to which Poirot responds "But you might not be speaking the truth" – a point he repeats, albeit with an impatient gesture rather than words, when Sheppard says that Poirot knows about the stranger (Kent) because "I told you so".

So Sheppard lying is contemplated by Poirot and subtly flagged for readers. But for Sheppard to have revealed in the narrative what his real thoughts were or what he did before or after 8.50 pm or that he was the blackmailer and murderer (not just assistant and narrator) would have undermined the mystification and those omissions cannot *of themselves* seriously be regarded as cheating.

However, it could well be cheating if the author has either (as the second category would claim) broken the 'rules' of detective fiction – those relevant to the narrator issue being Van Dine's Rule 2 and Knox's Commandments 1 and 9 – or has misled readers by abuses of plotting or clueing.

Van Dine's Rule 2 is "No wilful tricks or deceptions may be placed on the reader other than those played legitimately by the criminal on the detective". In other words, tricks can only be placed (meaning 'played') on the reader if they are played legitimately on the detective. Sheppard is constantly tricking Poirot by pretending that he is not the murderer and in chapter 23 he even assembles those tricks in one place by giving Poirot 20 chapters of his narrative, presumably intending to 'trick' him into thinking that, because he is writing it, he cannot be the murderer. If tricking Poirot like that is 'legitimate', there would be no breach of the 'rule' by Sheppard playing the same legitimate 'narrator' tricks on the reader.

Unfortunately, from an analytical perspective, we do not know whether the trick is 'legitimate' because the 'rule' begs the question of what 'legitimate' means. So one could argue that Sheppard, in not revealing his thoughts and deeds to Poirot, has not acted legitimately and that the 'rule' has been broken. However, the real issue here is surely not an analytical one but the soundness of the 'rule' itself because the word 'legitimately', if interpreted so as to fetter the author's mystification and deception of readers, undermines the very aim of a puzzle. So, like a number of Van Dine's other 'rules' which have been broken often, Rule 2 should be ignored or at least, allow for a more permissive interpretation of 'legitimately' than Van Dine envisaged.

Knox's Commandment No. 1 is "The criminal must ... not be anyone whose thoughts the reader has been allowed to follow". He clarifies this "in view of some remarkable performances by Mrs Christie"[3] by saying that "the author must not imply an attitude of mystification in the character who turns out to be the criminal". So

Sheppard would not be entitled to think *I wonder who murdered Roger Ackroyd*, although he could be mystified about the sub-plots. The novel does not transgress this rule.

Knox's Commandment No. 9 is "The stupid friend of the detective, the Watson, must not conceal any thoughts which pass through his mind". This 'rule' *as written* looks as if it has been broken. But Knox explains that its purpose is to give the reader a "sparring partner" against whom he can pit his brains to see who can come second-best to the detective – the "doddering fool" of a Watson or the reader. So, since it operates where the Watson is a "doddering fool" or "stupid friend" rather than a murderer, it is not intended to apply where the Watson *is* the murderer.

Therefore, ignoring Van Dine's Rule 2, there was no breach. But did the author mislead by abuses of plotting or clueing, meaning did she (Sheppard) either (1) lie to us or (2) omit events which, without giving away the murderer's identity, ought fairly to have been mentioned contemporaneously?

As to issue (1), Sheppard's narrative is remarkably clever in generally avoiding lying to us, *as readers*, by using two devices: (a) the way in which he records *facts* and (b) his use of *saying* things to other characters.

With device (a), he tries to ensure that in recording facts he always tells the truth – even if not the whole truth. The best example – indeed probably the most famous passage in the Christie canon – is where, having just murdered Ackroyd, he does not tell us that but writes "The letter had been brought in at twenty minutes to nine. It was just on ten minutes to nine when I left him, the letter still unread. I hesitated with my hand on the door handle, looking back and wondering if there was anything I had left undone. I could think of nothing. With a shake of the head I passed out and closed the door behind me". In chapter 27 he mentions most of this passage (although puts "letters" in the plural) and refers to his clever sentence after finding the body "I did what little had to be done" without saying that this involved retrieving the dictaphone and putting the grandfather chair back. But he does not lie.

There are two other examples. In chapter 6 Sheppard tells Inspector Davis "the whole events of the evening as I have set them down here" and in chapter 7 he tells Poirot "all the facts I have previously set down". What is notable is that he is not purporting to tell Davis or Poirot *all* the facts, just the facts which he has "set down". That is clever. Subject to one point.

In chapter 13 Poirot says that Sheppard did not mention Caroline overhearing Ralph in the wood. If Sheppard had told Poirot *all* the facts "previously set down", this should have included Caroline's remarks from chapter 3. Perhaps the author meant Sheppard to tell Poirot all the facts *of the evening* (as in the Davis sentence) which would exclude Caroline overhearing Ralph. But nothing turns on this since Poirot learns of it in chapter 11 (out of 27), well before Sheppard's exposure.

However, there are two occasions where it could be argued that he lies. One is when he writes in chapter 4 "I hate interfering in other people's affairs". Mrs Ferrars would surely not have agreed. The other is when, on the morning after her suicide, he "suddenly remembered" that he had seen her the day before talking with Ralph, when he was struck "disagreeably" (chapter 2). He later says (chapter 27) that he thought she was confiding in him and that "the idea persisted". It is hard to believe that, if seeing her gave him a disagreeable, persistent idea, he could only have *suddenly* remembered that this happened the day before. His claim of a *sudden* remembrance gives the (incorrect) impression that, whatever was disagreeable about Mrs Ferrars speaking to Ralph, it did not relate to her, making it more difficult – though not significantly so – to spot that his motive derived from blackmailing her.

Device (b) relates to Sheppard saying things to other people. Thus he does not lie to the reader by claiming 'I had done x' when he had not. Instead he uses the device of lying to another character, saying 'I told y that I had done x' when he had not. This is what was meant by saying earlier that we, *as readers*, are not generally lied to – only the other characters are.

Thus, he does not say as a *fact* that he came into a legacy (invented to explain the money from Mrs Ferrars) or did not notice that the letter had gone. Instead he *says* these things to Poirot. The author is consistently careful about this and thus Sheppard says things to Raymond (that he is expecting a summons to a confinement case), to Ackroyd (that he has put the latch across the window and that Caroline gave him the idea that Ferrars had been poisoned), to Davis (that he closed the window) and to Ursula (that he has no idea of Ralph's whereabouts).

So, having concluded that there was no significant deliberate lying, issue (2) is whether Sheppard omitted material events which, without revealing his role as murderer, ought fairly to have appeared contemporaneously in the narrative.

One thing he fails to reveal until chapter 23 is that he has already prepared 20 chapters of his narrative. But that hardly constitutes cheating since we know what is in those chapters. Nevertheless, a curiosity is that in chapter 18 he says "I know now that the whole thing lay clearly unravelled before [Poirot]". How can he say that, in a chapter given to Poirot, when he is incredulous, *after* Poirot has read it, that the murderer will be found at Poirot's meeting that evening? A similar curiosity arises in respect of various sentences in chapter 14, which look as if they should have been written later such as "To Poirot alone belongs the renown of fitting those pieces into their correct place" and "I see now that I was unbelievably stupid about these boots".

There is one area, however, where a charge of cheating seems at first arguable. This relates to Sheppard's second meeting with Ralph (when he advises him to hide) about which we know nothing until chapter 24. It is that meeting which Poirot has in mind when accusing Sheppard in chapter 12 of hiding something.

That second meeting is in a different category from the first one (the afternoon meeting at the Three Boars) which Sheppard does reveal, even if he does not tell us about Ralph's marriage or taking his shoes. If one accepts that a murderer-narrator cannot be expected to tell the whole truth, it seems legitimate for Sheppard to have withheld those points in chapter 3.

However, we weren't told about the second meeting *at all*. What we were told in chapter 7 was that after Ackroyd's death Sheppard went to the Three Boars to tell Ralph but that he had gone out and never returned. When Sheppard has to "make a clean breast" of the meeting in chapter 24, it seems unaccountable to the reader that he did not mention it before. The author could easily have provided an incomplete version contemporaneously. So, readers who would have been prepared to regard an incomplete version of the meeting as legitimate (as with the first one) may well feel that not mentioning it at all is cheating because it deprives them of evidence they should have had earlier.

But, taking the author's side, that is to misunderstand the 'second meeting' clue, which is a double one. One element is, of course, the existence and content of the meeting – and no harm is done there because we do find out about it before Sheppard's exposure. But the second element is the key – Sheppard's unaccountable failure to mention it, which is highly suspicious and thus, rather than being intended to mislead, provides an important clue against him. An oddity is that we are never told where or when the second meeting took place and, with Poirot saying "supposing … that [Sheppard] met [Ralph] in the street on his way home?" (chapter 24), one even wonders if it was fortuitous.

In conclusion, Sheppard's two devices are therefore generally very effective and the charge of cheating fails. Some readers may, however, wonder about Poirot's fairness in omitting Sheppard from "a list of suspected persons" (Mrs Ackroyd, Flora, Blunt, Raymond, Ursula, Parker and Miss Russell) which he reads out at the start of the denouement in chapter 23. Presumably he would argue that it was just 'a' list and that he didn't use the words 'the' or 'all' (Ralph and Kent are not in it); and that he had stopped Caroline coming to the denouement by saying "See you, all these people tonight [which would include Sheppard] are suspects".

Clues

This is a puzzle which proliferates with high-quality clues. Time is crucial for much of the evening of the murder, from the moment the post is brought in at 8.40 pm. Indeed, Poirot says that it was a "little discrepancy in time" that first drew his attention to Sheppard "right at the beginning". The discrepancy was Sheppard leaving the house at 8.50 pm but not passing the gates until 9 pm when the church clock chimed, even though the walk should only take five minutes.

Sheppard leaving at 8.50 pm is in chapters 4, 5, 7 and 13 and his being at the gates at 9 pm is in chapters 4, 5, 8 and 13. The linking clue, that the walk should take five minutes, comes from Sheppard in chapter 8, which Poirot overdoes by saying that "everyone" agreed that it took five minutes (chapter 26). Poirot also says, after referring to a drop in temperature that night (chapter 7), that it was "chilly" and not a night to "dawdle". So it is odd that Inspector Raglan calls it a "dry, fine night" (chapter 8). However, this 'church clock' clue is excellent, not just because it is built up over chapters but also because it is hidden deceptively in Poirot asking how long it takes to get from the gates *to* the study window (not the reverse) in the context of Kent's appearance.

This, then, is Poirot's starting point and Sheppard is in his sights. But time also helps Sheppard by giving him his apparently unimpeachable alibi, which is that he was at home with Caroline from 9.10 pm (as he was) and yet the murder must have happened after 9.30 pm – when Ackroyd was heard by Blunt and Raymond – and, so it seems, after 9.45 pm because Flora, in the sub-plot of her theft, says she saw Ackroyd alive then.

This alibi diverts our attention, at least until the main psychological clue in chapter 17, from many simple points about Sheppard which may or may not be intended as textual clues where he shares his thoughts about being, for example, upset, uneasy, worried, startled, grumpy and greedy.[4]

He even almost warns readers about his techniques of deception and misdirection by saying "Fortunately words, ingeniously used, will serve to mask the ugliness of naked facts" (chapter 14). The best example must be his thought, when discovering the body, that "Ackroyd was sitting as I had left him in the arm-chair before the fire" (chapter 5). This is a very telling sentence because, if Ackroyd was sitting as Sheppard had left him and was now dead, it follows that that is how Sheppard left him. How the author must have pondered over this 'Ackroyd sitting' textual clue, wondering if she was giving too much away, particularly when readers might look back and spot another textual clue, the 'unread letter' clue: what might explain the letter being unread when Sheppard left the study – Ackroyd being dead?

The main psychological clue against Sheppard comes in chapter 17 when Poirot, knowing he is the murderer, considers the murderer's psychology: an ordinary man without murder in his heart but with "a strain of weakness" which tells when a goldmine opens up and he greedily overreaches himself before becoming his normal, kindly self again once the dagger is removed.

Caroline assumes that Poirot is talking of Ralph who is the last person referred to before Poirot's hypothesis. Moreover, Ralph has "a strain of weakness"; he "may be weak"; and he has "a weak nature" (chapter 3, 7, 17). Caroline's misdirection is reinforced two chapters later when Flora says about Ralph and herself "We were both weak! … We're weak, miserable despicable things" and in chapter 22 when Sheppard refers to "the innate weakness of Ralph".

What readers may miss, partly because of that misdirection, is that shortly before Poirot's hypothesis Caroline had said about Sheppard: "Take James here – weak as water, if I weren't about to look after him ... You are weak, James ... With a bad bringing up, Heaven knows what mischief you might have got into by now". It is real bravado by the author to offer such an important clue so close to Poirot's hypothesis. She evens dares readers to spot the 'weak as water' clue by having Sheppard record after Poirot's speech "I cannot try to describe the impression his words produced".

Readers can also miss this key clue because of Sheppard's alibi, which is not affected when we learn that Flora did not actually see Ackroyd at 9.45 pm. What matters to Sheppard is that Ackroyd was heard at 9.30 pm. It is because of that that some readers will pause when, after Flora's admission, Poirot says "It seems now that Mr Ackroyd was murdered, not at a quarter to ten, but *before*. Between ten minutes to nine, when Dr Sheppard left, and a quarter to ten".

Why, we ask, does he go back as far as "ten minutes to nine" when Flora's admission does not affect Ackroyd still being alive at 9.30 pm? This 'Poirot timing' clue indicates that he thinks that Ackroyd could have been dead from 8.50 pm, so that the alibi based on him being heard at 9.30 pm does not work.

Various clues combine to break it, the first being the 'dictation' clue reflected in Ackroyd's language at 9.30 pm: "The calls on my purse have been so frequent of late that I fear it is impossible for me to accede to your request". Davis says "A demand for money. It may be that we have a very important clue". And we do – though not because of Davis' misdirection towards a demand but because the language was "distinctly odd" if Ackroyd was, as Raymond assumed, with Sheppard. Poirot spots that this language could not be conversational and that Ackroyd was dictating. But to whom, if not Raymond, as Blunt had assumed?

That brings us to the 'dictaphone' clue – a rare exception to the excellent clueing of the murder plan, which is a pity because the dictaphone is its most famous tangible feature.[5] We first learn of it when Raymond tells us (chapter 8) that "Mr Ackroyd had some idea of purchasing a dictaphone … but nothing came of it. Mr Ackroyd did not make up his mind to purchase". That last sentence reads oddly – as if the author is trying to avoid saying "Mr Ackroyd made up his mind not to purchase" – but, whatever she intended, Raymond has said that "nothing came of it", without any qualification such as "as far as I am aware".

Despite that, Poirot reveals in chapter 23 that Ackroyd inquired of The Dictaphone Company because, as he explains, "Mr Ackroyd had promised to invest in a dictaphone, you remember". However, we do *not* remember that. What we remember is Raymond saying that nothing came of it. But Poirot also reveals that, having inquired, he learned that Ackroyd *did* purchase a dictaphone.[6] So, if he was speaking into it at 9.30 pm, why wasn't it found among his effects?

In answering this, Poirot refers to two "facts" in chapter 25. The first is the 'telephone call' clue. He had said in chapter 8 that, when he could interpret the call (made by the steward to Sheppard), he would know everything – a point he repeats in chapter 12, although Sheppard declares it "utterly irrelevant". Poirot rightly concludes that the result of the call was that the murder was discovered that evening and that the murderer, knowing that it would be, could be present.

As to the caller's identity, Poirot says to Sheppard in chapter 26 that he had a vague notion of how it was worked when he saw Caroline on the first day (in fact Sunday) and asked what patients he had seen on Friday. He learned (as readers did in chapter 11) that the fourth patient was an "American steward off the liner". Who more suitable, asks Poirot, to be taking a train to Liverpool? However, it would be surprising if the 'steward' clue were spotted other than by a very astute reader because it is so well hidden in Caroline's misdirection that the patient in whom Poirot was interested was Miss Russell, which is reinforced two chapters later by Sheppard, although Poirot evades Sheppard's enquiry about her, cleverly saying that he was interested in "only one patient".

Poirot's second fact is the 'grandfather chair' clue, which Sheppard marks with an X on his plan in chapter 7 (though the X is not in some editions and nor, in some, is the window). Sheppard says about the chair being moved "Surely it isn't important" and, when Poirot notes in chapter 25 that the chair stood between the door and the window, Sheppard is quick to say "The window". However, Poirot has already realised that the chair would obscure little of the window whereas it hid the table. So he supposes that there had been an object on it which the murderer could not take away after the crime but which needed to be removed later – hence the telephone call.

Four people were there before the police, by which time the chair was put back – Parker, Sheppard, Raymond and Blunt – and each denies moving it. Poirot eliminates Parker as he would be on the spot whenever the body was found and so could have removed the object without the telephone call ploy. However, he keeps Raymond and Blunt under suspicion because, if the body was found in the early morning, they might be on the scene too late to deal with the object and so needed a pretext to be there – though readers may think that, as residents, they could have invented one to knock on Ackroyd's door that *evening*, irrespective of Sheppard saying that he wished not to be disturbed. If so, they too could have been eliminated, leaving only Sheppard.

Poirot then asks what object needed to be removed. Why not the dictaphone? But a dictaphone has a certain bulk. The murderer must have had a receptacle able to hold it, which is where the 'black bag' clue comes in. Sheppard had brought it not only for dinner (referring to an emergency confinement case that is not referred to again) but also after the telephone call.

But *why* remove it? Because it would reveal, as Poirot says in chapter 25, that, if a mechanical device such as a simple alarm clock had been applied to it, earlier dictation could have been played back at 9.30 pm – with Ackroyd dead. However, such a device could only have been applied by someone who knew of Ackroyd's purchase and had the necessary mechanical knowledge.

It is at this point, with Poirot referring to "necessary mechanical knowledge", that all readers should suspect Sheppard – even if they dismiss the suspicion because he is the narrator – in view of his mechanical turn of mind. It is in chapter 20, while we are unaware of Ackroyd's dictaphone, that we are given the 'mechanical' clue. There we learn that he has a workshop in his house, that he has a love of machinery, that he has made a wireless set and other little inventions and that he is adjusting the interior of – of all things – an alarm clock with a delicate mechanism. Poirot even says "Decidedly, you should be an inventor by trade, not a doctor". These points should leap to mind as Poirot refers to mechanical knowledge.[7]

For Sheppard to apply a timing device, he must know that Ackroyd has a dictaphone. How does he? Poirot says that he "knew Ackroyd well enough to know that he had purchased a dictaphone" (chapter 25). That sounds rather feeble. Perhaps the more likely, but unclued, truth is that Ackroyd told Sheppard because he needed the dictaphone mended.

So those are the clues enabling Poirot to break the alibi. We also know from the 'silver table' clue that Sheppard could have taken the Tunisian dagger from that table. He opens the lid and is still bending over the table when joined by Flora, who is later certain that the dagger was not there.

There are also clues relating to Sheppard's incrimination of Ralph. The most significant one, perhaps the most significant clue of all for readers, must be the 'second meeting' clue, namely Sheppard's failure to tell us until chapter 24 of his second meeting with Ralph. His failure to have told us in chapter 6 seems so completely unaccountable that it is plainly suspicious.

Second is the 'boots' clue. We know that the shoe prints on the study windowsill were from Ralph's shoes because the studs of his second pair left at the Three Boars had the same pattern. He could not have worn that second pair because they were being cleaned. So, in order to incriminate him, Sheppard must have used the first pair, taken during his first meeting with Ralph. However, since Ralph went out at about 9 pm, Sheppard could only have taken the first pair if Ralph had a *third* pair to wear when he went out. So, did he?

Poirot thinks it unlikely that he would bring three pairs of *shoes* to stay at the Three Boars so that any third pair was likely to be *boots*. In order to disguise his interest in the 'boots' clue, he asks Caroline to find out whether Ralph had black or brown boots, emphasising the colour, which is nice misdirection – although he later asks Ursula directly whether Ralph was wearing shoes or boots that evening. Once he learns from Caroline that Ralph has black boots, he knows that the murderer could have used Ralph's first pair of shoes.

Third is the 'open window' clue, suggesting that the murderer entered that way. Poirot says in chapter 7 that, with the door locked and (according to Sheppard) the window closed, only Ackroyd could have opened the window and that, if he admitted someone that way, it must have been someone well known to him (such as Ralph). In fact the clue is a false one because Sheppard had not closed the window but, even if he had, Poirot misses the point that, if Ackroyd was alive (to open the window), he might not yet have locked the door and so the murderer could have entered through it and then, after locking it, opened the window when leaving.

Fourth are the clues relating to Ralph's hiding place. In chapter 24 Poirot reasons that a nursing home in Cranchester would be where a doctor would hide Ralph. Readers had been given two clues relating to Poirot's reasoning. One is the 'Mah Jong' clue in chapter 16. Caroline tells Sheppard that, after Poirot had looked at their map, he noted that Cranchester was the only big town nearby. So, she says, Ralph must be there, at which Sheppard knocks over his Mah Jong pieces and objects to the theory. The other is the 'invented nephew' clue in chapter 21 where we learn that Poirot has told Caroline that his (invented) imbecile nephew might have to go into an institution, which we later learn was a pretext for asking her about homes for the mentally unfit in the Cranchester area.

A final 'clue' relating to the murder plot, the 'fingerprints' clue, turns out not to be a clue at all (despite Raglan saying in chapter 12 that it is a better clue than the 'telephone call' clue) because the fingerprints on the dagger are Ackroyd's, so explaining their awkward position on the handle. Indeed, they hardly constitute a red herring because they are never deployed to deceive us but just, so Poirot suggests, "to make a confusing case even more confusing".

As for the clueing of the blackmailer, Ackroyd tells Sheppard in chapter 4 that something Mrs Ferrars had said made him think that the blackmailer might be among his "household". Although he dismisses the idea after raising it, the thought naturally remains with readers, not least because Sheppard repeats it in chapter 6, causing the police to suspect Parker and causing readers to suspect Ursula since it is in the context of a discussion about her in chapter 10 that Sheppard points out that the blackmailer was not necessarily a man.

Poirot, however, knows it was Sheppard, even though, unlike readers, he does not have the imaginative 'well considering' textual clue where Sheppard writes that Mrs Ferrars' manner had been "normal enough considering – well – considering everything" (chapter 2). Instead Poirot refers to two facts in chapter 26. First, that, as the doctor who had attended Mr Ferrars, Sheppard would know best how he had been killed. And, secondly, that there was no trace of the legacy which Sheppard claimed to have received in chapter 3 – but this is the first we are told that the legacy is a lie.

For Poirot, therefore, as we saw earlier, "the whole thing lay clearly unravelled before him" (chapter 18) by Wednesday lunchtime (subject just to the wireless message from the steward on Friday). So it seems a little surprising that he says after supper on Wednesday that Sheppard's narrative, which he had received that afternoon, had helped him "considerably" (chapter 23). He never really explains why. His main comment is about Sheppard's reticence but, since he specifically refers (chapter 24) to Sheppard's failure to mention hiding Ralph, it is hard to say if he was giving a more general 'reticence' clue about the narrative.

Perhaps also, reading the narrative, he enjoyed Sheppard recording that he went "mechanically" on his round (chapter 2), that he noticed the sound of the silver table lid being shut "quite mechanically" (chapter 4), that he agreed "mechanically" about Caroline's memory (chapter 11) and that Poirot's tidiness was "purely mechanical" (chapter 19). Of course, since Poirot does not know until chapter 23 that Sheppard has been writing a narrative, he has not had the readers' disadvantage of spending 22 chapters thinking that Sheppard is above suspicion because he is the narrator.

The two main sub-plots also have clues to be fitted into the jigsaw. Poirot finds two after crawling about in the summer house – the 'goose quill' clue (a quill being used for sniffing drugs across the Atlantic, as it was by Kent, who had an American accent) and the 'cambric' clue (a scrap of stiff white fabric – resonant of Blunt seeing a "gleam of white" disappearing into the bushes – suggesting a maid's apron and thus Ursula's presence there).

He also finds a third clue in the goldfish pond – the discarded gold 'wedding ring' clue inscribed "From R., March 13th". This indicates that Ralph had married in March; that, since he was seen going towards the house at 9.25 pm, he was the person that Ursula (by then dismissed after telling Ackroyd of her secret marriage) was meeting in the summer house; and that she was therefore the girl he had married and with whom he had argued in the wood.

Those sub-plots also seem to offer clues, which turn out to be red herrings. Thus Sheppard wonders as a result of the 'disturbed papers' clue what papers on Ackroyd's desk could have caused Ursula's dismissal and yet the papers are only relevant in the sub-plot of Mrs Ackroyd searching for Ackroyd's will. As Poirot knows from the 'half hour' clue, Ackroyd would not have seen Ursula for half an hour just to dismiss her for disturbing papers. In the second sub-plot we have the 'undetectable poisons' clue, with Miss Russell asking Sheppard about poisons when she is really interested in cures for her son's drug addiction, having been prompted by an article that Friday in the Daily Budget (which should have been dated 17, not 16, September – chapter 15).

However, the real essence of the clueing is in the murder plot in which Sheppard is very cleverly clued by a series of factual, tangible, personal and textual clues, some openly presented but others expertly concealed, the best among a high-quality field perhaps being the 'church clock' clue.

The brilliance is that, despite all those clues and despite wondering why Sheppard is in the story at all (rather than Hastings) – itself a clue? – we do not treat him as a suspect. This is because the dictaphone provides him with such a strong alibi, because some clues are so cleverly concealed, because his apparent temperament and laconic writing style deflect suspicion and because we naturally assume that such a person, particularly given his role as narrator, just cannot be the murderer.

4

The Big Four

Solution

This book is, uniquely for Poirot and its narrator, Captain Hastings, a thriller, not a detective story. But it is interspersed with tales of detection and it has various allusions to the Sherlock Holmes stories.

The thriller element involves Poirot's ultimately successful attempts to foil the ambitions of the "Big Four", "a gang of international criminals or something of that kind" (chapter 1). They aim "at nothing less than the disintegration of civilisation" (chapter 3) and "world domination" (chapter 5).

The story starts in July and it takes until the following June, an unusually long time for one of Poirot's investigations, to defeat the Big Four at their headquarters at Lago di Carezza, 4,000 feet up in the Dolomites.

We never have to solve a puzzle about the Big Four's identity because we are given the information. Number One is a Chinaman, Li Chang Yen, who is the brains and controlling and motive force. Number Two is the richest man in the world, Abe Ryland, the American Soap King. Number Three is Madame Olivier, a French scientist – although there is some misdirection towards her secretary, Inez Veroneau (note the initials "IV", as in the Roman numeral for four), who is Poirot's old Russian antagonist, Countess Vera Rossakoff.

Number Four is "the destroyer", described by Poirot as "the executive" of the organisation. He is English and his main talent is his mastery of disguise. He plays at least 11 characters in the novel and his height, size, complexion, teeth, nose, eyebrows and beard are infinitely variable. By chapter 14 Poirot has established that he is one of four character actors. But we do not have to work out which he might be since the first lead takes us to Claud Darrell and by the end of the chapter we know that Darrell, who has been to China and America, is Number Four. We also learn that he has a memorable habit enabling Poirot to recognise him whatever his disguise, namely that he fiddles with his bread at the table: quite unconsciously he gets a little piece between his fingers and dabs it round to pick up the crumbs.

In the final chapter (chapter 18) Poirot confronts Numbers Two, Three and Four at their headquarters, which he has surrounded with police and Secret Service men. Madame Olivier knows that they can only get away by blowing up the mountain and killing themselves as well as Poirot and Hastings, who escape just before an explosion, which makes the mountain seem to dissolve.

The bodies of Numbers Two, Three and Four are recovered, although Number Four's body is quite unrecognisable, the head blown to pieces. Poirot wishes it were not so: "I should have liked to be *sure*", suggesting a doubt about his death. Number One commits suicide on hearing news of the disaster.

That is the story of the Big Four. As a thriller, and with the possible exception of locating their headquarters, it poses no puzzle for us. For that, we need to consider the murders committed by the Big Four which appear episodically in the book. There are seven victims. Number Four committed the first four murders and probably the fifth but we are not told who committed the final two, which do not bear Number Four's theatrical hallmarks.

The first victim is Mayerling, a Secret Service man who is unexpectedly heard in Poirot's bedroom. He sways into the sitting room and falls, later scrawling a "4" a dozen times on a sheet of paper before being carried to Poirot's bed to sleep. When Poirot and Hastings are out, Number Four kills Mayerling by forcing him to inhale prussic acid. This is undetected by the doctor, who cannot explain the cause of his asphyxiation. An attendant from Hanwell Asylum (in fact Number Four) then identifies the victim as an escaped lunatic suffering from acute persecution mania. We assume – since we are not told – that Mayerling's mission was to tell Poirot about the Big Four, who wanted to prevent this and to prevent Poirot from knowing Mayerling's true identity.

The second victim, still in July, is an old seafaring man, Jonathan Whalley, who lives on Dartmoor, and, in a letter to John Ingles, says he needs £200 to escape the Big Four. His throat is cut by Number Four, who cleverly poses as a butcher's delivery man on whom a trace of blood would attract no attention. He also incriminates Whalley's lodger, a recently released jailbird called Robert Grant by wearing a duplicate pair of the boots which he had given Grant when pretending to be from a Prisoners' Help Society. We are not told why the Big Four are after Whalley.

The third victim, in what we can deduce is November, is a former globetrotter called Paynter, who lives in Worcestershire with his Chinese servant, Ah Ling, and impecunious nephew, Gerald. He has written a book called *The Hidden Hand in China* with information about Li Chang Yen. He complains of feeling unwell after dinner and is attended by Dr Quentin (Number Four), who gives him an injection, later claimed to be strychnine which was used as a stimulant in the days before research debunked the claims that it acted as one.[1]

Next morning Paynter is found dead, having fallen into the gas fire, his face and head charred beyond recognition. On the floor is a newspaper on which he has scrawled "Yellow Jasmine" and two lines at right angles, to which the addition of a further downward line would complete a "4". His book is gone.

It transpires that he had not felt ill but been made suspicious by a curry which Ah Ling had served at dinner and which was found to contain enough opium to kill two men. Quite why Paynter should be so suspicious of a curry (of which Poirot says he ate none) as to call Dr Quentin (and so be murdered) is not persuasively explained. It is said that he was "acting in obedience to the suspicions Dr Quentin had aroused". But when had Dr Quentin done this? Perhaps on the one occasion when he had visited before but we are not told.

It also transpires that Paynter was not poisoned by the curry but by Quentin's injection, which he admitted giving in case the hypodermic mark was noticed. The injection did not contain strychnine but yellow jasmine (a potent poison). Quentin later returned by the window, which he had left unlatched, to find the book and to shove Paynter's head into the fire. And it was Quentin who added opium to the curry before handing it over to be analysed.

Hastings asks why Quentin shoved his head into the fire. Poirot explains – and this may be what the author meant to be the murder plan's ingenious feature – that, if you shot or stabbed a man after he were dead, it would be apparent that the injuries were inflicted after death; but with his head charred, no one would hunt about for *obscure* causes of death. This hardly sounds convincing since one surely *would* hunt around for obscure causes of death, given that, as Inspector Japp says, one can't hold a live man's head in a fire.

The fourth victim, in what we can deduce is December, is a brilliant young American chess player of worldwide reputation called Gilmour Wilson, who succumbs to heart failure during a match with the Russian champion, Dr Savaronoff. Wilson, who played White, was moving a bishop when he died and a burn scar is later noticed on the hand in which he held that piece.

Savaronoff's niece, Sonia, says that her uncle, not Wilson, was the intended victim because he feared the Big Four. But in fact the real Dr Savaronoff died at least three years before. Number Four had been impersonating him – but for how long, since he was acting as Dr Quentin only last month? – surpassing his disguise skills with a "peculiar formation" of the head. He had been doing so in order to claim a fortune left to Dr Savaronoff by a former lover.

However, Wilson challenges him to a match and, after repeatedly refusing the challenge, Number Four finally has to give in when the newspapers complain about unsportsmanlike behaviour. But, since he could not sustain the fiction of playing the match as Dr Savaronoff, he concocts a memorable murder plan to electrocute Wilson during the match, bringing it to an abrupt end after he has had to play only two moves as Black.

The game is played on a small table, inlaid with squares of silver and black to represent a chessboard, which is set upon a certain spot on the floor. A thin metal rod is inside one of the white bishops and, when it is placed on one of the silver squares, a current passes through Wilson's body, instantly killing him and leaving the burn mark on his hand. Poirot says that the murder plan was worked from the flat below, presumably – although we are not actually told this – by a wire underneath the silver square passing down the leg of the table and through a nail hole in the rug on the floor to an electricity source.

Of course, the plan will only work if Wilson moves the white bishop to the right square. There was no problem about this since chess has various regular opening gambits, enabling early moves to be predicted. Provided Wilson was to use the Ruy Lopez opening (of which Poirot says he was fond and "certain" to use), he would be electrocuted on White's third move – as he is – so that Number Four only has to learn Black's first two moves. Although the plan is not foolproof because it depends upon Wilson being White and using the Ruy Lopez opening, it is certainly the book's most ingenious and memorable event.

It is, however, subject to a curiosity. We are told that Dr Savaronoff fell foul of the Bolsheviks at the outbreak of the Revolution and was reported killed (and Poirot later confirms that he did indeed die). If so, why did he remain Russian champion for three years before his unexpected reappearance? Surely other Russians would have contested the honour. It is surprising that, when Savaronoff (Number Four) reappeared, almost unrecognisable from three years of pretended hardship in Siberia, he could resume the title of Russian champion and do so without playing any match before his game with Wilson.

The fifth victim, in January, is Flossie Monro, who had known Claud Darrell (Number Four) well and even had a photograph of him, which she offers to allow Poirot to copy. However, she is run over by a car and dies in hospital – a straightforward murder without ingenuity – and, when Poirot gets to her flat, it has already been searched. An empty photograph frame has a new price label marked "4 shillings" stuck on the back by, says Poirot, Number Four.

The final victims are killed in May – John Ingles, the one Englishman able to tell Poirot about Li Chang Yen, and his Chinese servant. Ingles, who was on the SS *Shanghai*, is assumed to have fallen overboard but Hastings is sure that he was killed by the Big Four. Later his Chinese servant is knifed in the street. Again there is nothing for us to solve about these straightforward murders.

Plot

This book, whose title brings to mind the Sherlock Holmes story *The Sign of Four*, is a loosely plotted thriller in which tales of detection are tossed into the adventures of Poirot and Hastings as they try to defeat the Big Four. It is very episodic as a result of being constructed, not as a coherent work, but by compiling 12 short stories which had appeared about three years before in *The Sketch* magazine in 1924.[2]

The melodramatic adventures take Poirot and Hastings to various parts of England and Europe and include investigating the disappearance in Paris of a leading British scientist, John Halliday, who is impersonated as a hotel guest by Number Four; being warned off there by a menacing man (Number Four) in a buttoned up overcoat; being captured there by Number Three; and escaping her clutches by threatening her with a blow pipe disguised as a cigarette containing a tiny curare dart – it being lucky that she chose that particular cigarette to give Poirot from his cigarette case.

Hastings then goes into "the house of the enemy" by becoming one of Ryland's secretaries where, after decoding a letter, he is ambushed at gunpoint in a quarry by the second footman, James (Number Four), before his rescue by Poirot. Later, in the mistaken belief that his wife Cinderella (whom he had met in *The Murder on the Links*) has been kidnapped in South America, he is lured to Chinatown and forced to lead Poirot into a baited trap, which Poirot avoids by throwing a smoke bomb.

Then in March they are decoyed to Hertfordshire to investigate the attempted poisoning of a Mr Templeton – perhaps by his son Micky (Number Four). They escape by scrambling down some ivy. On returning to London, a catastrophe occurs when Poirot is apparently killed by an explosion at his flat.

Hastings, believing Poirot dead, is warned off by a bearded man in a Soho restaurant (Number Four) and again about ten days later by Countess Vera Rossakoff. Then, prompted to return to South America by a letter from Poirot (written before his apparent demise), he boards a boat to Buenos Aires, watched by a man in a fur coat (perhaps Number Four), from which he is disembarked to a waiting destroyer (a nice use of 'destroyer', given Number Four's title) before meeting Poirot, who is alive after all, at a villa in the Ardennes.

Then they travel to an Italian hotel near the Big Four's headquarters and, while Poirot is sipping his coffee on the terrace (despite being muffled up to the ears), a bulb of anaesthetic is broken under their noses by the man from the next table (Number Four). They are taken to the headquarters to confront three of the Big Four but escape before the explosion which kills Numbers Two, Three and, seemingly, Four.

These adventures, in what was to become the James Bond style, are very much out of character for Poirot and Hastings. We have to suspend disbelief on numerous occasions. In particular, the Big Four's incompetence in trying to kill Poirot is staggering. Surely between September and March they could have despatched him as efficiently as they despatched Flossie Monro.

Despite this and a lack of ingenuity with most of the murders and a weakness in much of the clueing, the story is somehow more engaging than it is entitled to be and it does have elements which remain in the memory, such as the chess murder, Number Four's habit with breadcrumbs and Poirot's brother, Achille, about whom an astonished Hastings is first told by Poirot in chapter 15.

Achille lives near Spa in Belgium – Poirot's twin but without a moustache: "Do you not know that all celebrated detectives have brothers who would be even more celebrated than they are were it not for constitutional indolence?", he says, alluding to Sherlock Holmes' brother, Mycroft, who is first mentioned by Holmes, to Watson's "very great surprise", in *The Greek Interpreter* and has a greater facility for deduction than Holmes but no ambition or energy.

Surprisingly, given the importance of convincing the Big Four that Poirot is dead, Achille does not attend his funeral. But at last he appears in the final chapter. The Big Four believe they have captured Hercule, only to be told that they have merely captured Achille, who has dark eyes, not green, and a false moustache which, when snatched off, reveals an upper lip disfigured by a scar. Hercule, they are told, is outside with the police and Secret Service.

At the very end we learn that, unlike Mycroft Holmes, Achille is just a fiction. It was Hercule who had been captured but the whole crux of his plan was to make the Big Four believe that they had captured Achille and that Hercule was outside the headquarters directing operations. Hence belladonna in the eyes to change their colour, the sacrifice of the moustache and a real scar, the inflicting of which had caused Poirot much pain two months before.

They are helped to escape from the headquarters by Countess Vera Rossakoff, who does so in return for Poirot finding her child – a strange bargain for she believes the child to be dead. But, amazingly, Poirot then produces a photograph of the child. With considerable foresight, he had investigated the Countess's antecedents, had discovered that there were discrepancies in the story about the child's death and had then traced, acquired and photographed the child: "and so, when the time came, I had my little *coup de théâtre* all ready". This is enormously impressive planning by Poirot but it depends on being "fortunate", as Poirot tells the Countess, that Numbers Two, Three and Four left them alone to make the bargain. And what would Poirot have done if the child had in fact died? Or he had not been able to find it?

The Countess is a relatively memorable character – a flamboyant lady for whom Poirot had a sneaking fondness even though she was arrayed against him. Hastings describes her as "our old antagonist … who had engineered a particularly smart jewel robbery in London" – a reference to a short story *The Double Clue*.[3] For Poirot she is "A woman in a thousand" – the equivalent therefore of Irene Adler in the Sherlock Holmes story *A Scandal in Bohemia*, which begins: "To Sherlock Holmes she is always *the* woman".

The Big Four themselves are not much described beyond caricature: the reclusive Chinaman; the unscrupulous American; the fanatical French woman; and the elusive Englishman, who is a supreme character actor encountered by Poirot or Hastings on various occasions – as the man from the lunatic asylum; the man in the buttoned up overcoat in Paris; James the footman; Dr Quentin; Dr Savaronoff; Micky Templeton; the bearded man in the Soho restaurant; and the man from the next table in the Italian hotel. They also learn of Number Four's role as the butcher's boy; as the man from a Prisoners' Help Society; as the guest pretending to be Halliday; as the person who composed the letter sent by Hastings to Poirot to lure him to the baited trap; and as the probable murderer of Flossie Munro. He may even be the man in the fur coat who sees Hastings getting onto the boat for Buenos Aires.

Nearly all of Number Four's appearances are very short cameos and they all demonstrate the episodic nature of the plot. Even Hastings confirms this when he refers to "the adventure of the Baited Trap" as if it were a separate episode which, of course, it originally was. The plot also has a strange pace, resulting from the interweaving of the tales of detection into the thriller – occasionally slowed down to try to provoke thought and mystification (as with the second, third and fourth murders) but mainly speeded up to try to carry us along, as in fairness we are, with the adventures of Poirot and Hastings.

However, on the whole the storyline is too unrealistically melodramatic and the characters, even most of the main ones, far too sparingly depicted to engage or satisfy us. There is no sense of mystification at all in the attempts to defeat the Big Four and the detection tales are so short that even at their slower pace they do not in fact allow time to generate any real mystification or allow the reader to participate in the detection, although we are sometimes deceived into failing to identify Number Four (as with Dr Quentin or Dr Savaronoff).

Moreover, this is not a book in which the author makes the most of her skills of deception. Certainly we do not for one moment believe that Poirot is killed in the catastrophe from which he is resurrected, in the way that Holmes was in *The Empty House*.

Strangely, despite the catastrophic nature of this event, we are not told what explosive device was used to cause the flash of blue flame or what the scale of the explosion was, let alone how Poirot escaped being killed.

That is not the only curiosity. Why does Halliday ask if any letters had come for him? Although mentioned three times in chapters 5 and 6, its significance is never explained. When was the door to Paynter's study locked? Despite Japp hypothesising about the key being on the inside, we are not told what actually happened. And who is the man wearing a greatcoat, muffler and blue spectacles who gets off the train at Bolzano in chapter 17? We are never told.

Clues

As we have seen, we never have to solve any puzzle about the identity of the Big Four, so there are no clues about that. However, we have to credit Poirot for narrowing Number Four down to four people. He does so by identifying gifted character actors aged about 30, of more or less nondescript appearance, who left the stage within the last three years. He could have narrowed the field further if he had looked for actors with the medical knowledge needed to impersonate Dr Quentin and conduct surgeries for a month.

However, even though Number Four is identified as Claud Darrell, we wouldn't know him if we saw him. Either he would have to give himself away with the 'breadcrumbs' clue, as he does when being Micky Templeton and the man in the Italian hotel. Or he would have to make himself known, as he does by taking four cigarettes from his cigarette case (when he is the man in the buttoned-up overcoat in Paris) or when he puts four little heaps of salt on Hastings' plate (when he is the bearded man in the Soho restaurant).

The most important clue in this weakly clued novel is one which Hastings gets from John Ingles' Chinese servant who lies dying of a knife wound. It is a clue to the Big Four's headquarters, not that we realise it then since the dying man's broken sounds convey nothing to Hastings. He thinks he catches the word "hand", then the word "Largo" – so he thinks of "Handel's Largo" – and then another Italian word "*carrozza*", which he thinks means 'carriage', then "two or three more words of murmured Italian", which he does not reveal.

Although he puzzles over the words, we hear no more of them until he mentions them to Poirot in the Ardennes. He says that the additional Italian words were something like "Cara" and "Zia". Poirot reacts to these previously unrevealed words by saying that "Cara Zia is very important, very important indeed" but he says no more except that the English know no geography.

Later, as they are bound for the Big Four's headquarters, he explains that they are travelling to "Karersee, the new Italian name for Lago di Carezza", a well-known summer resort in the heart of the Dolomites. This, he says, is where "*Cara Zia*" comes in as well as "Carrozza" and "Largo". He says that the "Handel" was supplied by Hastings' imagination – possibly some reference to the information coming from the 'hand' of Mr Ingles. However, it is very doubtful that anyone – even a geography student – would have interpreted the 'Cara Zia' clue correctly and it would be generous to describe the pointless use of the words 'hand' and 'Handel's Largo' as legitimate misdirection.

Although Hastings fails to solve this important clue, he does solve a clue when acting as Ryland's secretary. It is in the form of a coded letter giving the time and place of a rendezvous (in fact a trap). Hastings decodes it by reading every fourth word. However, he does not have the actual letter. He had "unobtrusively" jotted down the words given to him by Ryland's stenographer.

She had remembered the letter word for word – a suspicious feat (although Hastings does not spot this), given that it is 42 words long, that she seemingly read it only once, that she had no reason to remember it "word for word" and that it was crucial that her memory was so accurate since otherwise the decoding of the 'coded letter' clue by reading every fourth word would not have worked. In fact the decoding does not actually work because "11 per cent" and "4 per cent" are each written as three words. The decoding would only work if they had been written as '11%' and '4%', with the percentage signs not counting as words or being ignored entirely.

As to the clueing of the seven murders, we assume, since Ingles had been going to China to do what he could against the Big Four and had information which his servant tried to convey, that the sixth and seventh murders are the Big Four's work. But we are given no more clues than this to those murders.

By contrast, we are given more direct clues to their involvement in the other murders. These are explicit in the case of Whalley and Wilson (since Whalley's letter to Ingles and Dr Savaronoff's niece expressly refer to the Big Four). They are more imaginative in the case of Mayerling (the clock stopping at four o'clock), Paynter (the two lines at right angles to each other) and Flossie (the four-shillings price tag on the photograph frame – which is the only clue relating to her murder). But none of these 'figure 4' clues as to the *whodunnit* mystify or deceive us because they are explained straightaway or shortly after being given. There is, however, some additional clueing of the *howdunnit* in the tales of Mayerling, Whalley, Paynter and Wilson.

In the first tale, when Poirot and Hastings return to find that their unexpected guest, Mayerling, is dead, Poirot notes that both bedroom windows, which had been shut, are now open. Hastings suggests that someone entered that way but Poirot says that, if only one window was open, he would not be so intrigued. On then seeing that the sitting room window is open as well, he pronounces that Mayerling was forced to inhale prussic acid. The murderer then opened all the windows because the acid has a strong smell of bitter almonds. With no trace of the smell to guide the doctor and no suspicion of foul play, death would have been put down to natural causes. The 'open windows' clue is not bad as a pointer to an odorous murder weapon but it is explained so quickly after Poirot expresses his intrigue that we have no chance to reflect on it.

In the second tale, there is a "very confused" series of bloody footprints in the living room where Whalley had his throat cut – rather too confused a red herring to lead us to realise, although Poirot manages to do so, that Number Four had tried to implicate Grant by using a duplicate pair of his boots.

The real clue to that murder is a frozen leg of mutton in the larder. Since it is Monday (as we are told), it must have been delivered that day because, had it been delivered on Saturday (there presumably being no delivery on a Sunday), it would not have remained frozen over Sunday during the hot weather. This explains how someone other than Grant could enter and leave the house unnoticed that day – as a butcher's delivery man (Number Four) in a horse and trap on whom a trace of blood would attract no attention. The 'leg of mutton' clue is rather good, the best in the book, and Poirot's detection excellent.[4]

In the third tale Japp's observation that one can't hold a live man's head in a fire because he would scream the house down is important because we then know that Paynter must have been dead when his head was put into the fire. But why was he killed? Half way through the tale Poirot says "I have not the clue – the motive". Japp suggests a motive for the impecunious nephew, Gerald, but Poirot accuses him of dragging "the red kipper across the trail" because Japp really suspects the Chinese servant. This is of itself a red herring because, as Poirot later says, if Ah Ling had been the murderer, his face would have remained impassive when Poirot traced a "4" in the dust instead of becoming a mask of terror. In fact the murderer's motive was to find and steal Paynter's book and, presumably, to prevent him writing it again.

However, it is the words "Yellow Jasmine" scrawled on the newspaper by Paynter which form the main clue. Paynter's house had a large quantity of yellow jasmine growing up its walls and it was thought that the dying message had referred to this. Poirot announces surprisingly early in the case that it is "now quite clear to me – all but the words, yellow jasmine". However, by the next morning, his researches have revealed that yellow jasmine's relevance is not as a plant but as the potent poison which was in the injection given by Dr Quentin to Paynter, although only readers with a knowledge of poisons would be able to interpret the 'yellow jasmine' clue without Poirot's help.

Indeed, quite how Paynter himself knows that he has been injected with yellow jasmine, or that it is a poison, we are not told. Did Quentin tell him? Why would he? What we do know is that Quentin was not the regular doctor but a locum doing a month's work in place of Dr Bolitho. But we get no clues that Number Four had been posing as Quentin until the end of the tale when Poirot says that the arrangements with Bolitho were made by correspondence, that the original locum was taken ill at the last minute and that the real Dr Quentin is probably abroad. We are not told how Poirot knows any of this.

The best clue in the third tale, since we do not realise that it is one, is "the Mystery of the Curry", as Poirot describes it at one stage. The 'curry' clue – that the curry was given by Paynter for analysis to Quentin – is stated in such a matter of fact way in the narrative that we are just not prompted to think that Quentin might have tampered with it *after* it had been given to him by putting powdered opium in it. So we do not spot that the curry was only poisoned after the dinner in order to implicate Ah Ling.

Finally, we have the fourth tale (the chess problem) in which Poirot relies not so much on the 'changed man' clue – that

Savaronoff was so changed that his friends hardly recognised him – but on four other clues where his powers of deduction are amazing, particularly since the murder plan is so unusual

First is the 'white bishops' clue. After simply weighing White's two bishops, he pronounces (before readers get a chance to wonder why he is triumphant) that a thin metal rod was passed up the middle of the one clutched by Wilson.

Second is the 'chess table' clue. After examining the table, he pronounces that, when the white bishop was placed on one of its silver squares, the current passed through it from the flat below. That deduction is supported by the third clue, the 'nail hole' clue – a hole in the beautiful rug on the floor made by a nail which was no longer there. However, Poirot's reliance on the 'chess table' clue is not very persuasive because the table he examines is actually "perfectly innocent", being merely a substituted "duplicate" of the "special table" which was used for the match.

Fourth is the 'Ruy Lopez' clue, derived from the opening with which Wilson started the match. Poirot reads a chess book which explains the opening and, for the reader's benefit, he actually lists the opening moves set out in the book.[5] However, these would only be understood by chess players who were aware of the 'descriptive' chess notation used during that period (it was largely replaced by 'algebraic' chess notation in the latter part of the 20th century), which makes the 'Ruy Lopez' clue rather difficult to spot even for the most astute reader until it is explained.

Poirot, however, realises from the 'Ruy Lopez' clue that moving a bishop is White's third move in the opening and he knows, as readers do, that Wilson was clasping a white bishop when he died. So, provided that Number Four can just learn and make Black's first two moves in that opening, Poirot deduces that White could be electrocuted as early as his third move (the bishop move B-Kt5, using the notation of the period) and that, since that move would be made "before any complications of defence set in",

Black (Number Four) would not have to be a real chess player at all. A brilliant murder plan.

In fact, since Savaronoff told Poirot that Wilson was killed on his "third or fourth" move, he could actually have been killed on his *fourth* move because this is also a white bishop move (the retreating B-R4), provided that the appropriate silver square was wired and Number Four could remember to make Black's most commonly played third move, which is P-QR3 (attacking the bishop). Indeed it would have been more in keeping with all the references to the figure "4" throughout the book for Wilson to have been killed on White's fourth move.

5

The Mystery Of The Blue Train

Solution

Poirot investigates the murder of Mrs Ruth Kettering, the 28-year-old daughter of American millionaire Rufus Van Aldin. She is strangled with black cord on the night of Tuesday 14 February on the Blue Train, the luxury express which ran from Calais to Nice via Paris and Lyons.[1]

After Ruth's death, her features are disfigured by a heavy blow and she is robbed of the necklace recently given to her by her father. It includes the three largest rubies in the world, the centre stone being the 'Heart of Fire'. Poirot, who was on the train, is asked by Van Aldin, who was not, to investigate.

Ruth had told her father that she was going to the Riviera but not that she was meeting her lover, the Comte de la Roche. A letter from him, found in her handbag, shows that he was looking forward to her bringing the Heart of Fire.

The two main suspects (for the murder or robbery or both) are the Comte and Ruth's estranged husband, The Hon. Derek Kettering, who was also on the train. However, the suspects also include three other passengers (Madame Mireille, with whom Derek had had an affair; Ruth's maid, Ada Mason; and Katherine Grey, who is visiting relations) as well as a brilliant jewel thief known only as 'the Marquis', who may be the Comte or Derek.

One person who was not a passenger and who does not seem to be a suspect, since he is never interviewed by Poirot (quite a clever device), is Van Aldin's secretary, Major Richard Knighton. Although clues point to him being the Marquis, it is a surprise when he is revealed as not just having stolen the jewels but also as having murdered Ruth, aided by his accomplice, Ada Mason, who is really an actress called Kitty Kidd.

But why, as Van Aldin asks in the penultimate chapter (chapter 35), did he kill Ruth: "Surely a clever thief could have stolen the jewels without running his head into a noose"? His question is a good one, even though he foreshadowed her being "robbed and murdered" for the rubies in chapter 4. Poirot's answer is that the Marquis had killed before, that he was a killer "by instinct" and that he believed in leaving no evidence behind. However, none of this motivation is clued for readers (there is no reference to a murder with his other robberies) and it sounds unconvincing because a clever thief with "an intense passion for famous and historical jewels" is unlikely to prejudice his theft of them by committing a murder which will increase detective scrutiny of the theft.

It is also odd that the Marquis steals the jewels with such a complex plan on the Blue Train. This may be because, after he has failed to rob Van Aldin of the jewels in Paris, his stolen jewels handler, M. Papopolous, advises him that "The direct attack – It answers sometimes – but very seldom". However, just because an attack against Van Aldin failed, it does not follow that an attack against Ruth would fail or that Ada could not, as Ruth's maid, simply steal the jewels and disappear. It is also unclear how Knighton knew that Ruth would take the jewels on the train when she did not know that they were to be her father's "little surprise" for her.

Subject to all these (important) points, the murder plan is clever (though too elaborate) for two reasons. First, as well as it appearing that Knighton was never on the Blue Train, it also seems that Ada had disembarked before the murder. Secondly,

Ada provides us with a prime suspect – a tall, dark man wearing an overcoat and hat whom she pretends she saw going into Ruth's compartment while the train stopped at the Gare de Lyon in Paris.

The Comte is a ready-made candidate for this prime suspect. He "was to be the scapegoat" (chapter 35) but Ada was not to be too certain in identifying him in case he had an alibi. In fact he does, albeit one that Poirot breaks. But, before Poirot does so, the murderers are fortuitously given a second prime suspect, Derek, whose height and build are not unlike the Comte's and who was seen by Katherine entering Ruth's compartment just before Lyons.

In fact, what happens is this. Ruth and Ada have adjoining compartments with a communicating door. On reaching Paris, the train makes its slow way round the *ceinture*, the railway which encircled Paris connecting its main stations. Knighton boards during one of the "interminable stops and waits". Ruth is surprised but unsuspicious. Knighton, perhaps pointing her to something out of the window, strangles her before the train reaches the Gare de Lyon and then drops off with her scarlet morocco jewel-case.

One would think this sufficient since the authorities will suspect train robbers ("apaches"), as indeed they do. But the plan is considerably elaborated. Before Knighton drops off the train, he and Ada strip off Ruth's outer clothes and roll up her body in a rug which Ada has brought (chapter 10). Presumably Ruth's face has been disfigured by then but we are not told when this occurs. The body is then put in Ada's compartment among the cases.

At the Gare de Lyon (with Knighton no longer on board), Ada buys a dinner basket for Ruth. The purpose, Poirot suggests, was to stop Katherine visiting Ruth. He does not say why this would stop her but he may mean that, if she saw the basket being delivered, she would think that Ruth wanted to be alone. That cannot have been part of the original plan because Ada could not have expected Ruth and Katherine to become friends. So, a better reason might be to prevent Ruth's failure to have dinner in the dining car from looking suspicious.

Ada, who is the same height as Ruth, then changes into Ruth's distinctive clothing and, when the conductor makes up Ruth's bed after the train has left the Gare de Lyon, he believes that Ada is Ruth as she tells him that she has left her maid in Paris. Although he is deceived, it is this conversation which, according to Poirot, explains the disfiguring of Ruth's face: although the conductor would not recognise Ada in Ruth's clothing, there was a danger that, when Ruth's body was found, he might realise that she was not the woman who had spoken to him. The disfiguring of a victim's face for the purpose of concealing, not the identity of the victim, but the earlier impersonation of the victim by someone else, is a clever device.

However, the disfiguring does seem unnecessarily brutal when the priority was the theft. And, since it only took place because of Ada's conversation with the conductor, surely she could just have avoided speaking to him face to face, given that she was either, according to Katherine and Poirot (chapters 10 and 35), looking out of the window while he made up the bed or, according to the conductor himself (chapter 11), sitting on the bed in Ada's compartment.

Nevertheless, we therefore think that Ruth was alive when the train left the Gare de Lyon so that the murder happened between Paris and Lyons. Since, as Poirot says (in chapter 35) "the crime is not supposed to have been committed until nearly twelve hours later", Knighton and Ada are safe because they were (supposedly) in Paris at the time – Knighton seemingly never having been on board and Ada apparently having got off there. But it is odd to think that the medical evidence could be wrong by as much as 12 hours or that this was part of the murderers' plan: as long as the murder was thought to have happened at any time after the train left Paris, they were safe.

Be that as it may, Ada next moves the dead body back into the bed in Ruth's compartment. Then, before getting to Lyons, she changes into a man's clothes and disembarks there, going back to Paris where she has been registered at The Ritz the night before by one of Knighton's female accomplices. Her alibi is completed by Knighton saying that he spoke to her at The Ritz.

Ada is lucky that, when Derek enters Ruth's compartment shortly before Lyons – and he could have done so at any time between Paris and Lyons (why did Ada not bolt the door?) – he does not find Ada dragging Ruth from one compartment to the other or changing out of Ruth's clothes or into the man's clothes or, worse still, that he does not try to wake the dead Ruth since he had entered the compartment to "have it out with her once and for all".

So, although the murder plan is clever, it is also a mixture of over-elaboration, unnecessary brutality and luck. Knighton also makes an extraordinary mistake by leaving his cigarette case, marked with the initial 'K', on the train. This does not immediately expose him, with the other Ks on the train (Ruth and Derek Kettering, Katherine Grey and Kitty Kidd), but it does seem incredible, given his intricate plan and willingness to kill because he believes "in leaving no evidence behind him", that he loses the case during his very short time on board. It is also disappointing, knowing that the Marquis has "an intense passion for famous and historical jewels", that he disposes of them for money.

Plot

This novel is an expanded version of a Hastings' short story *The Plymouth Express*[2] but it is in fact the first Poirot novel to be written in the third person.

In *An Autobiography* the author says that she "always hated" the novel and that, although she would not publish a book if she thought it was *really* bad, she had "come near it" with this novel, which she thought "commonplace, full of clichés, with an uninteresting plot".[3] But, actually, it is on the whole a nice easy read for those not troubled about plot analysis.

Following an opening which conjures up danger in the backstreets of Paris, it is set not only in London and on the Blue Train but also on the picturesque French Riviera and in Katherine's village of St Mary Mead in Kent.

Although the main characters are perhaps more stereotyped than normal, there are three minor characters of note – Mr Goby, a private investigator with the memorable characteristic that he looks at objects rather than at the person he is addressing; George, Poirot's intensely English valet (called Georges with an 's' by Poirot), who decided to work for Poirot because His Majesty thought very highly of his abilities; and Miss Amelia Viner, an elderly resident of St Mary Mead, who is memorable because her powers of observation suggest that she may be a fictional prototype for Miss Marple.[4]

It is in St Mary Mead that we meet 33-year-old Katherine Grey. Having been a ladies' companion for ten years, she has inherited a fortune and is visiting relations, the Tamplins, in Nice. At dinner on the fateful evening she sits with Poirot, who only enters the story in chapter 10. Dinner is a very short affair: Poirot converses with her for about one minute before he polishes a fork and she rises from the table. Food seems to have been forgotten.

Following the murder, he suggests to her that they are investigating the affair "together" (chapters 11 and 20), that they are "good friends and have no secrets from each other" (chapter 26), that they are "colleagues in this affair" (chapter 30) and that the affair is their own "*roman policier*" (chapters 20 and 32). Although she never seems to engage fully with this, she does give Poirot help, even though it comes "from such an entirely different angle".

That is because she appears to have a sort of sixth sense. When she sees Derek at Cook's in chapter 8, "A cold shiver passed over Katherine; she had a haunting sense of tragedy, of doom impending ". She is not the only one with this facility. Derek himself has "a sense of fatality" (chapter 9) and in chapter 10 Ruth tells Katherine that "something horrible is going to happen".

However, the most extreme example involves Katherine. In chapter 26, while sitting in Monte Carlo's Casino Gardens, she has a vivid impression that the dead Ruth is standing beside her, wanting to tell her something important. We are not told what but Poirot says in chapter 35 that it came to her that Ruth was trying to tell her that Knighton was the murderer. What should we make of this? Since Katherine never reveals what 'Ruth' said and there is no mention of her discussing it with Poirot, it is not offered as a clue. But if it had been, we could hardly have taken it seriously. Although Poirot just says "One cannot explain these things", Van Aldin's reaction is "Extraordinary".

Despite its easy readability and reasonably good pace up to about chapter 29 (out of 36), the novel never really engages us. We know from chapter 2 that the Marquis has very probably stolen the rubies. The mystery is his identity and whether he is also the murderer but the mystification engendered by those issues is not very puzzling. We don't believe that the Comte is the murderer (he is too obviously offered up to the police). We don't believe that Derek is the murderer (he is too obviously offered up to the reader). Katherine seems too genuine to be the murderer, just as Mireille seems too temperamental. With rather too much predictability, the stereotyped suspects seem too obvious or too unlikely – other than Ada – but Knighton saw her in Paris. So we are not sure what to believe. However, we don't much mind.

One reason for this is that, after Derek's arrest in chapter 28, Poirot's investigation drifts patchily towards a conclusion in a way that gives readers no real help save for a newspaper cutting about a wartime jewel robbery. We are taken back to St Mary Mead where Katherine is staying with Miss Viner and Poirot visits the Russian Embassy and The Ritz in Paris and

Katherine, Mr Aarons (a theatrical agent) and a Harley Street doctor in London.

We are given no information about the timescale for all this other than that Derek is in prison (chapter 31) – is he awaiting trial? – and we have no real sense of what Poirot has been doing. Then in chapter 34 Knighton is suddenly revealed as the Marquis without warning.

Even Poirot's "Explanations" in chapter 35 are rather unsatisfactory. He starts by referring to the disfigured face, which he describes as the "one point that puzzled me". It would have been interesting to see how he intended to carry on logically from there but, irritatingly, he is interrupted by Van Aldin who asks when he began to suspect Ada. His flow of reasoning gradually becomes pretty jumbled, perhaps because further interruptions from Van Aldin result in the jigsaw being pieced together in a rather random fashion, giving the sense of a mishmash of points and ideas rather than of a logical presentation.

Perhaps strangest of all is Poirot not even mentioning the point which gave him (so he says in chapter 36) the "first inkling" of the truth, namely Lenox Tamplin's suggestion in chapter 28 that the murderer need not have been a passenger but may have got on and off while the train was in a station.

Despite the jumble, we recognise two good pieces of misdirection. The first is the tall, dark man in the overcoat and hat. Might he be the Comte or Derek or someone else? In fact he doesn't exist. The second is the train's location when the murder happened. We are repeatedly pointed away from Paris – by the conductor, the Police Commissary (Monsieur Caux) and the medical evidence in chapter 11, by Poirot's theory in chapter 15, by the Examining Magistrate (Monsieur Carrège) in chapter 17, by Derek in chapter 26 and by Poirot in chapter 28 where he says "And we know this much, that a few moments after leaving Lyons Mrs Kettering was dead". All the time we are being cleverly conditioned to a belief, shared by Van Aldin in chapter 34, that the murder happened shortly before or possibly after the train left Lyons.

However, despite this cleverness with the misdirection, there is so much looseness in the plotting (and clueing) that the lack of discipline becomes positively dissatisfying for readers who are trying to solve the crimes and who can hardly be expected to go back and check the accuracy of everything they are told. The main examples will suffice.

As we know from chapter 10, Katherine saw the dinner basket being received "by the maid". Consistent with this, Poirot explains in chapter 35 that Ada got the dinner basket and *then* changed into Ruth's clothes. However, only a handful of paragraphs before this, Poirot had said that it was Ada "dressed in her mistress's very distinctive clothing" who purchased the dinner basket.

Also in chapter 10, who is the person seen with "intense surprise" by Ada in the train corridor before it reaches Paris? We are not told. Is it the lady who is "very heavily made up in a bizarre fashion" seen by Katherine in the same paragraph? Again we are not told who this is. The only candidate seems to be Mireille because her make-up is unusual but Katherine felt she had seen the face before and there is no sign that she had ever seen Mireille. We expect to find out since "It was a face not easily forgotten, as Katherine was to know when she saw it again". But there is no reference to Katherine seeing it again.

In chapter 12 Katherine realises that she forgot to tell Poirot that she saw Derek going into Ruth's compartment. So she tells him this in chapter 20. Yet he shows no real reaction to this apparently key piece of information. It is as if the author thinks that Katherine had already told Poirot in chapter 11.

Also in chapter 20, Van Aldin, describing Ruth's reaction to the tall, dark man getting onto the train, says "But we have the maid's word for it that she was both startled and dismayed at the

Count's appearance at the station in Paris". But that is not what Ada said, either when examined in Van Aldin's presence (chapter 14) or when asked to recognise the Comte (chapter 17). Although she rather thinks (chapter 17) that the Comte was the man, she is "not sure" (as she repeats in chapter 23) and she never says that Ruth was "dismayed".

A particularly odd omission relates to Kitty Kidd (Ada), an obviously significant lady with two 'K's in her initials and who, so Mr Aarons tells Poirot in chapter 31, is a male impersonator and character actress and has taken up with a man called the Marquis. But, despite Kitty Kidd turning out to be Ada, we never learn how Poirot knew to ask Mr Aarons about her.

However, the most extraordinary omission occurs in chapter 34 when Poirot, Van Aldin and Knighton are on the Blue Train. Poirot starts to reconstruct the crime and suddenly says "*Mon Dieu*, but that is something I have not thought of!". At his urging, the three of them get off the train at the Gare de Lyon. But, after being held up at the barrier, Poirot appears "stricken with paralysis" by another idea and asks them to return to the train, saying "I have been an imbecile". We are never told why he behaves in this idiosyncratic way. Perhaps it was to let the French police get on at Paris so that they could wait in the next compartment until Knighton's exposure.

Clues

There are a lot of clues in this story, some quite good but none particularly special and too many which have weaknesses, including two, one relating to Derek and the other to the Marquis, which seem misleading.

The 'missing jewel case' clue points to a robbery (chapter 14) and the prime suspect, at least for the police, is the Comte. But the only clue against him is the letter found in Ruth's handbag (the 'Comte letter' clue) and Poirot clearly thinks in chapter 15 that the Comte would have searched her bag to remove it if he had been the murderer. So he is not the *murderer*. But Poirot seems to think he could still be the *thief*. This seems odd because it was surely just as important for the Comte to remove the letter even if he was only the thief.

Our inclination to discount the Comte as thief, as well as murderer, is fortified in chapter 19 when he thinks "A fully matured scheme had been rudely brought to naught", presumably meaning that he had schemed to steal the rubies but failed (and so was not the thief). This seems confirmed when Poirot learns in chapter 22 that he has an excellent imitation set of the jewels (which Poirot obtains by the dubious device of intercepting a package mailed by the Comte at a Bureau de Poste). So, by chapter 24, with the 'imitation set' clue, Poirot has "no doubt" that the Comte meant to steal the rubies and substitute them with his imitation set but that someone got in ahead of him.

Nevertheless, Poirot still pursues him, breaking his alibi by getting his servant to admit that the Comte did not arrive at his villa until Wednesday 15 February (Poirot mistakenly calls it January). Poirot describes the undoing of the alibi as "one guess confirmed". But, frustratingly, we never learn what the Comte actually did on the night of 14 February. Presumably he found that he had been beaten to the jewels. But did he realise that Ruth was dead?

Poirot's other "guess" is that Mireille entered Ruth's compartment and found her dead. But she refuses to answer his questions and, like the Comte, we never learn for certain. However, in the next chapter Poirot tells Lenox that "someone else" (i.e. singular) had found Ruth dead and we assume he means Mireille. Notably, Lenox asks "And they [plural] did not rouse the train?", using 'they' generically because she doesn't know the intruder's gender. But, even though Poirot *does* seem to know, he replies in the plural "Doubtless they had their reasons", which avoids revealing the intruder's gender.

Having become the main suspect in chapter 15, the Comte is replaced in that role by Derek when Poirot has "A New Theory" (the title of chapters 23 and 33). We know that Derek has a financial motive: he is in "very low water financially" and will be in a "nasty hole" if Ruth divorces him (chapter 5), as she plans to do; and yet, if she dies, he will inherit the "couple of millions" settled on her by Van Aldin (chapter 6). On the other hand, Van Aldin offers him £100,000 not to defend Ruth's divorce petition (chapter 7), which undermines his financial motive even though he declines the offer.

Derek purchases his Blue Train ticket just after seeing "several roads that he might take – one in particular. If he shrank from it, it was for the moment only. Desperate ills need desperate remedies" (chapter 9). This 'desperate remedies' clue stays with us and, when it transpires that he is neither murderer nor Marquis and went into Ruth's compartment just "on impulse", we regard it as misleading. The worst he was doing was "more or less spying on my wife" (chapter 26), which hardly merits the dramatic language used.

Indeed, readers will think it highly unlikely that Derek is the murderer because of his demeanour after Ruth's body is found. In chapter 12 he is "quite unconscious of the fate that had befallen her. Of that there was no doubt. He did not know" and, when he learns that the police want to see him, "an expression of utter astonishment came over his face". Caux later says that, on breaking the news to Derek, "Oh, it came as a surprise to him. He was overwhelmed" (chapter 16). So, because of the 'Derek demeanour' clues, we disregard Mireille's attempts to suggest that he is the *murderer*.

However, we do wonder for a time if he is the *thief*. This is partly because of the 'French speaker' clue. We know (chapter 1) that the Marquis is a well-bred Englishman who speaks very good French and we learn (chapter 21) that Derek speaks French so well that he could be taken for a Frenchman.

But, more significantly, he knows that Ruth had the rubies with her. That is suspicious because, although Mireille told him about Van Aldin's purchase of the rubies, which she assumed were for Ruth, and about Ruth going to meet the Comte, she never said that Ruth would have the rubies with her. Moreover, he knows that they were stolen because, in an important exchange with Poirot in chapter 17, he says that, if he had killed Ruth (and inherited a fortune), he would have had "no need to steal the jewels".

Poirot accepts this logic but, once Derek has left, he says that Ruth had no opportunity to tell Derek about the jewels and that no one else would have done so. So, he asks (in italics for emphasis): "*Then how did he know about them?*" (and, indeed, how did he know they had been stolen?). An excellent question but, frustratingly, this seemingly key 'stolen jewels' clue against Derek is never explained away.

The final clue for Poirot's "New Theory" is the cigarette case of soft blue leather bearing the initial 'K', which he reveals to Katherine in chapter 21. It is probably the book's most memorable clue because it is so surprising that the murderer left such an incriminating item. Almost as surprising is Poirot's revelation of it to Katherine because there was no reference to him finding it in chapter 11, even though we were told he had found four of Ruth's auburn hairs (the 'auburn hairs' clue) on the rug in Ada's compartment.

The relevance of the 'K cigarette case' clue, in the context of Poirot's "New Theory", is Ada's answer in chapter 23 about who owns it. On being shown it, she looks startled (probably recognising it as Knighton's) but implicates Derek by saying that she thinks (but can't be sure) that Ruth bought it for him.

So, with the 'Ada answer' clue, Derek is now the main suspect. Poirot even says in the next chapter that he suspected Derek "from the very first", although that is an odd claim for two reasons. First, he adds in that paragraph that he thought that the tall, dark man apparently seen by Ada was the Comte (so why did he first suspect Derek?). Secondly, he then adds that he realised that the man might not be the Comte but Derek because Van Aldin had once mistaken the Comte for Derek; Van Aldin did indeed do that (chapter 5) but there is no record of him mentioning this to Poirot.

Nevertheless, with the "New Theory" pointing to Derek, readers will assume that, when Poirot warns Katherine in chapter 26 about a man more dangerous than the Comte, he is referring to Derek, particularly since he and Katherine were discussing Derek just before the warning. But the key point about the 'warning' clue is that Poirot does not name Derek. Those who spot this may also spot that the juxtaposition of Derek with the warning cleverly misdirects us away from the person being discussed before Derek, namely Knighton.

However, readers would do extremely well to focus on Knighton because for the first 20 chapters he does not appear much and in chapter 21 Poirot says he approves of him. So, what points to him by the time of the 'warning' clue? We know he became Van Aldin's secretary two months ago (chapter 3) just after Van Aldin began negotiating the purchase of the rubies (chapter 15), that he was in Paris on the fatal night (chapter 13) and that the 'K' cigarette case could be his. We also have the 'Clanravon jewels' clue, knowing from what he told Katherine in chapter 21 that he was at a house in Yorkshire when Lady Clanravon's jewels were stolen (as Katherine must later have told Poirot).

Some other clues may only be seen in retrospect, such as him prompting Katherine in chapter 21 to believe that the Comte is "of course" the person who "did it" and textual clues which would be spotted only by the most astute reader. Two good examples are in chapter 13. Knighton is "overjoyed" on 15 February (after the successful robbery) – a strong adjective just to describe his (claimed) pleasure that Van Aldin is now working hard – and he is "careful to make his voice as natural as possible" when telling Van

Aldin of Ada's (untruthful) statement that Ruth had met a friend unexpectedly on the train.

The final clue against Knighton before the warning relates to the Marquis' walk. We know that the Marquis walks in a "leisurely" way from chapters 1 and 2. We also know from chapter 3 that Knighton limps, suggesting that he cannot therefore be the Marquis. Then in chapter 21 Lenox tells Katherine that, when Knighton left her mother's hospital after recovering from being shot in the leg during the War (12 years before), he was "completely dot and go one" (i.e. he limped) even though the doctors had said that "he wouldn't limp or anything". The clue is not that Knighton limps (which we know) but that the doctors thought he would *not* have to do so (as Lenox presumably tells Poirot in the conversation referred to in chapter 32).

Readers would do very well to spot this clever 'limp' clue, which is probably the best in the book because it is hidden in Lenox's description of Knighton's time at the hospital and requires readers to spot a negative and remember the Marquis's "leisurely" walk. For those who do not remember it, there are a couple of reminders – though after the warning – when we are told that that the Marquis has a "young walk" (chapter 28) and "the light springy step of a young man" (chapter 32). Whether or not reminders are needed, those who correctly interpret the 'limp' clue – as showing that Knighton might not have to limp (so that his limp might be "camouflage", as Poirot puts it in chapter 35) – will realise that he could be the Marquis after all.

However, Poirot is further ahead of readers because by the time of the warning he regards Knighton as the *murderer*. But why? In chapter 35 we learn that he focused on Knighton because of his suspicions about Ada, which had begun with the 'Ada answer' clue. He explains that Ada had said that the cigarette case "was one which Mrs Kettering had given to her husband". In fact she had not said that. As noted earlier, she had said (chapter 23) that she thought (but couldn't be sure) that Ruth bought it for Derek.

Nevertheless Poirot, treating her as having said it, thinks it "most improbable" that Ruth would have bought it for Derek, given the terms they were on, such that it awakened a doubt in his mind about the "general veracity" of Ada's statements. That would be a sweeping conclusion to draw from the 'Ada answer' clue, even if it had been founded on an accurate premise, and it is the more unsatisfactory because it is through that general suspicion about Ada that Poirot comes to suspect Knighton.

But, even though Poirot now suspects Ada, he has the problem of two people indicating that Ada left the train and stayed in Paris – the conductor (who had apparently been told by Ruth that she had left her there, which, of course, the dead Ruth could not gainsay) and Knighton (who had told Van Aldin in chapter 13 that he saw Ada at The Ritz after the train left Paris).

Looking first at the conductor's evidence, the answer is that Ruth, who was "tall and slender, with a jaw and chin line that bespoke hardness and determination" (chapter 4) was impersonated by Ada, a "thin, tall woman" (chapter 10) who "looked bonier and more acid than ever" (chapter 23). The placing of these descriptions sufficiently far apart that we tend not to link them is good clueing. However, the 'thin tall' clue is unnecessarily complicated by Ada having been the person to whom the conductor handed the tickets, meaning that Poirot has to explain why he did not recognise Ada when she purchased the dinner basket and said she had left her maid in Paris. To do so, Poirot asserts, as if it were fact, that on the earlier occasion the conductor's "impression had been merely that of a gaunt, black-clad female". In fact, the conductor had never said what his impression was.

Readers would do well to spot the impersonation on the basis of the 'thin tall' clue. But they would have to be even more astute to spot it by reference to the rather clever 'disfigured face' clue which conceals Ada's impersonation of Ruth whose body was, as indicated by the 'auburn hairs' clue, in the rug.

Those who do spot that Ada could have impersonated Ruth still face the second part of Poirot's problem – Knighton's sighting of Ada in Paris. But Poirot notes the "rather suspicious fact" that Ada had been in Ruth's service for only two months (chapter 14) and the "curious coincidence" that Knighton too had been two months in Van Aldin's service.

Based on the 'two months' clue and supposing that the 'K' cigarette case was Knighton's, the answer to his "chief stumbling block" could be that Knighton and Ada were working together. He considered that, if they were and she recognised the cigarette case as his, she would act precisely as she had done when asked about it: at first taken aback, she would then evolve a theory agreeing with Derek's guilt. When she later confirms in chapter 24 that she is "almost certain" that the tall, dark man was Derek, Poirot says "The expected has happened". There was only one explanation for her "sudden certainty": she had been instructed by someone, namely Knighton.

That is the clueing position up to the 'warning' clue. We then get more clues about the Marquis. In chapter 27 we learn that he had committed robberies in Switzerland the previous autumn. We know that Knighton was in Switzerland two months ago (chapter 3) and, with that 'Switzerland' clue in mind, realise that he could be the Marquis. When Poirot refers to this in chapter 35, he adds that Knighton speaks French like a Frenchman and was in America, France and England when the Marquis was there. But we were not given those clues.

However, we do learn from Caux in chapter 27 that the Marquis "works behind the scenes, you understand. He has underlings who do his dirty work for him". These sentences are highly important – providing the book's most significant clue, especially for readers who do not yet have the answer to Poirot's chief stumbling block – because they suggest (or, for some readers, confirm) the solution that two villains were working together, more specifically an "underling" (the suspicious Ada) despatched to do the "dirty work" by the Marquis (Knighton) who was lying about having seen her.

But the 'underling' clue does more than suggest that there were two villains. It explains why a woman handed the rubies to Papopolous in Nice after the robbery in accordance with the Marquis's plan. And, for those who spot that Ada's dirty work did not just involve stealing the jewels but impersonating the murdered Ruth, it shows that the Marquis planned a murder, not just a theft.

There is, however, a further reason why the 'underling' clue is so significant, which is that it is so misleading. It is clearly saying that the Marquis "works behind the scenes" with his underlings doing his "dirty work". So readers who have deduced that Knighton and Ada are in league will fairly assume that Ada not only impersonated Ruth but murdered her. Yet, according to Poirot in chapter 35, it was the Marquis, not Ada, who strangled Ruth with the cord.

The fact that the Marquis is, according to Poirot, a killer by "instinct" is not clued. Although Poirot's valet, George, tells a tale in chapter 27 about a son of the Duke of Devize's (so spelled) – a kleptomaniac who was "vicious through and through" – this is not referred to again and we are never told whether Knighton was the Duke of Devize's son.

The clinching clue that Knighton is the Marquis is probably the 'newspaper cutting' clue. We know there is a clue among Miss Viner's cuttings in chapter 30 when Katherine has "a puzzled, worried look". It is the cutting reporting that there had been a jewel robbery at Lady Tamplin's villa while she ran it as an Officers' Hospital during the War. And, of course, Lenox had told us, when giving us the 'limp' clue, that Knighton had been at the hospital.

There is in fact one final clue to which Poirot refers in chapter 35. It follows from the 'limp' clue. He says that he had visited the surgeon who thought that Knighton would not limp and later mentioned the surgeon's name in Knighton's hearing; and yet Knighton said nothing (the 'Knighton silence' clue) even though it would have been natural for him to have said that he had been attended by that surgeon during the War.

However, although we know that Poirot had had an interesting interview with Lenox and visited a Harley Street doctor (chapter 32) and mentioned the doctor's name in front of Knighton (chapter 33), there was no reference in those contexts to Knighton's limp. So only the most astute reader would have derived a clue from Knighton's silence. It is a pity that the 'Knighton silence' clue is so inaccessible because Poirot says that "that little point, if nothing else, gave me the last final assurance that my theory of the crime was correct".

Nevertheless, readers ought not to need that clue in identifying Knighton as the Marquis. Having been given the rather obvious 'newspaper cutting' clue as well as the 'K cigarette case' clue and knowing of his presence in Switzerland and Yorkshire, even the most passive readers will suspect him of being the thief, although it may be a surprise to find that he was working with Ada and involved in the murder. And being the Marquis is all that Poirot accuses him of at the end of chapter 34. Readers will not automatically assume that the Marquis and the murderer are the same person and it is only in chapter 35 that Knighton is revealed as the murderer as well as the thief.

6

Peril At End House

Solution

Poirot and the narrator, Captain Hastings, investigate the murder of Maggie Buckley, who is shot on a Monday in August 1931 after her arrival at End House, which overlooks the harbour at St. Loo in Cornwall.[1] The imposing house is owned by Maggie's cousin, a 22-year-old lady called Nick Buckley.

Nick, whose parents had died when she was young, had lived there as a child with her brother Gerald and her grandfather, Sir Nicholas Buckley, who was popularly supposed to have sold his soul to the devil and so, like the devil, was known as 'Old Nick'. She went everywhere with him and so was called 'Young Nick' or 'Nick', though her real Christian name was Magdala, a family name of which there were many in the Buckley family (chapter 2). When Sir Nicholas, a gambler, died six years ago, he left hardly anything but End House and, when Gerald died three years later, it came to Nick.

On the Saturday before Maggie is shot someone apparently tries to shoot Nick in the garden of the Majestic Hotel in St. Loo where Poirot and Hastings are on holiday. A bullet strikes the terrace beside them, just before Nick hurries into sight. Poirot, who picks up the bullet, finds a bullet hole in her hat. It appears that she has been shot at by an unseen gunman with a Mauser pistol and had a lucky escape.

Nick says that she has already had three escapes from death in as many days. First, a heavy picture, hanging over her bed, whose wire had been tampered with, had fallen during the night while she was out of bed. Secondly, a boulder roared down the cliff path but just missed her. Thirdly, the brakes of her car went wrong but she only ran into a laurel hedge.

When Nick cannot then find the Mauser pistol which her father brought back from the War, Poirot, who is convinced that an assassin is trying to kill her, urges her to get a friend to stay with her at End House immediately. Nick suggests a Yorkshire cousin, Maggie, who is about her age. Maggie arrives at 5.30 pm on Monday and that evening she meets Poirot and Hastings when they come to End House for a party, involving dinner followed by a quayside fireworks display to be watched from the garden overlooking the harbour.

After dinner, during the display, Maggie is found dead in the garden, having been shot three times with the Mauser pistol, which cannot be found. She is wearing a black dress (like Nick) and Nick's distinctive Chinese shawl of vivid lacquer red. So, the assassin has apparently mistaken Maggie for Nick in a fifth attempt to kill her. "They were misled by the shawl" explains Poirot.

The rest of the story is essentially a mixture of trying to identify who has been attempting to kill Nick (mistakenly murdering Maggie) and of trying to prevent him or her from succeeding in any further attempt. In chapter 8 Poirot moves Nick to a nursing home for her safety. However, a sixth attempt is apparently but unsuccessfully made when Nick eats a chocolate, poisoned with cocaine, from a box sent to her at the nursing home.

In listing the suspects surrounding Nick in chapter 9, Poirot gives them each a letter from "A to J" (the title of that chapter). They are (A) Ellen, Nick's housekeeper, (B) her gardener husband, (C) their ten-year-old child (who, he says, can be ruled out), (D) Mr Croft, who rents the lodge at End House, (E) his wife, (F)

Frederica Rice, an old friend of Nick's, (G) Jim Lazarus, an art dealer who accompanies Frederica, (H) Commander Challenger, who seems devoted to Nick, (I) Charles Vyse, Nick's lawyer and nearest relation, and (J) an unnamed "outsider" but with a link via one of "A to I".

Frederica had been practically Nick's greatest friend. Before undergoing an appendix operation six months earlier in February, Nick had even made her residuary legatee in her will. However, she had come to hate Frederica when Jim Lazarus, who had once been attracted to Nick but had then gone off her, fell in love with Frederica instead.

By chapter 12 – after we learn that Nick had been secretly engaged to the recently deceased aviator, Captain Michael Seton, whose fortune she is due to inherit – Poirot concludes that her assassin is motivated by the money she will receive. So, he narrows his suspects to two – Frederica, Nick's residuary legatee (who had not, Poirot thinks, been at Tavistock, as she had claimed, before arriving in St. Loo – though nothing turns on that) and Vyse (who would inherit End House under Nick's will – or, if there were no will, her estate as next of kin). However, after the unsuccessful sixth attempt, he says "But those two – it is too simple – too easy, that. There is another twist still".

In fact there are no more attempts on Nick's life. Indeed, the murderer's only victim is Maggie whose murder does not seem to involve any real ingenuity since she is simply shot with the missing Mauser pistol, wearing the shawl and with no shots being heard because of the fireworks display.

However, what is undoubtedly ingenious is the misdirection at the core of the story as to the intended victim's identity. For, despite the apparent attempts on Nick's life, it was Maggie, not Nick, who was the intended victim all along – and it is Nick who, in a most impressive and expertly concealed solution, turns out to be her murderer. The ingenuity in Nick's plan was that all the attempts on her life were false and cleverly concocted solely to camouflage the apparently mistaken (but in fact deliberate) killing of Maggie by giving the impression that she was just the victim of an error by the killer.

Nick's motive derived from her passionate devotion to End House. The house was in a poor state with a leaking roof and Nick needed money for it but could not get it. It was heavily mortgaged after paying two sets of death duties following the deaths of her grandfather and brother.

Then, in September, nearly a year before, she met Captain Michael Seton, an intrepid aviator and the nephew of Sir Matthew Seton, the second richest man in England. Captain Seton took her flying but was never attracted to her. Instead he fell in love with Maggie (whose real name was also Magdala) and became engaged to her at about Christmas time. Only one person knew – Nick – because Maggie had otherwise kept the engagement secret at Seton's request for fear of irritating his uncle, who was known as a woman-hater.

Some months later, before going on a round-the-world flight, Captain Seton made a will, leaving everything to his fiancée, "Magdala Buckley" (Maggie), unaware that Nick's name was also Magdala. He wrote to Maggie about the will and, says Poirot, Maggie would have read the letter to Nick.

Then "about a week ago" (i.e. on about the Monday before the murder), Sir Matthew Seton died unexpectedly, leaving his fortune to Captain Seton, who was himself then reported missing during his round-the-world flight on Tuesday (i.e. the next day). If Captain Seton were to die as well, the fortune inherited from his uncle would go to "Magdala Buckley" under his will.

So, if Nick could, by reference to her known previous acquaintance with him, pretend to be the "Magdala" in the will, she would inherit. But this pretence would necessarily involve killing the real Magdala. So she arranges for Maggie to come and stay the following Tuesday.

Then the supposed attacks on her life start to give the impression that her life is in danger – on the Wednesday before the murder, says Poirot (chapter 12). She cuts through the picture wire, probably invents the story of the boulder and tampers with the car brakes.

Then she sees in the newspaper that Poirot is staying at the Majestic Hotel and on Saturday (by when there is still no news of the missing Seton) she makes him a witness to the fourth attempt with "the bullet through the hat that falls at my feet". The result is Poirot's request that she send for a friend and so she asks Maggie to come a day earlier, on Monday, without mentioning to Poirot that she had already asked her to come on Tuesday.

By the evening of Nick's party that Monday, Captain Seton's chances of being found alive are reckoned to be very low. Nick enters the dinner conversation about his overdue flight but at 9 pm she leaves (pretending to have heard the telephone) to listen to the news and learns of Seton's death.[2] So she takes (presumably from Maggie's room) the letters which Seton has written to Maggie (it is convenient that Maggie has brought them with her), selects those she needs to indicate that she, Nick, was the recipient and puts them in her own room, returning to dinner at 9.20 pm. The letters she selects could have been meant for her because, instead of starting with Maggie's name, they begin with "Darling" or "Dearest Love" or the like.

Then, while watching the fireworks that cold summer's evening, Maggie and Nick come in to get their coats. Maggie can't find hers and Nick tells her to use the shawl – "The Fatal Shawl", as chapter 8 is called. Maggie goes back out and, stealing after her, Nick shoots her with the pistol, goes back inside and hides it in a secret panel of whose existence she thinks nobody knows.

So in fact the murder plan does involve more ingenuity than at first appears – using the fireworks display in Regatta Week to drown the noise of the shots (but what would she have done if Seton had died later that week, after the fireworks displays on Monday and Tuesday?); purloining the letters (perhaps Nick had asked Maggie to bring them); wearing a dress of the same colour as Maggie's (even though Frederica had never seen her wear a black dress before); hiding Maggie's coat (one assumes, though we are not told this), so forcing her to wear the shawl; and concealing the pistol in the secret panel.

Then on Thursday, Poirot learns of the further attempt on Nick's life with the poisoned chocolates. This was part of the same scheme. If an attempt was made on Nick's life *after* Maggie's death, that settled the question that her death had been a mistake and that Nick was the intended victim.

So Nick telephoned Frederica, asking her to send a box of chocolates to the nursing home. She filled three of them with the right amount of cocaine (concealed in her wristwatch). She ate one and was ill – but not too ill, knowing how much cocaine to take and what symptoms to exaggerate.

Nick chose the hated Frederica in order to implicate her for the murder. So, when telephoning her, Nick used an unusual voice so that Frederica might seem doubtful, as she does, about whether it was Nick who telephoned. With Frederica's motive for murdering Nick coming from Nick's will and with Nick placing the pistol (from the secret panel) in Frederica's wrap, the incrimination was complete.

However, her removal of the pistol from the secret panel was witnessed by a concealed Inspector Japp and she is exposed by Poirot as he reveals the totally unexpected solution. Some readers may spot that the 'Magdala' in Captain Seton's will is Maggie (not Nick) more quickly than Poirot seems to (chapter 18). But even those readers will still do very well to conclude from that that Nick is not the intended victim but the murderer.

Plot

If one regards *The Murder of Roger Ackroyd* as a one-off masterpiece in the 1920s, Agatha Christie's glorious golden decade really starts with the present book and its ingenious deception. But it is a curious start, partly because of the role of a wasp in the fake shooting attempt at the beginning of the story.

We can later work out what the plan for this supposed attempt involves. Nick spots Poirot and Hastings on the hotel terrace and fires a bullet towards them, presumably through her hat; the bullet strikes the terrace beside them and Poirot picks it up; she then hurries into sight and chats to them, telling them of her three escapes from death; and she leaves the hat so that Poirot can notice the bullet hole. What she must hope is that, on seeing her hurrying into sight with a bullet hole in her hat just after the bullet has struck the terrace, Poirot will think – as he does – that he has witnessed a fourth attempt.

But during that period something else also happens. While Nick is chatting to Poirot, a wasp flies past her face. She flinches and remarks that she hates it when bees and wasps "come right past your face", implying that this had happened earlier. This remark – although opportunistic because Nick could not have *relied* on a wasp flying past her face as part of her plan – seems to convince Poirot about the attempt because he tells her in the next chapter that "it was not a wasp that flew past your face this morning – it was this bullet".

However, despite Nick repeating the idea that it was a wasp (chapter 8), the chances of her mistaking a speeding bullet passing through her hat for a wasp buzzing past her face seem most unlikely since the bullet would have whisked through the hat at such speed that, if she felt a sensation at all, she would hardly have attributed it to a wasp. So, although Poirot has good reasons for deducing that a fourth attempt was made (the bullet, the three previous attempts and the hole), it does not really make sense for him to treat Nick's reference to wasps as providing another reason for that deduction.

The fake shooting also seems unrealistic. This is not so much because Nick was lucky that Poirot even picked up the bullet (which Hastings assumed was just a pebble). Nor is it because no one saw a gunman "within a dozen yards of Hercule Poirot" (which he attributes to the garden having plenty of cover). Nor is it because no one heard a shot (which he attributes to the speedboat noise in the bay). Rather, it is because he was not more worried. His reaction to picking up a bullet which has struck the terrace beside him should surely be to think that he – or Hastings – is under attack but there is no such reaction.

Nevertheless, the reader's attention is quickly engaged by the fake shooting and the story then moves at a highly readable pace throughout its 22 chapters, increasing in drama and comprehensively deceiving us as to what is actually happening. The deception is so successful because the plot is constructed to ensure that readers never even think of Nick as a suspect.

This is achieved partly through readers being conditioned to believe that an "assassin" or "would-be murderer" is after Nick; partly through Poirot's various indications that Nick, not Maggie, was the intended victim; and partly through readers being directed to his list of suspects ("A to J") among which, he says, "there must be the name of the murderer" despite it excluding Nick.

The misdirection away from Nick is emphasised when Poirot writes out his list again in chapter 18, although this further list is rather a millstone because against each suspect he puts various questions (about 40 in total), some of which are never answered despite his claim in the final chapter that he has answered them. In fact, he adds "In all but a few isolated questions the result was simple and convincing". But what about the "isolated" ones? Were the answers tricky or unconvincing? And which questions were they?

Beyond this, the plotting is surprisingly simple for a story with such a clever solution. There are various reasons for this. First, with the story comprising one large deception, no real effort is directed at individually mystifying twists and turns. Secondly, Maggie's simple shooting does not require the intricate plotting or impressive clueing of the murder plans in some other stories. Thirdly, while the storyline never really comes across as episodic, it unfolds in quite an episodic way (the fourth attempt, the story of the earlier attempts, Maggie's murder, the Seton story, the chocolates attempt and the denouement – in fact, a double one). Fourthly, the author concentrates on the main deception, giving relatively scant attention to the interweaving of sub-plots.

One element of the main deception, however, is not simple, namely the sixth attempt with the poisoned Fuller's chocolates. Nick explains that she ate the chocolate because the box appeared to have come from Poirot; the accompanying card was in his handwriting and it used the same words he had used when sending her flowers. But it then appears that the box was delivered by Jim Lazarus, on behalf of Frederica, who claims that Nick asked her to get the chocolates on the telephone. Then, to add to the mystery, we learn that a second box of Fuller's chocolates had arrived by post (with no name inside), that this had been taken up to Nick's room with the first box, and that no one knows which of the two boxes had supposedly come from Poirot.

Readers will find all this as mystifying as Poirot, who considers the options in chapter 18. But the outcome is disappointing because, although the card turns out to be the one which Poirot sent with the flowers (and Nick put in the chocolate box), we are never told who sent the second box of chocolates or why. Mystification is frustrating when the mystery remains unexplained.

Less important are two minor errors in chapter 17 concerning the mystery. First, Poirot refers twice to the assassin having failed four times but, since he undoubtedly regards Maggie's murder as an attempt on Nick in chapter 8, the assassin had already failed five times. Secondly, Hastings prompts the nursing home orderly by saying that the nurse had said that the chocolates had arrived at 6 pm but the nurse is not interviewed until *after* the orderly.

There is also an oddity about Captain Seton's will. In chapter 16 his solicitor, Mr Whitfield, tells Poirot that the fortune passes to "his affianced wife, Miss Magdala Buckley absolutely" under the will, which is legal because Seton's intention is "plain" and it is properly witnessed. He adds that he has therefore written to Miss Buckley (obviously meaning the living one, Nick). But why did Whitfield assume that *she* was the "Miss Magdala Buckley" mentioned in the will? The intention of the testator was not in fact as 'plain' as he thought.

The only significant sub-plot concerns the Crofts, the (supposedly) Australian couple renting the lodge by the gates to End House. Mrs Croft prepares a forged version of Nick's will, leaving everything to herself, which Mr Croft then substitutes for the real will which Nick had made before her appendix operation (the one with Frederica as her residuary legatee). However, in a sort of mini, first denouement (prior to the main one in which Nick is exposed) Mrs Croft is revealed by Inspector Japp as the "Cleverest forger we've ever had, Milly Merton". There is no interweaving of the Croft sub-plot with the main one; it is "a different business altogether" (chapter 22).

There are other mini sub-plots, if they can be called that. One concerns the supplier of the cocaine used in the chocolates. He is Commander Challenger, who is in league with his uncle, Dr MacAllister – though it is unclear how Poirot knows this.[3] Another, running from chapter 2 until the end, concerns Lazarus' offer of £50 for the portrait of Nick's grandfather which was worth at most £20. His plan was that, if Nick got a valuation which showed that he had offered more than the portrait was worth, then next time he offered to buy a picture, she would not get it valued –

a clever idea because one picture was worth at least £5,000 and he presumably intended to offer a lesser sum.

The final mini sub-plot concerns Frederica's estranged husband, who turns up demanding money and whose dreadful, hardly human face is seen by Hastings pressed against his hotel window in chapter 18. In an equally bizarre incident in chapter 19 the husband appears outside End House at the denouement and shoots at Frederica, grazing her shoulder, before being shot and killed himself. Strangely, we are never told who shot him. The sub-plot is as unnecessary as it is bizarre and detracts from the otherwise sound double denouement.

Nevertheless, it does allow Poirot to suggest that he was right to have had a "J" (the unnamed outsider) on his list, meaning the husband. And the husband does explain Frederica's comment after learning about Nick's poisoning "The other, yes, but not this" (chapter 17) – presumably meaning that he could have shot Maggie, mistaking her for Frederica, but would not have poisoned Nick.

However, there is a further twist when Poirot reveals Nick as the murderer, admitting that he had made a grave error, which he remedies by adding "K" to his list. This stands for "A person who should have been included in the original list, but who was overlooked", with "K" being Nick.

Clues

Poirot starts by concluding that that the person trying to kill Nick is not a *stranger* but someone *known* at End House. That is because, if he had been seen at the house on his visit to fray the picture wire, he would only have had an excuse for being there if he was known as one of "the friends of the house".

Poirot then gets "indisputable proof" that no *stranger* was responsible for Maggie's murder when Nick's Mauser pistol cannot be found (chapter 9). The "logic of Poirot's deduction" (as Hastings describes it) is that the only reason why the murderer had used Nick's pistol for the attempted shooting was that he had planned to give her death the appearance of suicide (by placing it by her dead hand); but there was no such pretence with Maggie's murder; and the reason for abandoning the pretence was that the murderer *knew* that Poirot would not be deceived by it. For the murderer to *know* this (and we now come to the conclusion of the "logic"), he must be someone who "knows, in fact, what we know!". Thus Poirot focuses on people who are not strangers but who surround Nick, leading to his list lettered "A to J".

Apart from the reasoning being rather difficult to follow as a matter of logic, the 'absent pistol' clue does not really provide a compelling basis for the deduction, let alone "indisputable proof". Even if one accepts that the murderer took the pistol because he intended to make Nick's death look like suicide (rather than because he just needed a pistol to commit the murder), the abandonment of the pretence might be explained by him simply being unable to think of a convincing way to make the murder look like suicide; and the absence of the pistol might be explained by a stranger simply having taken it with him or thrown it into the sea, as Poirot actually goes on to say he would have done himself. So, his 'friends of the house' clue in chapter 5 seems like a much better basis for concluding that the murderer is not a stranger.

Nevertheless, satisfied that the murderer is not a stranger, Poirot focuses on motive. He had said earlier (chapter 4) "Until I can get some glimmering of the *reason* behind all this, I am in the dark". Then in chapter 9 he says "*Voilà* – it is always that we come back to! Motive! We must find the motive if we are to understand this crime". With motive being so important, he analyses the motives for murder, telling Hastings that, excluding homicidal mania and killing done on the spur of the moment under the impulse of an ungovernable temper, there are four motives for murder.

These are gain (in which he includes, with an awkwardness that readers will spot, gaining a property which is financially worthless but deeply cherished); hate (or love turned to hate), which he describes as "the *crime passionel*"; jealousy, which he rightly separates from the previous motive but on the rather odd ground that it may not necessarily be "a sexual emotion"; and, lastly, fear, where the victim knows something which the murderer fears will ruin his life.

Poirot concludes the chapter by saying that the motive in this case cannot be obvious and that he is going to think overnight. The following morning he asks Hastings three questions: (1) Why has Nick been sleeping badly lately?; (2) Why did she buy a black evening dress – she never wears black?; and (3) Why did she say last night "I have nothing to live for – now"? (in fact she had said "I don't want to live – now" but nothing turns on this).

Poirot regards Nick's weariness of life as a "psychological change", which he attributes to the telephone call which she (apparently) took at the end of dinner. When Seton's death then appears in the morning newspaper, Poirot says that he knows the answer to the three questions because "it stared me in the face" at breakfast (while Hastings was reading the newspaper) and by the end of the chapter Nick has said that she was engaged to the dead airman.

However, readers should spot that Seton's death does not in fact provide the answer to at least his second question. This is because Nick was wearing her black dress *before* dinner, with Frederica making her point about never having seen Nick in a black dress, and therefore *before* she learned that Seton was dead. In other words, she was *not* wearing the dress in reaction to that news.

Readers who spot this interpretation of the 'black dress' clue will be mystified by it and expect Poirot to be so too. But, frustratingly, he never focuses on it and in the final chapter, after saying that Nick wore a black dress because she and Maggie had to be dressed alike, he just adds rather dismissively that a girl would not buy mourning before she knew her lover was dead. More could have been made earlier of the 'black dress' clue but, because it was treated as a clue to Nick's psychological change rather than to her murder plan (which it is), one feels that rather a good clue is not as good as it should have been.

Nevertheless, with Poirot believing that the Seton relationship answers his three questions, he also believes that he has found the obscure motive, namely money: someone is after the money which Nick will inherit from Seton. And money does turn out to be the motive, though not for that reason.

In chapter 22 Poirot says that Nick was "passionately and fanatically devoted to her home" but needed money for it. Now one understands his awkward reference to this motive and remembers Vyse insisting in chapter 6 (twice) that Nick was fanatically devoted to the house. Indeed, Nick herself spoke of her "love" for it in chapters 1 and 5, although she then downplayed this by adding that she wouldn't want to sell it because she was "fond" of it. "One of the two is lying" says Poirot and, since he seems to regard Vyse as an unlikely liar, the 'home devotion' clue points to Nick lying and to her unusual motivation.

In fact that clue about Nick lying was perhaps not needed because there had been some explicit references by then. In chapter 2 Poirot himself describes her as "a polite little liar" when she pretends (so he thinks) to have heard of him. Frederica says in chapter 2, in relation to Nick's story about the car brakes, that Nick is "the most heaven-sent little liar that ever existed" because Lazarus thought there was nothing in Nick's claim (we are not told why), despite Mott's Garage saying that her car *had* been tampered with. Then later, when told by Poirot in chapter 5 that Nick had been shot at, Frederica smiles – a gentle, pitying, incredulous smile – and asks "Did Nick tell you so?".

There are other small clues about Nick's psychology: a hint of recklessness (chapter 1); inheriting the spirit of her grandfather 'Old Nick' (chapter 3); being an engaging young devil (chapter 5); and being in the wildest of spirits just before the murder (chapter 7). But the clue which finally causes Poirot to suspect her is contained in a letter written by Maggie to her mother after her arrival at End House on Monday. After reading the letter for a second time in chapter 18, the light bursts upon Poirot and he knows "All that matters".

So what strikes him? In the letter Maggie says "I cannot see why she [Nick] should have telegraphed for me in the way she did. Tuesday would have done as well". Poirot says that reference to Tuesday "*could only mean one thing*" – namely that Maggie had been coming to stay on Tuesday *anyway*. That is a fair interpretation of Maggie's words but it is not the only one. She could just have meant "I don't see why it was so urgent that I couldn't have been asked to come on Tuesday". However, adopting Poirot's interpretation, Nick had suppressed the truth by not telling him, when he urged her to send for a friend, that she had *already* sent for Maggie. As a result, he saw Nick in a different light and started looking critically at her statements as if they were not true.

It is indeed odd that Nick didn't reveal that Maggie was already coming and one wonders *why* she didn't. What benefit, in terms of her murder plan, did she get? Poirot says "It seemed to her less suspicious". But, although it might perhaps have looked slightly less suspicious if Maggie was only at End House because Poirot had suggested it (*if* that is Poirot's point), the advantage to Nick seems far too small to explain her odd behaviour, which makes the 'Tuesday' clue, as the basis for looking critically at Nick, feel a bit contrived.

It is also interesting to note about the 'Tuesday' clue that in chapter 10 Poirot claims to have said "all along" that Nick has been holding something back (which he did in chapters 4 and 6), adding that this missing factor is the "keystone of the mystery!". However, the first person to suggest that Nick had left something unsaid was Hastings in chapter 3 and he did so in the context of Nick asking Maggie to come on Monday (without revealing that she had already asked her). So, credit is really due to Hastings on this point, especially when we learn in chapter 11 that what Poirot thought had been left unsaid was not the Tuesday point but Nick's relationship with Seton.

Readers who do not spot the 'Tuesday' clue nevertheless know from Poirot's reaction to Maggie's letter that there is a clue of some kind in it. Some readers may assume that what has finally struck Poirot, when he sees the name "Maggie" signing the letter, is a point that they will probably have spotted some time ago (but which he has not mentioned), namely that Maggie is an abbreviation of Magdala so that both Nick and Maggie share that name.

The reason why some readers will probably have spotted this comes from a couple of clues in Seton's letters to Maggie (chapter 13). His third letter is dated 2 March. Readers may be drawn to it by the opening sentence in which he says that he ought not to write two days running and yet the date of the previous letter is 8 February, not 1 March. Therefore a letter is missing and, because of the 'two days running' clue, readers may focus on the 2 March letter to try to understand why this may be.

That letter is only five lines long but Seton twice mentions Scarborough, which is where we know Maggie had been (chapter 10). This 'Scarborough' clue makes us wonder if he had met Maggie there (not just Nick, whom we believe to be the recipient of his letter) – perhaps even been in love with her before Nick – which for the first time puts Maggie, who had until then just been an innocent victim, in our thoughts in a Nick/Seton context.

Then we see in the sixth letter – and this precedes Whitfield telling Poirot about Seton's will three chapters later – that he has made a will in favour of "Magdala". Of course, we assume that he is referring to his apparent fiancée, Nick, remembering (from chapter 2) that her real name is Magdala. But what some readers may also remember is that there have been lots of Magdalas in the Buckley family – the 'Magdala' clue – and with Maggie now in their thoughts because of the 'Scarborough' clue, they may wonder, long before Poirot seems to, whether Maggie might also be a 'Magdala'.

That is not to say that readers should at that stage understand the significance of Nick and Maggie having the same real name from the perspective of Seton's engagement. But we do then get hints about the engagement when first Ellen (chapter 13) and then Frederica (chapter 15) seem genuinely surprised on being told that Nick and Seton were engaged.

For those readers who have not spotted that Maggie may be an abbreviation of Magdala (or that she therefore has the same real name as Nick or may even have been Seton's fiancée), a clue is provided when Hastings mentions that "Maggie" can be one of various abbreviations for "Margaret" (chapter 18). This 'Margaret' clue is really too obvious a pointer to Maggie's name being, like Nick's, just an abbreviation – though for 'Magdala', not 'Margaret' – and even readers who had not spotted the abbreviation idea by chapters 13 or 15 will surely do so now. Given that 'Maggie' is the very name in the story, it would have been more subtle if Hastings had used names other than Margaret/Maggie as examples of how a female name might be abbreviated.

Seton's letters also provide other clues. Poirot wonders why Nick selected so few (six) letters to keep and whether there was any peculiarity about those retained. Not all readers will regard the 'few letters' clue as persuasive (because six is quite a lot) but an astute reader would realise that the retained letters mentioned no name in their greeting so that Maggie or Nick could have been the recipient. The 'letter greeting' clue is clever and suggests that Nick did not select the 1 March letter because it began "Dear Maggie".

Better still, and perhaps the best clue in the book, is that Seton's letter of 2 March makes no reference to the appendix operation which Nick underwent on 27 February. Had that letter been written to Nick, it would surely have expressed anxiety about the operation only three days before and yet most of us would not think of the 'appendix' clue because we are focusing on why the letter of 1 March is missing.

Although we are not told that the operation was on 27 February until the final chapter, we had been told (chapter 18) that Nick's will was dated 25 February and that on that day, according to Poirot in chapter 14 (although this is not quite what Nick had said), she went into the nursing home for the operation. That date is still close enough to the 2 March letter for the absence of anxiety to be surprising and thus for astute readers to spot the 'appendix' clue.

So, even though the 'Tuesday' clue which causes Poirot to suspect Nick feels a bit contrived, there are some imaginative clues among Seton's letters to Maggie. Otherwise, the story is not strongly clued, with the abbreviation of Magdala being signposted too obviously by the 'Margaret' clue and with the rather good 'black dress' clue being frustratingly unaddressed as a clue to the murder plan until the final chapter.

Beyond the 'black dress' clue, the paucity of murder plan clues is explained by Maggie's shooting being so simply plotted. But there are other murder plan clues, the most important and evocative of which is the 'fatal shawl' clue, which explains how Nick cleverly managed to give the impression that, despite Maggie being shot, she was the real target. Another is the 'twenty minutes' clue, being the time that Nick was supposedly on the telephone during dinner (when she took Maggie's letters after listening to the news); Poirot thinks that 20 minutes is a long time for a telephone call and that, if he can find out what happened then, "we shall find the clue we seek" (chapter 10). And then there is the 'secret panel' clue whose existence is revealed by Ellen (chapter 12) but vehemently denied by Nick (explaining why the pistol was missing after the murder but later available for incriminating Frederica).

As to the incrimination, Poirot explores with Ellen in chapter 12 why she had asked him after the murder if anyone had been hurt (although she had in fact asked Hastings, not him, in chapter 8). She says she didn't think the victim would be Maggie because "Nobody hated *her*". Hastings thinks there is "a clue" in her words and expects Poirot to follow it up. To his surprise, Poirot does not but changes the subject. It would have been more realistic if Poirot had followed up the 'Nobody hated *her*' clue and, with Ellen having been surprised in chapter 8 that Maggie had been hurt rather than Frederica, asked her *who* hated Frederica. His change of subject is an unsatisfying way of keeping Nick's hatred of Frederica hidden until chapter 22.

The clueing of the sub-plots is weak. A scrap of paper demanding money is found by the police when searching the grounds of End House, leading Hastings to ask "An important clue?" (chapter 15). In fact the 'scrap of paper' clue is the only one relating to the sub-plot in which Frederica is shot at by her husband; the handwriting on it turns out to be his, causing her to sway in chapter 15 when, as she later indicates (chapter 20), she recognised it,

As to the Crofts, when Japp unveils Mrs Croft as Milly Merton in the first, mini denouement, this does not seem to be clued at all. The only relevant facts are that Poirot regards the Crofts as too "typical" to be Australian (chapter 5); that Mr Croft is "too good to be genuine" (chapter 14); that his fingerprints are unknown to the police (chapter 16); and that he is unknown in Melbourne (chapter 16). However, this does not stop Poirot from describing exactly how the Crofts' plan worked, although it is not clear *how* he knows – perhaps from the (unknown) answers he receives to his chapter 18 telegram. When, in the next paragraph, Lazarus asks how he got wise to all this, he does not answer by reference to the Crofts but by explaining how he arrived at Nick's guilt.

7

Lord Edgware Dies

Solution

Poirot and the narrator, Captain Hastings, investigate the murder of George Alfred St Vincent Marsh, fourth Baron Edgware, who is stabbed with a corn knife in the back of the neck between 10 pm and 11 pm on the evening of 29 June in the library of his house at 17 Regent Gate near Regent's Park.

The immediate suspect is his wife, an American actress, Jane Wilkinson, who had left him soon after their marriage three years earlier. Before the murder she had persuaded Poirot to ask Edgware to divorce her so that she could marry the Duke of Merton, adding that she would kill him herself if Poirot wouldn't help. She was also heard uttering threats against him by Bryan Martin, the actor. And she had, according to Edgware's butler (Alton) and secretary (Miss Carroll), called at Regent Gate at about 10 pm, announced herself as Lady Edgware, entered the library, shut the door and left ten minutes later.

However, doubts soon arise about whether it was actually Jane who called there – partly because she would not have uttered threats and then announced herself at the house; partly because Alton cannot have recognised her, having only worked there for six months; partly because Miss Carroll admits that she only saw the back of the caller's head; but mainly because between about 8.45 pm and 11.30 pm Jane appears to have been at Sir Montagu Corner's dinner party in Chiswick, after dropping in at the Piccadilly Palace Hotel at 8.30 pm to visit a friend, Mrs Van Dusen, who was leaving for the United States.

At the dinner party she wore a white taffeta evening dress whereas the Regent Gate caller wore a black walking dress and hat – black being a colour never worn by Jane. There were 13 at the dinner and, as Inspector Japp says, unless 14 people (which must include the butler and Jane) are lying, she didn't do it.

By this stage it will be plain to readers not only that Jane was impersonated by the Regent Gate caller but that the impersonator was an American girl who was the theatrical rage in London that June, Carlotta Adams, whose programme ended with impersonations of well-known personalities, including Jane. A few days before the murder Poirot and Hastings had seen her performance. Jane had also been in the audience, applauding Carlotta's imitation and inviting her afterwards to her suite at the Savoy.

Carlotta's presence at Regent Gate is supported by evidence: when she left her flat at about 7 pm, she was dressed like the Regent Gate caller; her attaché case contained a golden wig in Jane's shade and style; she had bought a new black hat, shading one side of her face, from her friend Jenny Driver; she had been excited at lunch with Jenny because she was to take part in a hoax; and she had written a letter to her sister, Lucie, in America which appeared to suggest that Edgware's nephew, Captain Ronald Marsh, had told her that her performance as Jane would take in Edgware himself and that he had asked her to take part in a bet on which she could make ten thousand dollars.

However, on the morning after Edgware's death, Carlotta too is found dead after taking an overdose of veronal from a small gold box, initialled 'C.A.' in rubies. So it appears that, by pretending to be Jane, she had unwittingly provided a scapegoat for the real murderer – the impecunious Marsh, who had lived at Regent

Gate until quarrelling with Edgware and who had asked him unsuccessfully for money on the morning of his death.

The involvement of Marsh, who would inherit Edgware's title, seems clear when his alibi – that he was with the Dortheimers at the opera – is undone. He admits that during an opera interval he took a taxi to Regent Gate. He says he met his cousin Geraldine, Lord Edgware's daughter, by chance at the opera and told her about his financial problems, that she suggested he should have her pearls and that they took a taxi to fetch them at once, returning just before the curtain rose again. However, although she confirms this, he could still have entered the library and murdered Edgware while she fetched the pearls.

But then, after Marsh's arrest, another murder occurs following a lunch party at Claridge's at which Poirot, Hastings and Jane are present, with a young actor, Donald Ross, who had been at Corner's dinner party. Near the end Ross wants to speak to Poirot but he has already left.[1] So Ross telephones him later, saying that something seems odd about Edgware's death. But he can only add "It was Paris set me off. You see …" before he is stabbed at the base of the skull, as Poirot finds when he later 'springs up' the stairs of Ross' flat.

The arrested Marsh cannot have killed Ross and it is not even clear by the start of chapter 30, when Poirot tells us the "real story" of what happened, who are the most likely suspects for Edgware's murder from among Carlotta, Jane, Marsh, Geraldine, Jenny Driver, Bryan Martin, Alton, Miss Carroll and the Duke of Merton. Even Jane herself appears only twice (chapters 11 and 25) between chapters 6 and 30 and so the "real story" is a real surprise.

The assumption throughout that Carlotta impersonated Jane at Regent Gate rested on a gigantic deception because it was at Corner's dinner that Carlotta impersonated Jane (for a bet); and it was Jane, in a reverse impersonation (pretending to be Carlotta impersonating Jane), who could therefore go to Regent Gate (unknown to Carlotta) with an alibi and murder her husband.

As she explains in a "Document" after her trial (chapter 31), her plan in telling people (like Poirot and Martin) about killing Edgware was that "if you speak the truth in a rather silly way nobody believes you". And she seemed to have an excuse for saying she would kill him based on his refusal to agree to a divorce – although he had in fact already agreed (even before she asked Poirot to get him to do so) in a letter, which she pretended not to have received.

Her murder plan was cleverly and intricately organised, involving boldness with the murder and precision with the steps that she and Carlotta would take in order for Carlotta, unwittingly, to give her an alibi. Readers who wonder when they agreed those steps (since there would not have been time at their Savoy meeting after Carlotta's performance) learn in the Document that the idea was broached at a second meeting, although that is the first that we have heard of such a meeting. Jane told Carlotta that it was a bet and Carlotta, who was to get ten thousand dollars for impersonating Jane successfully, fell for it.

On the day of the murder Carlotta left her flat in the morning, taking her small suitcase containing the items (chapter 9) enabling her to impersonate Jane. The suitcase was "more of an attaché case" and, a bit confusingly, it is referred to as a suitcase and as an attaché case, making us wonder for a while if there were two cases. She had lunch with Jenny Driver from whom she purchased a hat in order, she told Jenny, to shade the left side of her face.

At some point that day she also took a room at the Piccadilly Palace Hotel (where she and Jane would later swap clothes). She did so in the name of Mrs Van Dusen, saying she was taking the night train to Liverpool (explaining why she would not be there that night). In order to disguise her appearance when playing the fictional Mrs Van Dusen, she wore not only her new black hat (one assumes) but also some pince-nez, gold-rimmed and rather severe for someone very short-sighted, which Jane had borrowed from her maid, Ellis, and which she must have given to Carlotta, perhaps at their second meeting.

At 6 pm Jane told people that she was not going to Corner's dinner. Since it was a key part of her plan to be seen there, one wonders why she said that (before later pretending to change her mind). Although we are not told, perhaps she wanted to make it look as if anyone who thought she wasn't going (such as Marsh and Martin) could have implicated her by taking advantage of her apparently not having an alibi when the murderer called at Regent Gate.

When Carlotta returned to her flat at 6 pm (as herself), she did not have the attaché case, which she must have left at the Piccadilly Palace. In her flat she wrote a letter to her sister. In it she referred to Marsh and then to Jane saying that "she" had said that her show would take in Edgware himself before asking her to take on something for a bet on which she could make ten thousand dollars. When leaving her flat at 7 pm to return to the Piccadilly Palace, she was wearing the black clothes and hat which Jane would later wear and carrying her black handbag containing the letter which she forgot to post.

At about 8 pm Jane left the Savoy and at 8.30 pm arrived at the Piccadilly Palace to say goodbye to her fictional friend Mrs Van Dusen (chapter 6). There Jane and Carlotta changed clothes and swapped handbags. Then Carlotta, dressed in a fair wig (Jane being fair) and a white taffeta dress, went to Chiswick, arriving at 8.45 pm, where, with the dinner table lit only by candles, she impersonated Jane, whom no one at the dinner knew very well.

Meanwhile Jane paid Mrs Van Dusen's bill. She was wearing a dark wig (Carlotta being dark), Carlotta's black clothes and the pince-nez and so looked like Carlotta's portrayal of Mrs Van Dusen. She then had Carlotta's suitcase put on a taxi and went to Euston railway station. She removed her dark wig in the lavatory, made herself up, put the pince-nez in her (i.e. Carlotta's) handbag (so one presumes, though we are never actually told when she does this) and, as a fair-haired lady, put the suitcase in the station cloak-room at 9 pm.

Before going to Regent Gate, Jane then telephoned Chiswick, asking to speak to "Lady Edgware". Carlotta rose from the table and answered the call. It had been arranged that, if all had gone well, Carlotta was to say something like "Yes, that's right" (chapters 6, 7, 15, 30), which she did. Poirot says that the call happened at 9.30 pm (chapter 8) but in fact neither Jane nor Japp nor Corner's butler (chapters 6, 7, 15) gave him the time.

Having established that her alibi was working (which was the real reason for the call, though Carlotta did not know this), Jane went to Regent Gate, still wearing Carlotta's clothes, including the new hat shielding the left side of her face from Alton's gaze, and committed the first murder with a corn knife which, like the pince-nez, she had taken from her maid Ellis.

She then returned to Euston, picked up the suitcase at 10.30 pm and changed from fair to dark again under the new hat. But, since she was supposed to be in Chiswick, she could not return to the Savoy where she was to meet Carlotta on her return. So she went to the Lyons Corner House in the Strand and prepared for the second murder because she could not let Carlotta reveal her false alibi.

She put a small gold box (initialled 'C.A.' in rubies and engraved 'C.A. from D. Paris. Nov 10th. Sweet Dreams') into Carlotta's handbag which she was carrying. She had ordered the box from Paris two days before the murder – a rush order to be collected next day, as indeed it was by a short, middle-aged woman wearing pince-nez, who turns out to be Ellis, Jane's maid.

The box contained veronal and Jane's purpose in putting it in Carlotta's handbag was to show that Carlotta took this dangerously uncertain drug which could have killed her accidentally. When the box was mentioned in the newspapers after Carlotta's death, the waitress at the Lyons Corner House recalled seeing it at about 11 pm in the hand of a lady who was dark, dressed in black, wore a new hat and had an attaché case.

It was perhaps while putting the box in the handbag that Jane found the letter to Carlotta's sister referring to the bet. She opened it because, according to Poirot (although Jane never explains this herself), she scented danger. Having done so, she cleverly realised that, if she tore the double sheet in two, removed the page referring to herself and tore the 's' off "she", which was the first word on the remaining page, in order to turn that word into "he", it would read as if Carlotta was taking on the bet for *Marsh*, not Jane, and so read as an accusation against him. Then she replaced the letter. But she forgot to take back the pince-nez, which were later found by Poirot in the handbag.

At the agreed time, with Carlotta having left Chiswick at 11.30 pm, Jane walked towards the Savoy and they entered the hotel at the same time (11.45 pm). They changed clothes (and swapped handbags) in Jane's suite. Jane suggested a celebratory drink in which she put veronal. When Carlotta returned home just after midnight, she was very sleepy. She tried to ring a friend (we are never told who) but gave up because she was too tired. She went to bed and, as she was doing so, she remembered that she had not posted her letter. So her maid put it in the late fee box at the post office. Carlotta never woke again.

The murder plan, with its pinpoint precision and criss-crossing of Jane and Carlotta, is fantastic. The brilliant solution may seem a little incredible, with so much needing to work smoothly, but a potential brake was cleverly built into the plan by Jane's telephone call to Chiswick since presumably, if she had not received the correct answer, she would not have committed the murder and the impersonation could have been explained away as a joke or bet. Although Jane was spotted by the waitress, this did not upset her alibi since the person in the Lyons Corner House was thought to be Carlotta. However, as we shall see later, it was an error to have left the pince-nez in Carlotta's handbag.

Among all the cleverness, Jane is most proud, she says in her Document, of tearing off the page of Carlotta's letter and leaving "he" instead of "she". But, ironically, that was never part of her murder plan. It was pure fortune that Carlotta had written a letter which could be altered to incriminate Marsh.

Although there is a third murder, it forms no part of this ingenious solution. It simply involves Jane going to Ross' flat, with no time to think of an alibi, and stabbing him as he speaks to Poirot on the telephone, perhaps – we are not told – with the corn knife again, although she says in her Document that she put that knife back after killing Edgware. Her motive was that she realised that she had somehow given herself away to him.

Her motive for killing Edgware is less apparent, given that he had agreed to a divorce, so enabling her to marry the Duke. The answer is that the Duke, as a pillar of the Anglo-Catholic Church, had a "queer sort of prejudice" against divorce and would not marry a woman whose husband was alive. Readers would do very well to spot this motive because, even though we knew that Merton was a "violent Anglo-Catholic" (chapter 2), few would know that this meant that he would not have regarded a divorce as sufficient. Indeed, Anglo-Catholics debate their beliefs among themselves.

Plot

The deception on which the magnificently plotted murder plan is built is Jane's alibi – her apparent presence at the dinner – and it works wonderfully well because it is so tightly constructed. The central significance of that alibi is reflected in the United States title *Thirteen at Dinner*. Marsh actually says that "Lord Edgware Dies" would be a good title for a crime novel but, while it sounds dramatic, it is not imaginative and the United States title is better.

That title also reflects the superstition (based probably on Jesus being the first to rise at the end of the Last Supper[2]) that, if 13 people sit down to eat, the first to get up will die within a year. Thus, Ross gives a nervous cackle when telling Poirot that he was first to rise at the end of the dinner (chapter 15). This causes Hastings to feel uncomfortable after he is murdered "as one always does when superstition is proved justified" (chapter 27) – though, as Poirot later points out (chapter 29) he may have got up first at the end but actually Jane (who is condemned to death) was the first to get up when she was called to the telephone. In fact, Poirot should have referred to Carlotta but the point still applies because of Carlotta's death.

Hastings' narrative is generally most engaging and, although the story loses some pace during the third quarter, with nothing happening for a fortnight in chapter 23 (out of 31), he makes us smile in chapter 14 by recording Poirot's comment that he is helpful because there is reflected in his mind "exactly what the criminal wishes me to believe".

Beyond the double murder plan and its mutual impersonation idea, there are a few inter-related sub-plots which bear on the murders. They are also generally speaking tightly constructed, within themselves and into the main plot, but their mystifying inter-relationship makes it hard to give neat individual descriptions of them. They relate to Marsh, Geraldine, Martin, Alton and Edgware himself.

Edgware was aged about 50. He looked bad-tempered and bitter and his eyes had a queer secretive look about them. He enjoyed the macabre and his taste was peculiar; Poirot thought he practised "many curious vices"; Hastings noticed an expression of fury on his face; and Jane thought he was "a queer man". He "terrorised" his daughter, Geraldine, and treated Marsh, so Carlotta thought, in a shameful way – leading on to the sub-plot in which Geraldine suggested that Marsh should take her pearls, so bringing them both to Regent Gate only shortly after the murder.

When Poirot asks five "psychological" questions in chapter 14, the first three are about Edgware (1) Why did he change his mind and agree to a divorce? (2) What happened to his letter which Jane claimed not to have received? (3) What was meant by the expression seen on his face by Hastings? Poirot concludes that Jane did receive his letter and that his fury at having to give in to her explained his expression but, on question (1), *why* did he have to agree?

Poirot suggests (chapter 29) that blackmail was involved and that facts about him might have emerged which, while not entitling Jane to a divorce, could be used by her as a lever coupled with a threat of publicity. We can make a guess about those facts, with the word "queer" being used two dozen times in the story and the vaguely effeminate softness of his handsome young butler's voice. However, we are never actually told about the "odd" way that Alton entered Edgware's service (chapter 16) or why Miss Carroll does not like him but cannot tell Poirot why. But one should not overdo this because "queer" is also used two dozen times, without any equivalent implication, in the author's novel *Why didn't they ask Evans?* published the following year.

If Jane had really not received the letter, it might have been suppressed by Bryan Martin. He had been, and probably still was (chapter 28), in love with Jane but, having been rebuffed, he might have suppressed it in order to stop her getting divorced and marrying the Duke of Merton rather than him. Instead, he visited Poirot to try to poison him against her. After pretending that he needed his help because he was being shadowed by a man with a gold tooth, he told Poirot that he could see Jane killing quite easily.

There is a chance that Martin himself murdered Edgware when Marsh, who was outside Regent Gate during the opera interval, says he saw Martin enter the house. In fact it was Alton (who resembled Martin). Although Alton had seemed suspicious after staring at Poirot with startled fear after the murder, it transpires that, in a sub-plot in which a £100 worth of French banknotes is taken from Edgware on the day of his death, Alton stole them and, when he later let himself back into the house, Marsh wrongly identified him as Martin.

Although the main plot and sub-plots are tightly constructed, some journey times do seem surprising today. Even allowing for less traffic in the 1930s, it is hard to believe that Jane could have arrived at the Piccadilly Palace at 8.30 pm, changed clothes with Carlotta and got to Chiswick by 8.45 pm. Chiswick was not even regarded as part of London then: Sir Montagu Corner "would not live in London for a million pounds" (chapter 15).

There are other curiosities. In the fifth paragraph of the book Hastings says that he will begin his narrative at a London theatre because this is where Poirot began his resumé, whereas in fact Poirot's resumé began at Jane's Savoy party. In chapter 7 Japp says that "both" Miss Carroll *and* the butler "swear by all that's holy" that Lady Edgware called at Regent Gate but five sentences later he says that Miss Carroll is "the only one" who is positive without adding that, as he may mean, she's the only 'credible' one. Also in that chapter Poirot asks Japp whether it was a man or woman who rang Jane at the dinner. Japp replies "A woman, I think she said". But what Jane actually said was that "a voice" spoke and that "they" rang off. In chapter 11 Poirot tells Jenny that Carlotta left Regent Gate at "five" past ten but Japp and Alton told us (chapters 5 and 7) that the lady had left at *ten* past. However, none of these points affects the substance of the plotting which, generally speaking, is magnificent.

Clues

Although readers are led to believe in chapters 14, 26 and 27 that Poirot's detection will be based on his five "psychological" questions, the first three do not relate to the murder plan (as we have seen), which leaves us with (4) What were the pince-nez doing in Carlotta's handbag and (5) Why did someone telephone to find out if Jane was at Chiswick and who was it?

As for question (4), Hastings says in the second paragraph of the book that Poirot viewed the case as a failure. He swore that it was the "chance remark" of a passer-by on the Euston Road, who had just come out of the cinema, that put him on the right track. The passer-by had commented to his companion (chapter 27): "Idiotic story. If they'd just had the sense to ask Ellis right away". Those readers who do not recall from chapters 4, 6 or 11 that Ellis was the name of Jane's maid, or therefore spot the 'Ellis' clue, are reminded when Poirot summons her in chapter 28.

We learn then that the pince-nez found in Carlotta's bag belonged to Ellis. Knowing also, as Poirot does (from chapter 24), that the short, middle-aged lady who collected the gold box in Paris wore pince-nez, he deduces that Ellis, who was short (chapter 28) and middle-aged (chapter 4), was sent to Paris by Jane to fetch it. So Carlotta had in her handbag two items (the pince-nez and the gold box) which had been in Ellis' possession – "Ellis and therefore Jane Wilkinson", as Poirot puts it in chapter 30. Thus the pince-nez and the gold box reveal a seemingly inexplicable connection between Jane (via Ellis' items) and Carlotta and so lead Poirot to the mutual impersonation idea.

The 'pince-nez' clue also leads Poirot to deduce that Jane borrowed "something else from Ellis besides *des* pince-nez ... A corn knife". We know from chapter 28 that Ellis suffered from corns but, although there was no reference to a knife when we were given the 'corns' clue, Jane confirms in her Document that it was the weapon she used to stab Edgware.

Quite a large clueing burden is therefore placed on the 'pince-nez' clue, especially as Poirot says (chapter 30) that leaving them in Carlotta's handbag was Jane's "one mistake". However, very few readers would have spotted that Ellis even wore pince-nez until we are told this at the end of chapter 28, given that the only reference is in chapter 4 when she is introduced as "a neat middle-aged woman with glasses and primly arranged hair" and that we are misdirected by Poirot's remark in chapter 27 that Miss Carroll was the only person connected with the case who wore glasses (indeed, pince-nez, as we learned in chapter 7). Moreover, readers were never even told that Mrs Van Dusen wore glasses or pince-nez until Poirot's explanations in chapter 30 when he says that Carlotta wore glasses when pretending to be her.

It would therefore be no surprise if readers missed the meaning of the 'pince-nez' clue, especially since they might just have been in Carlotta's handbag for her performances. In fact there is a much better clue to the mutual impersonation – the 'Paris' clue, perhaps the best clue in the entire Christie canon, which is not only ingenious but also wonderfully concealed both when it is presented and more generally among various other references to Paris.

The starting point (chapter 15) is Corner's remark that Jane (in fact Carlotta) made several intelligent remarks about Greek art at his dinner party. Our surprise at this, knowing that Jane has "the brains of a rabbit" (chapter 12), is offset by Hastings' immediate misdirection that Jane had probably just responded with suitable attention to Corner's own remarks.

The next step occurs when, at the lunch party at Claridge's (chapter 25), Jane (the real Jane) makes a "chance remark – a rather humiliating gaffe" after someone utters the phrase "judgment of Paris", intending to allude to the mythological tale, referred to in Homer's Iliad and elsewhere, in which Paris, son of the King of Troy, has to judge who is the fairest of Hera, Athena and Aphrodite and so entitled to a golden apple. Jane, however, takes Paris to be the only Paris she knows – "the Paris of fashion and frills!" – and says "Why, Paris doesn't cut any ice nowadays. It's London and New York that count". It was an awkward moment, with everyone hastily talking to someone else.

It is noticeable in retrospect that Ross, who had been at Corner's dinner, drew in his breath sharply and then answered only in monosyllables when Hastings tried to speak to him. In fact, although we don't learn this until we get the "real story" in chapter 30, Ross had realised that the cultured, well-read Lady Edgware who had discussed Homer and Greek civilisation at Corner's dinner was not the same Lady Edgware who made the humiliating gaffe at Claridge's.

That is why at the end of the lunch Ross wants to speak to Poirot. He tells Hastings that "something rather queer has happened" and that "it might – just might – be very important". It is by no means clear to readers at that stage what Ross' concern is. This is because Jane's gaffe is excellently concealed by the textual device of Hastings apparently referring to it (in paragraphs either side of the gaffe itself) only to support his impression that the Duke of Merton, who flushed at the remark and seemed to draw away from Jane, was no longer quite so intoxicated with her.

However, by the end of that chapter, when Ross telephones Poirot, just before being murdered, and says "It was Paris set me off. You see …", readers know that Paris is the clue. They will presumably also assume, as Poirot rightly does in the next chapter, that Ross' concern was prompted by Jane's gaffe.

They would, however, do extremely well to spot the inconsistency between the gaffe and Corner's earlier remark, not least because Ross' concern might have been connected with any one of numerous other references to Paris to which readers are regularly misdirected. Thus Edgware was due to go to Paris the day after he was murdered (chapter 4) and he had been there several times the previous autumn (chapter 17) including twice in November (chapter 27), which was the month engraved in the gold box (chapter 10); not only did that engraving refer to Paris but the box had been bought there (chapter 24); Carlotta and Geraldine had both been there that November (chapters 10 and

27) and Geraldine had also been there when Edgware married Jane (chapter 24); the Duke of Merton was there (or supposed to be there) at the time of Edgware's murder (chapter 4); Carlotta intended to meet her sister Lucie there (chapter 10); and even Japp pursues his investigations there, drawing a blank (chapter 18).

But any reader astute enough to see through the Paris references, and through Hastings' misdirection and textual concealment, and spot (as Ross does) that the significance of the gaffe is not Paris as such, but the gaffe itself *about* Paris because of its inconsistency with Corner's remark, will have interpreted a really first-rate clue to the mutual impersonation and murder plan.

There is, however, one aspect of this excellent clue which should make the reader pause for thought. This is the reaction of Jane who, following the gaffe, "looked serenely up and down the table without the least consciousness of having said anything amiss". Since we are told as a fact that she had not "the least consciousness" of having said anything amiss, it is not obvious why she should then murder Ross.

Although Poirot says that she had overheard Ross asking if he could speak to him and she was quick and shrewd enough to realise that she had somehow given herself away, the truth is that Ross did not even refer to the gaffe, let alone to Paris, when asking Hastings. Even in her Document Jane is not sure how Ross spotted her: "Something about Paris being a person not a place".

That is hardly a persuasive basis for Jane's decision to commit a murder which could not be put down to the arrested Marsh. It would have been better if Ross had said something to have justified her actions. As it is, with readers being told as a fact that she did not know that she had given herself away at the time of the gaffe and with Ross not saying anything to alert her to the cause of his concern, the 'Paris' clue is not really one to Jane being *Ross'* murderer.

But that is not its purpose, which is to expose, though in a brilliantly disguised way, the mutual impersonation idea and so act as a clue to Jane being *Edgware's* murderer. Although Poirot describes the pince-nez as Jane's "one mistake", her gaffe, a fortnight after Marsh's arrest, was surely as important.

The next major clue is Carlotta's letter to her sister, Lucie. Readers know that the 'Carlotta letter' clue is going to be significant when it is not only fully set out in a cable from New York in chapter 20 but the original is also sent to Poirot, and a facsimile of one of the middle sheets reproduced, in chapter 23.

That sheet, as Poirot spots almost immediately, has a ragged left side edge (unlike the others which have clean edges) indicating that it had been torn. It must have been a double sheet of which one of the pages was missing, having been, as Poirot correctly deduces, removed by the murderer. Since the page before the missing page talked of Captain Marsh and since the first word on the page after the missing page was "he", it had naturally been assumed that the "he" who had asked Carlotta to take on something for a bet on the latter page was Captain Marsh. In fact, as a result of Poirot's deduction, the "he" of the latter page might not be the Captain Marsh of the former page but another man who had proposed the hoax and was referred to on the missing page.

This appears to be not only a clever clue in Marsh's favour but also a good deduction by Poirot, who criticises the murderer's lack of order and method in not cutting the sheet but tearing it. Readers may, however, be rather mystified by the ragged edge being explained so quickly instead of being allowed to linger for their own detection. In fact, the author has been cleverer than we at first realise because, while we think that Poirot has solved the mystery of the ragged edge (with the murderer being a "he"), there is in fact more to it.

This is because, as Poirot says three chapters later, "The page had to be torn". Although he never, even later, *explains* why it had to be torn (rather than cut) beyond saying that Jane tore the 's' off "she", his point must be, as one sees when looking at the reproduced page, that, if the page had been cut in a straight vertical line, it would not have been possible to cut the 's' off "she" without also cutting off the first letters on a number of other lines.

But the clue contains an anomaly in that the reproduced page shows a very short diagonal line abutting the top left side of the 'h' of "he". This line cannot be part of the 'h' itself, as one sees when looking at the other examples of the letter 'h' on the page. Perhaps therefore it is the untorn residue of the top curve of an 's'. However, any reader who was astute enough to consider the possibility of an 's' would probably have had to reject it because, with every single other example of the letter 's' that appears on that page in Carlotta's handwriting – and there are seven of them – the bottom curve of the 's' is at least as near to the next letter as the top curve including the three words ('said' twice and 'some') which begin with an 's'. In other words, if the page was torn in the way shown in the reproduction and the short line was the top curve of an 's', the bottom curve of that 's' should also have been visible. Logically, therefore, because of the absence of a bottom curve, an 's' cannot have been torn off. So no one could actually have interpreted the 'Carlotta letter' clue correctly on a proper analysis of the reproduced page.

Poirot does, however, and he tries to give readers some help with the mutual impersonation idea when murmuring "candles" and something that sounded like "douzaine" at the start of chapter 28. Since he later says (chapter 29) "I followed every step of it – the candles – the dim light – Mrs Van Dusen – everything", the 'douzaine' clue must be a reference to Mrs Van Dusen. The 'candles' and 'dim light' clues are references to the lighting at Corner's house (in the dining room, with its candle-lit table, and the first-floor room respectively) where, as had been clued in chapter 7, none of the people were "close friends" of Jane's and some didn't even know each other.

We also get a couple of other clues. One is the 'attaché case' clue – Carlotta taking the case with her in the morning, not having it when returning at 6 pm, but bringing it back last thing (chapter 9) – the explanation being that she must have left it at the Piccadilly Palace. The other is Poirot's question (5) about why Jane was telephoned at Chiswick, the answer to the 'Chiswick call' clue being that it was Jane herself telephoning to check that her alibi was working.

However, although that telephone call has a proper place in the murder plan, Carlotta's attempt to telephone a number in Victoria just before her death is not clarified. This is most surprising, given that Poirot's eyes gleamed with excitement when told of the attempt (chapter 9), he referred to it as a possible clue (chapter 11) and both Marsh and Martin had Victoria numbers.

Similarly surprising is that we get no clue about Jane's expertise with a corn knife despite Poirot saying that the murderer knew where to strike vital nerve centres at the base of the skull, adding "It almost implies medical knowledge" (chapter 5) and using the word "scientific" (chapters 11 and 15). So, how did she acquire it? The answer in her Document is that she was shown what to do by a doctor in San Francisco. But using the Document to reveal this, when Poirot does not and when the answer is wholly unclued, is weak.

As to the other suspects, Marsh was brilliant in the O.U.D.S. (chapter 2). Some readers may guess that this is the Oxford University Dramatic Society – so that the 'OUDS' clue is perhaps one to Marsh having impersonated Jane – but we are not told what O.U.D.S means and instead it is Marsh himself who reveals (chapter 13) that he had once been celebrated for acting female parts.

As for his opera alibi, Poirot suggests to Japp (chapter 18) that he should find a driver who picked up "a fare – or more probably two fares – yes, two fares" from Covent Garden. As a result Japp finds the taxi driver who took Marsh and Geraldine to Regent Gate and back. One wonders how Poirot made such an insightful suggestion and the answer is the 'opera' clue in chapter 16. There Japp had mentioned Marsh and Geraldine's visits to the opera as separate events in separate paragraphs but this had caused Poirot to think that they might have been together at one of the intervals.

Then we have Bryan Martin's pretence to Poirot that he was being shadowed by an ugly man of about 30 with a gold tooth. Readers will have realised that he had some ulterior purpose for visiting Poirot because Poirot's reaction from the outset suggests that he considered the story to be pretty absurd. He did so because of the 'gold tooth' clue: according to Poirot, no man of only about 30 would have a gold tooth because this type of dentistry was by then already "hopelessly old-fashioned".

As for Alton, we learn in chapter 16 that Edgware's front door key is missing (the 'missing key' clue). Regent Gate had three keys: Edgware's key, which he "always" carried, but which was missing; one in the hall drawer which was taken by Geraldine to the opera and used when getting the pearls; and Marsh's key, which he had lost but found recently and had used, after waiting at first in the street, to follow Geraldine into Regent Gate. The only key that turns out to be a clue is the missing one but only in the sub-plot of Alton's theft; his use of a key which Edgware always carried, in order to let himself back into Regent Gate, suggests that he could use it because he found Edgware dead and so was able to steal the banknotes.

Which brings us to the final clue, the small gold box with the initials C.A. in rubies and the engraving 'C.A. from D. Paris. Nov. 10th. Sweet Dreams'. The 'gold box' clue has its place in the plotting (to make it appear that Carlotta took veronal) and the clueing (because it was collected in Paris by someone wearing pince-nez, Ellis) and the detection (because it told us of Carlotta's – though in fact it was Jane's – presence at the Lyons Corner House).

However, the *engraving* is a complete red herring. Poirot spends some time – as do readers – wondering who D might be – Geraldine (who is called Dina on a couple of occasions)? Donald Ross? Jenny Driver? The Duke of Merton? Hastings even calls it "the mystery of the initial D" in chapter 27. But, despite the mystery being mentioned a few times, the disappointing answer, suggested by Poirot in that chapter and confirmed in Jane's Document, is that the D was just put there "to make it all much more difficult".

So, the engraving is not a red herring in the sense of one placed to deceive us into thinking of it as a clue to the villain when in fact it fits into the plot in some other way. Rather, it is a red herring placed to deceive us into thinking of it as a clue to the villain, as indeed we do, when in fact it has no genuine place in the plot at all.[3] That might make some readers wonder whether just 'making it more difficult' was a sufficiently credible reason for its introduction.

8

Murder On The Orient Express

Solution

Poirot investigates the murder of Samuel Ratchett, a rich American who is stabbed in his sleeping compartment in the Istanbul-Calais coach on the Orient Express on its three-day journey across Europe.

The murder occurs on the second night when the train is between Vincovci and Brod (in the former Yugoslavia but now in Croatia), having been brought to a standstill at 12.30 am by a winter snowdrift. Since no one can have left the train after the snowdrift, the murderer must still be on it.

With the ordinary carriages being locked and the only relevant occupants of the Athens slip coach and the Bucharest-Paris coaches being Monsieur Bouc of the train's operating company (Compagnie Internationale des Wagon Lits) and Dr Constantine – who both assist Poirot – he must seek the murderer in the Istanbul-Calais coach from which the less evocative United States title *Murder in the Calais Coach* gets its name.

A plan of that 16-berth coach is provided at Part 2 chapter 1. In it on the fatal night, in addition to Poirot and Ratchett (in first-class compartments Nos 1 and 2), are 12 other travellers. So the coach (with eight first-class, single compartments and four second-class, double compartments) is almost full.

The occupants of the other six first-class compartments are: No. 3 – Mrs Hubbard; No. 12 – Countess Andrenyi; No. 13 – Count Andrenyi; No. 14 – Princess Dragomiroff; No. 15 – Colonel Arbuthnot; No. 16 – Cyrus Hardman. Ratchett's compartment is towards the middle of the coach, with Poirot on one side and Mrs Hubbard (with a communicating door) on the other.

The six occupants of the four second-class, double compartments are: Nos 4/5 – Edward Masterman (Ratchett's valet) and Antonio Foscarelli; Nos 6/7 – Hector MacQueen (Ratchett's sectetary), with No. 7 being unoccupied, though Poirot sleeps there on the first night (when Mr A.M. Harris does not turn up) before he moves to No. 1 after Bouc goes into the Athens slip coach when it joins at Belgrade; Nos 8/9 – Hildegarde Schmidt, with No. 9 being unoccupied; and Nos 10/11 – Greta Ohlsson and Mary Debenham.

At 12.37 am on the second night, Poirot is woken by a cry and the ting of a bell from Ratchett's compartment. The train is stuck in the snowdrift. He opens his door. The conductor knocks on Ratchett's. A voice replies "*Ce n'est rien. Je me suis trompé*". The conductor says "*Bien Monsieur*" and scurries off to Princess Dragomiroff. Poirot returns to bed and can hear Ratchett moving.

Just after 1.15 am he hears another bell tinging, then the voices of the conductor and Mrs Hubbard, who insists that a man has been in her compartment. As he drops off to sleep, he is woken again, perhaps by something falling against his door. He opens it and sees a woman wrapped in a scarlet kimono embroidered with dragons retreating from him. He then sleeps until morning.

In the morning, at 11 am, with the train still at a standstill, Ratchett is found dead – stabbed, with no sign of a struggle. His door is locked and chained on the inside but his window is open. If the murderer's plan was for the open window to suggest that he had left that way, the snow had defeated it because he would have left traces in the snow and there were none.

Dr Constantine's view that death occurred between midnight and 2 am is supported by a dented gold watch in Ratchett's pyjama breast pocket whose hands had stopped at 1.15 am – just before Mrs Hubbard said she saw the man in her compartment. He had been drugged (as his empty glass tells the doctor) and stabbed a dozen times – with at least three blows capable of causing death and one or two others being so slight as to be practically scratches. One blow was almost certainly struck with the left hand while some others were obviously right-handed. "Two people" murmurs Poirot.

But it transpires, in a breathtakingly innovative solution, that *all* 12 travellers did it – though not quite all, since, in a final twist, we learn that the Wagon Lit conductor, Pierre Michel, had participated rather than Countess Andrenyi.

Ratchett's real name was Cassetti, as Poirot discovers by cleverly revealing the words "*-member little Daisy Armstrong*" on a charred fragment of paper in his ashtray. Some years before he had kidnapped and murdered three-year-old Daisy Armstrong in the United States, where she had lived with her parents, Colonel Armstrong and his wife, Sonia, daughter of the actress, Linda Arden.

After Daisy's dead body was found ($200,000 having been paid in ransom money), Sonia gave birth to a dead child and died herself; her husband shot himself; and Daisy's French nursemaid, Susanne, wrongly accused, threw herself out of a window. But Cassetti was acquitted on a technicality, changed his name and left the United States. His murderers were a self-appointed jury of 12 people who condemned him to death and acted as his executioners.[1]

They all had connections to the Armstrong family which are gradually revealed in the following order:

1. Hector MacQueen: son of the district attorney in the Cassetti case
2. Princess Dragomiroff: Sonia's godmother
3. Countess Andrenyi: Sonia's younger sister (whose husband, Count Andrenyi, stabbed Ratchett on her behalf)
4. Mary Debenham: Sonia's younger sister's governess
5. Antonio Foscarelli: the Armstrongs' chauffeur
6. Greta Ohlsson: Daisy's nurse
7. Edward Masterman: Colonel Armstrong's valet
8. Pierre Michel, the conductor: Susanne's father
9. Colonel Arbuthnot: Colonel Armstrong's best friend
10. Hildegarde Schmidt: the Armstrongs' cook
11. Cyrus Hardman: in love with Susanne
12. Mrs Hubbard: Sonia's mother, the actress Linda Arden.

These connections explain the murderers' motivation, although it is not as convincing for MacQueen whose motivation the author tries to bolster by adding that he had seen Mrs Armstrong "more than once – she was a lovely woman" and later adding that he had "always adored" her.

The murder plan was brilliantly conceived and plotted. Hardman, who worked for an American detective agency, tracked Ratchett down. MacQueen and Masterman got jobs as his secretary and valet. They knew that he would be travelling on the Orient Express on which Michel was working. With Hardman (in the end compartment) saying that no one came along from the rear carriages, that no one else got on the train and that nobody could have passed his compartment without being seen, there was no chance of incriminating any innocent passenger who did not have an alibi.

MacQueen arranged for Ratchett to travel when Michel was on duty. The murderers meant to engage every compartment in the Istanbul coach. They even booked berth No. 7 in the name of a mythical Mr A.M. Harris because it would have been awkward for a stranger to share with MacQueen. But there was one compartment they could not get (No. 1) because it had been booked long beforehand for Bouc, who moved out for Poirot after the first night.

Before the journey, threatening letters were sent to Ratchett. On the night of the murder a note was placed in his compartment saying "*Remember little Daisy Armstrong*" to ensure he understood why he had been threatened. A narcotic was then administered to him without his knowledge (so that he could not cry out or struggle), probably by Masterman before he retired to bed to read the (fictional) novel *Love's Captive* by Mrs Arabella Richardson.

In the final chapter, Poirot reckons that it was not Ratchett who spoke French at 12.37 am since he was by then lying in his drugged sleep. We are not told who did speak French or who Poirot later heard moving in the compartment. Perhaps, but again we are not told, this was when the note was burnt; it should have been destroyed but instead survived as the charred fragment.

Poirot fancies that each person in turn entered Ratchett's compartment through Mrs Hubbard's and struck, very close upon 2 am. Since such a convoy of murderers would have been seen by Michel, the conductor, he must have been privy to the plan. Everyone – strong or weak – could use a dagger and it made no noise. The murderers themselves would never know which blow actually killed him; indeed two of the wounds must have severed blood vessels and yet did not bleed as one would have expected, meaning, according to Constantine, that Ratchett was already dead when the blows were delivered.

Although Poirot does not explain why he thinks the murder happened at 2 am, he may reckon that, if he had been awake, he would have heard the activity associated with the murder and that, since he did not (despite being awake between 12.37 am and the unspecified time after 1.15 am when he saw the woman in the scarlet kimono), he allowed himself the maximum time to fall asleep after seeing her, but without going beyond Constantine's limit of 2 am.

It is a feature of the superbly innovative nature of the solution that, despite Arbuthnot's belief that "Trial by jury is a sound system" (Part 2 chapter 8) and the gradual revelation that more and more of the suspects are connected with the Armstrong family, it remains counter-intuitive to believe that they were *all* involved.

Our instinct is reinforced by Hardman, and then Bouc, who both say in Part 3 chapter 8 that they cannot *all* be in it. We assume, of course, that Constantine is right that Ratchett was stabbed by more than one person. But we naturally think that we are still carrying out the traditional process of working out who the murderers are from *among* all the suspects. As Hardman says "They can't all be in it; but which one is the guilty party is beyond me".

And this remains our perspective until the end. Even when Constantine thinks (Part 3 chapter 3) "If they are all lying", we do not spot how small a jump it would then be for us to think 'If they all did it'. The solution is dangled in front of us but we don't spot it because it is so original.

Plot

The true version of events described by Poirot (which we can call Version 1) is not, of course, revealed until the final chapter. The murderers had intended, by their false clues and testimony, to lead the police to a different solution (Version 2). In combining two versions, the plot is magnificently constructed, as it has to be in order to create false, interconnecting stories for 12 murderers.

However, the construction is particularly brilliant in this novel because the author not only interweaves Versions 1 and 2 but also interweaves a further version aimed at deceiving Poirot when the murderers learn he is on the train (Version 3) and then yet a further version (Version 4) when, as a result of the train being stuck in the snow, they realise that Version 2 is not going to work. Then there is a final version (Version 5) which Poirot propounds in the final chapter before revealing the true solution.

The skill with which the five versions are interwoven is of the very highest standard of construction. Although Poirot never refers to 'five versions', the care which the author has taken to ensure that a murder plan and the false versions could work on the Orient Express, and with the placing of passengers in particular compartments, the order in which their evidence is given and the order in which the clues are revealed shows that great thought was given to these matters. The purpose of the murderers (and the author) is to cause real mystification and they succeed wonderfully well.

Various features are common to the false versions. First, Hardman, from the detective agency, says that he had been asked to protect Ratchett from a "small dark man with a womanish voice"; and Mrs Hubbard claims to have heard a woman's voice in Ratchett's compartment at some time before 1.15 am.

Secondly, it appears as if the man whom Mrs Hubbard had (falsely) claimed was in her compartment just after 1.15 am had been dressed as a Wagon Lit conductor because she later finds a button from a conductor's tunic there. This seems confirmed by Princess Dragomiroff's maid, Hildegarde Schmidt, who says she almost collided with him as he left Mrs Hubbard's compartment and that he was small and dark and had a weak voice like a woman's.

Thirdly, when this fake conductor's uniform is later found (in Schmidt's suitcase), it has a key for unlocking compartment doors. So it appears that the fake conductor, who must have joined the train at Vincovci (Part 3 chapter 1), could have got into Ratchett's compartment from the corridor (if the door was not chained – which it was not when Greta Ohlsson opened it at about 10.40

pm); lock it and chain it behind him; murder Ratchett; go through the communicating door to Mrs Hubbard's compartment whether it was locked on her side or not; and then lock Mrs Hubbard's door on the way out into the corridor so that it was locked when Michel answered her bell.

The murder would therefore, under that originally intended false version (Version 2), have been regarded by the police as "*an outside job*" with the small, dark man with the womanish voice having been 'seen' by one of the murderers leaving the train at Brod where it was timed to arrive at 12.58 am (Part 3 chapter 3) – Ratchett's open window being intended to be spotted by the authorities as deliberately misleading.

In Part 3 chapter 3 Poirot imagines that, under that originally intended false version, "two things only" would have been different from the version actually presented because of the snowdrift (Version 4), namely Mrs Hubbard would have said that she heard the man in her compartment just before 1 am (rather than just after 1.15 am) and the uniform would have been found in one of the toilets – a conspicuous place to show how clearly the trick had been played.

He does not refer, as one of his "two things only", to Ratchett's dented gold watch. So one assumes that it was always in Version 2 and intended to be spotted as a false clue ("it is common enough in detective stories"), allowing the police to take pride in spotting it and to confirm their belief that the murderer left the train at Brod at 12.58 am.

The dented watch, as an obvious false clue, also fits neatly with the waking of Poirot at 12.37 am by the cry, followed by the voice speaking French. This must be a Version 3 embellishment, rather than part of Version 2, because in the final chapter Poirot describes it as "a comedy played for my benefit".

It is not clear when the murderers decided to embellish their plan with the Version 3 'comedy' but it cannot have been in reaction to the train becoming stuck since that happened at 12.30 am and there would not have been time for them to concoct and execute it within seven minutes. But it must have been after the train was at Belgrade (between 8.45 pm and 9.15 pm) when Poirot's valises were moved from berth No. 7 to the compartment next to Ratchett's.

What Version 3 depends on is Poirot first spotting that the dented watch is a false clue (as he does, not only because it is a common device but because a pyjama pocket is a most uncomfortable and unlikely place to keep a watch); then, secondly, thinking that, since Ratchett spoke no French (as MacQueen had said twice), the voice he heard at 12.37 am could not have been his; and, thirdly, concluding that he must already have been dead, which would tie in with the false murderer passing through Mrs Hubbard's compartment just before 1 am and leaving the train at Brod at 12.58 am.

However, despite all the thought that the murderers have given to Version 2 (and the embellished Version 3, which Poirot spots as false because Ratchett could not have cried out if he were heavily drugged), neither is going to work when at 12.30 am, before the train even reaches Brod, it gets stuck in a snowdrift.

When that happens, the murderers must rethink. Poirot imagines that they had "a hasty consultation" and decided to proceed. Although they would all now come under suspicion (since no one could have left the train), their evidence had been worked out before, so that, if suspicion fell on one person, he or she would be cleared by the evidence of others, such as mutual alibi testimony from persons with whom they seemed unlikely to have had prior acquaintance.

In addition, to confuse the issue further (in Version 4), two so-called 'clues' – a pipe cleaner and a handkerchief initialled "N" – were dropped in Ratchett's compartment; and a 'red herring' was drawn across the trail – the woman in the scarlet kimono seen by

Poirot and apparently by others. So, in fact, more than "two things only" were different from the originally intended Version 2.

Exactly when the "consultation" at which this was all agreed happened is not clear. It must have been after 12.30 am (when the train came to a standstill) and presumably after the 12.37 am 'comedy' (since it would have taken time after the standstill to arrange the consultation as well as to make the decision). But it must have been before 1.15 am since it was just after this that the plan proceeded, with Mrs Hubbard's complaint about a man in her compartment taking place later than originally intended, perhaps because it took the extra 20 minutes or so to decide what to do.

And this, then – the confusing intermixture of Versions 2 and 3 and finally 4 – is what greets Poirot. Further discoveries are made during that day. First, the dagger – a cheap affair, sham Oriental, with an embossed hilt and a tapering blade – is found in Mrs Hubbard's rubber sponge bag, hanging on the handle on her side of the communicating door; presumably the fake conductor had slipped it into the sponge bag after shutting the door behind him.[2]

Secondly, the uniform apparently worn by him is found in Schmidt's suitcase. Clearly if there was a fake conductor, he could not retain the uniform. So where could he hide it? Since Schmidt says he collided with her, he would have known that her compartment was empty. So where better to hide it?

Thirdly, the scarlet kimono is found in one of Poirot's own valises.

Then in the final chapter, before Poirot reveals the true solution, he proposes "an alternative theory" (Version 5). This version, which allows the real murderers to go free, is a sort of hybrid between Versions 2 and 3, and has the murderer, an outsider, leaving the train at 12.18 am rather than 12.58 am.

He suggests that the murderer joined at Belgrade or possibly Vincovci by the door left open by Arbuthnot and MacQueen who were on the platform. He wore a Wagon Lit uniform over his clothes and had a pass key enabling him to enter Ratchett's compartment despite the locked door. He stabbed Ratchett, who had had a sleeping draught, with "great ferocity".[3] He left through the communicating door to Mrs Hubbard's compartment, putting the dagger into her sponge bag but losing a button of his uniform. He slipped out, putting the uniform into a suitcase in an empty compartment and then, in his ordinary clothes, left the train just before it started off (from Vincovci at 12.18 am).

But Poirot faces questions about the credibility of Version 5. What about the watch that stopped at 1.15 am? His brilliant answer is that Ratchett failed to put it back at Tzaribrod, so it still registered Eastern European time, one hour ahead of Central European time – meaning Ratchett was stabbed at 12.15 am, not 1.15 am.

What about the voice that spoke French at 12.37 am? Surely that was Ratchett or his murderer? Not necessarily, says Poirot. It could have been someone who had gone to speak to Ratchett, found him dead and rang the bell but then, afraid of being accused, spoke, pretending to be Ratchett.

Did Mrs Hubbard also fail to put her own watch back? No, says Poirot. At 12.15 am she heard the man pass through, but unconsciously, then (at 1.15 am) had a nightmare about a man in her compartment, awoke and rang for the conductor.

What about Schmidt nearly colliding with the fake conductor at about 1.15 am? Poirot says that she did see him – but earlier – while the train was at Vincovci but pretended, having recognised the handkerchief as the Princess's, to have seen him later with a confused idea of giving the Princess an alibi.

Having heard Version 5, Constantine says it will not hold water. He is right since, clever as it is, it fails to account for various points (such as the sleeping draught and differing wounds) while Poirot's ideas about how Mrs Hubbard and Schmidt saw the fake conductor one hour earlier are very unconvincing.

So he then gives the true solution (Version 1). Having heard it and an emotional speech from Mrs Hubbard – "Society had condemned him; we were only carrying out the sentence" – Bouc and Constantine say they prefer Version 5, which is the solution they will offer to the Yugoslavian police.

Despite the brilliance of the plotting, there are a few minor points that are not quite right. In Part 2 chapter 1 we learn that the train left Vincovci 20 minutes later than its scheduled time of 11.58 pm; so, when Poirot says it left at 12.10 am in Part 2 chapter 5, this must be an error for 12.18 am. In Part 2 chapter 2 MacQueen refers to the "young English lady" in the compartment next to his but he is next to Masterman, Foscarelli and Schmidt. In Part 2 chapter 15 Bouc refers to Michel saying that "the door into the corridor of Mrs Hubbard's compartment was locked"; he must mean *from*, not *of*, her compartment but, more importantly, Michel did not say this when Bouc was present – only when Poirot was (Part 1 chapter 5). And in Part 3 chapter 4 the Countess says that Colonel Armstrong's name was Robert whereas in Part 2 chapter 8 Arbuthnot says it was Toby and in the final chapter Mrs Hubbard says it was John.

Finally, in Part 3 chapter 8 Bouc says that of the 12 passengers in the Istanbul coach (he must be excluding Poirot and Ratchett) nine have a proved Armstrong connection. He must mean MacQueen; Dragomiroff; both Andrenyis (the Count by marriage); Debenham; Foscarelli; Ohlsson; and Masterman. But who is the ninth since no connection has yet been proved for Mrs Hubbard, Hardman, Arbuthnot or Schmidt?

Clues

As Poirot says in Part 1 chapter 7, "One cannot complain of having no clues in this case. There are clues here in abundance". He is right about that and, given their number, it is impressive that the standard of clueing is generally good, though much supported by his (admitted) guesswork.

The key clue is the 'charred fragment' clue since, as Poirot says, "With no clue pointing to the Armstrong case, there would be absolutely no reason for suspecting any of the passengers on the train". He is alerted to it by the quite good 'flatter match' clue, there being two burnt matches, one flatter than the other, in Ratchett's ashtray. Since Ratchett only had a box of the rounder kind, the flatter match must have been used by someone else to burn an incriminating paper. After revealing "*-member little Daisy Armstrong*", Poirot says that "Armstrong" is "the clue to the mystery". But, while the 'charred fragment' clue is key, it is not mystifying since it is explained so promptly.

Having explained it, Poirot's first thought was that the assembled company was very varied, with many classes and nationalities. This 'varied company' clue pointed to the United States since only there, he says, might there be such a household. In Part 2 he had asked all (but one) of the passengers who did not seem to be actual or naturalised Americans whether they had been to the United States. Countess Andrenyi, who was in fact American but appeared on her Hungarian husband's diplomatic passport, said she had not been there with him. Masterman, Ohlsson, Arbuthnot and Schmidt each denied having been there, although the truth may have been on their passports which Poirot had.

He then embarked on a scheme of "guessing" – that is, casting each person for a part in the Armstrong drama. It was, he explains, not only unlikely but *impossible* for so many people connected with the Armstrong case to be travelling by the same train by coincidence, especially when the trains were usually almost empty at that time of year, as shown by the rather good 'empty train' clue (which had appeared various times in Part 1 chapter 2).

In fact the murderers meant, says Mrs Hubbard, to engage every carriage (she means compartment) in the Istanbul coach, even trying to stop a stranger sharing MacQueen's compartment by booking berth No. 7 in the name of Harris, an imaginary passenger, whose failure to arrive enables Poirot to occupy that berth on the first night. Poirot spots the 'Harris' clue – anticipating his failure to arrive and thinking it "significant" – as revealed by his remark "I read my Dickens" – a reference to Mrs Harris, an imaginary friend of Sairey Gamp in *Martin Chuzzlewit*. An oddity is that, although the murderers were troubled about No. 7, they left the berth with Schmidt (No. 9) empty, despite her key role in the fake versions.

Thus, Poirot concludes, "They were *all* in it". If the passengers were a self-appointed jury – recalling Arbuthnot's comment in Part 2 chapter 8 that "trial by jury is a sound system" (the 'jury' clue) – the whole case fell into order because a jury is composed of 12 people and there were 12 passengers and 12 stab wounds of varying degrees of ferocity (the 'twelve wounds' clue) made by a dagger, which everyone could use. The 'jury' clue is very good because it is not obviously a clue and yet it almost a dead giveaway to the solution.

So, who were the jury?

(1) **Pierre Michel**: Poirot knows that he must have been privy to the plan and yet, since he had been with the Compagnie for over 15 years, he could not have been directly connected with the Armstrong household. Supposing, says Poirot – making one of his 'guesses' about Susanne, who killed herself – that she had been Michel's daughter; that would explain everything including the place for staging the crime. However, this is some 'guess', since the only clue we have for his Armstrong connection is the 'French' clue – that Susanne was French. It also means that one of the 12 passengers must be innocent.

(2) **Hector MacQueen**: Poirot doesn't need to guess at MacQueen because he admits his connection. But a few paragraphs later he goes further with the quite good 'But surely' clue. When told that Cassetti has been identified by the charred fragment, he says "But surely – I mean – that was rather careless

of the old man?". Despite his quick thinking after his first two words, readers will spot that he was about to say "But surely that was burnt!". Poirot says that, when MacQueen learned that the letter was not burnt, he must have told the others, who agreed to deny any Armstrong connection. That makes sense.

(3) Princess Dragomiroff: What does not make sense therefore is Princess Dragomiroff freely admitting (Part 2 chapter 6) she was Sonia's godmother and a friend of her mother. Otherwise there is no clue to her involvement except the handkerchief in Ratchett's compartment with the initial 'H' which, after some misdirection towards other suspects, is revealed as the symbol for 'N' in Russian, 'Natalia' being her first name. In fact, the 'handkerchief' clue turns out to be false, aimed at causing confusion, with the murderers knowing that, because of her social position, frail physique and alibi given by Schmidt and Michel, she was in a practically unassailable position.

(4) The Andrenyis: Countess Andrenyi is the first passenger for whom Poirot has to 'guess'. His guess is pretty impressive and based, first, on a spot of grease on her husband's diplomatic passport, which says that the Count is "accompanied by his wife. Christian name Elena Maria; maiden name Goldenberg; age twenty", and, secondly, on a wet label on her suitcase.

Poirot cleverly wonders if 'Elena' on the passport is really 'Helena', with the 'He' turned into to a capital 'E' and a spot of grease applied to cover up the alteration. He finds confirmation of this in the wet label, which had been soaked off and put on again to run over the first initial. The guess he makes, based on the 'grease spot' and 'wet label' clues, is that she is really Helena Goldenberg, Sonia's younger sister and the younger daughter of Linda Arden.

However, we could not make such a guess because we only knew that Poirot thought that Sonia had a younger sister, not that she was called Helena, let alone Helena Goldenberg. And, when he says that Princess Dragomiroff lied when saying that she "thinks Helena married an Englishman", the Princess did *not* give the name Helena – she only said that Sonia had a younger sister.

As for Goldenberg being the sisters' maiden name (and Linda Arden's real surname), 'Linda Arden' was just an acting name (based on Rosalind and the Forest of Arden in Shakespeare's *As You Like It*). That 'Linda Arden' clue is quite good in suggesting that the real surname of Sonia and Helena's mother was not Arden. But, as for what really is, Poirot's reasoning that it "may have been" Goldenberg because she "quite likely" had central European blood in her is very unconvincing.

Nevertheless, both the Count and Countess swear that the Countess is innocent and the Count's "earnestness" is the rather weak clue leading Poirot to conclude that she is innocent and that the Count, so to speak, took her place.

(5) Mary Debenham: The next person he tackles is Arbuthnot, though in respect of Mary Debenham's connection. They had caught his attention when he had heard him say to her "I wish to Heaven you were out of all this" on the Taurus Express from Aleppo to Istanbul and "Not now. Not now. When it's all over. When it's behind us – then –" on the platform at Konya. Poirot had also noted that Arbuthnot called her by her first name so that they were "well acquainted" but pretending not to be. We later learn that they are in love.

Poirot was made suspicious about Mary not only by those 'well acquainted' clues but by the clever 'Taurus delay' clue. She had been very concerned when the Taurus Express was delayed, fearing she would miss her Istanbul connection for the Orient Express. And yet, when that train was stuck in the snowdrift, there were no signs of her earlier anxiety. Although she says that her original concern was about causing inconvenience to waiting friends, she cannot explain why she was then calm when the Orient Express was delayed.

Also, hidden in that same conversation, when she refers to telephoning friends, she uses the words "long distance". Poirot says that her familiarity with that expression suggests she had lied about never having been to the United States. But the 'long distance' clue is not as good as it should be because, although he says three times that she said she had never been there, she did not say that. He asked everyone who was not an actual or naturalised American except her.

Nevertheless, he gets one further clue, which "practically told" him that she was Helena's governess.[4] He undersells himself here because Helena did not 'practically tell' him in a way that anyone other than a very astute reader would have spotted and Bouc thinks it "another miraculous guess". What she did was describe her governess in a way that could not be Mary – English, or rather Scotch, a big, red-haired woman who couldn't have been more than 40 – but then, when giving her name quickly, she said it was Miss Freebody. In doing so, she unconsciously gave Mary away since there was a shop in London called, until recently says Poirot, Debenham and Freebody (the department store). With the name Debenham in her head, she clutched at the first name to come to mind, which was Freebody. This 'Freebody' clue is a good one, but only for readers who know the name of the store.

(6) Antonio Foscarelli: Next Poirot calls for Foscarelli and makes what Bouc calls "another of these famous guesses of yours", suggesting that he was the Armstrongs' chauffeur, which he admits. Poirot does not explain what clued his guess but we know that Foscarelli was an agent of Ford motor cars. In the last chapter Mrs Hubbard says that he had suggested the idea of all 12 killing Ratchett. This contrasts with Poirot's expectation (Part 2 chapter 10) that the murder, being carefully planned and staged, was not Foscarelli's sort of crime, which shows how wrong Poirot's psychological analysis can be.

(7) Greta Ohlsson: Poirot then suggests that she was Daisy's nurse, which she admits. Again, he does not explain what clued his guess but we know that she is a trained nurse and that she said that the nurse's name was Stengelberg – which sounds Swedish, like Ohlsson.

(8) Edward Masterman: Then Masterman admits that he was Armstrong's batman and valet. So no 'guess' is needed but Poirot had the clever 'sleeping draught' clue – Masterman's claim that Ratchett took the draught himself, and yet he would hardly have done this (and so been unable to defend himself) when he had been threatened and slept with an automatic under his pillow.

(9) Cyrus Hardman: Then Poirot asks if Hardman was the gardener or butler, though it is not clear if he is being serious. Hardman denies this, adding (how does he know?) that the Armstrongs didn't have a garden. But he must have a connection, having aroused Poirot's suspicions with the 'detective methods' clue: if he really had been asked to protect Ratchett, the only way to have done so was to have spent the night in his compartment or in some spot where he could watch his door, rather than sitting in the end compartment peering out.

In the final chapter Poirot says he imagined that Hardman had loved Susanne. The clue, he explains, is that when he spoke to Hardman about foreign women (Part 2 chapter 15) "Sudden tears came into his eyes, which he pretended were dazzled by the snow". In fact we were not told about *tears* but that "He blinked as though the snow hurt his eyes". So, the 'tearful eyes' clue is not really fair and, indeed, when Poirot first mentions Susanne to Hardman (Part 2 chapter 9) as "the girl who threw herself out of the window", he shows no emotion, saying "Sure. That's a good point, that".

(10) Colonel Arbuthnot: In addition to the 'well acquainted' clues (and his refusal to explain his conversations with Mary), the pipe cleaner in Ratchett's compartment was identical to those he used, as the only pipe smoker on the train. But Poirot spots the 'pipe cleaner' clue as false, saying he can "think of eleven other explanations" for its presence than Arbuthnot's guilt. He says it was dropped to confuse the issue by incriminating Arbuthnot who had the strongest alibi (being with MacQueen) and whose connection with Armstrong, as his best friend, was probably hardest to prove.

(11) Hildegarde Schmidt: Poirot could 'guess' Schmidt's connection because he senses a good cook "instinctively". He also found it odd that she should be a Princess's maid, having suggested (Part 2 chapter 15) that it would be more usual for the Princess to employ a smart French woman than the homely Schmidt. So he lays a trap, asking Schmidt (Part 2 chapter 15) whether she is a good cook to which she replies "Yes, indeed, all my ladies have said so. I –" before stopping, perhaps realising that she has given herself away because, if you are a *lady's maid*, your employer seldom learns if you are a good cook. The 'good cook' clue is a good one, at least for those who know what a lady's maid does – or, rather, does not do.

Poirot also makes a cryptic remark (Part 2 chapter 13) in relation to his belief that the Wagon Lit uniform may be in Schmidt's baggage: "If Hildegarde Schmidt is guilty, the uniform *might* be found in her baggage – but if she is innocent it *certainly* will be". He never explains this 'uniform' clue (if it is one) and readers need to think hard to interpret it. Perhaps he means that, if her fake conductor story is true (so she is innocent), then the obvious place for him to dispose of the uniform is her compartment because, having collided with her, he knows it is empty and so the uniform will certainly be found there. But, if her story is untrue (so she is guilty), she might hide the uniform in someone else's baggage (to incriminate them) or in her own (to make the story look true). In fact, since the uniform is found in her baggage, she could be guilty or innocent under the 'uniform' clue, so it does not help readers.

(12) Mrs Hubbard: The person in the compartment communicating with Ratchett's was most open to suspicion. So, to act as a rather ridiculous American mother who could not possibly be a murderer, an artist was needed. And the Armstrong family *had* an artist – Sonia's mother, Linda Arden. Thus (the argument presumably runs) Mrs Hubbard must really be Linda Arden.

She claims that, because her sponge bag was hanging on the handle of her communicating door, she could not see if the door had been bolted (Part 2 chapter 4). So she asked Greta Ohlsson, who had come in for aspirin at 10.40 pm, to check that it was, which Greta says she did. But, when the dagger is found in the sponge bag (Part 2 chapter 14), a sentence reads "About a foot above the handle was the door bolt". Only a very astute reader would spot its significance, despite Poirot's brow being furrowed, which is that, if the bolt was *above* the handle from which the sponge bag was hanging, it could not have been obscured by the sponge bag and so Mrs Hubbard *could* have seen it.

This very good 'sponge bag' clue is enhanced by readers getting another chance to spot it when Mrs Hubbard, who refuses to stay in her compartment (No. 3) after the murder, is moved to a compartment in the Athens slip coach (No. 12) – exactly the same, but facing the other way. There, when Poirot hangs the sponge bag on the door handle, he says "The bolt is just underneath the handle – the sponge bag masks it" (Part 2 chapter 14) – exactly as Mrs Hubbard had previously claimed.

In the final chapter Poirot explains that, although her claim that she could not see if the door was bolted would have been true in an even-numbered compartment where the bolt was under the handle (No. 12), it would not have been true for an uneven-numbered compartment (No. 3) where the bolt was above the handle and so could not be masked by the sponge bag. Mrs Hubbard admits that the slip about the sponge bag was "silly", that they had tried it on the way out (in an even-numbered compartment) and that she never thought of the bolts being in different places.

Looking at the two quoted sentences in Part 2 chapter 14, we see that this is very cleverly clued. Even as Poirot furrows his brow, readers are misdirected away from the clue by being made to think that he is wondering how the fake conductor got into Mrs Hubbard's compartment if the door was bolted.

Although the excellently presented 'sponge bag' clue is the best in the book, it has one weakness – that there doesn't seem to be a good reason for Mrs Hubbard to pretend that she could not see if the door was bolted. The only logical reason is that it gave Greta the opportunity to corroborate that it was. But why would that be needed when the fake conductor's uniform had a pass key, so that he could go through the door whether it was bolted or not? So, perhaps the purpose of the sponge bag allegedly obscuring the bolt was to give Poirot and the astute reader a clue to Mrs Hubbard having lied, so that presumably she could not be trusted more generally.

Other Clues

Poirot says (Part 1 chapter 7) "This compartment [Ratchett's] is full of clues, but can I be sure that those clues are really what they seem to be?". So, he clearly expects false clues and, in addition to those considered against individual passengers, we have the artificial threatening letters written only to be produced as evidence; the dented gold watch pointing to 1.15 am; and the "small dark man with a womanish voice". But perhaps the most memorable and evocative of all the clues, despite its irrelevance to the murder, is the 'kimono' clue.

We are not told exactly what time Poirot saw the woman in a scarlet kimono retreating towards the dining car, only that he was dropping off to sleep, having earlier been woken just after 1.15 am (Part 1 chapter 5). Michel, who says he saw her between 2 am and the morning (Part 2 chapter 1), remembers Poirot opening his door and looking out for a second.

MacQueen says he saw her going towards the dining car while he was talking to Arbuthnot in his compartment (Part 2 chapter 2) between the train leaving Vincovci (at 12.18 am) and returning to his own compartment (at "getting on for two o'clock" according to MacQueen or "a quarter to two" according to Arbuthnot). Arbuthnot recalls a woman passing MacQueen's compartment roughly within the last hour of their discussion (Part 2 chapter 8). Although he did not actually see her, but smelt her scent, Poirot believes he is referring to the woman in the scarlet kimono (Part 2 chapter 13).

The final person who saw her is Mary Debenham, who had woken at about 5 am, and seen her down the corridor (Part 2 chapter 11), although the reference to 5 am strikes an odd note against the other timings. Other oddities are that, even though Hardman was awake all night, with his door ajar, and even noticed the conductor stirring at 5 am, Poirot does not ask him whether he saw the woman; and he tells Mrs Hubbard that she had entered either her or Ratchett's compartment (Part 2 chapter 4) and yet no one had suggested this.

Eventually the kimono is found in one of Poirot's valises (Part 2 chapter 15). He had predicted that it would be found in the baggage of one of the men but the reasoning behind his cryptic remark is never explained. Nor are we ever told who did wear the kimono. Poirot suspects it belonged to the Countess as there was only a chiffon negligee in her baggage but she could *not* have been the person to wear it if, like Poirot in the final chapter, we are "impressed" by the Count's word of honour that she never left her compartment that night.

What Poirot does know, however, is that the purpose of "the mythical woman in the red kimono" (as he describes her in the final chapter) was to confuse the issue by drawing a "red herring" across the trail. However, it is not right for him to use the word 'mythical'. The woman may have been 'mythical' as far as Michel, MacQueen, Arbuthnot and Mary Debenham were concerned. But Poirot actually saw her. So someone must have worn the kimono.

9

Three Act Tragedy

Solution

Poirot investigates the murders of Reverend Stephen Babbington, Sir Bartholomew Strange and Mrs de Rushbridger, each of whom dies of nicotine poisoning. The pure alkaloid of nicotine, used in rose-spraying solutions, is an odourless liquid, a few drops of which can kill instantaneously.

The first murder occurs at a party given by the actor Sir Charles Cartwright at his home, Crow's Nest, in Loomouth, Cornwall. There are 12 guests and, as they enjoy cocktails mixed by Cartwright, the local vicar, Stephen Babbington, collapses and dies. Cartwright suggests that he might have been murdered and, although Poirot (who is one of the guests) thinks not and no poison is found in his glass, an exhumation later reveals nicotine poison.

The second murder occurs at a party given by Sir Bartholomew Strange, a specialist in nervous disorders, at his home, Melfort Abbey, in Yorkshire. There are 11 guests and, as Strange drinks a glass of port at the end of dinner, he has a seizure and dies. The police are called because this time a doctor is present who suspects poison. The inquest verdict is 'Death by Nicotine Poisoning' but again no nicotine is found in the glass.

There is an obvious suspect for this murder, John Ellis, Strange's new butler, who disappears next morning. Readers will assume that he is too obvious and attention focuses on the seven people (other than Strange) who were at both parties – Angela Sutcliffe, Freddie and Cynthia Dacres, Muriel Wills, Oliver Manders, Lady Mary Lytton Gore and her daughter Hermione, known as Egg. But Egg becomes part of the investigating team with Cartwright, his friend Mr Satterthwaite and Poirot, none of whom were guests at Strange's party.

The third murder occurs at Strange's sanatorium. The victim is a patient, Mrs Margaret de Rushbridger. She had apparently sent a telegram to Poirot saying that she had information about Strange's death but, before Poirot can get to her the next day, she dies of nicotine poisoning after eating a chocolate from a box posted to her the day before.

Since the murders occur in that order, the reader's natural assumption is that Babbington's murder is the principal one and that the other two flow from it. There is therefore much focus on finding the motive for Babbington's murder. In fact, however, the principal murder is Strange's while the other two are only secondary. That is a clever device, which is complicated further by there never seeming to be any reason for murdering Babbington.

So, what was the murderer's plan? Looking first at the murder method, this required no real ingenuity. With 11 chapters still to go, Poirot reckons that the victims' cocktail and port glasses contained nicotine and that, while the guests were looking at the victims, the murderer simply exchanged the offending glasses for ones containing genuine drinks. As for the third murder, *all* the chocolates on the top layer were tampered with by the murderer, who was lucky that the box arrived so efficiently in the post and that Mrs de Rushbridger ate one a couple of hours before Poirot arrived.

A potential weakness, relating to all three murders, concerns the pungency of nicotine. It seems odd to Poirot that Strange did not taste anything unusual since "Pure nicotine has a most pungent and unpleasant taste" (Third Act chapter 5). So, how does the author get round this?

In Babbington's case, he takes a sip and chokes a little, probably because he doesn't like cocktails, but despite this he takes another determined mouthful. In Strange's case, he had "influenza last spring and it left him with his sense of taste and smell a good deal impaired". In Mrs de Rushbridger's case, although the chocolate must have tasted horrible, she was surprised and swallowed it because "One doesn't like spitting a thing out" (says the Matron) and "if a liquid runs suddenly down your throat, it is difficult" (says Poirot). The author clearly had to think about the pungency issue but one is left feeling that Babbington, at least, did not need to take a second mouthful.

As to the murderer, there is the possibility that – as well as the disappearing Ellis and the seven people known to be at both parties – someone, who was at the first party, was also present, *unrecognised*, at the second. If so, who?

The answer is Cartwright himself – the actor, playing the part of the stooping, middle-aged butler, Ellis, with his belladonna-darkened eyes, his whiskers and a painted birthmark on his wrist. Ellis was never real and after the murder he left by a secret passage in the Abbey, vanishing completely. For very many readers, the revelation that the murderer is Cartwright, who had been the most active of the investigating team, will be a genuine surprise.

Of course, Strange would have recognised Cartwright because they had known each other since boyhood and been at Oxford "together" (despite Cartwright now being 52 and Strange 55). So Cartwright must have persuaded him, as a joke or wager, to allow him to impersonate a butler, the culmination of which would be the spoofing of his guests. And, if Cartwright was identified before he poisoned Strange's glass, nothing irrecoverable would have occurred and everything could have been passed off as a joke. All very clever.

Moreover, Cartwright built into his murder plan a scheme for implicating Manders. His purpose perhaps (though this is never clarified) was to implicate one of the seven, thus focusing attention on a *connection* between both deaths and therefore away from Ellis, who was not present on the first occasion.

He arranges for Manders to be at Strange's party in suspicious circumstances by sending him a letter apparently written by Strange. He puts a newspaper cutting about nicotine poisoning in Manders' pocketbook. And he finds some letters written by Ellis (which Cartwright has faked) suggesting that he knows who the murderer is. Manders' implication is rather obvious and Cartwright is lucky that Manders even goes to Strange's party and tears up the forged letter before it can be analysed. If he had not done so, Ellis could, Poirot suggests, have torn it up when valeting him. But what if Manders had left it at home?

The reader's greatest difficulty in even treating Cartwright as a suspect is that, until the denouement, it seemed that he was in Monte Carlo when Strange died and so had no opportunity to kill him. He went there in the First Act chapter 5 and Satterthwaite met him there in the next chapter just after Strange had died. His return to England is never clued and only in the final chapter does Poirot produce his passport (not previously referred to) showing when he returned.

Another weakness is Cartwright's motive for the principal murder of Strange. Cartwright is clearly in love with Egg but doesn't ask her to marry him. Poirot says that there must be some "obstacle" to the marriage and he then identifies one out of the blue in the final chapter. He says that Cartwright had married when very young but could not get divorced because his wife was in a lunatic asylum under the name of Gladys Mugg, wife of Charles Mugg. Although we knew that Cartwright had changed his name from Mugg when taking a stage name (Third Act chapter 12), we knew nothing about a wife or lunatic asylum.

Indeed only Strange knew. But, despite sympathising with Cartwright, even he would not see him bigamously marry an unsuspecting Egg. So Strange had to be removed, enabling Cartwight to marry without fear of his bigamy being exposed. An almost entirely unclued motive – and, even when Satterthwaite and Egg discuss why Cartwright had never married (First Act chapter 4), no clue is given that he was married already. Indeed, he had "always managed to steer clear of matrimony".

Looking at the legal context of the motive, it was the law at the time, under the Matrimonial Causes Acts 1857 and 1923, that the only ground for divorce was adultery.[1] So married couples who did not want to commit adultery could not get divorced unless there was evidence that one of them had been adulterous. The law was satirised by the humourist A.P. Herbert in *Holy Deadlock* in 1934 (so the issue was topical). He became a Member of Parliament in 1935 and, after his introduction of a Private Members Bill, the law was liberalised by the Matrimonial Causes Act 1937, which extended the grounds for divorce to include cruelty, desertion and incurable insanity as matrimonial offences.

The purpose behind mentioning the English legal context is to explain why in the United States, where the book was published as *Murder in Three Acts*, Cartwright's motivation is different. His motive in that edition is fear about losing his freedom. In the final chapter we learn that Cartwright (not his wife, who is not mentioned) had, as Charles Mugg, been in a mental home suffering from egomania. Although discharged after four months, Strange was not satisfied about his mental condition and Cartwright was convinced that he was planning to have him restrained again.

Of the two different motives, one assumes that, even though the United States edition was published first (1934 rather than 1935), the author had originally given Cartwright the English motive because, if he had been given the United States one, that would have been equally well understood on both sides of the

Atlantic and there would have been no need for different editions. The English motive, however, would not have been generally understood in the United States because insanity had been a ground for divorce there for many years in at least 20 states[2], thus explaining why the motive based on the English legal context had to be changed in the United States edition.

Turning to Babbington's murder, Poirot's stumbling block is that he cannot see how Cartwright could have ensured that Babbington took the poisoned cocktail glass from the tray. So, how did he murder Babbington? The answer depends on his motive. In the Second Act chapter 7, Cartwright, Satterthwaite and Egg identify five motives for murder – gain; revenge; homicidal mania; crime passionel; and fear. In the United States edition, where that chapter has the same discussion, there is also a reference to motives in the final chapter in which Poirot identifies just three – fear, gain, a woman.

However, none of those motives applies with Babbington. The poisoned glass was not intended especially for him but for *anyone* present (even Poirot, as he alarmingly points out in the novel's final line) except for Cartwright himself, Strange (who did not drink cocktails) and Egg (to whom Cartwright handed an innocent glass). The murder was just a dress rehearsal for the principal murder. Cartwright, obeying his actor's instinct, tried out his murder before committing it; and the dress rehearsal went well – the nicotine worked, Babbington died, the glass was switched and no foul play was suspected.

So that is the story's central idea – that readers should naturally assume that the first murder is the principal one when it is only a dress rehearsal. Poirot may describe the dress rehearsal motive as "reasonable" and "natural" but it leaves one with a slight sense of incredulity and he admits that this was the only time he had come across such a motive. Nevertheless, its originality deserves real credit and only the most astute reader would have detected it.

216

There is also a novel motive for the third murder. Cartwright, when disguised as Ellis, had given Strange a telephone message that Mrs de Rushbridger had arrived at the sanatorium. Strange had then "chaffed" (talked jestingly to) Ellis. This was seen by Beatrice, a housemaid, who had told Satterthwaite, who in turn had told Cartwright. Cartwright wanted to direct attention away from the chaffing (which Strange no doubt only did because he knew Ellis' true identity) and what better way than by focusing on the *content* of the message about Mrs de Rushbridger and away from Strange's *reaction* to it?

So early one morning Cartwright left for Yorkshire from where he sent Poirot a telegram, apparently from Mrs de Rushbridger. saying she had information about Strange's death. Then he returned to London and posted the poisoned box of chocolates, which arrived the next morning before Poirot could get to Yorkshire from London. So it looked as if the murderer's motive was fear of exposure resulting from information that Mrs de Rushbridger might give.

However, the actual motive, although in the fear category, is more subtle than that. Because she could in fact give *no* relevant evidence, Cartwright's diversion towards her and away from the chaffing could only work if she were dead since, if she were interviewed, it would be clear that she could tell them nothing. So she was murdered for the novel reason that she knew nothing.

Plot

The story is, like a play, structured into three Acts, the First Act being called "Suspicion" (five chapters), the Second "Certainty" (seven chapters) and the Third "Discovery" (fifteen chapters, with the final one entitled "Curtain"). One murder occurs in each Act, as the title of the novel perhaps anticipates.

The title of the First Act refers to the *suspicion* that Babbington was murdered. Perhaps the title of the Second Act refers to the *certainty* that Strange was murdered. Another interpretation might be that the *suspicion* about Babbington's death turns to *certainty* but in fact this does not happen. Even as late as the Third Act chapter 5 Poirot feels that Babbington perhaps "died a natural death after all" while in chapter 7 Egg says to herself in relation to Babbington "How odd it would be if he wasn't murdered at all". It is only in that chapter that we have any real *certainty* that Babbington was poisoned. And in the Third Act, we have the *discovery* of the murderer.

Babbington's murder really needs no plotting at all – no clever murder plan, no clues – because Cartwright is not seeking to kill any *particular* person. It is hard to build engagingly around a murder that requires no real plotting and this makes the story feel lightweight from an early stage. The task of detection is also rather uninspiring because none of the seven people at both parties is a convincing suspect. The exposure of Cartwright as the murderer provides a much more inspiring solution than the investigation leading to it.

Nor is the story helped by a slightly clumsy exposition during which Strange recounts some of Cartwright's past to Satterthwaite, who must know much of what he is told because he had a financial interest in one of Cartwright's plays years before and they had been friends ever since. The author even seems to recognise this clumsiness in saying "It had been a long speech".

It is only when one realises that the whole purpose of the story has been for Babbington's murder to have no motive – or, rather, a novel one – that one sees how very clever the author has been. But one has to wait a while for that and until then the author's main device for mystification is Manders not being on Strange's guest list but, in the Second Act, running his car (chapter 2) or motorcycle (chapter 5) into an Abbey wall and then being asked by Strange to stay the night – all being part of the murderer's attempt to implicate him.

Another plotting weakness is the lack of pace, the only exception coming in the penultimate chapter when Poirot goes to Cartwright's London flat but, instead of pursuing his original aim (whatever that was), he follows Miss Milray, Cartwright's housekeeper, to Loomouth and then up and up to an old stone tower in the garden of Crow's Nest.

She knows – although we know nothing of this until the end – that Cartwright dabbled in chemical experiments in the tower and that quite a lot of his rose-spraying solution had gone. When she learned that Babbington had died of nicotine poisoning, she concluded that Cartwright had used his chemical apparatus to extract the pure alkaloid and devotedly decided to destroy the apparatus. But she is foiled by Poirot who shows a surprising degree of athleticism in following her.

That, however, is not the biggest surprise in the story. The biggest surprises relate to Cartwright's behaviour. One concerns his motive for killing Mrs de Rushbridger. Poirot says that it was "extremely uncharacteristic" of Strange to have chaffed his butler and so attention had to be directed away from this (towards Mrs de Rushbridger). However, although Strange had not chaffed his previous butler, the chaffing struck Satterthwaite as only "a little odd" and "somewhat uncharacteristic" and could have been explained by Strange being in very good spirits that evening. But instead *Cartwright himself* makes the chaffing an issue from which attention had to be diverted by saying "It *was* uncharacteristic ... he'd never have spoken like that". If Cartwright, who knew Strange better than Satterthwaite, had dismissed the chaffing as insignificant, that would probably have been an end of the matter.

Another odd aspect of his behaviour is urging that Babbington was murdered. Having devised a plan for Strange's murder with a suspect, Ellis, who (though too obvious for readers) is good enough for the police, why does he go on about Babbington being murdered when no one else – not even Poirot – has this suspicion at the outset? Poirot's answer is that he was "gratified" that the suggestion was not taken seriously (and so he could be confident about getting away with Strange's murder). But one cannot help feeling that he would have done better to have kept quiet, *especially* as he was going to murder Strange.

Another reason for Cartwright stressing Babbington's death, Poirot suggests, was that, with the doctor suspecting poison in Strange's case, Strange's death would then be presumed to have followed from Babbington's poisoning (rather than been motivated independently). However, although one can see the sense of Cartwright creating suspicion about Babbington's death *if* he were a suspect for Strange's murder, he was not a suspect. So why do so, *especially* when he had poured Babbington's drink? One can only assume that Cartwright behaved as he did because he was defying Poirot to spot the truth.

Poirot does not actually appear very much in the book – only in 10 chapters out of 27 including, by an astonishing coincidence, in one Second Act chapter in Monte Carlo just as Satterthwaite has read of Strange's death.

There are also unexplained features about Poirot's behaviour. At Cartwright's party, before Babbington's death, he looks "grave and a little sad". Why? He was looking at Manders but his later comments about Manders do not explain why he looked like that. Then he says to Satterthwaite in Monte Carlo that there is something he does "not quite understand" but does not say what. Although they were talking about Cartwright and Egg, Poirot doesn't know enough about their relationship then to be wondering why they could not marry. And we never find out what he did not quite understand.

Frustration is also caused by a letter which Cartwright receives from Egg in the Second Act chapter 1. He had received one letter from her after getting to Monte Carlo ("Just giving me the news and all that") but her second letter concerned Strange's death. He introduces the letter to Satterthwaite by saying that Egg was in the house when Strange's murder happened. Indeed she was – but the letter doesn't say that and nor do the press clippings which he and Satterthwaite then read. So how does he know?

Moreover, in the letter Egg is worried about someone who had nothing to do with the murder but against whom things might look odd. She does not name Manders or say that the police suspect him. But six chapters later she and Cartwright say that the letter spoke of the police suspecting Manders. And in the same chapter she lists the seven suspects and says "That makes six suspects" and yet she gets the figure of seven correct in the next chapter.

Clues

Except for the motive for Strange's murder, this is quite a well-clued story, with a mixture of clues ranging from those that seem so obvious that they don't really look like clues, via the two best ones – the 'director' clue and the 'dress rehearsal' clue – to clues which the most astute reader would find difficult to interpret correctly.

At the start of the book, even before the First Act, there is a list of credits, the first being "Directed by Sir Charles Cartwright". This, of course, is not seen by Poirot (who is credited with "Illumination") but for readers this imaginative 'director' clue is quite a determinative one to the murderer's identity.

Readers could be forgiven for thinking that the credit is just a reference to Cartwright's direction of the investigation since, when it is being planned in the Second Act chapter 7, he is described as being "in command, directing a production" and four chapters later Poirot says "Continue your investigations which Sir Charles is so ably directing –". However, the credits don't relate to the investigation; they suggest that Cartwright is directing the tragedy.

Poirot then invites himself on to the investigating team, to which Cartwright reacts "rather nervously" (a clue in itself). It seemed obvious to Poirot that the murderer of Babbington and Strange was present on both occasions and so was one of the seven. But he is then "visited by a curious sensation" and has a "feeling" (disappointing from a clueing perspective) that the obviousness was an "arranged obviousness" (Third Act chapter 15). So, who other than the seven might have been present on both occasions?

The answer comes in the 'actor' clue. Right at the outset, in the novel's third paragraph, before we even know that Cartwright is an actor, we are told that there was something that did not ring true about his appearance as a "Retired Naval man". After that, there are so many references to his acting (including Strange's important remark in the first chapter that he is "a better actor in private life than on the stage!") that his acting almost doesn't seem like a clue. But the 'actor' clue is crucial to the motive for Babbington's murder (the actor's instinct for dress rehearsal) and to his performance as Ellis.

Ellis was not, of course, present (as Ellis) at Babbington's murder and after Strange's murder Satterthwaite regards him as "a very clumsy red herring" (Second Act chapter 3). But he is no red herring. He is clearly suspicious and probably isn't a real butler since Alice the parlourmaid had never worked with a butler like him before and says that he "arranged the work different".

The 'real butler' clue is the first main clue about Ellis: he is not a real butler but impersonating one – and who better to do so than an actor? For those who spot the 'real butler' clue, other clues confirm that the actor is of Cartwright's class – that Ellis had been with the best families, had a gentlemanly way with him and knew about well-known people in society – and perhaps even confirm (for those who had also spotted the 'actor' clue) that the actor is Cartwright himself (since he is the only candidate), thus explaining not only Strange's remark to Lady Mary that he would surprise her that night (with the spoofing) but also the 'chaffing' clue – Strange's uncharacteristic chaffing of Ellis.

A couple of clues that Ellis is in disguise are more obscure, namely that bright light made his eyes water and that he wore glasses when going out but not when on duty. The 'watery eyes' and 'glasses' clues are not explained (and so may not even be clues) but Poirot does say in the final chapter that Ellis' eyes were darkened with belladonna. Perhaps he deduces this from the watery eyes since belladonna makes the pupil sensitive to light. But the relevance of wearing glasses when going out remains unclear. Is it that they would protect the eyes from sunlight? Or is Cartwright worried about being recognised?

The second main clue about Ellis (indeed a clue that he is Cartwright) comes with the discovery of the letters suggesting that Ellis knows who the murderer is. The letters – which Cartwright faked and wanted found – are discovered by him in the crack under the gas fire in Ellis' room. However, the process by which he finds the letters (which were missed by the police), prompted by a splash of ink (which may not even have been made by Ellis), is so incredible that readers must wonder if he *knew* he would find something in the crack and so must have put them there. Although Poirot does not mention this as a clue, he does exclaim, when learning how the letters were found, *"Ah, mais c'est magnifique, ça!"* and readers will assume he is mocking.

However, there is a final Ellis clue which may throw readers off the track – the strawberry birthmark on his left wrist, about the size of a sixpence and rather the shape of Australia. It was seen by Muriel Wills, as Ellis served vegetables to her at dinner. She later tells Cartwright, who asks her where the mark was. She gets him to stretch out his wrist and she puts her finger on the spot.

In view of the unperturbed way in which Cartwright offers his wrist, but mainly because he has no mark there, anyone astute enough to suspect him may now have doubts. Only at the end do we learn that the birthmark had been painted on. Although the 'strawberry birthmark' clue was noticed only by Miss Wills,

Cartwright had intended it to bulk largely in Ellis' description and it is quite a good false clue suggesting that Ellis is not Cartwright.

Miss Wills then asks Cartwright to pretend to hand her a vegetable dish so she can be sure which wrist the mark was on. This satisfies her that it was the left wrist but she then smiles with satisfied malice. She does so, Poirot explains, because, as Cartwright talked, it "suddenly" occurred to her that he was Ellis. Her request that he pretend to hand her a vegetable dish was not intended to establish which wrist the mark was on but was just a pretext to test his hands – hands held in the same position as Ellis' – and this confirmed Ellis' true identity. Even though we knew she was a good observer of hands (because she comments on Babbington's), it is hard to believe that any reader would have made the same deduction about the 'malicious smile' clue as Poirot.

Cartwright, however, is troubled by the malicious smile and thinks "The Wills woman knows something". Readers will wrongly assume that he is troubled as an investigator rather than as a murderer but Poirot has a rather different explanation for Cartwright being troubled. He says: "First Mr Satterthwaite – now Miss Wills. Attention *must* be drawn away from that vital point. It must be focused elsewhere". By "elsewhere", he means on Mrs de Rushbridger.

One can understand the reference to Satterthwaite, who had focused on Strange's chaffing of Ellis, and how attention might be diverted away from that by Cartwright running Mrs de Rushbridger "for all he is worth as a red herring". However, the reference to Miss Wills is much less clear, partly because Cartwright never told Poirot about her malicious smile (only that she knew something) but mainly because it is hard to see how murdering Mrs de Rushbridger would neutralise *Miss Wills* knowing something.

Nevertheless Poirot, thinking that Cartwright is the murderer and having been told that "The Wills woman knows something", gives a party at his suite at the Ritz where (for some unexplained reason) he is staying. During the party Cartwright collapses but this turns out to be a sham tragedy in which Poirot has persuaded Cartwright to participate in order to show how easy it is to exchange glasses while all eyes are on the victim.

Later Poirot explains that he had an additional aim. He wanted to watch the expression on one person's face when Cartwright fell. He does not reveal then whose face it was but he says that he saw on it "an expression of the utmost surprise" and that he now knows who the murderer is.

Naturally readers assume that the surprised expression must be on the face of the murderer who had not tried to poison anyone. It does not occur to us that it might be on the face of someone who is not the murderer but who thinks Cartwright is. Looked at from that perspective, which of the suspects might have that expression? Well, we have the clue that "The Wills woman knows something" and, if the expression were on her face (as it was), why would she be surprised at Cartwright collapsing unless she thought he was the murderer? The 'surprised expression' clue is clever but only the most astute reader would realise that we were being given such a clue.

As to the motive for Strange's murder, this is almost entirely unclued. The nearest one gets to a clue is Cartwright's love for Egg, described by Poirot as "a terrible absorbing passion that comes to a middle-aged man and which is usually inspired by an innocent young girl". His passion is similar to the 'actor' clue, in the sense that there are so many references to it that it hardly seems to be a clue. But it is a clue because it was in the proverb *Cherchez la femme*, so Poirot says, that he found the motive for Strange's murder (in the United Kingdom edition) in the form of Cartwright's lunatic wife.

However, for readers, this 'Egg passion' clue is not sufficient because Cartwright's passion is only a clue to part of the motive.

Since we get no clue that there is another significant part (that Cartwright is married), the 'Egg passion' clue really takes us nowhere. But for Poirot, it justifies saying at the denouement to Cartwright "You wanted to marry her" and deducing that, not having done so, there must be an "obstacle" to the marriage and that "It could only be the fact that you already had a wife". That deduction is likely to be beyond the reach of the most astute reader, not least with Angela Sutcliffe saying (Third Act chapter 8) that Cartwright wasn't "a marrying man".

Poirot's reference to *Cherchez la femme* does not occur in the United States edition and it is at that point in the final chapter that the different motive is introduced in an amended section lasting for about three pages, with some consequential amendments in earlier chapters, which prepare us slightly better for the motive than the United Kingdom edition does.

In the Second Act chapter 2 of the United States edition (but not the United Kingdom edition) we get two small motive clues – the 'breakdown' and 'M' clues. First is Cartwright saying that he retired from the stage two years ago because he had had a breakdown. Second is a note in Strange's diary, the day before his murder, "Am worried about M – Don't like the look of things".

The diary does not say who M is but it is not the actress (mentioned in the First Act chapter 4) with whom Cartwright had an affair since, although her name begins with 'M' in the United Kingdom edition, it begins with 'R' in the United States edition, presumably to avoid confusion with the 'M' clue. In fact, the 'M' in Strange's diary stood for Mugg, Cartwright's real name. It is noteworthy that the author did not, when spotting the need for the 'breakdown' and 'M' motive clues in the United States edition, put some equivalent motive clues into what was probably the original version.

Despite the two small United States clues, it is only in the final chapter that we learn that in Cartwright's last three plays he had acted the role of a powerful person and that his public speeches showed traces of egomania; that when he had retired with his breakdown and supposedly gone on a cruise, a patient called Charles Mugg was admitted to a private mental home; and that, after his discharge four months later, Strange was not satisfied about his mental condition and was planning, so Cartwright believed, to put him under restraint.

As for Mrs de Rushbridger's murder, Poirot says that Cartwright made "a colossal – a childish – error!" (almost as if it were the main clue), which was that she could hardly have sent him a telegram saying she had information about Strange's death when she had not heard of his connection with the case because, so Poirot asserts, no one in that part of the world knew of it.

However, the 'Rushbridger connection' clue is only a clue to the telegram being sent by someone else. It could have been sent by any of the seven, who were all at Poirot's party and must have known of his connection. So, although the telegram was an error, the clue is not as colossal as he implies.

Although Poirot knows the murderer's identity, he still does not know why Babbington was killed. He says "Until I know that I can prove nothing" (Third Act chapter 11). But a "superb idea" comes to him two days later (chapter 14) when Egg tells him she is going to the dress rehearsal of a play by Miss Wills called "*Little Dog Laughed*". Then Poirot sees the motive, crying "*Mon dieu!*".

This 'dress rehearsal' clue, flagged by Poirot's cry, is good and cleverly obscured by him saying, when she asks why he is so excited, that she had just told him she was seeing "*Little Dog Laughed*"; he does not mention 'dress rehearsal'. Oddly, though, when he tells Cartwright, Satterthwaite and Egg at the denouement that a chance word from her showed him the light, he does not say what it was and, surprisingly, none of them even asks him.

As to the seven people present on both occasions (other than Cartwright/Ellis), some readers may wonder whether Miss

Wills' malicious smile is an overly obvious clue to *her* being the murderer. However, the clues against her and the others are so lightweight that one never thinks of them as genuine suspects.

Poirot dismisses Wills and also Sutcliffe and the Dacres because it was impossible for them to have known that Babbington would be at Cartwright's party. But why was this impossible? Cartwright or Miss Milray could have told them that the Babbingtons were coming. And would that matter anyway if the murderer wasn't particularly trying to kill Babbington?

As for the other three, Poirot could find "no evidence whatsoever" that they had murdered Babbington and, although we are told that Egg's father was a "wrong 'un" and born with a "kink", it's unclear whether this is supposed to be a psychological red herring. Even Manders, "by far the most possible suspect" according to Poirot, is unconvincingly drawn as such, despite being cold and not kind and "riding for a fall".

Poirot lists the other clues about him in the final chapter: he had displayed "all the signs of high nervous tension" at Crow's Nest; he had a distorted view of life owing to private troubles; he had an inferiority complex ("a frequent cause of crime"); he was at an unbalanced age ("twenty-five at a guess"); he had quarrelled with Babbington two years ago; and there were the peculiar circumstances of his arrival at the Abbey and his incredible story of the letter from Strange. This is either all pretty weak stuff or *too* suspicious.

The main (but also far too obvious) clue against Manders is a tangible one – a newspaper cutting about nicotine poisoning falling out of his pocketbook. Cartwright had put it there while valeting him as Ellis – but what if the 'nicotine cutting' clue had not fallen out or no one had seen it fall?

The story, which is short on genuine tangible clues, has a final physical clue in the apparatus by which Cartwright obtains the pure alkaloid of nicotine, which we know can be extracted from rose-spraying solution. When rose-spraying solution is first mentioned in the Second Act chapter 2, Cartwright remarks "Roses. Now where have I heard – ?". But we are never told why he would make a remark which might point to the source of his murder weapon. In fact, it doesn't really point to it because we never get any clue that *he* uses a rose-spraying solution. The nearest we get is knowing that he may be a gardener because Mrs Babbington lectures him on gardening.

The person who does know that he uses a rose-spraying solution is, we learn in the final chapter, Miss Milray. She is not a suspect because she was not a guest at Strange's party and her striking features made it impossible for her to be there unrecognised. But there is a sort of attempt to make us suspect her in the penultimate chapter as Poirot follows her to Loomouth and up to the stone tower where he stops her destroying Cartwright's chemical apparatus.

Beyond the 'chemical apparatus' clue, the nearest one gets to thinking she is suspicious occurs when she and Egg collide by a London newspaper stand in the Third Act chapter 7. Her face distorts with emotion when reading that Babbington's exhumation has revealed that he died of nicotine poisoning. Her explanation for being upset – that she had known Babbington all her life – is "not quite satisfying" to Egg, who also notices five chapters later a "queer note in her voice" when congratulating Cartwright and Egg on deciding to marry.

This is the nearest one gets to a 'clue' that Miss Milray knows something. Indeed the reason for her distress only becomes clear in the final chapter when we learn that she thought that Cartwright had made the poison with the apparatus which she then devotedly tries to destroy. But we knew nothing of this until Poirot told us. Nor could we have guessed that she was so devoted given that in the first chapter we were told that she was leaving Cartwright.

10

Death In The Clouds

Solution

Poirot investigates the murder of Marie Morisot, known as Madame Giselle, a rich Parisian moneylender who blackmails her clients. She is killed on an airliner, the *Prometheus*, on its midday Universal Airlines flight from Le Bourget (Paris) to Croydon (London) on 18 September 1934.[1]

There are 11 passengers in the 18-seater rear car and the seating plan (a diagram of which is provided) shows that they occupy seats (starting at the rear): 2, 4, 5, 6, 8, 9, 10, 12, 13, 16 and 17. Poirot, "a little elderly man", is in seat No. 9 while Giselle is in seat No. 2 in the back row.

Shortly before landing, Giselle is found dead in her seat, with a puncture mark on her throat, on the jugular vein. It is at first suggested that she has been stung by a wasp since one was flying about before being killed by Jean Dupont (seat No. 6), who is travelling with his father, Armand (seat No. 5).

Then Poirot spots on the floor a little knot of fluffy silk, yellow (or orange) and black, attached to a thorn with a discoloured tip. Dr Roger Bryant (seat No. 10) asks with surprise if it is another wasp. It is not but is, says Mr Daniel Clancy (seat No. 8), a native thorn shot from a tribesman's blowpipe, which is later found pushed down behind Poirot's seat. We soon learn that the thorn had been dipped in the venom of a South African boomslang (a tree snake).

Inspector Japp thinks it mad to have used a blowpipe since the chances of success without being spotted were very low; and Poirot is troubled by the blowpipe being found in the plane when it could have been pushed out of a ventilator in one of the windows. By then it is obvious that the murderer wanted the blowpipe found because he had not used it at all but had thrust the thorn into Giselle's neck. So, who could have done this?

There are 11 suspects – the nine passengers (excluding Giselle and Poirot) and two stewards. But the only people who went to the back of the plane where Giselle sat were the stewards and Mr Clancy, who got a book from his coat. With the stewards, Mitchell and Davis, being "decent, sober men", Clancy, who suggested the blowpipe idea and owns one himself, is the most obvious suspect, although he returned to his seat long before the victim died.

The only other two passengers known to have left their seats are James Ryder (seat No. 4) and Norman Gale (seat No. 12). They both went to the toilet but this meant going forward rather than to the rear of the car. So very few of the 11 suspects had an opportunity to murder Giselle. As to motive, there are two areas of investigation. Who will inherit her wealth? And who owed her money and might have been blackmailed by her?

As to the first motive, inheritance, Giselle had a daughter, Anne Morisot, to whom she had left almost everything (nearly 8 or 9 million francs) in a will made many years ago. However, Giselle had not seen Anne since she was a baby; there is no photograph of her; and her whereabouts are unknown, though we learn (from Giselle's lawyer) that she may be about 24 or 25.

Readers will wonder whether Anne might be one of the three lady passengers – Lady Horbury (seat No. 13), Jane Grey (seat No. 16) and the Hon. Venetia Kerr (seat No. 17) – who are all about the right age. Venetia is the least likely because she has known Lord Horbury (aged 27) since they were children (chapter 12) and comes from an "authenticated" family (chapter 23). Jane, however, had been brought up in an orphanage in Ireland (chapter 16) while Lady Horbury had acted under a stage name before marrying (chapter 19). However, this is all misdirection because in chapter 23 the real Anne appears to claim her inheritance and we learn about her background.

Her parents were both from Quebec in Canada. Her father, George Leman, deserted her mother, Marie/Giselle, soon after the marriage. Giselle then went to France, leaving Anne to be brought up at the Institut de Marie in Quebec. Anne, now aged 24, left the Institut at 18 to start to work and came to Europe as a lady's maid. A month ago she married an American (or Canadian) from Detroit called James Richards whom she met in Nice.

After Giselle's death, her lawyer advertised in journals for Anne Morisot. Anne had read of the tragedy but, she says, did not realise that the victim was her mother or even remember what her mother's maiden name was. However, an advertisement was seen by the Principal of the Institut, who sent a telegram to Mrs Richards (Anne) in Europe, telling her of her mother's death and reminding her of her mother's maiden name. So Anne contacted Giselle's lawyer to claim her inheritance in Paris.

This seems satisfactory until Poirot remembers that he saw Anne on the plane. She was Lady Horbury's maid, Madeleine. Although her seat was in the *front* car, Lady Horbury had asked a steward to fetch her and then sent her to the rear of the plane to get her dressing case. In fetching it, Anne had gone past Giselle. But that had happened at an early stage in the flight and Giselle was alive long after Anne had returned to the front car. So, unless there was a delayed action of the almost instantaneous poison, she could not have done it.

Nevertheless, she could have been an accomplice to the person who did do it – perhaps her husband, Richards, flying under a false name, who would share Giselle's wealth with her. After all, we learned in chapter 11 that, three days before the murder, the blowpipe and four darts (each of which had a fluff of cerise red silk on it) had been bought by an American in Paris; and that the day before the murder an American had bribed a clerk at Universal Airlines to tell Giselle's maid, as she booked the flight, that the 8.45 am service (which Giselle usually took) was full and to give her seat No. 2 on the *Prometheus* at midday. However, if Anne were an accomplice, it would make no sense for her to be on the plane since suspicion would naturally fall on her as heiress. So the accomplice approach to the inheritance motive does not seem to help either.

The second motive arises from Giselle's moneylending. But the 20 or so entries in her black notebook were not very meaningful without her private papers which had been destroyed by her maid, Elise. However, Poirot reckons that five of the entries could relate to persons on the plane and, although there is some misdirection in relation to these, the only person with a clear motive is Lady Horbury, who had borrowed from Giselle and visited her in Paris on the night before the murder. She could not repay the loans and Giselle, who knew of her affair with the actor Raymond Barraclough, was turning nasty. But even though she had a motive, she had no opportunity.

So Poirot considers another approach to motive in chapter 21 by assessing, some three weeks after the crime, whether the 11 suspects have gained or lost from the murder. He reckons that four (the stewards and the two Duponts) have been unaffected and perhaps a fifth, Dr Bryant, unless he was a client of Giselle's; that two have lost – Norman Gale (whose dentistry practice has suffered) and Venetia Kerr (whose chance of marrying Lord Horbury has diminished with the evidence of Lady Horbury's affair being destroyed); and that four have gained – obviously Lady Horbury but also Jane Grey (with an increased salary), Ryder (who has written articles on the murder) and Clancy (a detective story writer, who is writing a book dealing with the murder).

Thus we have Clancy again. So it is no surprise when he is invited to dine with Poirot and Japp in the final chapter. But it is a surprise that the only other invitee is Norman Gale, who seems to have had no opportunity or motive and who has spent some chapters assisting Poirot along with Jane Grey (with whom he has been falling in love since the first chapter).

Nevertheless, it is Gale who is the murderer. He was the disguised American who bought the blowpipe and bribed the Universal Airlines clerk. Once the stewards had gone to the front car, he went forward to the toilet. There he put on his dentist's linen coat, which was in his attaché case, and padded his cheeks with dental rolls of cotton wool (also from his attaché case). Then, dressed like a steward, he seized a coffee spoon from the pantry and hurried down the gangway with a steward's quick run, as if taking a spoon to Giselle.

He then thrust the thorn into her neck, having dipped it in the boomslang venom, which he had acquired working on a snake farm in South Africa. Then he opened a Bryant & May matchbox and let a wasp escape from it; if Giselle cried out, the buzzing wasp would explain why. He then hurried back to the toilet, changed his coat and returned to his seat.

Very simple and, although daring, nobody notices a steward particularly, says Poirot (though presumably another steward would[2]), and the only person who might have recognised Gale was Jane, who would be adjusting her make-up while he was away. The wasp even provides a simple solution – that Giselle had been stung and succumbed to heart failure. Poirot describes this simple solution as "plan No.1" – the first of two solutions provided by the murderer.

However, its success, Poirot says, depended on the murderer retrieving the thorn. In case he could not, and it was found (as happened), he had prepared a second solution – the blowpipe solution. Poirot says that the most reliable way of placing a thorn in the jugular vein is *by hand* and that the blowpipe was intended, if the thorn were found, to convey the impression of *distance*.

But why, readers will wonder, was this second solution necessary? The thorn would not have been found (and the blowpipe solution would not have been needed) if Gale had thrust it into her neck and then, after her practically instantaneous death, simply retracted it and pushed it through a ventilator hole.

What Gale actually did with the thorn when murdering Giselle is never made entirely clear. Did he retract it and just throw it on the floor? Surely not. Did he leave it in the neck, hoping it would just fall out? Surely not (what if it didn't?) but this may be the most likely answer since in chapter 4 we are told that it was found where it would have fallen naturally from Giselle's neck.

And why make the thorn look like a wasp (by substituting the original cerise colouring of the silk with wasp colours)? Is it being suggested that anyone seeing the wasp-like thorn on the floor would assume it must be another wasp and ignore it? Surely not. Indeed, Poirot picked it up. So what was the point? This is never explained. What one can say is that Gale's simple murder plan is complicated unnecessarily by his blowpipe solution – which is seen through at once and is only the result of unnecessarily allowing the thorn to be found.[3]

As to Gale's motive, this derives from inheritance, not moneylending. We learn in the final chapter that he is Anne's husband of one month, James Richards (that is his real name), and we get an explanation of his motivation and strategy according to Poirot, which we can split (although Poirot does not himself do so) into nine steps: (1) Gale met Anne in Nice when she was there as Madeleine, Lady Horbury's maid; (2) she knew her mother's maiden name was Morisot; (3) Giselle was pointed out to him at Monte Carlo and her real name (Morisot) was mentioned; (4) he realised that a large fortune (Giselle's) might be got (via Anne); (5) he learned from Anne of Lady Horbury's connection with Giselle; (6) he planned to murder Giselle in such a way that suspicion would fall on Lady Horbury; (7) he bribed the clerk at Universal Airlines to get Giselle to travel on the same plane as her; (8) Anne could, after the murder, claim her inheritance and, since she would have gone to England by train (rather than on the plane with Lady Horbury), do so with a perfect alibi; and (9) he would then marry her, knowing she was infatuated with him.

This was entirely Gale's planning and it is never suggested that Anne was an accomplice. He was just using her. He had intended, Poirot says, that, once Anne had claimed her inheritance and become Mrs Richards, they would go to Canada, where she would die, leaving a fortune to her widower, who would return to England as Norman Gale, having speculated luckily in Canada.

However, his planning was complicated by two things – at the last minute Lady Horbury decided that Madeleine (Anne) should go with her on the plane (so she did not have an alibi); and he fell in love with Jane Grey. He intended to have both the money and Jane. To get both, he would need to marry Anne and acquire her money before marrying Jane; and he decided, says Poirot, "that no time must be lost".

So, after the murder, again according to Poirot, he frightened Anne by telling her that, if she came forward "at once" to claim her inheritance, she would be suspected (having been on the plane). He induced her to ask instead for a few days' leave from Lady Horbury and go with him to Rotterdam, where they were married and made wills in favour of each other.

Then about a month after the murder Anne claimed her inheritance. It would have been suspicious to ignore the Principal's telegram. By then she had been primed by Gale to say nothing of her role as lady's maid and to say that she and her husband were abroad at the time of the flight (and so not on the plane).

But, when she made her claim, Poirot was present. On learning this, Gale feared that Poirot might recognise Madeleine/Anne from the plane and get the truth from her. So he hustled her onto the boat train from Paris to Boulogne and forced her to take hydrocyanic (prussic) acid, leaving the empty bottle in her hand, so as to make her death look like suicide.

Gale's wish that no time be lost explains why he married Anne so soon after the murder (rather than waiting, as planned, until *after* she claimed her inheritance). "It was haste ruined your plan" Poirot tells him after saying that he was identified in Rotterdam as the man, Richards, who had married Anne.

The surprise about the solution is the murderer's identity. Nothing in the personality of Gale hints that he is the murderer and it is only in the final chapter that his "whole personality seemed to change" as he turned from a "handsome, vigorous young man" into a "rat-like creature". In particular, his thought processes in chapter 14 – about the effect of the murder on his dentistry practice and about going to Canada to make money – are inconsistent with his guilt or true personality since by then he must be thinking, as we later learn, that he will be wealthy (through Anne) after killing Giselle – whether he marries her at leisure (as planned) or in haste (as he later decides).

Plot

This story, called *Death in the Air* in the United States, is rather enjoyable, perhaps because of its novel use of airline travel. But it is also lightweight and frustrating. That may be because the murder plan is so simple, because Gale's personality seems unfairly portrayed, because so few, if any, of the suspects engages us as a possible murderer and because it is not clear why Gale left the thorn in the neck or changed its colouring or acted so hastily after the murder.

However, the main factor is probably that the plotting of his motivation and strategy contains too many unexplained assumptions. Poirot's summary of it, set out earlier in nine steps, is provided in an unusually long paragraph halfway through the final chapter and it is worth revisiting those steps.

Poirot tells us (1) that Gale (Richards) met Anne in Nice when she was there as Lady Horbury's maid. Fine. He also tells us (2) that she knew her mother's maiden name was Morisot (and so was lying about not remembering this). But why does Poirot say that? Of course, she would know the name if she called herself 'Anne Morisot' before marrying Richards. But did she?

We are never actually told. The implication is that she called herself 'Anne Morisot', not because Giselle's will used that name (since she might just have used the name by which she thought of her daughter) but because on each of the 30 occasions, after production in chapter 23 of the birth certificate (in the name of "Anne Morisot Leman") when she could have been 'Anne Morisot' or 'Anne Leman' in the text, she is called 'Anne Morisot' (by Jane Grey, Fournier of the Sûreté, Poirot nearly 20 times and in the narrative).

But can it be right, when we are never told what name Anne used (either at the Institut up to age 18 or afterwards up to age 24), for it simply to be assumed on 30 occasions that she called herself 'Anne Morisot' rather than 'Anne Leman' despite Leman being the last name on her birth certificate? Indeed, if she had used 'Morisot' as a surname (perhaps if her mother had placed her at the Institut *after* resuming that name), why would the Principal have thought it necessary to send her a telegram *reminding* her that that was her name?

Surely this suggests that Anne used the name Leman all her life until marrying Gale and one wonders how the Principal would have addressed her telegram if Anne were not married (chapter 23 says that she telegraphed Mrs Richards). Since she would hardly have written to her as 'Anne Morisot' to remind her of that name, she would presumably have written to 'Anne Leman'. So it is slack and confusing for there to be 30 references to 'Anne Morisot'. But, assuming that Anne *did* know that her mother's maiden name was 'Morisot', the next step (although Poirot doesn't say this) must be that she told Gale because otherwise the subsequent steps don't make sense.

Poirot's next point is (3) that Giselle was pointed out to Gale at Monte Carlo and her real name (Morisot) was mentioned. But why should he assume that Giselle Morisot was Anne Morisot's mother? Of course, Anne knew *after* the murder that her mother was the Morisot known as Giselle (because Gale told her not to make her claim "at once") but nothing is said about Anne knowing that *before* then, let alone telling Gale, until Poirot says so at the denouement.

Nevertheless, assuming also that Anne knew, and told Gale, that Giselle was her mother, Poirot's point (4) is that Gale realised that a large fortune might be got. But how would he know that Giselle intended to leave her fortune to Anne, despite not having seen her for over 20 years? We are not told.

Poirot's next points are (5) that Gale learned from Anne of Lady Horbury's connection with Giselle and (6) planned to murder Giselle in such a way that suspicion would fall on Lady Horbury. But how is he supposed to have done this? He does not take any steps on the plane to implicate her. He does not even hide the blowpipe down the back of *her* seat.

Poirot's next point is (7) that Gale bribed the clerk at Universal Airlines to put Giselle on the same plane as Lady Horbury. He presumably knew from Anne which plane Lady Horbury was taking. But there is nothing to explain why he assumed that *Giselle* was travelling that day – which is the biggest plotting weakness of all. Somehow, however, he did know the previous day when he bribed the clerk (chapter 11), *prior* to Giselle's maid ringing that afternoon to make the booking (chapter 10) – even though the maid herself did not know of Giselle's intention to fly until she returned to Paris that afternoon.

There is no need to consider Poirot's points (8) and (9) – that Anne, having travelled by train, would claim her inheritance with a perfect alibi and that he would then marry her – because the plan went wrong when Lady Horbury decided that Anne (Madeleine) should accompany her on the plane.

However, Anne's presence on it does produce another plotting problem – the lack of recognition on the plane. Since we are assuming that Anne knew she was Giselle's daughter, it is notable that she does not introduce herself as she passes her to get the dressing case. Maybe she does not see her or know what she looks like (if she wasn't in Monte Carlo when Giselle was pointed out to Gale). But much more surprising, almost unbelievable, is that Anne did not spot Gale (seat No. 12) – or that he did not spot her – as she spoke to Lady Horbury (seat No. 13) in the same row across the aisle.

Had they done so, she would surely have expressed surprise to him innocently about the coincidence, while he, not having expected her on the plane, would have been shocked, realising that her presence "seriously jeopardised" his plan because she now had no alibi. He may not even have proceeded with it.

Looking at Gale's thinking and Anne's role more generally, it feels as if the author, believing (rightly) that she has devised a cleverly simple murder plan with a well-concealed murderer in a novel setting, has contented herself with that. She has not gone on to think through or plot carefully what the murderer needs to do or know before and after carrying out his plan. That is the main reason why the story is not as satisfying as it could and should be.

Another reason is the narrative in the middle of the book. The narrative does recover quickly from a bitty and uneven exposition of the suspects in the first chapter but the pace is hampered by a lot of padding between chapters 12 and 20, representing nearly 30 per cent of this 26-chapter book. The padding is probably the result of the murder plan being so simple and of the author's wish to delay Anne's appearance until chapter 23. But she could have used those chapters to create mystification or give the suspects credible motivation. There are attempts to explore whether some might fit the five entries in Giselle's notebook but one senses that she did not have the appetite for this.

One thing she does do, in chapter 14, is describe Gale's thought processes, which are plainly disingenuous in the light of what we later learn about him. Moreover, since Anne was married a month before making her claim, the references to the passing weeks and days in chapters 21 and 22 mean that the wedding must have happened about three days after the murder, which is consistent with the "haste" of which Poirot accuses him. However, his thought processes in chapter 14 read as if he could only have thought that way *before* deciding to marry Anne and go to Canada but, since the chapter happens at least two Saturdays *after* the murder, by which time he and Anne have already married, the chapter is particularly misleading as to his thinking.

Very much on the plus side, however, is Poirot's dramatic realisation in chapter 24 that Anne, who claimed her inheritance in chapter 23, was on the plane as Lady Horbury's maid. Chapter 25 opens "This sudden revelation had an almost stunning effect on the three people sitting round the luncheon table" (Fournier, Poirot and Jane). And that is a very fair description since this realisation has the same dramatic, mystifying effect – as startling as in any Christie novel – on readers. After all, Japp had said in chapter 6 "Just as well she wasn't on that plane".

It would be a pity for stunned readers to go straight to chapter 25 after the revelation without thinking a little about its possible implications or at least trying to identify some of the questions it raises such as: How did we forget that the maid had come in to the rear car? What did she do when she came in? By what name did Lady Horbury call her? And, now that we know she was Anne, surely it can't be a coincidence that she was the maid of one of her mother's clients? Surely it can't be a coincidence that she was on the plane? Could she even be the murderer, with motive and opportunity?

When we do read on to chapter 25, we see Poirot's mental distress. His face is "contorted in agony" before he groans and drops his head in his hands. But in the end, although it is important to Gale's motive that Anne is Lady Horbury's maid, it *is* in fact a coincidence that she is on the plane because of Lady Horbury's last minute decision that she should go by air.

Finally, there are some minor points. First, when chapter 1 says that "the passengers in the forward compartment thought their various thoughts", this should be a reference to the rear compartment (and this has been corrected in later editions). Secondly, when the second steward (Davis) refers to the early service from Paris being at 8 am in chapter 2, he presumably means the 8.45 am service referred to by the senior steward in chapter 4, by the Universal Airlines clerk in chapter 11 and by Davis himself in chapter 17. Thirdly, the significance of Poirot nearly colliding with Lady Horbury's lover, Raymond Barraclough, when Raymond comes out of Anne's hotel in chapter 25 is unclear. One is left to speculate.

Clues

The obvious starting point is chapter 21 because it is entitled "The Three Clues". In it Poirot identifies these as the 'wasp' clue, the 'passengers' baggage' clue and the 'extra coffee spoon' clue.

Almost from the start Poirot is interested in the wasp. Having discarded the blowpipe as the murder weapon, he thought that the murderer had released the wasp to suggest that Giselle had been stung and suffered heart failure. If so, the murderer must have had a box for storing it until its release, at what Poirot calls "the psychological moment" (though it is hardly 'psychological'). Hence his interest in the list of passengers' possessions in chapter 8.

Having read it, he says that the list pointed "very plainly" to one person as the murderer, later adding that, having hoped to find a certain object on the list, he had done so. The item was Gale's empty Bryant & May matchbox. The 'empty matchbox' clue and the 'wasp' clue are really just different sides of the same coin – a mutual clue in which the matchbox explains the belated appearance of the wasp and the wasp explains the need for the matchbox.

This mutual clue is clever because, on the one hand, it points Poirot "very plainly" to the murderer as early as chapter 8 while, on the other, few readers will spot it as a clue at all, despite – though Poirot never says this – Gale also having a silver lighter on the list – so, would he also have needed matches?

Given the 'wasp' clue's significance, one wonders *why* Poirot thought the wasp so important in the first place. He just says that it was rather curious that no one noticed it until coffee was served. Whether or not that is good justification for regarding it as important (since it could have been elsewhere on the plane until then), one cannot complain of any unfairness to the reader, who is regularly alerted to the 'wasp' clue – and not just in chapter 21. As early as chapter 3, Poirot "seems very much interested" in the wasp and he asks nine of the 11 suspects about it. In chapter 7 Japp says that he is "always harping on" about the wasp. In chapter 19 he absolves Lady Horbury partly because of the wasp and in chapter 23 he tells Fournier not to forget the wasp.

The second of The Three Clues, the 'passengers' baggage' clue, is not related to the matchbox, which was in Gale's pocket, not his baggage. What Poirot spots from the 'passengers' baggage' clue is the white linen coat in Gale's attaché case. Why, he asks in the final chapter, take a dentist's coat on holiday? Because it resembled a steward's coat. The 'white coat' clue looks quite good, telling Poirot *how* Gale got to Giselle. But it is a bit unfair because Gale was *not* just on holiday; he had viewed dental instruments in Paris (chapter 3) and may have worn his white coat for that.

Poirot says in the final chapter that, because of the matchbox and contents of the attaché case, he was "convinced" that Gale was the murderer and that he then tried to gain his confidence by enlisting his help (in chapter 16). It is odd that, if by then he was "convinced", he should merely murmur "I think I know" at the end of chapter 16.

He murmurs that after ticking four names on his list of 11 suspects. We are not told which ones or why. Since he has just discussed Clancy with Gale and Jane, he may be ticking those three (but who then is the fourth?). However, we later wonder if he ticked the four people thought to have gained from the murder (Lady Horbury, Jane, Clancy and Ryder) but he did not know until chapter 18 that Ryder had gained. Then, when in the final chapter he lists "*four* persons who could have done the crime" as the two stewards, Clancy and Gale (oddly omitting Jean Dupont whom he has just called "a barely possible fourth"), we wonder if these were the four. We never learn.

The list of passengers' belongings also contains some items which might have been used as blowpipes. Those items, which are all mentioned in chapter 1, are listed in chapter 23 as Bryant's flute, the Duponts' kurdish pipe stems and Lady Horbury's cigarette holders. One item on the list which is not mentioned in chapter 1 or 23 is Jane's "Holder", which is listed between her cigarette case and matches and so was presumably a cigarette holder.

As for the real blowpipe, we know that Poirot regards the 'blowpipe' clue as a red herring, believing the murderer wanted it found, and he rejects it as a clue before itemising The Three Clues. However, one is still left trying to visualise where precisely the blowpipe was found. Chapter 3 says that it was pushed down "behind" seat No. 9. But where exactly is "behind" the seat? In chapter 7 Poirot refers to it being pushed down "beside" his seat, which is easier to visualise, although he then, confusingly, refers to "behind" in the same sentence. Moreover, as the author in effect admitted in chapter 12 of *Mrs McGinty's Dead*, a tribesman's blowpipe would be much too long to be pushed down into any seat (whether behind or beside).

Furthermore, it seems clear in chapter 3 that Poirot thinks that the murderer was trying to implicate, or at least play a prank on, *him*. But, although No. 9 was his seat, that is not where he was originally sitting. In chapter 1 he moved out of seat No. 17 to allow Venetia Kerr to sit there and so she may have been due to sit in seat No. 9. Readers may therefore wonder if his move is a clue to the murderer having intended to implicate her but this point is never made.

The third of The Three Clues does not come from the list of possessions. Indeed only two (out of well over a hundred) items from the list implicate Gale – the empty matchbox and the white coat – although perhaps a third could have done so if his face had been seen, namely the dental rolls of cotton wool in his attaché case, with which he padded his cheeks to play the steward.

Rather, the third of The Three Clues is the extra coffee spoon in Giselle's saucer, which Gale had taken down the aisle to her. It is surprising that Poirot puts the 'extra coffee spoon' clue in the same category as the 'wasp' and the 'passengers' baggage' clues since he never explains *why* it is so significant and he is already convinced that Gale is the murderer before he learns of the extra spoon in chapter 17. So, the 'extra coffee spoon' clue is weak. Perhaps he thought that the extra spoon could only have been brought by a steward and that, since the real stewards would know that Giselle already had a spoon, it must have been put there by a fake steward. However, that assumes that real stewards don't make mistakes – an odd premise given that Davis tells him that he laid two sets of fish knives and forks a week before.

A better clue known by chapter 21 is the ridiculous disguise which Gale proposed to wear in chapter 19 when Poirot wanted him to "blackmail" (Poirot's word) Lady Horbury into giving information about her indebtedness to Giselle. Poirot thought Gale's disguise as a blackmailer to be "singularly unconvincing" for someone who had acted in amateur theatricals and then performed convincingly as a blackmailer.

The 'ridiculous disguise' clue is quite good, revealing that Gale did not want to show himself as an actor who could have been the American in Paris or the fake steward. What is odd, though, is that Poirot describes the "ridiculous and impossible outfit" as Gale's "first mistake", which sits uneasily with Gale having given himself away with the wasp and matchbox and with Poirot saying "It was haste ruined your plan".

There are a couple of other clues against Gale. First, in chapters 14, 16 and 19 he thinks about going to Canada. That repeated idea seems innocent enough at the time but, when there are various references to Canada in chapter 23 (relating to Anne), some readers will wonder if there is a 'Canada' clue connecting those references to Gale's earlier thoughts. Beyond that, however, we are given no clues to suggest that Gale might be Richards or connected to Anne before Poirot provides the nine-step explanation in the final chapter.

Secondly, we learned in chapter 4 that the boomslang is a South African snake and in chapter 22 that at one stage Gale gave up his dentistry practice and went to farm in South Africa. Some readers may spot the 'South Africa' clue connecting the snake and the farm, although we are not told until the final chapter that Gale's farm was a snake farm.

There are a few clues (or rather red herrings) implicating some other suspects beyond the alternative 'blowpipes' – and Clancy is, as we have seen, perhaps the most obvious one. There are also red herrings relating to Ryder, who has a financial motive; Jane, who was brought up in an orphanage (and so might have been Anne); and the Duponts who have journeyed in wild places (and so might have acquired the native blowpipe were it not for another clue, the remains of a torn-off price ticket adhering to it). One also wonders why Jean Dupont tells Jane a tale about a man who abandoned his ill wife in Syria because he wanted to be in Iraq. In fact the story is irrelevant; it is just the author reminding her husband of an occasion when he abandoned her in similar circumstances.

As for Lady Horbury, Poirot absolves her in chapter 19 not only because of the wasp (which tells him that Gale is the murderer) but also because of her sex. He never clarifies his sex point but it is unlikely to relate to the blowpipe being bought by a man since she could have conspired with one; indeed, we are led to think of her lover, Raymond Barraclough, as the American who bought the blowpipe and bribed the clerk. However, if she is absolved because of her sex, readers are presumably getting a clue that the murderer is a man.

As for Bryant, Giselle's black book mentions a Harley Street doctor and Japp reckons that Bryant could have obtained snake venom. However, when Poirot sees him at his hotel in Paris, his secret is that he proposes to run off with a lady patient. And as for Venetia Kerr, she spots Poirot when he visits Horbury in Sussex (chapter 12) but we are never told what he is doing there.

That is it in relation to the generally unimpressive clueing of the suspects other than Gale, which is why it is hard to think seriously of them as being credibly motivated. In Gale's case, although the clueing of his likely guilt and his murder plan is more impressive and, generally speaking, quite good (personality aside), the clueing of his motivation is actually worse than that of the other suspects and, it is fair to say, pretty much non-existent.

There are a few other aspects of Poirot's detection which are worthy of note. In chapter 7, when Japp says that only about two people in a hundred would be likely to have any knowledge of snake venom, Poirot says that this "makes one thing, at least, perfectly clear" but he never explains what this is.

In chapter 24 he makes various points about Anne's background and then remarks abruptly that he has an idea that, without knowing it, he has just said something of significance. Although readers then look back at what he has just said, the significant point (that she had a job as a lady's maid) is well concealed among various others and readers will do well to spot the 'lady's maid' clue. But readers' main sense will be that it is a curious skill to know that you have said something significant without knowing what it is.

The clue which prompts Poirot to identify his significant point is Jane needing to file a jagged fingernail. The reason why Lady Horbury got Anne/Madeleine to come to the rear car was because she had a broken fingernail and wanted the nail file from her dressing case. However, she did not say this aloud and it is hard to see how Poirot, sitting in the seat behind her, with its high back (chapter 4), could have known this or therefore used Jane's 'jagged fingernail' clue to prompt him to focus on Anne's job as a lady's maid.

However, the most unreal aspect of Poirot's detection occurs after he realises that Anne is Lady Horbury's maid. He is rightly stunned and in his subsequent mental struggle he spends 30 or so paragraphs telling Fournier and Jane that his ideas might have been wrong. During those paragraphs he does not explain – and is not even asked about – those ideas and it seems unrealistic that he completed that conversation without explaining any of his thinking.

The final step in Poirot's agonising thought process is that, despite Anne appearing to be guilty because she had concealed that she was Lady Horbury's maid (and so was on the plane), his first supposition – that Gale was guilty – could still be right, given one "premise" which, if correct, meant that Anne should not (as far as Gale was concerned) have been on the plane at all.

Poirot's point, which he does not convey at all clearly, must be that Gale would only have gone ahead with the murder if he expected that Anne would *not* be on the plane since her presence there would seriously jeopardise his plans because of suspicion falling on her as heiress; and yet she *was* on the plane but the murder still happened. So, how could Gale be the murderer?

The answer comes with Poirot establishing that his "premise" is correct, the premise being that Anne, who would usually go by train and boat, was only asked to accompany Lady Horbury *at the last moment* – unknown to Gale, who did not expect her on the plane and who cannot have spotted her on the one occasion that she left her seat in the front car to attend to Lady Horbury.

Finally, as to Anne's murder, this is so subsidiary that there is no real murder plan, plotting or clueing. Gale just forced Anne to swallow hydrocyanic/prussic acid, a weakly acidic but highly poisonous solution, and left the empty bottle in her hand. In the absence of clues, Poirot tricks Gale by saying that he left his fingerprints on the bottle, to which Gale says "You lie. I wore …". It is hard to believe that Gale, who devised a cleverly simple murder plan for Giselle, would have reacted that stupidly.

11

The ABC Murders

Solution

Poirot and Captain Hastings, who narrates most of the story, pursue a serial murderer who kills his victims in alphabetical order. Before each murder, he writes to Poirot, warning him of the date and town of his next killing. He signs his letters "ABC" and he leaves with each victim a copy of the *ABC Alphabetical Railway Guide* (familiarly known as an 'ABC') open at the page of the town where the murder has occurred.

The first letter warns Poirot about Andover on 21 June (a Friday, so it is 1935). That day elderly Mrs Alice Ascher is killed in her tobacco shop by a blow on the head. The most obvious suspect (but for the later assumption that there is a serial ABC murderer) is her estranged German husband, Franz.

The second letter warns Poirot about Bexhill-on-Sea on 25 July. That morning Betty Barnard, a 23-year-old waitress at the Ginger Cat café, is found on the beach strangled with her own belt of thick knotted silk. She was killed between 11.30 pm and 1 am. The most obvious suspect (but for the ABC murderer) is her jealous boyfriend, Donald Fraser.

The third letter warns Poirot about Churston on the 30th (a Friday, so it is now August, as we are later told in chapter 14). But, since it is wrongly addressed to Poirot at "Whitehorse" (instead of

"Whitehaven") Mansions, it doesn't arrive until the evening post that day. By then Sir Carmichael Clarke has already been killed by a blow on the head. The most obvious suspect (but for the ABC murderer) is his brother, Franklin Clarke, who will inherit Sir Carmichael's fortune when his wife, Lady Clarke, dies of her incurable cancer.

The fourth letter warns Poirot about Doncaster on 11 September. That day George Earlsfield is stabbed in the Regal cinema. It appears that the ABC murderer has slipped up with his alphabetical scheme by killing Earlsfield, who had been sitting close to Roger Downes. Interestingly, although Downes' Christian name does not begin with a D, no one makes anything of this.

Indeed, no one spots that the Christian names of the first three victims (Alice Ascher, Betty Barnard and Carmichael Clarke) each begin with the same letter as their surnames. Everyone assumes that the murderer's serial intention is to match the first letter of the *surname* to the town.[1] Thus Betty is referred to as Elizabeth on various occasions and Poirot asks Hastings to escort Alice Ascher's niece, Mary Drower, in Doncaster because her name begins with D.

As the ABC murderer comes to public prominence, readers have an advantage over Poirot, press and police in identifying him because in various chapters, which are not part of Hastings' personal narrative, the story of Alexander Bonaparte Cust unfolds.

Cust lives in a shabby bedroom in Camden Town. His head has not been right since the War and sometimes he hardly knows what he is doing. His suitcase contains silk stockings, which a shabbily dressed man had sold to Mrs Ascher and Betty's mother and tried to sell at Sir Carmichael's house, Combeside. He lied about going to Doncaster, saying he was going to Cheltenham (another horse racing town), and afterwards, there was blood on his sleeve and a knife, sticky and red, in his pocket,

By chapter 27 (out of 35) Poirot and the police have nearly caught up with readers in identifying the shabbily dressed, blood-stained man as the murderer, learning his name in the next chapter. The police then find in his Camden Town room a block of notepaper of the sort on which the ABC letters were written (and, we later learn, the typewriter on which they were typed) as well as a quantity of hosiery and eight new ABC railway guides; and behind the hall stand they find the knife used in Doncaster with dried blood still on it.

And that is how things stand when Cust is committed for trial in November, at which point readers will feel that, while they have participated in an enjoyable chase for the ABC murderer, the author has not used her usual ingenuity. It is obvious who he is. So we don't seem to have a *whodunnit*. And, as the murder plans are so simple (even careless with Downes), we don't have a *howdunnit* either. Rather, we have, so Poirot seems to think, a *whydunnit*.

Although he never uses that term, he asks various *why* questions. *Why* did the murderer commit these murders? *Why* does he have an alphabetical complex? *Why* did he select these particular victims? *Why* has he selected Poirot as his adversary (by addressing the ABC letters to him)?

Even after the incriminating objects have been found in the Camden Town house, Poirot says that there is something that worries him very much: "It is the *why*? The *motive*". And, after Cust's committal for trial, Poirot says "Until I get at the reason for those letters being written to me, I shall not feel that the case is solved". But he gets no answers from Cust himself, when he meets him in chapter 33, because Cust does not know Poirot's name and, although he thinks that he committed the murders, he doesn't know *why*.

In the next chapter ("Poirot Explains"), we realise that we have been subjected to a gigantic deception, that Cust is not the ABC murderer and that we have been reading a *whodunnit* after all. The *why* questions (in particular, *why* the ABC letters were written to Poirot) have merely been the starting point for Poirot's brilliant unravelling of the solution to the *whodunnit*.

In retrospect, Poirot's pursuit of the *why* questions (while everyone else knows that Cust is the murderer) would seem contrived as a starting point for identifying the real murderer were it not for Cust having an alibi for the Bexhill murder. He was playing dominoes at an Eastbourne hotel until 12.10 am on 25 July and so, as Chief Inspector Japp says, couldn't very well have been strangling Betty Barnard 14 miles away in Bexhill between 12 am and 1 am. This is an "insuperable" problem for Poirot and, when we first learn of the alibi in chapter 31, we wonder if the rest of the story will involve Poirot working out how Cust committed the murder – perhaps a *howdunnit* after all.

But we are wrong and, when the deception is unravelled by Poirot, we find that there never was a true serial murderer motivated by an alphabetical complex and that the first, second and fourth murders were only committed as part of a series to distract attention from the single murder which the murderer really wanted to commit, that of Sir Carmichael Clarke.

The murderer is his jealous brother, Franklin Clarke, who was concerned that, when Lady Clarke died of her cancer, Sir Carmichael might marry his secretary, Thora Grey. If there were children, Franklin's chance of inheriting his wealth would vanish. So he devised the fantastic idea of a homicidal murderer and of focusing attention (through his warning letters) on a series of murders.

But it wasn't enough just to devise the series idea. He also wanted a stalking horse. In chapter 34 Poirot explains that Clarke chose Cust as a result of a chance encounter in a city coffee den where he played dominoes with Cust and noticed his shrinking and insignificant personality and learned of his bombastic Christian names and epileptic seizures and headaches.

The whole alphabetical plan sprang into his mind. Cust's initials and the fact that Sir Carmichael Clarke's 'name' (in the singular) began with a C and he lived at Churston were the nucleus of the plan, which was embellished with the warning letters being signed "ABC", the ABC railway guides and the selection of victims whose names began with A and B and who lived at places beginning with those letters.

The four murders were then carried out quite simply. With Mrs Ascher, he needed nerve, daring and luck but otherwise he only had to hit her on the back of the head, using a stick with a knob handle, with some wood removed and melted lead poured in. With Betty, he took her out once or twice and, for the murder, he admired her belt; she took it off; he passed it playfully round her neck; and pulled. With Sir Carmichael, his nightly walk from Elbury Cove offered the opportunity and Clarke reverted to the blow with the stick.

After that, with his object accomplished, he had no wish to commit more murders but, if they stopped, someone might suspect the truth. Therefore, having selected Doncaster, he pretended to stumble while leaving the Regal cinema, leaned over and stabbed a man in the row in front, sliding the ABC railway guide onto his knees. He wasn't concerned to choose a victim who began with D. There would be someone in the audience who began with D and it would be assumed that he was the intended victim.

Those four murders are joined as a series by the ABC letters. Clarke is clever with the B and C letters but he did not need to be with the A letter because the police treated it as a hoax until they found Mrs Ascher's body. However, after the B letter arrived, the police were taking the matter seriously, watching small tobacconists and newsagents in Bexhill.

So, having drawn Poirot's attention to Bexhill on the 25th in the B letter, he murdered Betty in the very early morning before people were awake – perhaps even (as Poirot suggests in chapter 34) before midnight the previous day.

By the time of the C letter, the first two crimes had not yet been connected in the public eye. But the police made the C letter public, with special press editions, so alerting everyone whose name began with C. However, the C letter did not arrive until the 10 pm evening post on the day of the murder, despite being dated three days before, because of Clarke misaddressing it, apparently in error. But he had done so deliberately so that it would go astray and the police could only get on the trail after the murder.

With the ABC mystery leaping into public prominence after the third murder, there was time, when the D letter arrived, to give ample warning to everyone in Doncaster whose name began with D. But, since any victim would do, Clarke didn't mind about the ample warning or being clever with the D letter.

His cleverness on this fourth occasion was in suggesting to Poirot, after the third murder, that a "special legion" should be formed, working under Poirot's orders, composed of the friends and relatives of the murdered people – Mary Drower, Megan Barnard (Betty's sister), Donald Fraser, Thora Grey and Clarke himself. When the next warning came, they might, by being on the spot, recognise someone as having been near the scene of a previous crime.

Although this turns out to have been foolish of Clarke – because, by pushing himself forward, he gave Poirot the chance to analyse his personality – it did give him (although this is never said in the story) a perfect excuse to be in Doncaster at the time of the fourth murder when otherwise, if he was seen, his presence would look very coincidental.

So the brilliance of the unexpected and highly satisfying solution comes not only in Clarke's magnificent and highly memorable scheme of concealing a principal murder in a series but also in his excellent planning. Beyond this, the brilliance comes most intricately of all in Clarke's incrimination of Cust.

What we did not know, but learn in chapter 34, is that, having selected Cust as his stalking horse, Clarke wrote in Cust's name to a hosiery firm asking for a consignment of stockings to be sent to him. He then sent him some ABC railway guides in a similar parcel. He then sent him a typed letter, purporting to come from the same firm, offering him a job. He then typed out some letters, to send to Cust at the appropriate times, instructing him where to go and who to visit. And he then sent him, again purportedly on behalf of the firm, the machine on which the letters had been typed – so that, with them being received *afterwards*, it would look as if Cust had typed and sent them to himself and that his story about instructions from the hosiery firm was a lie.

Then, having selected victims A and B, Clarke sent the Andover letter to Cust, directing him to go there on a certain date, and sent the first ABC letter to Poirot. Presumably he did similarly with the B and C murders. Then Cust got the order to go to Doncaster. Clarke followed him around and, when he went to the cinema, Clarke sat a few seats away. When he got up, Clarke also did so and, having killed Earlsfield, he collided heavily with Cust in the darkened doorway, wiping the knife on his sleeve and slipping it into his pocket.

From Cust's point of view, Poirot says that he was highly neurotic and extremely suggestible and that epilepsy sufferers often cannot remember what they have done. Having been at the scene of all four crimes and then found blood on his sleeve and a blood-stained knife in his pocket on returning from the cinema, Cust thought he was the killer and he hid the knife.

Plot

The format of this sixth Hastings novel is different from his earlier ones in that eight of the 35 chapters (after his explanatory Foreword) are not from his personal narrative. Four of the chapters (2, 16, 25 and 30) plus parts of two others (22 and 28) tell us Cust's story while the remaining parts of chapters 22 and 28 plus two other chapters (24 and 26) are told in the third person.

So Cust appears very little in the first half of the book. Indeed chapter 2 is only three paragraphs long. But his early introduction works well in creating intrigue almost from the outset. And the length of the chapter is exactly right – easily enough to engage us until he reappears in chapter 16.

Having had our curiosity aroused in that way turns out to be important when we read the chapters about the Ascher murder because, as Hastings rightly says in chapter 3, the murder of an old woman who kept a little tobacco shop seemed sordid and uninteresting. Indeed, without Cust in the background, chapters 5, 6 and 7 would be rather boring.

The same could also be said of chapters 10, 11 and 12 relating to the Barnard murder, though less so because those chapters are noticeably shorter than the Ascher ones. And readers who are not hooked by then will be by the end of chapter 13 which concludes "How little we knew what the future held".

As we read on, the plotting seems pretty simple – an episodic series of rather ordinary murders which are not mystifying (because we think we know the murderer) but which keep us engaged, partly through the early introduction of Cust, partly through the public concern in the murders and partly through our desire for answers to what we (wrongly) assume are the key questions, such as how will Cust be caught or how many will he kill before then or how will Poirot break the mystifying Bexhill alibi?

But in fact the plotting is not simple at all, although we don't realise this until chapter 34. The plot has been very cleverly constructed to direct us away from Clarke (and even away from the story being a *whodunnit*) by forcing us to focus on the wrong questions and by deceiving us comprehensively as to the type and identity of the murderer in various ways.

First, we are conditioned to believe that the murderer is a serial killer when he is not in the normal sense of that term. Thus, in chapter 3 Poirot suggests that Hastings would like "a series of murders". In chapter 8 we are reminded of Jack the Ripper (who is mentioned again in chapters 22 and 34). In chapter 9 we are told that the "chain" or "series" type of murderer is of great interest to Dr Thompson, the famous "alienist" (a rather obsolete term nowadays meaning psychologist or mental pathologist). And in chapter 14 Hastings tells Poirot that this is the first crime of this kind that they have worked on together, their other murders having been "private murders, so to speak" (though that is not the case with *The Big Four*).

Second, we are conditioned to believe that the serial killer is mad. In chapter 1 the word "madman" is used four times about the writer of the first letter. In chapter 8 Poirot agrees that he is up against "a homicidal maniac" and there are references to "madman" (twice), "acute mania", "insanity" and "madness". There are later references to "mad", "madman", "paranoia" and "lunatics" and press headlines after the third murder refer to a "Homicidal Maniac". But the high point is Poirot saying in chapter 18 "That he is a madman in an advanced stage of mania goes without saying". Even though Clarke is sane (as Poirot says in chapter 34), all the misdirection about a serial madman is legitimate because we are simply being told what the characters and the press think.

Third, and most significantly, we are conditioned to believe that the serial madman is Cust. In addition to the signs in chapters 2, 16, 22, 25 and 27, a most telling sign occurs when chapter 15 ends with a question about the ABC murderer "Where was he now?" and the next chapter starts "Mr Alexander Bonaparte Cust ..." – very clever and perfectly legitimate since it is us who (wrongly) connect the two chapters. So, when the meeting between Poirot and Cust in chapter 33 is described as being between "the two adversaries in the long drama", this is exactly what we assume the meeting to be.

Although we are cleverly misdirected away from Clarke towards the wrong questions, none of the misdirection towards *Cust* is subtle – we are *obviously* meant to regard him as the serial madman, with his unusual personality and behaviour and his presence in the murder towns. But, if that was all there was to it, then, although Clarke's guilt would provide an ingenious and unexpected solution, the story would not have been very demanding to plot.

However, that is not all there is to it because the plot doesn't just involve *misdirecting* us towards Cust. It involves Clarke *incriminating* Cust. Cust has the typewritten letters, the knife, the stockings, the ABC railway guides, the notepaper and the typewriter only because he got them from Clarke. He is not just a coincidental suspect but an integral part of Clarke's scheme. It is only when we realise this in chapter 34 that we see quite how brilliantly the author has plotted the incrimination.

She has even built in for the reader two elements of doubt about Cust's guilt, having correctly spotted the need for some weakness in the case against him to justify Poirot's *whydunnit* concerns – the first being his domino alibi for the Bexhill murder. Clarke himself even says in chapter 34 "That's been worrying me all along". Although he appears to be saying innocently that he is perplexed by the alibi, we later realise that he must be worrying about this weakness in his incrimination plan. The subtle double meaning of the sentence certainly makes it the best line in the book.

The second doubt comes with the author cleverly making the obviousness of Cust's guilt simultaneously *not* obvious by indicating that he lacked nerve and was too unattractive to have picked up Betty Barnard. This creates a real conundrum for readers. But particularly astute ones may spot Hastings saying in chapter 23 that he would not be of much avail during the special legion's patrol in Doncaster since "I was never likely to have set eyes on ABC".

Why does he say "never likely"? Surely, if ABC were Cust, he would more naturally have said that he had 'never' set eyes on ABC since he had not seen Cust. But he can't say that because he *has* met Clarke. The author must have thought carefully about this sentence, perhaps deciding she could risk it without giving the game away because readers would assume that Hastings has in mind that he may unknowingly have seen ABC somewhere.

But even those readers who don't believe that the murderer is Cust will do very well to work out that it is Clarke because of the author's success in conjuring up the public interest in the idea of a serial murderer. This is most apparent in chapter 17, with the newspapers being full of nothing else, with questions in Parliament, with Poirot being incessantly badgered for interviews, with hundreds of stories from imaginative people being sifted and with at least twenty people being detained and questioned. One has the very clear impression that the events in that chapter cover a number of days in which the Great British public turned itself into an army of amateur sleuths.

But there must be a doubt about the timing, with the third murder having become public on 31 August at the earliest, since chapter 17 ends with Poirot getting a letter from Clarke, which he cannot really have received after 2 September.[2] It is hard to believe that the public, parliamentary, press and police reaction in chapter 17 can all have occurred in 48 hours in 1935.

There are a couple of other date references where Hastings sounds a false note. In chapter 8, after the first murder, Hastings says that on 25 July the affair revived and he refers to the arrival of the second letter. In fact, however, it was the *murder* which took place on 25 July; the *letter*, as one can work out from the subsequent conference with the police, arrived on 22 July.

Secondly, Hastings starts chapter 23 by saying "I shall, I think, remember that 11th of September all my life".[3] This is the day of the Doncaster murder and, given his introduction, we expect him (and Poirot) to have a singularly dramatic day, with the special legion making an all-day session of it and patrolling the race course. But it is rather a disappointment. Nothing dramatic happens to them and by the time they reappear in chapter 26 the murder has already taken place elsewhere while in the meantime the St Leger has been won, so we learn in chapter 24, by Not Half at 85/1.[4]

There are some unexplained points as well. Why is Megan anxious to "excuse and explain" coming up to London in chapter 21 – had she perhaps been with, or following, Donald Fraser (rather than wanting to ask Clarke something, as she says)? Why does Lily, Cust's landlady's daughter, warn him in chapter 28 that a police inspector might be coming even though she seems to think that he is the ABC murderer – surely it can't be because "Women were very queer", as Cust suggests? Why does Poirot think about going to Eastbourne in chapter 32 – perhaps in connection with the alibi or to confirm that Clarke had not dined at the Splendide Hotel, as had appeared possible in chapter 13? And how can Poirot have told Hastings in chapter 33 that Cust had "shrunk" when he had not met him before?

Clues

The starting point for Poirot's detection is *why?* And his first clue is the first ABC letter. He says that it seemed to him at once that there was something "very wrong" about the letter and he equates his impression to that of an expert feeling that there is "something wrong" with a picture or a piece of furniture or the signature on a cheque. It is a feeling based on a host of small signs and details and on experience.

He says that he had assumed that what was "wrong" with all the letters was that they were written by a madman. But that later, when he examined them again, he realised that what was wrong was that they were written by a sane man; they were fakes, pretending to be the letters of a madman but in reality had been written deliberately to focus attention on a group of murders.

Readers know that Poirot thinks that the first letter is wrong because he says so in chapter 1. But the way in which it and the others were wrong ("as a picture is wrong – because they were a fake!") would be accessible only to an "expert" like Poirot. The reaction of most readers would be to wonder how they were supposed to interpret the letters in the way that he does – even knowing that he thinks they are wrong – which makes the 'wrong letters' clue disappointing, the more so because it is fundamental to his thinking.

Much better in relation to the letters is the 'misaddressed letter' clue, which is a double clue *if* one realises that the C letter was wrongly addressed on purpose. It not only reveals that the murderer wanted the letter to arrive after the third murder had been safely committed but also answers Poirot's question about *why* the letters were sent to him rather than to the police or the press: the murderer could not have arranged for the C letter to go astray if it had been addressed to Scotland Yard.

When that letter arrives in chapter 14, Hastings actually suggests that it was wrongly addressed to Whitehorse Mansions on purpose, rather than by mistake (though without suggesting why). But his idea is dismissed by Inspector Crome, who suggests that the writer had prepared the letter with a bottle of White Horse whisky in front of him and started writing "White" but then put "horse" instead of "haven". This explanation is admired by Poirot and the focus on the whisky is good misdirection, obscuring Hastings' suggestion.

However, Hastings was right and we get a clue to this in chapter 31 when Poirot says that Hastings has "a genius for stating the obvious", as he had rather predicted Hastings would do in chapter 1. In trying to work out which "obvious" statement by Hastings contains a clue, we look back at his last comment to Poirot, which was about the alphabetical selection of victims. But this was not what Poirot had in mind. It is only during Poirot's explanations that we realise that he was referring in chapter 31 to Hastings' remark 17 chapters earlier that the C letter had gone astray intentionally.

Although the 'misaddressed letter' clue is a good and quite memorable one, and the best in the book, the murderer's concern to ensure that the Churston murder was committed safely does not necessarily point to Clarke or to a 'private' murder since a serial killer could have had the same concern and deliberately sent the letter astray.

Nor does the belt with which Betty was strangled. When Poirot learns she was strangled with her own belt in chapter 9, he says "That tells one something, does it not?" and he seems a little frustrated that neither Hastings nor Crome understands what "valuable clue" (as Crome puts it) the belt has given him. His point, we later learn (chapter 34), is that she must almost certainly have been killed by someone with whom she was on friendly or affectionate terms because she is unlikely to have taken off her belt for a stranger. This 'Betty belt' clue is quite a good one – though a stranger could have forcibly removed the belt – but again it does not point to Clarke unless one can demonstrate that he was on friendly terms with Betty.

So what does? In chapter 17 Poirot says "When I know what the murderer is like, I shall be able to find out who he is". And that proves correct because, when Poirot identifies the points against Clarke in the penultimate chapter (in addition to his motive), those points essentially relate to what Clarke is like.

First is his "daring adventurous character". It is not clear where Poirot gets this from. Lady Clarke does say that he has "knocked about the world so much" and he tells Cust that he has had two near escapes from drowning. But a daring adventurous character is not obviously derived from those comments. Perhaps Poirot derives it from his second point, Clarke's "roving life". We know from chapter 18 that he had a kind of roving commission in the East to purchase things for his brother but it is hard to see how this incriminates him.

Third is his "partiality for England", which had showed itself "very faintly in the jeer at foreigners". By this Poirot presumably means Clarke's single one-liner in chapter 15 when he questions why people would want to go abroad to the Riviera when they could visit Elbury Cove. Again it is hard to see where this takes us beyond, perhaps, Poirot being chosen as the private addressee of the ABC letters because the writer wanted to jeer at a foreigner.

Fourth is his "attractive free and easy manner", which enabled him to pick up Betty Barnard – a better point in principle but we are never actually told that he had such a manner, only that he had the "resolute competent manner of a man accustomed to meeting with emergencies" (chapter 15) and a "pretty wide experience" of young ladies (chapter 18).

Fifth is his "methodical, tabular mind" (like the murderer whose crimes were listed by alphabetical progression). This is clued by his having made a list of tasks for the special legion in chapter 18 – hardly a clue of any weight, though improved by his list being enumerated by the headings A, B, C, D (as the ABC murderer might have done) rather than, say, 1, 2, 3, 4.

Sixth, and finally, is his "boyish mind", mentioned by Poirot in chapter 18 and Lady Clarke in chapter 20 and shown by his love (in chapter 18) of a book by E. Nesbit, which Poirot suggests is *The Railway Children*. The relevance of the 'boyish mind' clue is twofold, as Poirot indicates five paragraphs before listing his six points. First, the jeering ABC letters were, according to him, "schoolboy-like" (and so written by someone with a boyish mind, like Clarke – although in fact they could have been written by anyone pretending to be mad). Secondly, the choice of an ABC railway guide suggested, as Poirot explains even earlier in the chapter, that the murderer was a "railway-minded man" so that, because small boys love trains, the murderer might have an undeveloped, boyish mind, like Clarke.

In fairness to the author, Poirot does say to Hastings in Chapter 8 "The ABC, that is a clue for you"; and the link between the ABC railway guide and a "railway-minded man" on the one hand with Clarke's love of an E. Nesbit book on the other provides rather an imaginative clue. However, quite a bit of supposition and benevolence towards Poirot is needed from readers to take his two deductions from the 'boyish mind' clue as seriously as he seems to.

Indeed, the six individual points made by Poirot about Clarke's personality are either not very well clued or do not really incriminate him in any serious way. Having said that, when looked at in combination – and Poirot does rattle them all off in one paragraph – they seem a bit more compelling.

Poirot mentions a different (non-personality) type of clue against Clarke in the final chapter when he is asked whether there was any point in the questions which he asked the special legion in chapter 32. He had asked the five members one question each and he says that one thing he learned was that Clarke was in London when the first letter was posted (from "WC1").

But readers could not have deduced this from Poirot's question for Clarke or from the answer. Poirot had asked what Clarke thought of the ladies' hats worn at Ascot and he had replied that he hadn't gone to Ascot but that from what he could see of the hats worn by people driving in cars, they were an even bigger joke than usual. This does not reveal that Clarke was in London when he saw the hats. But, even if it did, we are not told the dates of the Ascot meeting in June 1935 (and so cannot judge whether this happened when the first letter was posted). And, even if we had been told, we were not given the date when the first letter was posted anyway. So, although Poirot may know these things, readers are not helped by the 'Ascot hats' clue at all.

There is, however, one thing, beyond the motive, that may help readers with Clarke. It occurs in chapter 21 after Poirot spots a connection between the first three murders, namely the presence of a stockings salesman in each location (chapters 6, 18, 21). The realisation that there is this link between the murders, which he says cannot be a coincidence, is good detection. The "clue of the stockings", as he later describes it, is really the first break he has had and one would expect his detection to result in applause all round. Instead, Clarke, who reacts first, cries "That a man came selling stockings proves nothing". That unimpressed reaction will jar with some readers, who may start wondering about him – though in fact Poirot does not mention Clarke's reaction later (and so it was probably not intended as a clue).

Poirot's second break comes in the form of the 'Thora letter' clue written to Clarke by Sir Carmichael. In chapter 23 Clarke shows this letter, which refers to Thora, to Poirot so that he can see that her relationship with his brother, who thought of her like a daughter, was perfectly above board. This looks like an act of chivalry but it is more likely that he was trying to indicate to Poirot that there was nothing between Thora and his brother which might have put his potential inheritance at risk or therefore given him a motive.

However, the ploy backfires because Poirot's interpretation of it is precisely the opposite of what it seems Clarke wanted. The letter may have referred to "daughter" but Poirot reckons that it clearly displayed Sir Carmichael's absorption in Thora. However, with Clarke apparently showing him the letter in order to rely on a diametrically opposed interpretation of it, one suspects that not many readers would have interpreted it as Poirot does.

Related to the letter is the question which Poirot asked Thora as a member of the special legion in chapter 32. He asked whether she would have married Sir Carmichael in the event of Lady Clarke's death and she said no. Poirot says in the final chapter that he had wanted to see Clarke's face when asking this question and that he saw malice and anger in his eyes.

However, it is not clear what Poirot deduces from this malice and anger, particularly as Thora's answer does *not* support Clarke having a motive. If anything, it does the opposite. So, does Poirot perhaps think that the anger was directed towards Thora, thus telling him that Clarke could hardly have had chivalry in mind when showing him the letter? Whatever the answer, the reader's problem is that there was no reference to Clarke having an angry expression when Thora answered in chapter 32.

As to Poirot's questions for the other three members of the special legion, he explains in the final chapter that "some of them" were simply "*une blague*". Thus he asked Mary Drower whether she had a young man and she said she was not sure. He asked Megan Barnard whether she wanted to find out the truth and she answered no – presumably because, as we learn in the final chapter, she feared that Donald Fraser had murdered Betty.

Which leaves Fraser himself. Poirot asked him when he took his holiday and he said the first two weeks in August. Poirot later says that this made it "unlikely" (hardly a strong word) that he had anything to do with the Churston crime. But why should this be? That murder happened on Friday 30 August. Is Poirot suggesting that Fraser could only have committed it while he was on holiday? Could he not have taken Friday off from his estate agent's firm and gone to Churston, returning on Saturday? And, if working on a Friday would stop him committing murder that day, this would have applied also to Friday 21 June, when Alice Ascher was killed.

So, where do we stand by this stage, with none of Poirot's five questions having helped readers at all? The truth is that the clueing is not of the same standard as the magnificent solution or brilliant plotting.[5] Beyond the motive, the only clues which specifically implicate Clarke have weaknesses or are unpersuasive when considered individually and so the reader has to deduce the solution in stages in the following way: the 'wrong letters' clue points to a sane person who wants to conceal one crime in a group; of the people connected with at least one crime, some personality clues suggest, in combination, that Clarke is the most likely suspect; and he will inherit his brother's wealth. It is that final point which is really the biggest clue to him, as borne out by Poirot's emphasis on the motive (the *whydunnit*), which he describes in chapter 13 as "one very important clue".

Looking at the clueing this way, cumulatively rather than individually, it works better. But there doesn't actually seem to be any evidence, even circumstantial, against Clarke. As Poirot says in chapter 34, he was safe so long as no one suspected him.

However, Poirot did suspect him and the proofs were then apparently easy to obtain: the stick used in the Andover and Churston murders was found in a cupboard at Combeside; Clarke's photograph was recognised by two people who saw him leaving the Doncaster cinema; and he was identified by Betty Barnard's friend and a girl from the Scarlett Runner Roadhouse (between Bexhill and London) where we know Betty had dined with a middle-aged man on the evening of her murder (chapter 13).

The problem for readers is that we know nothing of these proofs until Poirot reveals them in his explanations. He also tells Clarke about another proof, namely that he had left a fingerprint on Cust's typewriter – a trick (since he had not left one) which causes Clarke to concede that Poirot has won.

This brings us finally to the last person ruled out by Poirot – Cust himself, the big red herring. We know that Cust has an alibi for the Bexhill murder and that he lacked nerve and the attraction to pick up Betty Barnard. But there is also one much more subtle clue indicating that he is not the murderer – the 'just glanced' clue – which Poirot does not mention because he would have been unaware of it. In chapter 22, as Cust is heading off to Doncaster, "He just glanced at the railway guide on the table and then left the room, suitcase in hand". Note that he "just glanced" at the guide; he did not take it with him. Why not take it if he was going to Doncaster to commit an ABC murder?

12

Murder In Mesopotamia

Solution

Poirot investigates the murder of Louise Leidner in Mesopotamia, the area between the Tigris and Euphrates rivers corresponding today roughly to Iraq. Most of the story is set in an expedition house occupied by the members of an American archaeological team, the University of Pittstown Expedition to Iraq. The team, led by Louise's husband Dr Eric Leidner, an American Swede, are excavating an Assyrian city, Tell Yarimjah, near Hassanieh.

The rectangular, one-storey expedition house is built around a courtyard accessed through an arch on its north side. As the plan (chapter 4) shows, the courtyard is surrounded by 23 rooms – six for the expedition's work (such as a laboratory and an antika-room for storing the finds), nine bedrooms for the expedition team including Leidner plus a separate bedroom for Louise, six rooms for their communal use and one bedroom for nurse Amy Leatheran.

Most of the rooms open onto the courtyard – chapter 4 says that they all do but the plan shows this is incorrect – as do most of their windows, except on the south side where there are also windows onto the outside country, with the corner rooms of Louise and Father Lavigny looking only onto the outside. In the south-west corner a staircase goes up to a flat roof running along the south side of the building. Outside the house are the natives' sleeping quarters.

The nine members of the expedition team comprise Leidner; Richard Carey; Anne Johnson; Joseph Mercado; Marie Mercado; David Emmott; Bill Coleman; Carl Reiter and Father Lavigny.

Nurse Amy Leatheran, who narrates the story, joins the expedition after its work has started. She is asked to do so by Leidner who tells her that Louise, whom he married less than two years ago, suffers from nervous terrors and would feel safer if a nurse looked after her. In fact, Amy fails to keep Louise safe because in chapter 10 (out of 29), about a week after Amy's arrival, Louise is murdered in her bedroom by a blow on the front of the head from a heavy quern (a grinder) which is found in chapter 25.

Even though more than two thirds of the book remains when Louise is killed, she is the character around which it revolves and Poirot refers in chapters 20, 22 and 27 to the importance of knowing what she was like. She was beautiful – though not young (aged between 30 and 40) and with a rather haggard face but lovely eyes – and worshipped by Leidner. She had to be the centre of attention and enjoyed exercising power over those who came under her irresistible spell. Everyone had to acknowledge her sway and, if conquest was too easy, she indulged her cruel side, turning ugly if she didn't get her way. She enjoyed getting at people and setting them against each other – not quarrelling herself but making others do so. She was dangerous, ruthless and temperamental, being nice one day but devilish the next. In short, she was, as suggested by Amy (chapter 6) and Dr Reilly (chapter 19) and noted by Poirot (chapter 27), a kind of *Belle Dame sans Merci* (as in the ballad by John Keats) – a beautiful lady without mercy – and, although the tension this year among the expedition team had not been so bad last year (when she accompanied Leidner for her first season), it was never like that before she came.

Her nervous terrors were caused mainly by receiving four letters threatening to kill her because she had married Leidner. They may have been written by her first husband, Frederick Bosner, who had married her in America in 1918 when she was 20. He was a German spy, as she discovered after only a few months, and she reported him to the War Department. He was sentenced to death but escaped, only to be involved in a train wreck. He was pronounced dead, although it was not certain that the disfigured body was his.

Louise then became fond of another man but she received what she describes as "an anonymous letter – from Frederick" saying that, if she married again, he would kill her. This happened whenever she got on intimate terms with a man, but no such letter came before she married Leidner. However, two days after that marriage she received the first letter telling her that, because she had disobeyed, she had to die. A month later she received a second, similar letter and shortly afterwards the Leidners narrowly escaped death by gas poisoning. Then just over three weeks ago, a third letter came with an Iraqi stamp on it and a week ago she found a note in her bedroom, saying "I have arrived".

Readers will wonder, when Louise mentions the original letter, how she could describe it as both "anonymous" and "from Frederick". One at first imagines that it was unsigned but that she recognised his handwriting. But she then says that it is hard to say whether the letters were in his handwriting and adds that the writer might have been his brother, William, who may have thought her responsible for his death and dedicated himself to revenge.

The letters were not the only cause of her terrors. One night fingers tapped on her window; then there was "a hand without an arm attached"; and then pressed against the window in the semi-dusk was a yellow ghostly face, which turns out in chapter 22 to be a mask, with eyes and mouth crudely painted and roughly smeared in plasticine.

Then, when Amy was walking with Louise, they noticed an Iraqi man trying to look into one of the windows, which caused Louise (who assumed it was her window) to clutch Amy's arm violently. And, later in the week, at about 2 am on Friday morning, Louise was petrified on hearing someone scratching on the wall of the antika-room next to her bedroom.

When Louise is finally killed at about 1.30 pm on Saturday, it is a complete mystery how this happened. She had gone to her room to rest at 12.45 pm and about two hours later, when Leidner, who had been on the roof throughout, came down to see her, he reeled out of her room about a minute and a half later calling for Amy, who entered to find Louise dead, in a heap by the bed.

The only door to the bedroom opened onto the courtyard where Emmott and the native boy Abdullah were working but neither had seen anyone enter. They were there from 12.45 pm to 2.45 pm save for a ten-minute gap at about 1.30 pm when Emmott went up to the roof to help Leidner whereupon Abdullah strolled out through the arch to chat to the other natives.

The natives did not see any stranger come through the arch and no one could have gained access via the windows to Louise's bedroom which looked onto the outside country since these were closed and fastened. So the murder must have been committed, probably during the ten minute gap, by one of the expedition staff (who may be Frederick or his brother William in disguise).

That afternoon Leidner accepts a suggestion made by the local doctor (Dr Reilly) and Police Chief (Captain Maitland) that he call in Poirot, who had been disentangling a scandal in Syria and would pass through Hassanieh the next day. Poirot arrives at the house after lunch on Sunday.

Without the ten-minute gap, the murder would be a fine mystery of the 'locked room' type where the victim is found alone in a room and it seems impossible to work out how the murder could even have been committed. Although the door was not locked, no one (other than Leidner when finding the body) was seen going in or out; the windows were closed and latched on the inside and, even if open, no one could pass his shoulders (only his head) through the bars; the walls were of solid mud-brick; there were no trapdoors or skylights; and there was nowhere in the room where someone could have hidden.

Indeed the book would be a better locked room mystery if there were no ten-minute gap, with the door being visible to Abdullah or Emmott throughout. And this could easily have been achieved because the murderer does not enter by the door. As Poirot reveals in chapter 28, it was while on the roof that Leidner murdered Louise at 1.30 pm.

Poirot explains that Leidner called Emmott up to the roof and, while talking to him, noticed that "as usually happens" Abdullah took advantage of his absence to leave the courtyard. Leidner detained Emmott for ten minutes and then, when Emmott was down again shouting to the boy, put his plan into operation.

He took from his pocket the plasticine-smeared mask used to scare Louise and dangled it over the parapet until it tapped on her window. She was half asleep when the mask attracted her. It was not dusk, so she recognised it for what it was. She was not frightened but indignant. She jumped off her bed, opened the window, put her head through the bars and turned her face upward to see who was playing the trick. Leidner was holding one of the querns which were on the roof and he dropped it on her at, says Poirot, "the psychological moment", which really just means that she was in the right position. With a faint cry, she collapsed onto the rug below the window.

Then Leidner, who had passed a cord through a hole in the quern, hauled it up, replacing it neatly, bloodstained side down, among similar objects on the roof. After working for an hour or more, he descended, entered Louise's bedroom, closed and fastened the window, moved her body to a position between the bed and the door and, having noticed a stain on the window-side rug, swapped it with the rug by the washstand. And then he acted as the overcome husband.

His murder plan does have weaknesses. Would Louise, with her nervous terrors, really have reacted to the mask with indignation, not fright; and would she actually have put her head through the bars rather than just grabbed the mask? What if she had not gone to sleep but gone out to see Richard Carey (who might have been expecting her, according to Miss Reilly in chapter 27)? Or if Amy had looked in on her before 2.45 pm? But, subject to those points, the murder plan is characteristic of the slightly far-fetched but impressive ingenuity of the typical locked room mystery.[1]

Leidner's guilt is also a genuine surprise because he never seems to be a suspect. Even in chapter 27, when Poirot says that anyone except Leidner, Carey and Coleman had the opportunity to commit murder and then goes on to dismantle the alibis of Carey and Coleman, he does not deal with Leidner's roof alibi, giving the clear impression that he is not even a suspect.

That impression will not surprise readers who are consistently conditioned to believe that he worships (chapter 3) and is devoted (chapter 6) to Louise. He collapses completely after her death and there are then more references to his devotion and worship in chapters 15, 18 and 20. Later he looks twice his age (chapter 22), almost a complete wreck (chapter 25) and then crumpled, torn and ravaged with grief (chapter 27). So why does he kill her?

The answer is that he is in fact Frederick Bosner, Louise's first husband. He had emerged from the train wreck with a new personality, that of a young Swedish archaeologist, Eric Leidner, whose dead body was badly disfigured and who was wrongly buried as Frederick Bosner. The real Frederick, who had not been disfigured, built a new life as Eric Leidner (somehow convincing the real Leidner's friends and colleagues) and succeeded in his new career.

Nevertheless, he never forgot the woman who had betrayed him. He still loved her passionately and his jealousy dictated that she should marry no one else. When he judged it necessary, he sent a letter. At last, when the time was right, he re-entered her life. She never dreamed of his true identity. She agreed to marry and no letter came to forbid this. But after the marriage, when its intimacy might awaken a memory, he wished to impress upon her that Leidner and Bosner were two different people. So he sent the first of the four letters, then another, and then arranged the gas poisoning. After that he was satisfied.

However, following nearly two years of marriage, Louise fell in love with Richard Carey, who could not resist her. Hence the third and fourth letters – because the jealous threat underlying them was always genuine: if she gave herself to any other man (as she had to Carey), Bosner/Leidner would kill her.

So that is the ingenuity of the solution: the victim is killed by her second husband who turns out to be the first husband she had betrayed. Of course, this ingenuity depends entirely on the unwitting victim not realising that her first and second husbands are the same person, which is hardly credible.

Two pre-emptive attempts are made, in chapters 9 and 16, to suspend our incredulity with some unconvincing reasons why Louise might not recognise Bosner: Louise says that she "mightn't recognise his face"; and Poirot says that his face, build and voice would have changed and that Louise visualised Bosner (if he was sending the letters) as an *outsider*, not one of her household. In the penultimate chapter his actual explanation is that she did not recognise him because "the upstanding good-looking young fellow is now a middle-aged man with a beard and stooping shoulders".

But does his explanation really work? How "young" was the "good-looking young fellow" at the time of the first marriage? In chapter 9 Louise says he was "a young man" then but nowhere are we given Bosner/Leidner's actual age. That, however, does not stop Poirot from asserting in chapter 16 that he would by now be a man of "fifty odd".

He also says in that chapter that Louise lived with him "some fifteen years ago" and Louise herself refers to "over fifteen years ago" in chapter 9. So Poirot must regard Bosner as having been about 35 at the time. This hardly sounds like a "young fellow" or "young man" but let us assume that 35 is correct. On that basis, since Louise met Leidner three years ago (chapter 9) i.e. 12 years after the first marriage, he must therefore have been about 47 when they met, which ties in with Leidner being "middle-aged" (chapter 2).

Although Louise was married for only "a few months" (chapters 9 and 16) to the 35-year-old Bosner, it is almost impossible to believe that the physical change in him over 12 years, before he resurfaced as the 47-year-old Leidner, was so great as to make him unrecognisable to Louise during nearly two years of her second marriage. And the more so when Leidner was "a man of great personality" who was able to dominate Louise "as before" (chapter 28).

The final element in Leidner's plan was Amy. In chapter 15 Poirot asked why he had employed a nurse (rather than the police or a private detective) when Louise had been threatened. He said he suspected that Louise had written the letters herself and so hadn't believed she was in danger. But in the final chapter Poirot says that the real reason was that he needed a *professional* witness, such as a nurse, to state that Louise had been dead for over an hour when he found the body – and so was killed when he was on the roof.

However, that doesn't really work because in chapter 11 another professional witness, Dr Reilly, puts the time of death at between 1.15 pm and 1.45 pm, saying 1.30 pm at a guess (when Leidner was on the roof). So Amy wasn't needed to make this point and Poirot's explanation for employing her, thus enabling her to be the narrator, is a rather weak and unnecessary one.

He is also most unpersuasive when assessing the possible motives of the other suspects. He says that each could be "credited with a motive" but his unconvincing, conditional suggestions are replete with the words "might" and "if" and he even deploys double negatives for Reiter and Coleman (he could not be sure they were not William Bosner). As for "Father Lavigny", he is an imposter, Raoul Menier, who steals from museums, substituting fake articles for genuine ones by taking wax impressions of them and getting duplicates made. Louise "may" have remembered some wax she had noticed (chapter 7) on a gold cup in the antika-room and hinted to Lavigny, who killed her. Poirot does better with the final suspect, Carey, who is in love with Louise and, unable to resist her, hates her for undermining his loyalty to Leidner. His hatred is the only definite motive beyond Leidner's incredible one.

Having assessed the motives of the suspects (even Amy, but not Leidner), Poirot says that this was his thinking until the murderer struck a second time, by killing Miss Johnson. She was killed (in chapter 24) because, Poirot says, Leidner had been watching her and realised that she had worked out the truth.

That night he substituted a glass of hydrochloric acid (from the laboratory) for the glass of water which she usually drank during the night and put the quern under her bed in order to suggest that she had killed Louise but then been overcome with remorse. Amy was woken by an awful sort of agonised choking groan and found Miss Johnson contorted in agony, with the corners of her mouth and the skin of her chin burnt a kind of greyish white.

Since it was hard to believe that anyone could kill herself in such a painful way, it was recognised that she must have stretched out an arm, found the glass in its usual place and, still half asleep, had drunk enough to be fatal. As Amy says, poisoning with hydrochloric acid is "one of the most painful deaths possible" and, with it being a strongly acidic solution, this is the nastiest murder method in the author's novels to date.

Plot

The structure of the book is unusual in that, although Amy narrates chapters 2 to 29, chapter 1 is written by Dr Reilly, who also writes a Foreword.

In it he says that he persuaded Amy to write her account because there had been the wildest and most ridiculous rumours about important evidence having been suppressed. We are not told what was suppressed but perhaps it related to Bosner's espionage and escape or to Leidner's true identity.

Reilly also says that the events took place some four years before. Since the book was published in 1936, he perhaps appears to mean 1932, but Louise was married in 1918 "over 15 years ago" (chapter 9), so it is 1933 at the earliest. Either way, we are told that the murder occurred just after the middle of March (chapter 13) and that Poirot then returned to England on the Orient Express and got mixed up in another murder (chapter 29). This is surprising because Christie readers know that that train got caught up in a winter snowdrift.

Reilly also refers to Amy's modesty about her literary style. Although her style is occasionally a bit forthright or matronly, she does make a few amusing bracketed asides and she gets credit for her characterisation of Louise and for her description of an authentic archaeological expedition house setting.

But overall she is much less engaging than the typical Christie heroine and readers will smile less than when Hastings is the narrator. She also jeopardises her credibility with an odd interlude in chapter 23 (entitled "I Go Psychic") in which she lies on Louise's bed, imagines herself as Louise on the fatal afternoon and waits to see who entered to murder her.

It is perhaps partly because of Amy's rather uninspiring personality that one senses almost throughout that the story is a bit dull. That sense may also result from Poirot coming into the story later than in any other book to date (chapter 13). But a more concrete criticism is that from chapter 3 Amy introduces the expedition members in a way that makes it hard to work out who is who.

That is because at times she gives only a person's Christian name or surname or nationality or occupation or a characteristic (that he is plump or talkative or young) so that it takes time to work out that, for example, David and the silent American and Emmott are the same person. This means that the reader has to do quite a lot of thinking across three or four chapters just to work out who is who, even though this could have been clarified openly since nothing turns on it. The result is a stuttering exposition, with frustrated readers unable to enjoy the story properly until they have identified the characters.

Having said that, the 'locked room' element is genuinely mystifying. One does, however, wonder – since, oddly, we are not told – *why* Leidner arranged the ten-minute gap with no one watching the door. He did not need it to commit the murder. Perhaps his purpose was to suggest that the murderer used the door during that gap. But his murder plan was clever enough without this elaboration which detracts from the locked room mystery. And the elaboration itself, requiring Abdullah to leave the courtyard in Emmott's absence (presumably so that Emmott would then be shouting at him while Leidner put his plan into operation), is not entirely fair on readers since neither Poirot (nor the reader) was told that this "usually happens" before chapter 28.

There are also problems at the end of the book arising from Poirot's explanations. Towards the end of chapter 26, with the suspects gathered, Maitland is impatient for Poirot to get on and, when he finally does so in chapter 27, entitled "Beginning of a Journey", he takes a very long time. His explanations in that chapter, by far the longest in the book, last at least twice – even three times – as long as his explanations in any other story to date. And yet at the end of it we learn that it really has just been a 'Beginning' because we still don't know who the murderer is.

Indeed by then, when Poirot rejects the idea that Lavigny killed Miss Johnson because she realised that his whole *personality* was a disguise (meaning that he was an imposter rather than someone whose distinctive appearance suggested he was impersonated by a stranger who came in from outside), the explanation has become far too convoluted – and a little unfair because, in describing Lavigny's distinctive appearance, Poirot refers to his sun helmet and sunglasses, which we had not been told about before.

And then suddenly, in chapter 28 ("Journey's End"), Poirot announces that Leidner's roof alibi is worthless and that he committed the murders. It might seem surprising, given the unusual length of Poirot's explanations, to describe this as coming out of the blue but this is what it does because there was no lead up to it in chapter 27.

Clues

"How's that for a coincidence?" asks Reilly when telling Leidner in chapter 12 that Poirot will be in Hassanieh the next day. Indeed it is. In response, Leidner asks Reilly to approach Poirot – an error, since Poirot is the cause of his undoing, but it might have looked odd if he had not.

Soon after arriving, Poirot says that, having established who benefits from a victim's death financially, he next suspects the victim's husband or wife. This is surely not a clue but, if it were, Poirot promptly eliminates Leidner on three grounds – his roof alibi; his financial loss (with Louise's money going to the Pittstown Museum); and his devotion to her.

In that chapter he tells Amy that she will be of great service to him because she has a neat and orderly mind and (in chapter 18) is a very good observer. Amy does then act as a kind of assistant, regarding Poirot and herself as the doctor and nurse in charge of a case. But she makes no inspired remarks of Hastings' inadvertent kind and she refuses to believe that Louise "cared like hell for

Richard Carey" (chapter 18), which shows that Poirot gives her too much credit for observation.

We try to follow Poirot's line of detection, particularly his clue in chapters 20, 22 and 27 about the importance of knowing what Louise was like. His aim in emphasising the 'Louise personality' clue is no doubt to elevate the story's 'psychological' element and he turns out to be right since it is her irresistible capacity to invoke others to love her (both Bosner/Leidner and Carey) – fairly clued in her descriptions – that prompts Leidner's jealousy motive.

But what Leidner himself is like is nearly as important. He says "I loved Louise and I killed her … if you'd known Louise you'd have understood". He (not her) turns out to be the person responsible for the tension during the expedition, as (in Poirot's words) "an obsessed fanatic plotting to kill".

The point at which Poirot puts himself in a league well beyond most readers' deductive powers comes in chapter 24 (in which Miss Johnson is murdered) when he says that "the truth is so clear – so clear". Only the most astute reader could have spotted the truth by then. So how does Poirot see it?

Here Amy does come into her own – by being in the right place at the right time twice. First, in chapter 23 she is on the roof with Miss Johnson, who tells her *"I've seen how someone could come in from outside – and no one would ever guess"* as she looks inward to the courtyard (the 'in from outside' clue); but Miss Johnson then refuses to explain her comment, at which point readers correctly predict that she will be the next victim. Secondly, in chapter 24 Amy is the only person to hear the last words of Miss Johnson who, despite swallowing hydrochloric acid, is rather incredibly able to utter in a strangled whisper, "The window … Nurse … the window" (the 'window' clue).

Amy tells Poirot about the two clues and they go onto the roof to look inward to the courtyard to see what Miss Johnson had seen. But they see nothing. Then, looking outward to the sunrise and the open country, Poirot sees the truth. He repeats in chapter 26 that it came to him when watching the sunrise.

He saw the truth (and this requires careful reading, even in retrospect) not because of watching the sunrise or the open country but because he was doing so on the *roof*, where he realised that Miss Johnson had deduced that Louise could have been killed from there *if* her window had been open. In causing him to go onto the roof, the 'in from outside' clue is important. But it is the combination of that clue with the 'window' clue which enables him to see the truth, so making that combination the book's most important clue.

However, readers will do extremely well to interpret this complex combined clue correctly. This is partly because Poirot directs us to the sunrise rather than the roof. It is partly because the words of the 'in from outside' clue are not very helpful: Miss Johnson's remark that *"someone could come in from outside"* suggests that someone or something had come in through Louise's window from the open country – but nothing did. And it is partly because we understood that her windows were not open but closed and fastened. So how had Poirot and Miss Johnson worked out that a window must have been open?

When Louise was murdered, Miss Johnson was in the living room and she heard, she thought, a very faint cry – the 'faint cry' clue. But she believed that this could not have come from Louise's room because her windows were closed. An experiment, with Poirot in the living room and Amy in Louise's room, confirms that Miss Johnson could not have heard a cry from Louise's room with its windows closed. However, Poirot conducts a second experiment when he is in Lavigny's room and Amy is in the dining room (the same distance apart as Louise's room and the living room). On this occasion, with Lavigny's window *open*, Poirot's faint cry *is* heard.

The purpose of the experiments is to interpret the 'faint cry' clue by showing that a noise can only be heard across a certain distance when a window is open but not when it is shut. Poirot says in chapter 28 that his experiments were not lost on Miss Johnson, who realised that, if she heard Louise's cry, her window must have been open, not shut. However, interpreting the 'faint cry' clue depends on knowing that the window in Lavigny's room was *open* during the second experiment. Although Miss Johnson must have known this, it is not a point made to readers, who must therefore next interpret the 'tablet' clue.

We learn in chapter 22 that during the second experiment Lavigny showed some tablets to Poirot, who said "I take one to the window to see better". He then pretended to stub his toe and cried out, which was when his faint cry was heard. Presumably what one is supposed to deduce from Poirot taking the tablet to the window in order to see it better is that the window was open.

However, deducing that it was open from the 'tablet' clue is extremely hard because we are not told that, if it were closed, the window pane would not admit enough light to enable Poirot to study the tablet. It is a pity that he did not say "I take one to the open window" because, even though readers would still do well to spot the relevance of the word 'open', it would be in the text and the 'window' clue as a whole could have been a really good one.

Even then, one still wonders how a reader who has got this far could interpret the experiments as Miss Johnson does since, when she was on the roof, she looked inward to the courtyard, not outward. Poirot's answer is that, because she worshipped Leidner, she wanted to stop Amy guessing her discovery and so looked *deliberately* in the opposite direction towards the courtyard and made a remark about Lavigny. In fact she didn't make any such remark, although she did turn her head. But what clue do we get that she *deliberately* changed the direction of her look in order to stop Amy guessing?

Amy says that, when she went up to the roof, Miss Johnson was "staring straight in front of her" (no direction is given). When Amy approached her asking what the matter was, "she turned her head at that and stood looking at me". So the assumption must be that she turned her head in response to Amy. For readers to interpret the 'turned head' clue as meaning that she *really* turned her head in order to stop Amy guessing her discovery, rather than in response to her question, requires an unreasonable degree of astuteness.

Nevertheless, the combination of the 'in from outside' and 'window' clues, with the supporting 'faint cry', 'tablet' and 'turned head' clues, is still a clever and carefully constructed one. But it is notable that, because Poirot conducted his second experiment in chapter 22, the idea of Louise's window being open must have occurred to him *before* he got the 'window' clue, even though he could not work out its significance until he got the 'in from outside' clue.

The combined clue's significance – that Louise could have been murdered from the roof because her window was open – is also well concealed and one can see why, in order to conceal it, the author got Poirot to conduct his second experiment in Lavigny's room. The concealment is, however, very contrived because in real life he would surely have conducted the second experiment from Louise's room where the murder happened, but with the window open.

As for clues about the *howdunnit*, one is the murder weapon, the heavy quern or grinder found under Miss Johnson's bed. On it is a dull, dark stain and a fragment that looked like hair but the 'heavy quern' clue raises three points.

First, Poirot saw the truth in chapter 24 *before* the quern was found. He had presumably noticed querns on the roof but he did very well to deduce that one was used as a most unusual murder weapon before that had been established.

Secondly, there was no actual reference to querns being on the roof, either when Poirot was there with Amy or when Amy was there with Miss Johnson. So, how could readers deduce that a quern was used? There is in fact an answer, which is that, when Amy went up to the roof in chapter 6, Leidner was there with "big things he called querns" and various other artefacts. However, only the most astute reader would have remembered this reference to querns, four chapters before there has even been a murder.

Thirdly, most readers probably don't know what a quern is, beyond being told in chapter 25 that it is a grinder. Plainly Amy had not heard of querns, which were used for grinding food and dyes. It may not matter if readers don't know exactly what a quern looks like but what does matter, if readers are to work out the murder plan, is knowing that a quern has, or can have, a hole through which a cord can be passed enabling it to be hauled up.

The other clue relating to the *howdunnit* is the 'plasticine-smeared mask' clue, which explains why Louise was attracted to the window and so opened it and stuck her head out. We know from chapters 6 and 9 that she had been frightened by a yellow, dead face, ghastly and grinning, pressed against her window pane and that in chapter 22 Poirot and Miss Johnson found a crumpled, plasticine-smeared mask, with eyes and mouth crudely painted, at the back of a cupboard. Although Poirot says straightaway that the mask had been *hidden* in the cupboard, readers would do well to deduce that it is connected to the murder rather than just to the history of frightening Louise.

The final clue relating to the murder appears to be the barely noticeable blood stain on the rug in front of the washstand in Louise's bedroom. Poirot later explains that, after Leidner had moved her body away from the window, he noticed a slight stain on the rug under it. So he swapped that rug with the washstand rug because, if the stain were noticed, it would be connected with the washstand – not the window – which, Poirot says, was very important because it must not be thought that the window played a part in the murder.

However, the 'bloodstained rug' clue isn't really a clue to the *howdunnit* because the rugs don't actually show that the murderer used the window. As Poirot himself suggests in chapter 17, the murderer may have got a little blood on his hands and gone over to wash them (dropping a spot of blood on the washstand rug before doing so). What can be said about this clue, however, is that Poirot finds an explanation for the stain which, if the rug had been swapped, would be consistent with his theory of the murder plan.

Generally speaking, we are given enough clues relating to the murder plan – getting Louise to open the *window* by dangling a *mask* from the *roof* so that she could be struck with a *quern* – but one can't help feeling that there is no relief at all from the need for considerable astuteness to interpret every single one of those clues. The fact that Miss Johnson managed to do so, and beat Poirot to it, is therefore extremely impressive.

But what clues do we get that Leidner *realised* that she had worked out the murder plan, so motivating him to kill her? In chapter 28 Poirot says that she "must have" come across unfinished drafts of an anonymous letter; that she "perhaps" made a reference to the letters, which Leidner understood; that she realised how he could have committed the murder from outside; and that Leidner who had been "watching her anxiously", realised she knew. Much of this is entirely unclued conjecture and, in particular, we are never told that the crumpled paper which she snatched in chapter 19 was a draft letter or given any indication that Leidner was "watching her anxiously" before her murder.

As well as giving Poirot the combined clue, Amy also gives him "a valuable clue" about Lavigny's role as faker and thief. She had remarked to Poirot and Lavigny, when they looked at the gold drinking cup in the antika-room in chapter 22, that there was "no wax on it today" (unlike when she had seen it in chapter 7). Poirot later explains that, when Lavigny responded by saying "Wax?", his *tone* was enough for Poirot to know that he was taking wax impressions of artefacts. But how could readers interpret this 'wax tone' clue when nothing was said in chapter 22 about Lavigny's tone?

The revelation that Lavigny is an imposter, and in league with the Iraqi seen by Amy and Louise trying to look through one of the windows in chapter 7 (into the antika-room, in fact, rather than Louise's room), will again be predicted by most readers (even if his real role as faker and thief is not). This is partly because one or two of his translations (of tablets and bricks) had been surprising; partly because he was found by Leidner in the antika-room at night in chapter 8, claiming to have been investigating after hearing a noise; and partly because he was seen talking to the Iraqi whom he then described in a glaringly different way from Amy.

Poirot says in chapter 27 that it soon became "apparent" that Amy's description of the Iraqi (rather than Lavigny's) was "substantially accurate". But how did it become "apparent"? Of course, readers (and Poirot) are inclined to believe Amy but, looked at objectively, there is no reason for it to be "apparent" that her description is to be preferred until one has other reasons for distrusting Lavigny.

13

Cards On The Table

Solution

Poirot investigates the murder of Mr Shaitana (first name unknown) – a man of uncertain origin who attempts a Mephistophelian effect, living richly and beautifully in Park Lane, and who knows a little too much about everyone.

He tells Poirot that he "collects" murderers whose crimes have gone unpunished and invites him to a dinner party to meet his "exhibits" on Friday 18 October. There Poirot meets Mrs Ariadne Oliver (a writer of detective fiction), Superintendent Battle (of Scotland Yard) and Colonel Race (of the Secret Service) – not real murderers but people whose jobs have involved them in taking life legitimately, whether in fiction, law or espionage. "Four 'sleuths', so to speak," says Battle, including Poirot in the group, in chapter 4.

However, Shaitana then says that there will be other guests and four more arrive – Dr Roberts, Mrs Lorrimer, Major Despard and Miss Meredith.

After dinner, the guests divide into two groups of four to play bridge, starting at about 9.30 pm. The four sleuths play in the smoking room while the other group plays in the drawing room. Shaitana, who does not play himself, sits in a chair by the fireplace in the drawing room. When the sleuths finish their game at 12.10 am and enter the drawing room, he is found dead in the chair, stabbed in the chest by a long delicate stiletto, to the apparent surprise of the four guests still playing in that room.

No one had entered the drawing room during the game and so one of the four players in that room must have committed the murder. Each player had left the bridge table at least once while being dummy – to get drinks or an ashtray or stoke the fire or look at their partner's hand. On one such occasion, while the three other players were concentrating on the game, the murderer must have struck.

In the Foreword the author warns readers that there are only four suspects, any one of whom, given the right circumstances, might have committed the crime, and that "an equal interest" should be attached to the four, "each of whom has committed murder and is capable of committing further murders". She adds that they are widely divergent *types*, that the *motive* driving each one is peculiar to that person and that each would employ a different *method*, so that the deduction must "therefore" be entirely *psychological*.

Readers therefore know, even before chapter 1, that the four suspects in the drawing room are the only suspects and that they are all past murderers. Poirot reminds us that at dinner Shaitana had referred to women poisoners, doctor's opportunities, shooting accidents and domestic accidents. There had been a "momentary silence" after that as those words went home to someone who thought that Shaitana had evidence of a past murder and was planning to expose one of his "exhibits" as the climax to the evening.

So the murder was an unpremeditated reaction, prompted by Shaitana's words, to fear of exposure for a previous murder, with the murderer opportunistically using Shaitana's stiletto which had been on a table by the drawing-room door.

However, the mere fact that the four suspects are different types who may be driven by different motives and employ different methods does not of itself mean that the deduction must *therefore* be entirely psychological. The reason that the deduction needs to be psychological is because there are, so it seems at first, no tangible clues.

Poirot's psychological premise is that the murder took "audacity and nerve" because Shaitana might cry out or another player might look up at what Poirot describes as "the psychological moment". Indeed we know that the murderer could have been seen from the bridge table because, although there was a big Chinese cabinet between it and the fireplace, Mrs Lorrimer saw Miss Meredith bend over Shaitana.

Poirot assesses the "character" of the suspects, partly through questioning, including asking their opinions of the other suspects as bridge players, and partly through looking at the bridge scorecards which they each kept. So, how well do they match the psychological requirement of audacity and nerve?

Dr Geoffrey Roberts is a middle-aged man of the world. The figures on his scorecard are rather flamboyant. He over-calls his hand disgracefully and deserves to go down more than he does. But he plays brilliantly and has complete confidence in his own powers to pull off a risky thing. As Poirot says, "His psychology fits very well with the crime".

Miss Anne Meredith, a pretty girl aged 25, is quite a good player but a bit too cautious. Her scorecard shows careful addition and her use of the back of the card (rather than using a fresh card for a new rubber) shows she is economical. Poirot regards her as timid – "the last type of person to carry out a bold and risky coup" – but nevertheless a person who, when fearing exposure, could murder, not through cool nerve but desperate panic.

Major John Despard, tall, lean and handsome, has plenty of nerve and would take a risk if there was a reasonable chance of success. But he likes to be sure before he speaks, to weigh the pros and cons before taking action and to know where he stands, as reflected by his scoring in the cancellation style.

Mrs Lorrimer, a well-dressed woman of 63 (first name unknown) is a first-class player, with firm handwriting and a mathematical brain. She has any amount of nerve but Poirot reckons that, if she committed a crime, it would be premeditated. So he regards her as slightly more unlikely than the others but, beyond this, he thinks that his personality analysis "does not help us much".

That is strange because most readers will have found his analysis in chapter 8 very helpful in identifying the most obvious suspect to commit an impromptu, risky, murder. Surely this is the over-calling Dr Roberts rather than Miss Meredith, who seems too timid, Major Despard, who would have needed time to be sure, or Mrs Lorrimer, who could only commit a premeditated crime.

Poirot, however, wants to look for evidence of the suspects having murdered in the past, which he starts to do in chapter 9. At first, this sounds like a surprising abandonment of the psychological approach in favour of a factual investigation. But, in fact, psychology remains important, not only because he continues until chapter 15 to seek psychological clues from the bridge game but also because it enables him to assess whether the suspects have previously committed what Battle describes as "the same *type* of crime".

Dr Roberts' victims appear to be Charles Craddock and possibly also his wife, who was his patient. Craddock believed (wrongly) that Roberts was having an affair with her and threatened to get him struck off. Craddock then died after contracting anthrax from an infected shaving brush. Anthrax was lethal unless treated with antibiotics whose commercial availability was only starting to develop in the 1930s.[1]

Presumably Roberts infected the brush in the Craddocks' dressing room after the threats (though, oddly, the parlourmaid says that Craddock was infected "already") and the anthrax entered Craddock's system through his facial skin, chafed from using a straight razor of the type that were common until the 1950s. Mrs

Craddock then went to Egypt and died from blood poisoning, after being inoculated against typhoid by Roberts, who may have introduced germs into her blood if she was being a nuisance and causing a scandal.

Anne Meredith lives in a cottage in Wallingford with a friend, Rhoda Dawes. At 18 she became a mother's help for a Mrs Eldon. She did this for two years before becoming a companion to Rhoda's aunt, Mrs Deering, which she did for three years. Two years ago she started to share the cottage with Rhoda.

What that resumé omits – because Meredith omitted it when talking to Battle – is the death of a Mrs Benson for whom she acted as a companion for a few weeks. Meredith broke a bottle of hat paint and Mrs Benson, who took syrup of figs, suggested putting the remaining paint in an old syrup of figs bottle. One night she drank from that bottle, instead of from her regular bottle, and died. Poirot thinks that Meredith swapped the bottles for fear of being exposed by Mrs Benson as a thief, which seems likely after she steals two pairs of stockings in a trap laid by Poirot.

Major Despard's victim is botanist Professor Timothy Luxmore whom he shot in the Amazon – either (according to Luxmore's widow) in self-defence or (according to Despard, who says he tried to shoot him in the leg) to stop him drowning in the river where he was heading in a fevered state.

The fourth suspect, Mrs Lorrimer, has been a widow for 20 years and doesn't seem to be associated with a mysterious death.

Armed with this information by chapter 24 (out of 31), do the past motives or methods make one suspect most likely to be the murderer? As to *method*, Shaitana was stabbed but none of the past victims were, so that doesn't help. As to *motive*, Shaitana's murder was motivated by fear of exposure and Roberts' and Meredith's past crimes were also motivated by fear, which contradicts what the Foreword says about the suspects' motives being peculiar to them, although there is perhaps a subtle difference in that Meredith feared exposure for theft while Roberts feared a professional complaint or scandal.

However, Despard's shooting was not, in either version, motivated by fear and so he can be discounted by reference to both motive and method, with Battle remarking that Despard, who killed by accident or in self-defence, "wasn't a murderer, after all" (chapter 24). This echoes Poirot's prediction in chapter 8 that one of the four would be innocent – again contradicting the Foreword, which says that all four are murderers. It also says that "an equal interest" should be attached to the four – which does not happen with Despard, thus again contradicting the Foreword.

So, if Lorrimer has no past crime, which of Roberts or Meredith is the more likely? Although Battle says that Roberts, having used "medical methods" before, would have used "the germ and not the knife" (chapter 19), he also says that he would know the right spot to shove the dagger in (chapter 8). Meredith's past murder, however, was what Battle calls "a *hopeful* kind of murder". It might work or not but it involved no risk while Shaitana's murder was audacious and purposeful. As Poirot says, "The two types of crime are not the same". So it must be plain to readers after the factual review (chapter 24) – and probably five chapters before – that Roberts, the obvious suspect after the psychological analysis, is now even more obvious.

Therefore the sleuths' dismissal of him as a suspect in chapter 19 seems to make no sense. And, if he is not the murderer, that just leaves Lorrimer, who suddenly claims, when Poirot visits her in chapter 25, to have killed Shaitana – a real surprise but an incredible one given how unlikely she is, psychologically and with no known past crime. However, she then says she murdered her husband, though we are not told her motive, merely that her reasons were her own. Fear of exposure for a past wrong seems an unlikely reason for murdering one's husband which, in terms of past motive providing a clue for Shaitana's murder, makes her an even less likely suspect, if that were possible.

Tenaciously (and correctly), Poirot refuses to believe she could have killed Shaitana unless she had planned it beforehand. She then admits to Poirot (but says she will deny doing so) that, not having long to live, she wanted to take the blame for Meredith whom she had seen bent over Shaitana with her hand on his breast and with a look of guilt and fear on her face.

The following morning Lorrimer is found dead, apparently having committed suicide after sending letters to the other three saying that she killed Shaitana. Roberts receives his letter first, just before 8 am, and dashes round to Lorrimer's house but we are told it is too late. When we then learn that Meredith had visited Lorrimer after Poirot's visit, we assume that she wrote the letters and somehow caused Lorrimer to take an overdose of her sleeping tablets; and her role as the villain seems confirmed in the next chapter when she dies during an unsuccessful attempt to drown Rhoda – the only person who could give a clue to the Benson (hat paint) incident.

So by chapter 30 everything seems to have played itself out, with Meredith as the murderer of Shaitana and Lorrimer. We applaud the author's cleverness in tricking us for so long into suspecting Roberts but feel a bit misled about being told that Meredith was not capable of a purposeful murder – clearly belied by her attempt to kill Rhoda – but not as misled as we would have felt if Despard or Lorrimer had been the murderer.

However, that is not the end because in a further twist it transpires that Roberts is the murderer after all – a very satisfying solution because it felt right for much of the book and yet by this stage it comes as a genuine surprise. Poirot explains that, when Meredith went over to the fireplace, she saw that Shaitana was already dead but dared not call out for fear – spotted by Lorrimer – that he had left a record about her Benson (hat paint) murder.

No description of Roberts' murder of Shaitana is given but one assumes that he would have noticed the dagger, been alert enough to purloin it and stabbed him while away from the bridge table. No particular ingenuity – though a lot of nerve – was required for this impromptu murder plan, although Roberts deserves credit for working out when best to commit it.

The risk that another player might look up from the bridge table would be much less likely during an exciting hand – such as a grand slam – when the players other than dummy would be focusing wholly on the game. So, in what the scorecards show was the final hand of the third rubber, Roberts bid a grand slam in a suit that his partner, Lorrimer, had bid first, so that she played the hand while Roberts as dummy went off to murder Shaitana.

That is clever. But Roberts' motive for murdering Lorrimer is unconvincing. Poirot says that he "lost his nerve" and became "uneasy" with Battle nosing about and so decided to blame Lorrimer. Roberts does say that it is not very pleasant to be under suspicion of murder but his loss of nerve is directly contrary to our understanding of his psychology.

Nevertheless, he "manages", Poirot says, to get a sample of her handwriting – we are not told how – forges the letters and arrives at her house with his story of the letter he has supposedly just received from her. He and the parlourmaid run up the stairs; he rushes into the room, takes a look at Lorrimer still asleep under the influence of her normal sleeping drug and says "Too late". But he sends the parlourmaid for brandy and hot water and then, according to her, tries to bring Lorrimer back but it can't be done. In fact, while she was gone, he had injected Evipan into Lorrimer's arm.

Plainly, with the forged letters and diversion of the parlourmaid, Roberts had given some thought to his murder plan and, subject to getting an example of Lorrimer's handwriting, it seems brilliantly simple. However, he should have expected her death to be carefully scrutinised and realised that it would be very risky to use a method that would leave a bruised arm and a substance that could be so easily detected. But then over-calling was part of his personality.

Plot

The titles of the author's Poirot books had so far been rather unimaginative. But *Cards on the Table* is different. The title refers, of course, to the bridge game during which the main murder is committed but also to the well-known expression for being honest about one's position. It is therefore a little surprising that it is not used in the latter sense until the sleuths' meeting in chapter 19. Race says that he'll play fair with the others and then Battle says "Cards on the table. That's the motto for this business. I mean to play fair".

However, having used it, the author does so again in that chapter and in chapters 20 and 24. But in the final chapter she overplays her hand by using further card references which look contrived. Thus, in relation to Roberts' murder of Lorrimer, Poirot says "This time the cards lay wrong for him" and later "And so – the gambler will gather in no more tricks. He has thrown his cards upon the table. *C'est fini*".

In the Foreword the author says that Captain Hastings (who does not appear in the book) considered the story "very dull". Indeed, one wonders whether the Foreword reveals a genuine anxiety about likely reader reaction to such an apparently simple plot and whether the reference there to "an argument in favour of this story" is a plea to readers to persevere.

If one takes Hastings' side, one can see why, with Roberts and then Meredith being such obvious suspects, he would have thought that the story lacked mystification. One can also see why he might have thought the third quarter of the book to be dull since from chapters 16 to 22 Poirot's focus is on the past crimes, none of which is very engaging.

However, Hastings is being too blinkered in his thinking. The author, in telling us that there are only four suspects and that the deduction must be entirely psychological, has imposed upon herself very confined parameters in which to plot and Hastings should be applauding her ambition and originality. He should also be recognising that whether she succeeds with her plotting depends more on the tightness of construction which, except for the contradictions of the Foreword, is generally very good.

Moreover, probably starting with Poirot's trap in which Meredith steals two pairs of stockings in chapter 23, the pace gradually accelerates. This continues with Lorrimer's claim to be the murderer, her accusation of Meredith, Lorrimer's 'suicide' and the attempted murder of Rhoda. Any dullness will surely have vanished even for Hastings by the end of chapter 27 and the story seems to have become more of a thriller than a detective story by chapter 30, with the apparent solution (Meredith as the villain) having been presented to us instead of being the result of detection. However, Poirot's detection comes to the fore in his explanations in chapter 31.

The author deserves credit for good misdirection in those final chapters. But there are a couple of slightly unsatisfying elements. After seeing Lorrimer's body, Poirot goes with Battle to Wallingford (where Meredith tries to drown Rhoda) and on his return goes straight to his flat. There he announces that Evipan has been discovered by the Home Office Analyst, Sir Charles Imphery. However, we are not told when Imphery's finding was reported to Poirot or when Poirot hinted to the police surgeon to look for Evipan.

Similarly, we do not know how or when Poirot instructed an actor, Gerald Hemmingway, to come to the denouement and pretend to have been cleaning Lorrimer's bedroom window at 8 am. Hemmingway claims to have seen Roberts jab something into her arm before she dropped back on the pillow. It is unsatisfactory that we are not told how this was arranged because it is that false 'evidence' which causes Roberts to admit that he injected Lorrimer.

Nevertheless, we feel that the plotting on the whole has been very satisfying, with the obvious suspect turning into an unexpected murderer. In particular, building the plot around only four suspects engages the reader's interest in detecting the murderer in a more focused way than is possible when there is a longer list of suspects or the prospect of an unexpected surprise.

The book also has humour and we are introduced to Mrs Ariadne Oliver who is the author's device for poking fun at some of her own characteristics and for expressing thoughts about various subjects including writing and police work. One of Mrs Oliver's stories is, we learn in chapter 2, *The Body in the Library*, which the author later writes herself, and she even refers (chapter 12) to being taken to Harrogate by a nurse who went home having forgotten about her – Harrogate and forgetfulness being vaguely reminiscent of the author's disappearance before being found at the Harrogate Hydro on 14 December 1926.

There are, however, some oddities in the book. In relation to the Benson (hat paint) incident, Battle says (chapter 19) that it must have happened "between the Isle of Wight and going to Miss Dawes" and that Meredith "went to Miss Dawes straight from the Isle of Wight". He refers twice to Miss Dawes but he must mean Mrs Deering. And the incident cannot have happened four years ago (as Rhoda says) or three years ago (as Mrs Oliver reports in chapter 19) because Meredith would have been with Mrs Deering. The author has clearly lost interest in these rather dull details, with Battle's mistakes even occurring in a paragraph where he says: "I've got her history taped out quite clearly".

He also seems to be wrong, along with Poirot, about when Shaitana was killed. They agree, only a few minutes after 12.10 am, that he had been dead "well over an hour". However, Roberts had said that he got up from the table three times, the last time

301

being at about 11.30 pm. Given the rate at which the hands were played between 9.30 pm and 12.10 am as estimated from the bridge scores, 11.30 pm would fit in pretty much exactly with when the grand slam would have been played in the last hand of the third rubber. So, if Shaitana was killed at 11.30 pm, he would not have been dead for "well over an hour" shortly after 12.10 am.

Clues

In chapter 31 Poirot says this case was one of his most interesting because there were "no tangible clues – only the people themselves". But immediately he contradicts himself by saying that there was "one tangible clue – the bridge scores", by which he means the scorecards on which each player kept score during the bridge game and which are reproduced in chapter 6.

From the start he showed a particular interest in these scores as well as in the hands played and he asked Roberts, Lorrimer and Despard how each hand was called and played, explaining in chapter 10 that he thought that the hands might be valuable landmarks in remembering other things.

Given his detailed interest in this, we try to follow the answers diligently, studying the scorecards and learning not only about the suspects' personalities but also – if we synthesise the information provided at different points – that four rubbers were played (the last unfinished); that they were scored in turn by Meredith, Despard, Lorrimer and Roberts; that Lorrimer's recollection of the hands was "magnificent", remembering every card, while Despard and Roberts could only remember two or three hands; that Lorrimer and Meredith had easily won the first rubber (with some good cards and over-bidding by the men); that Lorrimer and Despard had won the second rubber; that Lorrimer and Roberts had won the third rubber after a battle royal in which nearly 20 hands were played; that the fourth, unfinished rubber was a ding-dong battle, with Lorrimer partnering Despard again and neither side able to score; and that Lorrimer therefore won all the finished rubbers, that Roberts was a bit up and that Despard and Meredith must therefore have been a bit down.

Some readers will note that Poirot does not seek Meredith's recollection of the hands; that Roberts was not correct in saying that they had been one game all in the fourth rubber (since neither pair had scored); and that, as Despard amends the running total in respect of the eighth, ninth and tenth games of the second rubber from 440 to 410 to 480 (the figure is 480, not 450) and finally to 1060, he does not cancel out any figures (30, 70, 80) below the line.

However, despite our diligence, it transpires that Poirot has been after only one thing from the 'scorecards' clue (beyond the personality indicators). He had noticed that there was a score of 1500 points above the line in the third rubber, which could only represent one thing – the call of a grand slam – and he wanted to know how the bidding had gone because the risk of other players looking up from the cards was much less likely during such a hand and less likely still when doubled. So who bid it?

In chapter 11 Lorrimer explains that, after she had bid three diamonds and then five spades, Roberts "suddenly jumped to seven diamonds". She says that he had no business to make such a call, that they were doubled and that she never thought they would get the slam when she saw his hand go down. Her reference to seeing Roberts' hand go down is important because it would not otherwise be clear to a non-bridge player which of the pair actually played the hand and who was dummy (and therefore the potential murderer). Indeed, Lorrimer says "we" got the grand slam twice in the relevant paragraph while Roberts had said earlier (chapter 10) "I got a grand slam". So some readers might well be cleverly misled into thinking that Roberts had played the cards whereas bridge players will know from Lorrimer's description of the bidding that, because Roberts had bid the slam in the suit which she had bid first, she would necessarily have played it while he was dummy.

The reckless bidding of a grand slam causing the other suspects to focus on the hand while the bidder, as dummy, commits the murder is an excellent clue and is concealed about as fairly as it could be. When Poirot says "I am sure I am right … It *must* be that" at the end of chapter 11 (in which Lorrimer tells him about the grand slam bidding), he must have the 'grand slam' clue in mind, thus being a very strong pointer to Roberts, even without the personality clues which already make him the most obvious suspect.

Poirot then says that he next approached the matter from his "second angle – psychological probability". In fact, he does not then say much about the suspects' psychology – though he had in earlier chapters set out his views, including the important Roberts 'over-calling' personality clue.

Poirot then says that he next made "a second test" – which is a bit confusing given his earlier reference to a "second angle" – namely to get the suspects to tell him what they remembered of the drawing room, from which he got some "very valuable information". "First of all", he says, Roberts was by far the most likely to have noticed the dagger because he was a natural observer of trifles of all kinds. This 'observer' clue is quite clever and also fair because Roberts listed the items in the drawing room in more detail than the others.

However, the clue starts to deteriorate when Roberts asks Poirot whether he included in his quite long list the object which Poirot had in mind. Poirot's esoteric reply is that, if Roberts had mentioned it, it would have been "extremely surprising" and says "As I thought, you could not mention it". Some readers may assume that Poirot had the dagger in mind, wanting to see if Roberts would mention it (which he did not) or avoid doing so. However, Poirot never tells us what object he had in mind or what his purpose was in replying as he did, which leaves the 'observer' clue rather incomplete.

The clue becomes more obscure when Poirot suggests that perhaps Roberts could not mention the object "because it was not there to mention". He may mean, *if* he is referring to the dagger, that it had already been taken. However, that is not clear from his words which, he suggests, remind Roberts of the Sherlock Holmes incident (in *Silver Blaze*) where the dog did not howl in the night. But that does not work here because Poirot's words are never explained and seem only to have been included as a contrivance to allow him to refer to the Sherlock Holmes incident. The reader will sympathise with Roberts, who tells Poirot that he is "completely at sea as to what you are driving at".

By the time Poirot asks Meredith for her description of the room in chapter 23, he tells her that none of Lorrimer, Roberts or Despard has given me "the response I had hoped for". What does he mean? We are never told. Perhaps he was hoping that one or more of them would mention the dagger, in which case such honesty might suggest innocence. But none of the three mentions it.

Meredith does remember a case of Egyptian jewellery and Poirot suggests that this was at the other end of the room from the table which had the dagger on it. Readers will immediately think that Poirot has laid a trap about the dagger, which Meredith avoids by saying that she never heard which table the dagger was on. To their surprise, however, he comments that he would never lay a *piege* (trap) as gross as that. This comment is strange because in the next chapter he tells Battle that it *was* a clumsy trap for Meredith which, once avoided, would relax her vigilance before she then fell into the real trap by stealing two pairs of stockings from Poirot, so giving him the 'stolen stockings' clue which confirms her as a thief. But the fact is that the first trap was still a *piege*.

So, having "First of all" identified Roberts as the most likely observer, what other "valuable information" did Poirot get from his second test? Strangely he does not tell us but reverts to talking about Roberts' and Lorrimer's memory of the scorecards (rather than the room), saying that Roberts' forgetfulness suggested he had something else on his mind, which is not compelling, *if* intended as a clue, since Despard's recollection of the cards was just as bad.

In fact, Poirot had also learned from his second test that Meredith, a timid girl, was poor but fond of pretty things – "The temperament, is it not, of a *thief* rather than a murderer" (chapter 24). So he wonders if she had stolen from her employers. He had established that Mrs Eldon was untidy – the 'untidiness' clue being a good one to her assuming that any items stolen by Meredith had disappeared because of her own carelessness. But what if her next employer, Mrs Benson, had accused her of theft? That, he suggests, would be a motive for murder. However, it will seem illogical to readers for Poirot's reasoning, which starts with the express premise that Meredith does *not* have the temperament of a murderer, to end with the conclusion that she may have murdered Mrs Benson.

Poirot's "third test" was the discovery of the earlier murders to establish a similarity of method. Although none of those victims was stabbed, he says that Roberts' two murders, when examined "from the psychological point of view", were almost exactly the same as the Shaitana murder for two reasons.

First, they had also been "public murders", by which he seems to mean that they were committed while Roberts was openly carrying out his professional duties. But it is hard to regard this 'public murder' clue as a strong one since infecting a shaving brush in a victim's dressing room and giving an inoculation in a doctor's surgery are not directly comparable to the murder of Shaitana, which was genuinely committed in public in the sense that it was done in the presence of others.

Secondly, that Roberts' reaction with the past crimes was the same as in Shaitana's case – "Pushed into a corner, he seizes a chance and acts at once". Roberts did indeed act at once in relation to Craddock and he seized his chance with Mrs Craddock's inoculation, so this 'seizing a chance' clue fairly reflects what he did with Shaitana. But the clue is perhaps equally as applicable to Meredith's attempt to drown Rhoda.

One clue which Poirot does not explain clearly is his reference in chapter 8 to there being "a nuance" in the answers given by the four suspects when asked whom they thought was the murderer. Roberts thought Despard; Despard thought Roberts; Meredith thought that it couldn't be any of them but ruled out Lorrimer last; and Lorrimer refused to say.

Poirot says in the final chapter that Lorrimer's manner suggested that she had either committed the murder or knew who had. He does not use the word 'nuance' at that point but that is the only 'nuance' to which he could have been referring in chapter 8. However, there is nothing to enable readers to deduce such a 'nuance' either in the language or the manner of Lorrimer's refusal to answer what she fairly regarded as a most improper question.

Nevertheless, she did believe that Meredith had done it and we do get clues, more noticeable in retrospect, that Meredith might have feared exposure for the Benson (hat paint) murder – drawing in her breath in chapter 6; her hand shaking during the bridge game in chapter 10; her hand tightening on the chair in chapter 12; and pulling her hand away from Despard in chapter 13.

However, that still leaves us with her timidity – although other clues do make us wonder if she really was too timid to murder Shaitana. For example, her club was the Ladies' Naval and Military Club (chapter 6); and she was part of "the ski-ing lot" (chapter 14) – both of which suggest the opposite of timidity – and she even suggested that stabbing seemed more like a woman's crime (chapter 6).

Moreover, in chapter 17, Mrs Oliver says to Rhoda "Take care of yourself, my dear" – a normal farewell but one which readers may note because Mrs Oliver then says to herself "Now, why did

I say that?". We never get an answer but it might be a clue to Mrs Oliver expecting Rhoda to be in danger from Meredith since she had just learned of the poisoning in Meredith's past.

Poirot too regards Meredith as "dangerous" after Lorrimer tells him that she had seen Meredith murder Shaitana. He even says, coupling the Shaitana murder with the Benson (hat paint) murder, "With Mademoiselle Anne those two crimes will not be the end". So it will seem odd to readers that he does nothing when he sees a lady looking like Meredith going up the steps of Lorrimer's house just after he has left.

Even though he is not sure that the person is Meredith, readers would expect him to take action since he clearly thinks she could well be the murderer. Yet he goes home and, even after repeating to Battle that Meredith is "dangerous", just sits in front of his fire and goes to bed, knowing not what the morning would bring. Readers rightly guess that it will bring Lorrimer's death but will wrongly assume that Meredith, who was in fact the visitor, is the culprit.

Which brings us, finally, to Lorrimer's murder. Poirot establishes that she is very unlikely to have written the suicide letters because she went to bed after Meredith had left and would have had to get up again to post them herself because her servants had not done so. He then spots a dark, discoloured bruise on her arm (this 'bruised arm' clue being the key one in the Lorrimer murder) and realises that she has been injected intravenously.

He then asks what is said to be "an irrelevant question" – whether Roberts had had breakfast when he arrived at Lorrimer's. It is not clear why the question is irrelevant since Poirot says, once told that Roberts had not had breakfast, that he would therefore be back at home (having breakfast) and could be contacted. Perhaps the author meant that the question was irrelevant to the murder.

Anyway, having got the answer, Poirot rings him at home and asks him if he is well acquainted with Lorrimer's handwriting.

Roberts says that he doesn't know that he's ever seen it before. Poirot later says that this was an "awkward moment" for Roberts because, if the forgery has been detected, he must save himself by saying that he has never seen the handwriting. He says that Roberts' mind worked quickly but not quickly enough.

Poirot's point here will not be apparent to readers, who will be wondering what this 'awkward moment' clue told Poirot since it is hard to see what answer Roberts could have given other than his negative one, which might even be taken for the truth? Is Poirot suggesting that, if Roberts' mind had worked more quickly, he should have said "Yes" in case the forgery had not been detected? Surely not. How would Roberts benefit from this? And it would leave him open to suspicion if a forgery was discovered later.

However, faced with the 'evidence' of Hemmingway, the Evipan and Battle's reference to the Craddocks, Roberts throws in his hand. He killed Shaitana. But should he have thrown in his hand? There was no evidence against him for the Shaitana murder. There is the excellent 'grand slam' clue, the very helpful 'over-calling' personality clue and the quite clever 'observer' clue. But these are not evidence. And Poirot's clues based on the similarity of the Craddock murders, for which there is no evidence either, are not strong ones.

Roberts' downfall came from murdering Lorrimer who, unknown to him, was actually accusing Meredith. Even though he murdered Lorrimer because he surprisingly lost his nerve, one might have expected him to have bluffed it out more in the penultimate chapter. But, having admitted injecting Lorrimer (with, he claims, a simple restorative) in response to Hemmingway's 'evidence', there was probably no point in further resistance once told that the substance was Evipan since realistically no one else could have injected this.

14

Dumb Witness

Solution

Poirot and the narrator, Captain Hastings, investigate the death of Emily Arundell, a wealthy, elderly spinster, who dies on 1 May 1936 at Littlegreen House in Market Basing. She had lived there with her companion of about a year, Wilhelmina Lawson, her maid (Ellen), her cook (Annie) and her dog, a wire-haired terrier called Bob.

Under Emily's will of 21 April 1936, her estate passed to Miss Lawson rather than her three relations, Charles, Theresa and Bella, who knew that under her previous will they would each have inherited one third.

Charles and Theresa Arundell were the children of Emily's deceased brother Thomas. Charles, in his early thirties and unmarried, was in a hole financially while Theresa, aged 28–29 and engaged to Dr Rex Donaldson, needed money to maintain her extravagant lifestyle and to enable Rex to pursue his medical research. Bella Tanios was the daughter of Emily's deceased sister Arabella. She was married to a Greek, Dr Jacob Tanios, who had speculated with her money unsuccessfully. They lived in Smyrna but were presently in England.

Although Emily died on 1 May, Poirot does not become involved until 28 June on receiving a letter from her seeking his help in relation to "the incident of the dog's ball". He is intrigued by the letter being dated 17 April, so he goes to Market Basing, where he learns that Emily had died soon after writing it.[1]

Gradually the story is put together. Charles, Theresa, Bella and Jacob had stayed with Emily at Easter from 11 to 15 April. On Easter Sunday 12 April, Charles, having had a request for money refused by Emily, told her that she was "going about it the right way to get bumped off", although readers will feel, from his account of the incident to Theresa and Poirot (chapters 2 and 19), that he wasn't seriously threatening her.

On Wednesday 15 April, at about 1 am, Emily, who would wander round the house at night, fell down the stairs. She might have been killed but was only cut and bruised and had to spend a week in bed. The fall was attributed to her having slipped on Bob's black rubber ball, found at the top of the stairs.

Readers had learned in chapter 1 that a favourite game of Bob's was to lie at the top of the stairs with his ball between his paws and nose it towards the edge before sending it bumping down the stairs, to be picked up by someone who tossed it back up to him so that he could catch it in his mouth before doing it again. He often left the ball at the top of the stairs – Charles had stumbled on it there in chapter 1 and Hastings does so in chapter 8.

However, Emily could not recall slipping on the ball. She concluded, Poirot later suggests, that Charles had tried to kill her. So she had written to Poirot on 17 April, referring to "the incident of the dog's ball". But she had forgotten to post the letter and it was not until 27 June that it was found and posted by Ellen. So there was an innocent explanation for the mystery of the delayed letter.

Also on 17 April, Emily wrote to her solicitor, in a letter which she did post, asking him to draw up her new will in favour of Miss Lawson executed on 21 April. Poirot suggests she had two reasons – first, spite against her family, who were after her money; and secondly to protect herself against any further attempt by showing the will to Charles, as she did over the next weekend of 25/26 April (chapter 14), so indicating that murder would bring him nothing.

Then on 27 April Emily became ill. After dinner she participated in a séance with Miss Lawson and her friends, Isabel and Julia Tripp. In the darkness Miss Lawson saw a luminous ribbon issuing from Emily's mouth and a luminous mist (or, as the Tripps described it, a luminous halo or haze) around her head. That was the start of the illness from which she died four days later.

She had nearly died 18 months before from a similar attack, described as "jaundice" (chapters 7 and 8). However, she had recovered and had no more serious attacks until the fatal one. But what, readers will ask, actually killed her since jaundice, with its yellowing of the skin, is just a symptom of illness? We assume we will learn in chapter 9 when Poirot visits Dr Grainger but, astonishingly, he doesn't even ask. Although Hastings says (chapter 15) that Grainger thought that Emily had died "a perfectly natural death", he had said no such thing and, frustratingly, it is not until chapter 21 (out of 30) that we learn that Grainger believes that Emily died of yellow atrophy of the liver.

By then, nearly three quarters of the way through the story, this news is too late for readers who will have realised that, whatever illness supposedly killed Emily, she was in fact poisoned and that the luminous haze is relevant to this. What few readers will have worked out is that the poison was phosphorus.

The murderer, who had some chemistry knowledge, knew of Emily's liver trouble and that the symptoms of phosphorus poisoning would look like a liver infection such as yellow atrophy. It was not hard to get phosphorus ("Foreign matches – vermin paste", says Poirot) and a small dose would kill, with the victim's breath perhaps becoming phosphorescent (hence the "luminous ribbon") before she felt affected. The murderer simply opened one of the capsules which Emily took after meals (Dr Loughbarrow's Liver Capsules – a creation of the author) and placed the phosphorus inside, knowing that one day Emily would swallow it and that poison was unlikely to be suspected.

Poirot says "Oh! It was well-planned" in chapter 29 but minimal planning was needed – just putting phosphorus in a capsule. He is more accurate when later describing it as "child's play" but, in fairness, it was clever of the murderer, and inventive of the author, to spot how perfect phosphorus would be to use on someone with liver trouble.

However, the murder is not the only crime because Emily's fall arose from an attempt to kill her. When Poirot first visits the house, he spots, impressively, a nail in the skirting board at the top of the stairs, varnished so as not to show. Having learned that Emily would wander about at night, he suggests that the dog's ball would have given the criminal the idea of stretching a thread across the stairs. Although it could be tied on one side to a baluster supporting the banister handrail, something would be needed on the inner wall for attaching the thread, like a nail. If Emily fell, that would be blamed on the dog's ball placed at the top of the stairs by the criminal.

In chapter 20 Poirot learns from Ellen that a loop of thread had been round the nail. In chapter 22 he learns that on the night before the fall Miss Lawson had been woken by a tapping – which he suggests was the sound of a hammer on a nail. She had noticed a smell of varnish, before seeing in her looking glass a woman kneeling on about the third step with her head bent over something.

Like the murder, there is no clever plan for the attempt – just a thread across the stairs – so it is odd that Poirot describes it as "ingenious" (chapter 29). He is more sensible when saying "a child could have thought of it" (chapter 18). Indeed, it seems stupid of the criminal to have used the quiet of the night for tapping in and varnishing a nail opposite a door that was open (for Miss Lawson to see if Emily went downstairs) and by a passage that was lit (so it was not too dark during Emily's night-time walks). It is not surprising that the criminal was heard and smelled – and even (partially) seen – by Miss Lawson.

Poirot first lists the suspects in chapter 12 when saying that the thread could only have been tied after everyone had gone to bed, so that only the house occupants were suspects – "the guilt lies between seven people" – Charles, Theresa, Bella, Jacob, Miss Lawson, Ellen and Annie. But in chapter 25 he adds Rex Donaldson, having learned (chapter 14) that he had dined at the house that night. This is strange because Poirot is surely right that the thread could only have been tied after everyone had gone to bed – and yet Donaldson rose to leave the house at 10 pm. Perhaps he had in mind Hastings' idea (chapter 25) that Donaldson might have left a window open and returned later.

Miss Lawson is initially the most obvious suspect, as the beneficiary under Emily's will. But it will be pretty clear to readers by about chapter 22, as she tells Poirot about the nail and the varnish, that she is not the villain because she seems so genuinely surprised that someone had tried to kill Emily.

Various characters make comments to the effect that Charles (chapter 10), Bella (chapter 15) and Theresa (chapter 17) could commit murder and there are hints that Charles and Theresa's mother may have been a murderer, so they have "bad heredity" – but this is a red herring.

However, the comment about Bella, made by Miss Lawson – that she would "*murder* someone if he [Jacob] told her to" reflects more on Jacob than on her. Indeed, we know that Bella seemed "afraid" of Jacob: in chapter 15 she had looked "simply terrified"; in chapter 17 she had a "hunted, harried look" when saying she *must* tell Poirot something before changing the subject when Jacob came over; and by chapter 26 she has an "obvious air of terror". Certainly, by then, Jacob has taken over from Miss Lawson as the most obvious suspect.

For readers who exonerated Miss Lawson even before chapter 22, Jacob will have been the most obvious suspect since chapter 17, although, like her, too obvious. We know (chapter 8) that he and Bella visited Emily at the weekend after Easter (18/19 April) and that he had a special mixture made up for Emily, which she poured away (chapter 16); that he had visited Emily next Sunday (26 April) on his own (chapter 15) and may well not have told Bella about that visit (chapter 17); and that he showed a "momentary apprehension" (never explained) when Poirot wondered if he could ask him a question (chapter 17).

But in fact he is just the innocent target of attempts to implicate him by the murderer – Bella. She was not afraid of him. She disliked him. The one thing illuminating her life was the expectation of money on the death of Aunt Emily whom she planned to murder. She tried by staging the fall – and failed. Then she succeeded at the second attempt – but the money went to Miss Lawson.

Poirot was convinced that Bella, who was fairly sure he suspected her, planned to murder Jacob and to stage his pretended suicide and confession for Emily's murder after forging his name on a prescription and buying chloral hydrate, a sleeping draught, from the chemist. So Poirot wrote out his solution to the case and gave it to Bella, who killed herself with an overdose of the chloral hydrate, thinking this was best for their children (chapter 28).

As a personality, Bella comes across as almost too pathetic to be a murderer. Charles even says that she "is marked out by fate to be a victim" (chapter 19), though in a sense he is right because of her suicide. In fact, she kills herself *before* readers are told (in chapter 29) that she is the murderer. So, in what should be a clever piece of misdirection, she is not actually present as a suspect when Poirot assembles the others for the traditional denouement, which encourages us to think that she can't be the murderer. Unfortunately, however, Hastings, overdoes the misdirection, saying "Yes, there was no doubt of it. *One of these people was a murderer!*" – which turns out to be simply untrue, as Hastings would have known when he wrote the narrative.

Plot

The first thing readers notice is the title. It suggests the intriguing prospect that the "intelligent" and "almost human" Bob has witnessed a key event but cannot describe it. But in fact Bob did not witness the fall or murder or any clue left by the murderer. So the imaginative title doesn't seem to deliver what one expects (though see under Clues). However, it is better than the United States title, *Poirot Loses A Client*, because Emily was not Poirot's client or, at least, not treated by him as one until she had *already* been lost.

The second is the length of the book. Published in July 1937, it was the author's longest to date – and noticeably longer than her previous ten novels.[2]

The third is the structure of the opening. The first six paragraphs of chapter 1 are written "weeks and even months" after Emily died; then there is a flashback for nearly four chapters (from 10 to 17 April); and then a jump forward to 28 June when Hastings becomes the narrator (until chapter 30). Readers may well think that, if Poirot had received Emily's letter of 17 April on 28 June and then gone to Littlegreen House, only to find that she had died nearly two months ago, this would have made a more engaging opening than the first four chapters, which are pedestrian and mainly contain information revealed to Poirot (at length) over the next dozen or so chapters, causing Hastings to plead in chapter 18 "No, no, Poirot, don't go over it all again!".[3]

The problem is that the facts relate more to the background and Emily's family (what they are like and what they want) than to the crimes – which is unsurprising since, with such simple murder plans, there is so little evidence to gather and such little plotting to do. So the story is more about working out why people behaved as they did than about solving a mystifying *whodunnit*, which makes one feel one is reading a work from another genre. When Poirot says in chapter 12 that the drama "resembles, does it not, a novelette of older days?", he is correct, as the author plainly recognises. What is odd is her using her longest novel so far for such simple murder plans.

Readers will also be frustrated by not knowing what is even *thought* to have caused Emily's death until chapter 21; by some unconvincing analysis at the denouement; and by some of Poirot's other minor assumptions. Thus he calls the maid "Ellen" in chapter 8, though there has been no mention of her name. In chapter 9 he identifies Dr Grainger's house without any indication of how he could know this. In chapter 19 he says that Emily wrote to her lawyer on 17 April, without knowing that she had written to him (only that he was "sent for") or that she did so on 17 April. And he repeatedly describes the person who tied the thread as a "murderer" (though it is not yet certain that that person killed Emily), referring in chapter 18 to "a murderer – in intention if not in fact". But the "fact" is needed for murder – one cannot be a "murderer" until one has killed someone, which he finally recognises in chapter 22.

Other minor frustrations are Emily's father being called Charles in chapter 2 (he is John at least four other times including on his gravestone) and Bella's son being called John in chapters 16 and 17 (he is Edward in chapter 2), though he is changed to Edward in some later editions. And there is an oddity relating to Bob's trick with the ball: he noses it "slowly and slowly nearer the edge" (chapter 1). Should it not be 'slowly *nearer and nearer* the edge'? On the plus side chapter 24 contains a joke when Theresa calls Hastings "St Leonards" (a suburb of the town of Hastings on the English south coast).

Finally, chapter 18 is titled "A Nigger in the Woodpile" – a saying that refers to an unknown person or thing causing a problem. It is in quotation marks because Poirot uses the words before adding "There is – not a nigger – but a murderer in our woodpile". The title remains unchanged even though, for reasons of racial decency, British publishers of *Ten Little Niggers* changed that title to *And Then There Were None* from the mid-1980s. Perhaps it is not so easy to change a chapter title when Poirot uses the words – though it is not clear why he does when we already know there is a murderer in the woodpile.

Clues

In chapter 6 Poirot says "The Hercule Poirots, my friend, need only to sit back in a chair and think". Yet the opening clue for Poirot (in chapter 8) is a tangible one – the varnished nail at the top of the stairs. This 'varnished nail' clue sets him on his way to reconstructing "the incident of the dog's ball".

Readers know from the narrative that at 6.30 pm on the evening of her fall Emily put away Bob's ball in the drawer of the bureau (chapter 2) or table (chapter 8); that she went to bed after 10 pm; that Miss Lawson then let Bob out for his run; that Emily fell down the stairs at about 1 am (attributed to Bob's ball at the top of the stairs – the 'dog's ball' clue); and that, after she had been treated for her fall and returned to bed, she was woken by Bob barking for admission outside the front door at about 5 am.

In reconstructing the "incident" in chapter 9, Poirot makes two assumptions which (as we know from the narrative) are correct – first, that Emily remembered hearing Bob barking at 5 am; and secondly (which he admits is "guess-work") that Emily herself put away Bob's ball in its drawer. He therefore concludes that, because Emily had put the ball away and Bob went out "After that" and did not return until 5 am, it could not have been Bob – but must have been a human – who left the ball at the top of the stairs (in order for Bob – rather than the thread – to take the blame).

Poirot's deduction (based on his two assumptions) that it was a human – and that the 'dog's ball' clue was not a genuine one – seems like a very good one. It *may* also explain (though we are never actually told this) the sense in which Bob is a 'witness', namely as a provider of evidence with the 'Bob barking' clue (his barking at 5 am, revealing that he had been out all night). Ironically, though, his barking is the very occasion on which he is not 'dumb'.

An issue with Poirot's deduction is that, although his words "After that" rather imply that Bob went out soon after Emily had put the ball away, there was in fact a long gap between her doing so at 6.30 pm and Bob being let out after 10 pm. So, one wonders whether during that period someone else could innocently have taken out the ball and played with Bob, who simply left the ball at the top of the stairs before being let out. Poirot does not explore that possibility, perhaps because Emily might then have seen the ball on her way to bed.

One also wonders what entitled Poirot to make his two (correct) assumptions. He relies on "significant words" uttered by Emily after the fall (as reported by Ellen) – something about Bob's ball and a "picture ajar", as he puts it (chapter 9). He realised that, since one does not talk of a picture being "ajar" (only a door), she meant "a jar" (two words); and there had been a jar in the drawing room with a picture of a dog on it and written below were the words: "*Out all night and no key*". Thus, says Poirot, Emily in her feverish state thought Bob was like that dog – out all night – so could not have left the ball on the stairs.[4]

The 'picture ajar' clue is very contrived but its real problem is that it does not actually support either of Poirot's two assumptions – that Emily heard Bob *barking* or put the ball away herself. Nor are they supported by Ellen's only other relevant facts, namely that Bob occasionally went out until 4 am and then barked until he was let in; that that night he had come home at about 5 am; and that

Miss Lawson had hurried down to let him in *before* he could bark because she was afraid he would wake Emily.

So, although Poirot is right with his assumptions, he is not entitled to be on the basis of what he learned. However, his first assumption (that Emily heard Bob barking) links with a genuine clue of "supreme importance", as Poirot puts it in chapter 18. This is Ellen's statement that Miss Lawson hurried downstairs in an (unsuccessful) attempt to let Bob in before his barking woke Emily.

This 'stop Bob barking' clue means that Miss Lawson did not stage the fall. As Poirot explains in chapter 29, since she would not have inherited under the will in force before 21 April, her only motive for staging the fall on 14 April would have been to make Emily suspect her family and so change her will. If she had wanted to achieve this, she would have stressed that Bob was *out* that night, so it must have been a human who left the ball on the stairs. In fact she did the opposite by trying to *prevent* Emily hearing that Bob had been out. So, as Poirot says, she "*must* be innocent" of staging the fall.

This is a clever deduction because the reader's instinct will be that, by trying to conceal Bob's absence from Emily, Miss Lawson was acting nefariously, given that she is initially the most obvious suspect for her murder. An oddity, however, is that, having declared she *must* be innocent, Poirot then eliminates her on a different ground (13 paragraphs later in chapter 29) when saying that she would hardly have told him about the luminous ectoplasm (ribbon) if she was connected with the murder.

It was that evidence, coupled with that of the Tripp sisters about a luminous halo or haze, which provided the clue to phosphorus being the murder weapon, although only readers with a knowledge of chemistry could deduce this from the 'luminous' clues.

Poirot presumably had the luminous ribbon in mind when saying that "one statement" stood out from Miss Lawson's conversation (chapter 18). But Hastings (with good misdirection) asks whether he means that Emily had curry for dinner. In fact, Miss Lawson had not mentioned curry (it was Ellen) but Poirot responds "Yes, the curry has a certain significance, perhaps". However, he never explains what. Although Emily's taste for rich food was thought to have caused her illness, that cannot be what Poirot had in mind if he was focusing on the luminous ribbon as clueing the cause.

Although phosphorous was the murder weapon, it was administered in one of Emily's liver capsules. The 'liver capsule' clue is fairly presented by being referred to on half a dozen occasions in chapters 21 and 22, with Poirot even opening one of the capsules on the last occasion.

A key question is whether the murder (with the phosphorus capsule) and the attempted murder (with the thread) were executed by the same person – which brings us to the 'same outline' clue. At the denouement, Poirot says that both crimes had the "same outline" because both were simple, cunning, carried out efficiently and required a certain amount of knowledge, but "not a great deal".

Poirot's use of the 'same outline' clue, and particularly his reference to the murder requiring "not a great deal" of knowledge, seems designed to extricate him from two difficulties of his own making. The first is that in chapter 25 he had said that phosphorus poisoning is "a highly scientific one needing fully-specialised knowledge". Indeed, in chapter 29 he eliminates Ellen and Annie because their mentality was not adapted to phosphorus poisoning.

The second is that, despite having said in chapter 25 "There is the mark of one brain and one brain only in this", he confusingly then agrees with Hastings that the kind of person to have laid the original booby trap (the thread across the stairs) was not the kind to plan a scientific murder. "Exactly", he says, which leads Hastings to deduce, unsurprisingly, that the only logical solution is that the murder and the attempt were planned by two different people.

It is by referring in chapter 29 to both crimes having the "same outline" that Poirot extricates himself from this inconsistency and confusion. To do this, he has to backpedal from his remark that the murder was a "highly scientific one". He does so, without referring to that remark, by saying "The facts about phosphorus poisoning are easily learned". In other words, he resolves the inconsistency by indicating that phosphorus poisoning did *not* need "fully-specialised knowledge" – it was simple, like the thread across the stairs – but readers would do extremely well to realise this while reading chapter 25.

As to the remaining five suspects, he absolves Charles from the poisoning because, having seen the new will on 25/26 April, he knew he would not inherit. But what clues did Emily have that he had staged the fall? Poirot gives us two. One, of course, is Charles' remark about Emily getting bumped off. But, as Poirot says, it was made "lightly enough".

The other is that Charles had nearly disgraced the family name before, having forged Emily's name to a cheque. What we had actually been told, in relation to the 'forged cheque' clue, was that he was wanted by the police in a foreign country (chapter 11); he was sent down from Oxford for forging a cheque (chapter 14); there was a fracas with Emily and the local bank (chapter 14); and his troubles were always hushed up, once by sending him to Australia (chapter 15). Then Poirot adds "After forgery – a step further – murder!". Surely he cannot be serious. He must be describing Emily's thinking rather than his own because he later says the opposite when suggesting that Charles' psychology is such that his crimes will always be "crimes of weakness. To steal, to forge – yes, it is the easiest way – but to kill – no".

Nevertheless, this does seem to have been Emily's thinking and Poirot reckons that it is revealed by further clues – "the terms of her letter" (the one she sent to Poirot) and her subsequent actions. By her "subsequent actions", he means showing the will to Charles to protect herself, this 'self-protection' clue being described by Poirot as "absolutely conclusive". That is a good point but the same cannot be said about his reasoning based on "the terms of the letter".

He says that the "tenor" of the letter was that the business be kept private since the family's honour was involved. The letter does stress the need for privacy but there is no reference to this being based on family honour and it is not reasonably inferred from the 'tenor of the letter' clue. He adds that, from a Victorian point of view, this meant that someone of Emily's own *name* was indicated – preferably a *man*. These are two large leaps from the already shaky reliance on family honour.

One clue that Emily did not have relating to Charles was that some arsenic used for weeding at the house had disappeared and that he had paused in chapter 9 before saying "strychnine" (perhaps he was going to say "arsenic"). However, it was not Charles, but Theresa, who took the arsenic. Poirot says at the denouement that he "felt sure" it was her but he does not explain why. Whatever the answer, Theresa did not use the arsenic, which is a red herring.

Having absolved Miss Lawson, Ellen, Annie and Charles, Poirot falls back, for the four remaining suspects, on the "psychology" or "character" of the crimes – and what this said about the "personality" or "temperament" of the criminal. In doing so, he first concludes that, although Jacob and Donaldson were doctors who might have thought of phosphorus, the incident of the dog's ball seemed not to fit the masculine mind but to be essentially a woman's idea.

Why this should be so is not clear and readers will feel that this is weak reasoning, particularly as the sole basis for eliminating Jacob who seems such an obvious suspect because of Bella's apparent fear of him. However, we do get some clues to his true personality when we are told that he is a jolly, amusing man (chapter 1) and "a thoroughly nice fellow" (chapter 14) who would not hurt a fly because he is "much too kind-hcartcd" (chaptcr 19).

That leaves Theresa and Bella. He dismisses Theresa because her "type of person" (who had lived fully and selfishly and never been "thwarted") was not the type to kill – except in sudden anger. But his reliance on this 'never thwarted' clue should surprise readers because Theresa had told him that when she, Charles or Bella asked Emily for a loan, Emily would tell them to wait for her money until she was dead (chapter 13). So Theresa, with a constant need for money which Emily would not supply, was permanently "thwarted".

It is also surprising that he should dismiss her on personality grounds after just describing her as "bold, ruthless, and not over scrupulous", with "quite sufficient strength of mind to carry such a design through" and when readers know (chapter 2) that "For Rex she would do anything – anything!".

Nevertheless he is right about Theresa, which brings us finally to the clueing of Bella – a mixture of good and weak points but sufficiently fair that, even though Miss Lawson and Jacob are at times more obvious suspects and she never comes across as a convincing murderer (and is already dead at the denouement), readers should be disappointed if they do not spot her as the villain.

Poirot regards the most telling clue as her "personality" or "temperament" – so much so that he was, he says at the denouement, "convinced from the first moment I saw her that Mrs Tanios was the person I was looking for", which sounds like very impressive detection.

That first moment occurred at the start of chapter 16 and his meeting with her lasts until the end of chapter 17, which is when, with her hunted, harried look, she says she *must* tell him something but changes the subject as Jacob comes over. When Hastings wonders if she will tell them later, Poirot says "I rather fear – she may not", giving readers the clear impression that she will not tell them because of her apparent fear of Jacob.

However, he says at the denouement that, when Bella pretended she could not speak in front of Jacob, he realised that she did not fear him but disliked him and "at once, summing the matter up, I felt convinced that here was the exact character I had been looking for". Readers will have noted that Poirot was "at once" *convinced* about Bella at that point (the end of chapter 17) even though he had said, eight paragraphs earlier at the denouement, that he had been *convinced* about Bella when he "first" saw her (the start of chapter 16).

Before meeting her, he had heard from others that she was "dull" (chapter 10), "dreary" and "rather pathetic" (chapter 14). At the denouement he describes more fully why she was "the exact character" he was looking for. She was a "thwarted" woman – a plain girl, leading a dull existence, unable to attract the men she would like, finally accepting a man she did not care for and feeling exiled in Smyrna with that man, who had speculated with and lost her money.

So, while Poirot had deployed the 'never thwarted' clue for Theresa (to suggest she did not kill Emily), he now deploys the 'thwarted' clue for Bella (to suggest she did). But being 'thwarted' doesn't, on its own, seem like a convincing reason for murder.

A better adjective might have been 'stupid' – not just for using the quiet of the night to tap in and varnish a nail near a lit passage opposite an open door, but for leaving the nail there with the thread around it. Indeed, an oddity about the clueing of Bella is that Poirot does not rely on the 'stupidity' clue. So perhaps it was not intended as a clue but that would be surprising given Isabel Tripp's comment that Bella is "absolutely stupid" (chapter 11) and his comment that "stupidity" can go hand in hand with intense cunning (chapter 18).

So, what clues, beyond her personality, does he rely on? The first is her fear. He says that, as soon as he saw her, he realised she was afraid and that, when she saw he realised this, she pretended to be afraid *for* Jacob – saying that anything said against him was untrue and that Emily was *most* ungrateful in pouring away his digestive mixture. However, a little later – and this is the clue – she pretended to be afraid *of* Jacob. According to Poirot, a woman can be afraid *for* her husband or *of* her husband – but hardly both – and that he was not deceived by her 'change' over chapters 16 and 17.

This 'Bella fear' clue, based on her 'change', is too contrived because it is most unlikely that she would have pretended to be afraid *for* Jacob. After all, Miss Lawson had already told Poirot (chapter 15), *before* he meets Bella, that Bella was afraid *of* Jacob – so why not just continue that pretence with Poirot?

However, the next clue, which explains how Bella knew about phosphorus, is very good. Poirot says at the denouement that she "had a certain knowledge of chemistry, having assisted her father in the laboratory". In chapter 10 we were told that Bella's father was a chemistry professor but this was buried in a long paragraph dealing really with Bella's mother and Aunt Agnes. Then a dozen paragraphs later, we learn that Bella spent her time "helping her father or holding wool for her mother". Astute readers may spot that "helping her father" meant helping him with his chemistry. This 'chemistry professor' clue is probably the best in the book because it connects with Poirot's reference to scientific knowledge and is so cleverly, but fairly, hidden.

However, it is not until chapter 22 that Poirot gets 'proof' from Miss Lawson with the 'brooch' clue. She insists that, after being woken by the tap on the nail, the person she saw in the looking glass was Theresa – not because she saw her face but because on her dressing gown was a big brooch which she often wore with the initials 'T.A.'.

At first Poirot does not understand the 'brooch' clue but says that, as Miss Lawson was talking, he had "a feeling of unreality", as though something was *impossible* – which is an unnecessary and unconvincing introduction to his later appreciation of the clue's significance, which occurs during a discussion with Theresa in chapter 24. Having established that the brooches had become very common in the spring, he attaches Theresa's brooch to his lapel, looks in the mirror and appreciates the significance of the clue – though we are not told then what he has appreciated.

In chapter 25 we are told part of what he has realised. He cuts out a brooch shape from some cardboard and pins it to the coat worn by Hastings, who sees *in the mirror* a fair representation of Theresa's brooch with his own initials 'A.H.'. But then, when Poirot puts on Hastings' coat, Hastings sees that the initials are 'H.A.', not 'A.H.'. As Poirot explains in relation to Miss Lawson, "*So, if she saw the initials at all*, she must have seen them *reversed*". So, in fact the initials were 'A.T.', not 'T.A.' as suggested by the mirror.

It is odd that Poirot says "*if she saw the initials at all*" (and does so in italics) since there has been no question about this. It is odder still that Hastings does not then initiate a discussion with Poirot about what the initials 'A.T.' mean. Of course, Poirot knows but that final part of the 'brooch' clue stays hidden from readers because there are still four chapters until the denouement.

The clue also has other oddities. One is that the person who tapped in the nail wore a "dark dressing-gown" whereas the next night (of the fall), Bella's outer night garment was a "navy-blue kimono" (chapter 3). Readers who spot this will think that it can't have been Bella who tapped in the nail. Another, which is odder still, is that anyone should wear a brooch on a dressing-gown.

Having said that, the principle of a reflected clue is very clever and the 'brooch' clue is the most memorable in the story. A nice feature is the symmetry of 'A.T.' working just as well with Hastings' initials, allowing Poirot to reveal the clue (but not his interpretation) in the way he does.

When revealing his interpretation, he says that 'Bella' was a contraction for 'Arabella' and that 'A.T.' stood for Arabella Tanios.

The author had subtly flagged this possibility by telling us in chapters 3 and 10 that Bella's mother's name was Arabella but readers will do well to spot these 'Arabella' clues or to think of Bella simply on learning that the initials were 'A.T.'.

However, readers will surely have wondered who, if the brooch was not Theresa's, might own such a brooch, given that they became very common in the spring. And the answer is obviously Bella – who had a habit of copying Theresa's coats and hats as far as she could with her limited means – which should prompt readers into thinking how Bella could be 'A.T.'.

Indeed the 'copying Theresa' clue is so obviously determinative of Bella's ownership of the brooch that it may well, despite Poirot's focus on personality, be the main clue in the story. And it is flagged very clearly in the first chapter where Bella talks so animatedly that she even "forgot to watch Theresa".

What is less clear is where Poirot "observed" the habit, as he claims. He had been told about it by Theresa in chapter 14 but, when he first meets Bella, she is wearing a "rather depressed-looking cotton frock" (which hardly sounds like Theresa). So he must be relying on the hat she wears in chapter 23, which turns out in chapter 24 to be a cheap imitation of a hat worn by Theresa.

What is quite clever is that immediately before that, at the end of chapter 23, Poirot points out that a brooch can "be lost – or borrowed – or even stolen". He does not mention 'bought' but is surely prompting readers to imagine differing possibilities, including that one, for themselves.

Better still is his question to Hastings in chapter 23 about Miss Lawson saying she had seen Theresa on the stairs. He asks: "Did it strike you – reflect before you answer – did it strike you that there was something *wrong* with that statement of Miss Lawson's?". The suggestion that Hastings should 'reflect' on what Miss Lawson had seen in her looking glass is very pleasing and one guesses that the author smiled at her cleverness as she wrote it.

However, the 'brooch' clue relates only to staging the fall. It is not evidence for the murder. As Poirot explains at the denouement, an exhumation and post mortem might not prove phosphorus poison and, even it did, it was very doubtful that he could connect Bella with the purchase of phosphorus. That is why he gave her his solution to the case, believing that, if she then committed suicide, that was the best way out.

꙳

15

Death On The Nile

Solution

Poirot investigates the murder of 20-year-old American heiress Linnet Doyle on the Nile steamer SS *Karnak*. He is assisted by Colonel Race who had helped him in *Cards on the Table*.

Linnet was very rich, receiving a vast allowance from her American trustees and owning some exquisite pearls. She was also entitled outright to her late father's fortune on becoming 21 or marrying. And she had just married Simon Doyle, former fiancé of her oldest friend, Jacqueline (Jackie) de Bellefort.

Jackie pursues the Doyles on their honeymoon, which takes them up the Nile to the Cataract Hotel at Assuan where Poirot is staying. There Jackie tells him that she sometimes wants to shoot Linnet with her pearl-handled pistol. In order to give Jackie the slip, as Simon puts it, the Doyles go further up the Nile, on a seven-day trip on the *Karnak*, but Jackie (with Poirot and others) turns out to be on board. On the third day a boulder hurtles down the cliff at Abu Simbel towards Linnet. Had Simon not dragged her away, she would have been crushed but Jackie was on the *Karnak* and so could not have pushed it.

On the return from Wadi Halfa, on the fifth night, with the *Karnak* anchored at Abu Simbel again, Linnet is shot, as she is sleeping in her cabin between 12 am and 2 am, with Jackie's pistol held close against her head. Her pearls are missing and a letter J is scrawled on the wall in blood. Since she could not have scrawled it after being shot, the murderer had probably put it there to throw suspicion on Jackie. But Jackie has an alibi.

From 11.20 pm she was in the saloon on the promenade deck and was still there after 12 am when she threatened Simon with telling the other occupants, James Fanthorp and Cornelia Robson, how he had mistreated her. Embarrassed, Fanthorp left. Jackie got out her pistol and fired. Cornelia called Fanthorp back. A crimson stain was soaking Simon's trouser leg below one knee, where he held a handkerchief. Jackie kicked the pistol under a sofa and wept.

Simon, his face twisted with pain, told Fanthorp to get Jackie back to her cabin; asked Cornelia to fetch Miss Bowers (a nurse travelling with Cornelia's elderly cousin, Miss Marie Van Schuyler); and told them not to leave Jackie but to ensure she was safe with Bowers before bringing Dr Bessner to the saloon to treat him. With Jackie struggling, it took time before Fanthorp could get Bessner to the saloon where Simon was leaning against a window, his face a ghastly colour, and a handkerchief sodden with blood lay on the carpet.

Bessner pronounced that Simon, whose bone was fractured, could not walk. So he was carried to Bessner's cabin by Bessner and Fanthorp, with Cornelia joining in, having left Jackie with Bowers. There, after ten "purely surgical" minutes, Bessner injected Simon to make him sleep. Meanwhile Bowers had injected Jackie with morphine and would stay with her all night.

When, just before 12.30 am, Fanthorp returned to the saloon, he could not, he says, find the pistol. So it seemed that someone had taken it when he, Simon, Bessner and Cornelia were all in Bessner's cabin, and used it to shoot Linnet.

Another possibility that may occur to suspicious Christie readers is that Simon was not as incapacitated as the fracture suggested. They will work out that the activity involving Jackie, Bessner, Bowers, Fanthorp and Cornelia was all on the port side of the promenade deck (where the cabins of Bessner, Bowers and Jackie were) and so perhaps Simon had struggled with his fractured leg down the starboard side (where Linnet's cabin was) and shot her. But any such idea is roundly scotched as Bessner's initial view of Simon's fracture and inability to move is repeated in chapters 13, 14, 17, 20, 24, 26 and 29. So, if Jackie and Simon could not have killed Linnet, who are the other suspects?

As well as the passengers already named, five more had cabins on the promenade deck (Tim Allerton; his mother; Mrs Salome Otterbourne; her daughter, Rosalie; and Andrew Pennington) while three were on the lower deck (Linnet's maid, Louise Bourget; Guido Richetti; and Mr Ferguson).

Two can be discounted because they get killed – Louise and Mrs Otterbourne, a novelist with a secret supply of spirits. Louise is found dead under her bed, stabbed by a surgical knife, holding the corner of a thousand-franc note. Mrs Otterbourne sees her murderer and comes to Bessner's cabin to tell Poirot. However, before she can tell him, she is shot in the head with a Colt revolver. Poirot makes a "catlike jump" for the cabin door and sprints towards the stern but, despite this unlikely athleticism, the murderer cannot be seen.

Andrew Pennington, who owns the Colt, is (with his partner, Sterndale Rockford) one of Linnet's American trustees. They had expected to control her money until she was 21[1] and it is plainly suspicious when they decide to arrange a "chance meeting" with her in Egypt, as is Pennington's annoyance at her insistence on reading documents before signing (chapter 9).

In chapter 15 Poirot suggests that he had speculated with her money; that, having lost control of it on her marriage, he could no longer remedy the losses; so he had casually tried to get her to sign a document absolving him; but, having failed, realised that, if she died, the fortune would pass to Simon, who never read documents before signing. And by chapter 18 we know that Pennington had lied about where he was when the boulder fell at Abu Simbel.

Rosalie Otterbourne is suspicious for various reasons: she denies throwing anything overboard on the fatal night despite Miss Van Schuyler saying that she had; she is unconvincing when twice denying having seen anyone on deck at about 1.10 am; and she denies having a pistol despite the stewardess seeing one in her handbag. However, we later learn that it was her mother's supply of spirits (not the murder weapon) that she threw overboard and that she lied about not seeing Tim Allerton on deck because she loved him.

As for Cornelia and Bowers (Jackie's alibi witnesses), who are travelling with Miss Van Schuyler, Cornelia's father was practically ruined by Linnet's father but she has no spite; while Bowers reveals that Miss Van Schuyler stole Linnet's pearls. In fact the pearls, which Bowers returns, turn out to be an imitation set. The real set had already been stolen by Tim Allerton, a jewel thief travelling with his innocent mother. He had entered Linnet's cabin and swapped the sets just after 1 am, assuming that Linnet was asleep, though by then she was dead.

As to the other suspects, Richetti, who claims to be an archaeologist, is in fact a murderous rioter, who is being chased by Race; Ferguson, who thinks that Linnet is the sort of woman who should be shot, turns out to be Lord Dawlish – very rich but a communist; and the final suspect is not a passenger but a *Karnak* engineer, Fleetwood, who had also said that he would like Linnet dead – he had wanted to marry her previous maid, Marie, but Marie would no longer see him after Linnet found out that he was married with three children.

So what is the solution? The surprising answer is that Linnet was murdered by Simon. When Linnet met him, she went all out to steal him from Jackie. He didn't care for Linnet but wanted money and knew that, if he married her and she died, he would acquire a fortune. So Jackie, with whom he was still in love, worked out a plan, which involved her pretending to hate Simon and pursuing the Doyles after their marriage.

Then, for the final drama, she would be seen to fire at Simon and injure him so badly that he could not have murdered Linnet (though in fact the bullet would miss him); and he would insist, after she had fired, that she should not be left alone – so giving a perfect alibi to the most obvious suspect and giving him the chance to kill Linnet – "a kind of two-handed alibi", as she later calls it.

What happened was that Jackie, who was a good shot, fired at the saloon table. She seemed to have shot Simon in the leg – he was holding a handkerchief "close against the wound" and his trouser leg was soaking through with a crimson stain, which he created using red ink from a bottle of nail polish.[2] We are not told exactly how he produced this effect but perhaps the bottle was open within the handkerchief as he pulled it from his pocket, with the ink then being shaken into the handkerchief and through it into the trouser leg.

He then insisted that Jackie be taken away and not left alone. Poirot suggests twice (chapter 29) that Simon was then alone for five minutes before Bessner came – although no witness says this. But Simon only needed two minutes. He picked up the pistol from under the sofa, removed his shoes, ran silently along the starboard side and into Linnet's cabin, shot her, put the bottle of red ink on her washstand (since it mustn't be found on him) and then wrote a J in blood to incriminate Jackie, knowing she had a perfect alibi.

He ran back, dug the bullet out of the table with a penknife and flung it through the window, got Miss Van Schuyler's velvet stole, which was stuffed down a chair in readiness, muffled it round the pistol, fired into his leg and then inserted a spare cartridge to make it look as if only two shots (Jackie's shot and the shot that killed Linnet) had been fired.

The chair into which he then fell (now in genuine agony) was by a window and he threw the pistol (wrapped in the ink-stained handkerchief, with the stole folded around them) into the Nile and used a second handkerchief to tend his wound – the one seen sodden with blood. So he too has an alibi – at the cost of some pain but it was necessary that the wound should disable him.

But what if no doctor had been on board? Or if someone had woken Linnet to tell her about him being shot? Or if a starboard passenger had come on deck while he was running to and fro? After all, although the murderers had drugged Poirot's wine, both Tim and Miss Van Schuyler did leave their cabins to steal the pearls and Rosalie came from the port side to throw the spirits overboard.

And what if Cornelia had not witnessed the fake shooting? Poirot admires the "selection" of Cornelia but, although Jackie insisted she *stay* in the saloon, it is chance that she was there at the outset. The key thing was to ensure that everyone remained occupied on the port side for as long as Simon needed. And Jackie achieved this by overdoing her remorse, hysterics and struggling.

Overall, although the murder plan therefore involved some pain, risk and luck, it was brilliantly conceived and executed, with a two-handed alibi of great ingenuity. It was, as Poirot says, "an extraordinarily clever idea".

However, the plan goes wrong because Louise sees Simon run to and from Linnet's cabin. Poirot says she would have found it "easy enough" to work out what happened and she tries to blackmail Simon. He tells Jackie, who takes their money to Louise and kills her with Bessner's scalpel. However, Mrs Otterbourne sees Jackie enter her cabin and, when she comes to tell Poirot in Bessner's cabin, Simon shouts "You know the person who killed Louise Bourget, you say", so warning Jackie, who is in earshot. She acts like lightning, getting the Colt from Pennington's cabin (between her own and Bessner's), and fires into Bessner's cabin before dropping the gun and going into her own. It was risky but the only chance and well executed, though it was lucky that Jackie was in earshot, Pennington was not in his cabin, his gun was to hand and Mrs Otterbourne took so long to tell her story.

Plot

Published in November 1937, this was the author's longest novel to date, eclipsing even *Dumb Witness* published in July.

The Foreword refers to "a very elaborately worked out plot".[3] That is right. The plotting is extremely good not only because of the ingenuity of the murder plan but because it is combined so skilfully with the sub-plots and deceives us completely about the relationship between Simon, Jackie and Linnet.

Despite the length, paragraph after paragraph is directly relevant to the ingenious murder plan or one of the sub-plots. Although the main murder does not happen until chapter 13 (about 45 per cent of the way into this 31-chapter book), the exposition is very good, with a nice ending to the opening chapter, in which Mrs Otterbourne thinks it is not a matter of life or death whether she goes to Egypt. There, as the text says, she was quite wrong.[4]

The story then moves to Egypt and the author conjures a real sense of the Nile and its cataracts.[5] Gradually one appreciates the care with which the suspects have been put in particular cabins on the *Karnak's* promenade deck, a useful plan of which (referred to in chapter 16) is unfortunately not in all editions. We know that the plan is accurate because it follows the search for the pearls (chapter 22). However, there are some minor mistakes in the *text*. Cornelia is not in cabin 43 (chapter 13) but 41 (as on the plan); and neither Pennington nor Bessner – it is not clear who is being referred to in chapter 18 – is in cabin 40/41 since Jackie is in 40 and Cornelia in 41.

Unaccountably, Poirot and Race do not search Louise's cabin. Race just glances in and we are told, as a fact, "It was empty", despite Louise being dead under the bed. But this naughtiness is short-lived because the body is found at the end of the chapter.

As to the array of well-motivated suspects, the mystification is such that after three-quarters of the story, it is still hard to know who is the main one (though it is probably Pennington). Of course, it seems unreal to have so many characters with so much to hide on such a small steamer. But the only one who jars is the engineer, Fleetwood. The presence on the *Karnak* of the man who wanted to marry Linnet's former maid is an unnecessary coincidence because there was no need for Fleetwood or Marie to figure in the story at all.

On the other hand there is some excellent misdirection (chapter 18) when Race produces a thoughtful, well-constructed note on Linnet's murder, listing alibis, the probable course of events, possible motives and other points. He ends with two groups – "those who had a possible motive or against whom there is definite evidence" and "those who, as far as we know, are free of suspicion". Jackie and Simon are in neither category. They are just not suspects.

As for oddities, one is the boulder incident. Had Simon not dragged Linnet away, she would have been crushed. Well, why does he do so? He would not have been blamed for not getting to her in time and it would surely have been better than the risky, painful murder plan. Another concerns Race's thoughtful note. It is hard to believe that even the author could have constructed that note of about 800 words in only "some minutes", as we are told Race did.

Next, Race says (chapter 21) that the boat would have been deadly quiet when Linnet was shot and that any noise should have been heard. Why then didn't Miss Van Schuyler (in the cabin on the aft side of Linnet's) or Pennington (in the cabin backing on to Linnet's on the port side) hear the shot? According to Bowers, Miss Van Schuyler suffered from deafness – and yet she heard Rosalie on deck (chapter 16). Pennington says (chapter 18) he didn't hear any shot and so Poirot intends (chapter 21) to come back to him "with the kid gloves removed" and yet, when he has his session with him in chapter 26, he never even asks him about this.

However, the most curious aspect of that session is the conclusion drawn by Race: "Admission of fraud. Admission of attempted murder". Pennington's demeanour did suggest that he had taken financial risks but he said nothing about using Linnet's money, let alone admitting fraud, and he swears that he stumbled against the boulder accidentally three times.

Then we have Poirot telling Tim that, if he returns the pearls, there will be no case against him. That might be fine if *that* was his only crime. But Scotland Yard had spent three years looking for the perpetrators of a series of robberies.

Finally, the timing does not quite work. Fanthorp says (chapter 13) that it was at about 12.20 am that Cornelia went to get Bowers and at "actually half-past twelve" that he got back to his own cabin, referred to as the "ten minutes' interval" in Race's note. But that would allow only ten minutes for Fanthorp to rouse Bessner, take him to the saloon, help get Simon to Bessner's cabin, watch the "purely surgical" work (which on its own took ten minutes – chapter 12), go to look for the pistol before returning to Bessner's cabin (some three minutes later – chapter 12) and then get back to his own.

Clues

When Poirot reveals the solution, he starts with the 'pistol overboard' clue. The pistol was found in the Nile, with two bullets fired, inside a handkerchief stained with pink, wrapped inside Miss Van Schuyler's folded, dripping velvet stole, which was scorched, with several small holes in it indicating that the murderer had wrapped it round the pistol to deaden the noise of the shot.

Poirot's "preconceived idea", up to the point when it was found, was that the crime was committed by someone who had overheard the scene in the saloon, grabbed the pistol after the others had left and shot Linnet, before then scrawling a J in blood on the wall so that the crime would almost certainly be attributed to Jackie. "All so clear, is it not?", he says (chapter 16).

But, if the murderer wanted to incriminate Jackie (as suggested by the 'letter J' clue), why throw overboard such an incriminating piece of evidence – her own pistol – instead of leaving it to be found? So, he asks in chapter 18, "*Why* was the pistol thrown overboard?", adding "That is – that *must* be the starting point". In chapter 24 he even describes it as "the crux of the whole business".

It is therefore strange that he never explains why it was thrown overboard. He does say that the murderer took it away from the scene of the crime "because he *had* to … he had no choice in the matter" (chapter 28) and, when we later learn that Simon needed it to shoot himself, we can understand that.

But why throw it overboard after shooting himself, given that he had inserted the spare cartridge? If he had put it back under the sofa, it would look as if the murderer had taken it while he was with Bessner and replaced it before Fanthorp's return. Perhaps the answer is that, since he would still have been left with the scorched stole and stained handkerchief, he felt it best to fold everything into a bundle, made heavier by the pistol, and throw it overboard.

However, that uncertainty is more than compensated for by Poirot's next point – the 'scorching' clue. When he examines the stole's scorch marks and burnt holes in chapter 18, he realises that something is "odd" and he later asks Race if he remembers how Linnet looked with the hole in her head. Only the most astute reader would realise what his point is.

It is that, if the pistol had been fired at Linnet through the stole to deaden the sound, there would be scorching on the stole (as there was) but no burning on her skin. Yet there *was* scorching on her skin, so the shot which killed her had not been fired through the stole. But nor had the shot fired by Jackie at Simon. So the shot through the stole must have been a third shot. That is a brilliant deduction – and the scorching being *both* on Linnet's skin (chapter 13) and on the stole (chapter 16) is an excellent two-part clue to the third shot, fired by Simon into his leg, and the best in the book.

Poirot's next point is the 'nail polish' clue. In chapter 22 he finds two bottles of Nailex in Linnet's cabin. One, Nailex Rose, is empty but for some drops of dark red fluid while the other, Nailex Cardinal, is nearly full. He uncorks and sniffs them both and an odour of pear drops billows into the room. With a grimace, he says *"On ne prend pas les mouches avec le vinaigre"* (one doesn't catch flies with vinegar), adding that he is curious.

In chapter 29 he explains that he was curious about the Rose bottle, partly because Linnet's nails had always been the deep dark red Cardinal shade – not that readers had been told this – but also because the drops in the Rose bottle were not pale pink as one would expect with rose but bright red. Actually chapter 22 said "dark red" (not "bright red") but either way some readers may have realised then that the liquid in the rose bottle was not rose-coloured nail polish because rose is not dark (or bright) red.

But what was it? Poirot says that he had taken out the stopper and that, instead of the usual odour of pear drops, the bottle smelt of vinegar (hence his French proverb) suggesting that the fluid was red ink; which in turn suggested a link with the stained handkerchief because red ink washes out quickly but always leaves a pink stain, as with the handkerchief recovered from the Nile.

Nevertheless the 'nail polish' clue is not entirely satisfactory, despite Poirot's proverb being supported by his grimace, because we are told that he uncorked *both* bottles and that an odour of pear drops billowed into the room (so readers would do well to attribute it to one bottle). And even if they guess that he was suggesting a *separate* smell in the Rose bottle, they would do well to match vinegar with red ink. But they should work out that there is *some* connection between a Rose-labelled bottle and a pink-stained handkerchief and Race even helps by referring to "The Clue of the Blushing Handkerchief" in chapter 18.

Next comes the death of Louise, clasping the corner of a thousand-franc note. This 'thousand-franc note' clue enables Race to conclude that she had been blackmailing the murderer; and Poirot to say that she *had* therefore seen him, despite her denying this. When she denied it, she added, curiously, "Naturally if I had been unable to sleep, if I had mounted the stairs, *then* perhaps I might have seen the assassin …" (chapter 14). Poirot says she used those curious words to hint to the murderer that she *had* seen him. He describes this 'Louise hint' clue as "the crux of the whole matter" (chapter 29), presumably meaning the 'matter' of Louise's murder since he had already described the 'pistol overboard' clue as the "the crux of the whole business".

He goes on to say that, if the words were a hint, the murderer must have been present to hear them – as only Poirot, Race, Bessner and Simon were – which is a very sound deduction. Moreover, he says, she would not have needed to hint to Bessner because she could have spoken to him "in private at any time she liked" whereas she could only speak to Simon ambiguously because he was constantly attended by a doctor, in that doctor's cabin. So she was hinting to *Simon* – another very clever deduction.

Only the most astute reader would have made these deductions from the 'Louise hint' clue. But, in fairness, we were also told that, after saying "I might have seen the assassin", Louise threw out her hands appealingly to Simon, implored him and asked "What can I say?", to which he said he would look after her. It is really Louise's appeal and Simon's reaction that make the clue a very good one and a better one than her mere curious words.

The clue also benefits from some excellent misdirection because straightaway Louise goes on to explain why Fleetwood would like to kill Linnet. Readers will wrongly regard this as the key part of her evidence and this misdirection is improved further by the next topic which Louise discusses – the pearls being missing. By that point any reader who had thought about lingering on what had passed between Louise and Simon is likely to have been well and truly misdirected into the more dramatic revelations and away from the hint.

It is therefore a pity that there is an error in the 'Louise hint' clue. Simon was not constantly attended by Bessner (indeed, how could Bessner have been in constant attendance if Louise could have spoken to him "in private at any time she liked"?). From the time that Simon is moved to Bessner's cabin (chapter 12) to the time Louise hints (chapter 14), Bessner is absent from the cabin on various occasions – first, in chapter 13 when he is in Linnet's cabin examining her body with Poirot and Race; then when he is with them in the smoking room; then when, as he is leaving, he says he will have breakfast; and then when (seemingly having missed breakfast) he follows Fanthorp and Cornelia back to the smoking room, which he never seems to leave, making it odd that he later appears at the smoking room door in chapter 14 to tell Poirot that Simon wants to see him. So, Bessner's repeated absences from his cabin meant that Louise *did* have opportunities to speak to Simon unambiguously.

In chapter 24 we are told that Poirot has been "*sure*" since the death of Louise and that he now understands the significance of the pistol being removed from the scene of the crime – meaning that he must know by then that Simon couldn't leave it there because he needed it to shoot himself.

In that chapter he identifies six clues: (1) Jackie's statement that someone overheard their conversation at Assuan; (2) Tim's statement as to what he heard and did on the night of the murder;

(3) Louise's significant answers to Poirot's questioning; (4) the fact that Mrs Allerton drinks water, Tim drinks whisky and soda and Poirot (their table companion) drinks wine; (5) the two bottles of nail polish and the French proverb; and (6) the fact that the pistol was wrapped in a cheap handkerchief and a velvet stole and thrown overboard.

As for (1), this is a reference to the conversation in which Jackie told Poirot that she sometimes wanted to shoot Linnet; at the end of it she stared into the shadows and suggested that someone had been standing there. It is strange that Poirot puts this first because it is not a clue at all. Jackie was only pretending. As he says (chapter 29), it was just "a useful red herring".

As for (2), this brings us to the 'splash' clue. Various people thought they heard the splash of something being thrown overboard. Ferguson believed he heard a splash but couldn't be sure and, strangely, Poirot does not ask him when. Fanthorp thought he heard a splash at about 1 am and Richetti heard a big splash at what might have been 1.10 am. Those splashes must have been Rosalie throwing the spirits overboard. Mrs Allerton thinks she heard a splash and then someone running (or the other way round), probably within the first hour or so after going to sleep just after 10.30 pm, though it is not clear what she is referring to, with the murder being committed after midnight.

Among so many splash references, it is very hard to identify the real 'splash' clue and readers are unlikely to do so without Poirot prompting them to focus on Tim's statement. Tim's key point is that, after hearing Cornelia shouting for Fanthorp, he heard someone (in fact Simon) running along the deck and then a splash (in fact the gun in the stole) before he heard Bessner booming out instructions about moving Simon carefully to his cabin (chapter 15).

However, when Poirot refers to Tim's evidence in chapter 29 he says "He heard a pop – *followed* by a splash". But that is not what Tim said. He said he heard a splash. Poirot then asked him whether it was not a shot and he replied that it might have been because he did hear a cork pop and may have *imagined* the splash because of connecting a cork with liquid pouring into a glass. So, he does *not* say he heard both a splash *and* a pop (it was a splash *or* a pop). Poirot should have stuck with what Tim actually said – he heard a splash *before* Bessner boomed – and deduce that this splash was the pistol being thrown overboard when it should still have been under the sofa.

Clue (3) has been covered, bringing us to (4). In chapter 29 Poirot suggests that a sleeping drug had been slipped into his bottle of wine to stop him taking part in the events of the night. This had occurred to him (chapter 15) but he had attributed his deep sleep to the hot day and unusual tiredness. What the 'bottle of wine' clue shows is that the murder had been decided upon before dinner at 7.30 pm but it is a hard one to spot: the fact that the Allertons, who were not drinking wine, did hear noises does not necessarily mean that the reason why Poirot did not was because his wine was drugged, particularly when he had already explained his deep sleep on other grounds.

Clues (5) and (6) have been covered. So we can move to chapter 27 where Poirot runs over the list again, though in a slightly different order and with a few other differences, some of which seem minor – thus he refers to Louise's death rather than her significant answers; he refers to "my bottle of wine" but not to his companions; he refers to the two bottles of nail polish but not his French proverb; and he adds a new fact, the death of Mrs Otterbourne.

But one difference seems more important because he splits what was his sixth clue into three: "The velvet stole. The stained handkerchief. The pistol that was left on the scene of the crime". First, we have the stole from which we get the excellent 'scorching' clue. Secondly, we have the handkerchief, which Poirot now describes as "stained" (instead of "cheap") which is more helpful because the stain ties in with the 'nail polish' clue.

Thirdly, however, we have an error because the whole point of the 'pistol overboard' clue – "the crux of the whole business" – is that it was *not* left at the scene of the crime, Linnet's cabin, but thrown overboard. The error is odd since Poirot himself, when he refers elsewhere to "the scene of the crime", is clear that the pistol was *not* left there: his statement in chapter 24 about realising the significance of it "being *removed from* the scene of the crime" and his question in chapter 28 "Why had that pistol *not been left* on the scene of the crime?" (emphasis added to both quotations).

In the latter chapter Poirot says "For some time now I have known what I may express as the 'first half' of the murderer. Now I know the 'second half'' also". Although this confirms that he was "*sure*" that Simon was the first half in chapter 24, it also tells us that he was not sure then about Jackie. But that is surprising because Simon could only have pretended to bleed (with a bottle of red ink which he couldn't have had on him by chance) if he had known that he was going to be 'shot' by someone with whom he was in league.

Nor are we told what clues between chapters 24 and 28 enabled Poirot to identify the 'second half'. Perhaps the murder of Mrs Otterbourne helped. It was well executed and we knew from the 'good shot' clue (chapter 5) that Jackie was a good shot – which would also explain her accurate shooting in the saloon. Perhaps it was also the way that Mrs Otterbourne's murderer vanished. The murderer could not have gone forward or back along the deck because he or she would have been seen by Ferguson, Fanthorp or Tim. Poirot says that he or she could have gone a third way and he allows his listeners to misdirect themselves into thinking that the murderer could have swung over the rail onto the deck below. In fact he was thinking that the murderer could simply have gone into a cabin on Bessner's side (Jackie's).

As for personal clues against "the two halves of the murderer" (as Poirot calls them in chapters 28 and 29), very few readers will be impressed by the two points on which he relies against Simon in chapter 29 – that, when he spoke bitterly about possessive women (chapter 6), he was talking about Linnet, not Jackie; and that he overdid the devoted manner to Linnet in public.

Much better, in retrospect, are Simon's thought processes. In chapter 10 he thinks back to the first night at the Cataract Hotel: "What a fool he'd been to be rattled … After all, one could trust Jackie". Readers think that he no longer needs to feel rattled by the pursuing Jackie but he must be thinking about her executing the murder plan. Then on the fatal night, as she drinks in the saloon, "a faint line of anxiety" shows between his eyebrow and later "a queer sort of watchful look" shows on his face. Readers think that he is concerned because she may make a scene but it is because she will soon fire the shot. And after the shooting he has a "grateful look" when he learns that Bowers will stay with Jackie all night. Readers think he is concerned about Jackie's well-being but he is grateful because this will complete Jackie's alibi.

As for Jackie, there are two early clues. First, the 'penniless Jackie' clue. It seems odd that, even though she is "as poor as they make them", she can afford to follow the Doyles to Egypt. Poirot asks Simon how, but his answer that she must have sold her capital (chapter 6) sounds wrong to readers who know (chapter 1) that she is "absolutely broke". Second, the 'brainy Jackie' clue. It seems odd, given that the Doyles' *Karnak* trip is supposedly intended to give her the slip, that she is on board. Oddly, Poirot never asks her how she knew about the trip, merely saying when Linnet inquires (chapter 7), "She has brains, you know".

The 'brainy Jackie' clue, which Poirot gives us more than once, is important in relation to her role in Linnet's murder. Poirot thinks she could commit murder (chapter 7) but doubts if she could do the *act* of a cold-blooded murder (chapter 13). This probably means two things. One, that she could still commit murders of urgent necessity (Louise and Mrs Otterbourne); and two, that, even if she could not do the *act* of a cold-blooded murder (Linnet's), she could be involved in the planning, particularly where it was, as Poirot says, a "big fact" that she hated Linnet and wanted to kill her (chapter 13).

So the 'brainy Jackie' clue is quite a pointer to her taking part in a *joint* enterprise – Jackie, the planner with the cool, resourceful brain and Simon, the man of action who carried out the main murder with incredible swiftness and timing. Indeed, some readers may wonder early on if she and Simon are up to something together because of the 'same expressions' clue. Not only does he describe her as hot-blooded in chapter 6, as she had just done in chapter 5, but he compares her to the moon which he could no longer see once the sun (Linnet) had come out – the same simile which Jackie had just used – and to which Poirot responds by saying "*Tiens, c'est drôle, ça*".

A more telling example of the 'same expressions' clue comes when Poirot overhears Simon say "We've got to go through with it now" (chapter 8). Simon had earlier said the same to Linnet when she saw Jackie on the *Karnak* and thought about turning back. So, naturally, Poirot assumes that Simon is again talking to Linnet. But, after Linnet is murdered, some readers may wonder whether those words relate to the murder and, if so, then they clearly point to Simon's involvement in a joint enterprise.

However, readers will still do very well to spot his motive. In chapter 7 Poirot lists the most usual motives for murder: money (that is to say, gain); revenge; love; fear; hate; and beneficence. Simon's motive is a desire for money but this is not clued, other than in his dislike of needless expense (chapter 7) and in Poirot's remarkably prescient comment to Rosalie (chapter 2) that Linnet "may have been married for her money". Jackie's motive was her love for Simon (chapter 30); both that motive, and her hatred of

Linnet, are stated openly in the story. The motive for the other murders is, of course, fear of exposure.

The final point about the murderers is that, despite Poirot describing Jackie as the brains and Simon as the man of action, Mrs Otterbourne's murder reflects these qualities the other way round – Simon with the sense to shout out and so convey the danger and Jackie who, hearing him, "acted like lightning".

In looking at the murder plan clues overall, the 'scorching' clue is excellent and Poirot makes a brilliant deduction. He also does so with the 'Louise hint' clue, which is well concealed by some excellent misdirection, and the 'nail polish' clue, although the chain of reasoning required to interpret both those clues makes them feel a bit convoluted. And it is a pity about the few errors and uncertainties and that we didn't know until the denouement that Poirot had found a hole in the saloon table (from which Simon dug out Jackie's bullet).

As for the sub-plots, readers may spot, from the other thefts mentioned in chapters 1 and 20, that the unemployed Tim, who was annoyed about Poirot dining at his table, is probably the jewel thief who stole Linnet's pearls and substituted an imitation set. This is reinforced by the 'Tim temper' clue when he refers to the "blasted business of the pearls being missing" (chapter 20) – Miss Van Schuyler's theft of his imitation set having exposed his real theft.

But where are the real pearls? The search does not produce them but it gives us the 'Tim's cabin' clues – books, a wooden rosary and a tube of Seccotine (an adhesive). Poirot's theory is that the imitation set was sent to Tim by his accomplice in a book with a square hole cut out in the middle, that the rosary beads unscrew and that inside each is a real pearl, stuck with Seccotine. Readers could hardly have deduced this since, as Poirot says in relation to the beads unscrewing, "you would never think so to look at them".

As for Ferguson, Poirot identifies him as Lord Dawlish because "there was a picture in one of these papers" and during the search he found a signet ring with a coat of arms on it. It is impressive that Poirot knows Dawlish's coat of arms but it is not clear what "these papers" are.

As for Richetti, the clue that gives him away is a telegram about vegetables, mistakenly read by Linnet. As Race knows, vegetables form part of a new code used in the South African rebellion. Readers could not have known this or realised that he was a murderous rioter merely because he was, in Poirot's view, almost too word-perfect in his role as an archaeologist.

As for Pennington, with fraud and attempted murder taken as read by Poirot and Race, the remaining clue relates to the "chance meeting" with Linnet. Poirot tells Pennington in chapter 10 that he understands from Linnet that he came over on the *Carmanic* (in fact *Simon* told him this in chapter 6). Pennington concurs but Poirot later points out that the only recent transatlantic sailing labels on his luggage are from the *Normandie* which, Poirot remembers (most impressively), sailed two days after the *Carmanic* (meaning he was still in New York when he learned about Linnet's marriage). Had we not been told in chapter 1 that he had sailed on the *Normandie*, we might have felt aggrieved by the 'labels' clue because there is no reference to Poirot or Race looking at his luggage, let alone the labels, during their search. One might have expected some mention of them, as with Tim's rosary or Ferguson's signet ring.

Finally, as for the pearl-handed pistol seen by the stewardess in Rosalie's handbag, Jackie had a *pair* of the pistols and, with the first having been used for the murder, she had slipped the second into the handbag when realising there was to be a search for the pearls. Later she took it back, which is why it was not in the handbag. It is therefore a red herring as far as detection is concerned but it is important because, having confessed that Poirot's solution is right, Jackie uses it in the final chapter to shoot Simon and then herself.

16

Appointment With Death

Solution

Poirot investigates the murder of Mrs Boynton, a tyrannical American matriarch, who enjoys inflicting mental torture on others including her family with whom she is visiting Palestine.

She had been a prison wardress, marrying the prison Governor after his first wife died and becoming mother to his three children – two boys (Lennox and Raymond) and a girl (Carol) – before having her own child, Ginevra. After her husband died, she shut off the outside world. The four children had to live at home and avoid school, jobs and outside contacts, the only exception being when a cousin, Nadine, a trainee nurse, came to stay. She married Lennox four years ago but Mrs Boynton would not let them live away from home.

The Palestine trip is the family's first outing and the early chapters are set in Jerusalem, mainly in the Solomon Hotel, where Mrs Boynton, bloated like a distorted Buddha or gross spider in a web, presides over Lennox (aged 30), Nadine, Raymond (23 or 24), Carol (23) and Ginevra (perhaps 19). The children seem so cowed by her that, despite their ages, they can do nothing unless she agrees. But that does not stop Raymond saying to Carol in the story's opening line, *"You do see, don't you, that she's got to be killed?"*. And she is killed when the Boyntons go to Petra in Jordan.

However, the family are not the only suspects. They are joined on the Petra trip by Jefferson Cope, an admirer of Nadine's. Then two days later, on the evening before Mrs Boynton's murder, they are joined by another group who had also been at the Solomon Hotel and travelled together to Petra – Dr Sarah King (who falls for Raymond), Dr Theodore Gerard (a psychologist), Lady Westholme (a Member of Parliament[1]) and Miss Amabel Pierce (a suggestible former nursery governess).

On the day the Boyntons left the Solomon Hotel, Sarah, who viewed Mrs Boynton as pathetic and ludicrous, told her so. Mrs Boynton froze but, when she then spoke in her baffled fury, she looked not at Sarah but over her shoulder and said with venom "*I never forget. Remember that. I've never forgotten anything – not an action, not a name, not a face ...*".

At lunch on the day after Sarah's group had arrived in Petra, Mrs Boynton, with unexpected amiability, released her family by suggesting they go for a walk – except for Ginevra, who was told to sleep in her tent. So Lennox, Nadine, Raymond and Carol, accompanied by Cope, set off at about 3.05 pm, followed at about 3.15 pm by Sarah and Gerard, while Mrs Boynton stayed at camp, sitting in the mouth of the cave in which she slept.

In Part 2 chapter 5 Poirot refers to a plan of the camp and, although this is not appended, it is easy to understand. The cave next to Mrs Boynton's was used by Lennox and Nadine. The caves opened onto a ledge, below which were tents for Raymond, Carol, Ginevra, Gerard and Sarah. There was then a stream and across it was a big marquee (for eating and relaxing), with Miss Pierce's tent on its right and those of Lady Westholme and Cope on its left. Those tents faced the ledge, which was nearly 200 yards away.

At 3.45 pm Lady Westholme strolled along to Miss Pierce's tent to see if she too wanted a walk. They agreed to go in half an hour and Lady Westholme returned to her tent. At 4.15 pm, when they left, they called up to Mrs Boynton on passing under the ledge but they say she simply grunted at them.

Gerard returned to camp first at about 4.20 pm because of a malaria attack. He wanted a quinine injection but could not find his drugs case, which had been moved, or his hypodermic syringe. So he took quinine by mouth and slept.

Lennox was back next, at 4.35 pm; then Nadine at 4.40 pm; Carol at 5.10 pm; Cope, Lady Westholme and Miss Pierce at 5.40 pm; Raymond at 5.50 pm; and last, at 6 pm, came Sarah who could see Mrs Boynton still in her chair in the mouth of her cave.

When supper was ready at 6.30 pm a servant was sent to tell Mrs Boynton. But she could not move and Sarah pronounced her dead. The assumption was that, because she was taking medicine for heart trouble, she had died from the strain of the journey to Petra. Sarah did not disturb Gerard because of his fever but, when he examined the body at 9 am next morning, he noticed a mark on her wrist of the sort caused by a hypodermic syringe. Earlier, he had found the syringe he could not find the day before and he also noticed that his stock of digitoxin was much reduced.

Digitoxin is one of the active principles of *digitalis*, derived from the leaves of the foxglove. *Digitalis* provides an effective treatment for heart conditions and has, as Gerard explains, various active principles[2] – not only digitoxin, which he says is the most active poisonous constituent of *digitalis* leaves – causing death by quick palsy of the heart – but also digitalin, which was in Mrs Boynton's medicine (Part 2 chapter 2).

Her body is brought to Amman where Colonel Carbury hears Gerard's story and requests Poirot, who is on holiday there, to find out what really happened. Poirot asks when she was last known to be alive and Carbury, referring to an official-looking document, says that she was spoken to by Lady Westholme and Miss Pierce shortly after 4 pm and that each of Lennox, Nadine, Carol and Raymond had spoken to her when they returned.

Even though the last of them, Raymond, swears that his mother was alive on his return at 5.50 pm, Sarah is equally adamant that she was not. She says that, when she examined the body, Mrs Boynton had been dead for "over an hour. It might have been much longer" (which five chapters later Poirot converts to "at least an hour and a half and probably *two hours*"). Because Gerard did not examine the body until 9 am next morning, he can only be sure that Mrs Boynton died between 12 and 18 hours before he saw the body, meaning in effect between 3 pm the day before (18 hours before he saw the body) and 6.30 pm when Sarah examined it.

Having conducted his investigation, Poirot assembles various people in a hotel bedroom in Amman to hear his report. Present, in addition to Carbury, are the Boyntons (Raymond, Carol, Nadine, Lennox and Ginevra) and also three "outsiders" with, Poirot says, a "definite stake" in the case – Gerard (whose evidence began the investigation), Sarah (who examined the body and has a personal interest – Raymond) and Cope (who is intimate with the Boyntons).

Poirot forces Raymond to admit that Mrs Boynton was dead when he returned. He had not said so because he feared that she had been killed by Carol to whom he had spoken the story's opening words. But in fact Carol too had found Mrs Boynton dead at 5.10 pm and had similarly suspected Raymond.

Poirot then forces Lennox to admit that he also found his mother dead on his return at 4.35 pm. He mechanically picked up her wristwatch, lying in her lap, and put it on her limp wrist. And Nadine too confirms that she was dead on her return at 4.40 pm. She said nothing because she had seen Lennox replace the wristwatch and, on seeing the hypodermic mark on the wrist, thought that she had inspired him to commit murder by telling him on their walk that she was leaving him for Cope because of his mother.

As for the three outsiders, Poirot says that Cope had no opportunity or motive and that, since Sarah left camp before 3.30 pm, it was hard to see how she had an opportunity. In fact, though, with Gerard having said that the murder could have happened as early as 3 pm, both Sarah – and possibly Cope, who did not leave until 3.05 pm – would have had opportunities *before* leaving. As for Gerard, he would not have suggested foul play if he were the murderer.

That leaves Ginevra, since Lady Westholme and Miss Pierce are not in the room. But Poirot accepts that she would not have murdered Mrs Boynton with the cool logic used. So, if none of those in the room are guilty, who is?

Poirot says that, when Mrs Boynton was told by Sarah that she was pathetic, she recognised, in her baffled fury, a face from the past – a victim delivered to her. And her words *"I've never forgotten anything – not an action, not a name, not a face ..."* – ostensibly spoken to Sarah – were meant not for Sarah but the person behind her, Lady Westholme, whom she recognised.

Poirot suggests that before her marriage, Lady Westholme, who had met her husband on a voyage from the United States, had served a criminal sentence there in the prison where Mrs Boynton was a wardress. This is just intelligent supposition by Poirot, which makes the motivation feel weak, but he says that her crime must have put her career, ambitions and social position at stake. Mrs Boynton would have enjoyed torturing her before revealing the truth. While Mrs Boynton lived, Lady Westholme was not safe.

Poirot says that Mrs Boynton instructed Lady Westholme to meet her at Petra and that she wanted to interview her on the afternoon of her death, which explains her unexpected amiability in releasing her family. However, at 3.45 pm Lady Westholme went to Miss Pierce's tent to check on her as the only witness still at the camp likely to be awake. She found her sitting in the tent's entrance and they agreed to go for a walk in half an hour.

Having learned what Miss Pierce was doing, Lady Westholme returned to her tent, dressed as an Arab servant, went to Gerard's tent, looked in his medicine chest, chose a suitable drug, took the hypodermic syringe, filled it and went boldly up to her victim. She injected the drug into her wrist before hurrying away, changing and rejoining Miss Pierce.

On doing so, she pretended she had seen an Arab servant with Mrs Boynton and impressed her version of that event on Miss Pierce whose suggestibility Poirot later tests by getting her to recollect that he had sneezed when he hadn't. As a result, both ladies say that, before setting out at 4.15 pm, they saw from their tents Mrs Boynton abusing an Arab servant. It was understandable that Miss Pierce could not identify the Arab or hear what was said from 200 yards. However, although they could both have seen the incident from their tents, they could *not have seen each other*, their tents being on either side of the marquee, and so Miss Pierce would not have known that Lady Westholme was not at her tent but was in fact the Arab servant she had seen.

At 4.15 pm they went for their walk, passing below the ledge. Lady Westholme shouted to Mrs Boynton. Of course, she received no reply but she remarked to Miss Pierce how rude it was of Mrs Boynton to snort at them. This was accepted by Miss Pierce who would swear she heard Mrs Boynton snort.

Poirot says (twice) that Lady Westholme carried out her plan boldly. That is fair. Also it was quite clever of her, realising that she may be seen with Mrs Boynton by Miss Pierce, to dress as an Arab servant and later to call out to Mrs Boynton and influence Miss Pierce into believing that she had snorted.

But the only real ingenuity is the choice of murder weapon – the use of digitoxin, opportunistically taken from a doctor travelling with the party, to poison a victim who was taking a medicine containing digitalin. Gerard says that death might have been attributed to the victim having overdosed on her medicine or to digitalin being a cumulative drug whose effects can intensify after repeated doses. Moreover, he says, the active principles of *digitalis* may leave no appreciable trace. Poirot describes it as "a very clever murder! ... There is thought – care – genius" (Part 2 chapter 2).

That may be true in theory. But that ingenuity is not very satisfying. This is partly because we are not told how Lady Westholme knew that Mrs Boynton was taking a drug containing digitalin. But it is mainly because there is nothing to show that she knew about medicine or poisons or was proficient in using hypodermic syringes, and yet she chose from Gerard's case and injected Mrs Boynton with a poison that might be taken for the victim's own drug.

Another unsatisfying aspect is that she turns out to be the murderer at all. This is not because Carbury and then Poirot (in Part 2 chapters 1 and 3) point us towards a family member; nor because Poirot refers only to Gerard, Sarah and Cope as the three outsiders with a "definite stake" in the case; nor because, when dealing with alibis, he only mentions Lady Westholme and Miss Pierce in the context of an alibi for Cope. Indeed, that is all quite good misdirection.

Rather, it is because, first, she is so remote from suspicion by the time her villainy is revealed (she last appeared 13 chapters ago) that it is hard to feel enthusiastic about her being the murderer; and, secondly, because, when Nadine checks in Part 2 chapter 17 that Poirot believes "that one of us – here in this room" is the murderer, Poirot is "nodding slowly to himself". Since it is never suggested that he was nodding in respect of some separate thought process, this seems like a clear but misleading indication that the murderer is in the room – which Lady Westholme was not.

Plot

This book has two Parts followed by a short Epilogue. Part 1 (chapters 1 to 12) is set mainly in Jerusalem but ends with the murder in Petra. Part 2 (chapters 1 to 18) is set in Amman where Poirot undertakes his investigation and presents his report. The short Epilogue, set five years later, presents a much happier gathering of the Boyntons. Lennox and Nadine have children; Raymond and Sarah are married; so are Carol and Cope; and Ginevra is accompanied by Gerard.

The opening of the story (*"You do see, don't you, that she's got to be killed?"*) is a good, arresting one. Poirot overhears the words but it is not until eight chapters later, when he recognises Raymond's voice, that a waiter tells him that his name is Boynton (he does not give the Christian name, despite Poirot suggesting he had in Part 2 chapter 2).

Readers, however, learn that the speaker is Raymond in chapter 1 but it is 26 chapters later before they learn that his murder plan comes from an English detective story – "you stuck an empty hypodermic syringe into someone and it did the trick". Raymond is referring to Dorothy L. Sayers' *Unnatural Death* (1927) in which the murderer uses a hypodermic syringe to inject an air bubble into the victim's artery – an ingenious idea, though, if it was to work (which is doubtful), would have required injecting the bubble into the victim's vein.[3]

Despite the arresting opening, it is hard to regard the plot as engaging when the first nine chapters describing the Boyntons are so relentlessly grim. Life for the children is like being in prison. Lennox, exhausted with suffering, has parted company with hope. Nadine, though unafraid of Mrs Boynton, is as unhappy as she can be. Raymond is in a constant state of nervous tension. Carol knows the hopelessness of it all and is twice shaken by a storm of weeping. And the remote Ginevra doesn't always know what she's doing.

The ending has a similarly negative effect because of the convoluted nature of Poirot's report, which goes on for four chapters. Taking Part 2 chapter 15 as an example, he considers what might have happened in different situations – if Carol had found Mrs Boynton dead at 5.10 pm (rather than alive, as she claimed); if Carol had found her alive and murdered her; if Raymond had then found her dead at 5.50 pm (rather than alive, as he claimed); if Carol had not murdered her so that Raymond found her alive and murdered her himself; and if he had found her alive but not murdered her himself, with Sarah later giving the fatal injection. Although Poirot produces a logical analysis in that chapter and in the three further chapters, his report is unnecessarily long.

Having said that, one should add that the timing on the fatal afternoon, which is the crux of the plotting and allows for various outcomes, is carefully structured because we see, as we work back in time from 6.30 pm to 4.15 pm and look at the suspects in the room in turn – Sarah, Raymond, Carol, Nadine, Lennox, Gerard and Ginevra – that there was a time when each of them (other perhaps than Cope) had an opportunity to kill Mrs Boynton (had she not – as we slowly learn in relation to each such opportunity) already been dead.

The importance of timing is emphasised by Poirot making a timetable of the fatal afternoon's events, which is even set out twice (in Part 2 chapters 9 and 16). So one expects the timing to be the key element of mystification. But it doesn't really work satisfactorily because of some small errors.

Thus Poirot's timetable says that the Boyntons left camp at "3.5 approx" (meaning 3.05 approx). But in Part 2 chapter 15 Poirot says that Raymond left camp with the others at "about three-fifteen". Poirot's timetable says that Lady Westholme and Miss Pierce left camp at 4.15, which is what Lady Westholme had told him, but Carbury's document says that they spoke to Mrs Boynton "shortly after 4 pm". (More strangely, in Part 2 chapter 17 Poirot says that they started out at "four-sixteen", an odd time, which is not "*exactly twenty minutes*", to quote Poirot's italics, before 4.35 pm.) Poirot's timetable says that Lennox returned at 4.35 pm and Nadine at 4.40 pm, presumably because Carbury's document says she spoke to Mrs Boynton "about five minutes later". However, Part 2 chapter 5 says that Nadine came along "about quarter of an hour later". Poirot's timetable says that Lady Westholme, Miss Pierce and Cope returned at 5.40 pm but in Part 2 chapter 14 Cope says that they returned "about six". Poirot's timetable says that Raymond returned at 5.50 pm. And yet, just after being told this by Raymond, Poirot writes "R.B. 5.55?" rather than 5.50 pm.

Although these turn out to be minor errors, not affecting the careful structure, they are frustrating because one doesn't know while reading whether they are intentionally significant. However, there is a bigger error after Poirot sets out his timetable for the second time. He refers to the 20-minute gap between 4.50 pm when Nadine stopped talking to Mrs Boynton and 5.10 pm when Carol returned and says "Therefore, if Carol is speaking the truth, Mrs Boynton must have been killed in that 20 minutes" i.e. before 5.10 pm. But this makes no sense since what Carol said in Part 2 chapter 8 was that Mrs Boynton was *alive* at 5:10 pm, which Poirot actually confirms by saying in Part 2 chapter 15 "Let us suppose that Carol is speaking the truth, that Mrs Boynton was alive at five-ten". So he is getting confused, unsurprisingly when his report is so convoluted.

Cope also makes an odd mistake about timing when in Part 2 chapter 13 he says it was "yesterday" that Nadine said she would leave Lennox. It is plain from the next chapter that he is referring to the fatal afternoon because of his description of the subsequent events. But the murder cannot have taken place "yesterday" since Gerard examined the body at 9 am the next day; it would then have taken a day to move the body between Petra and Amman (Part 1 chapter 10); and it was not until the day after that Cope mentioned "yesterday".

Clues

For a story with such unsatisfying aspects to its solution and plot, making it perhaps the author's weakest Poirot novel of the 1930s, it is surprisingly rich in clues. The better ones are quite clever and lead to good deductions but there are some on which Poirot bases deductions which only the most astute reader could replicate. And the main clue, Mrs Boynton saying "*I never forget*", does point quite a large finger at Lady Westholme.

When presenting his report, Poirot says that the murder was not committed by the Boynton family as a group because their stories did not dovetail and there was no system of alibis. That is right but it is also supported by two specific clues showing that one family member believed that another was the murderer.

The first clue, showing that Nadine thought that Lennox was the murderer, is the 'Nadine lie' clue. In Part 2 chapter 7 she tells Poirot that she had told Lennox about leaving him for Cope *after* she had returned to camp. However, in Part 2 chapter 13, when she speaks to Lennox, he says she had told him about Cope *before* he returned. So, she had lied to Poirot in order to protect Lennox, fearing that he had reacted murderously after being told that she was leaving him because of his mother.

That clue, based on contradictory statements six chapters apart, is quite clever. But, unlike readers, Poirot was not privy to Nadine's chat with Lennox. So, how does *he* know she lied? He refers to Lady Westholme saying that Lennox walked as if he was slightly dizzy. But the 'dizziness' clue requires a leap to deduce that, because he looked slightly dizzy, he had been told that his wife was leaving him since he might just have caught the sun.

The second clue, showing that Carol thought that Raymond was the murderer, is the 'pronoun' clue. In Part 2 chapter 8 Carol tells Poirot that they had nothing to do with it. Poirot asks her to swear that their mother did not die "as a result of any action of yours?". She swears she never harmed her. Poirot later notes that she had only sworn for *herself* – so suggesting that, because she was not also replying for Raymond, she thought he was guilty. Using 'yours' as both a singular and plural word is another quite clever clue.

Carol's thought that Raymond might be guilty is unsurprising in view of his opening words and, although most readers will regard the 'opening words' clue as a red herring, with the speaker's identity revealed so soon, it is surely significant. And yet, when Poirot writes out a list of "Significant points" in Part 2 chapter 10, the words are not listed. Nevertheless, that list seems to provide a clear indication of the main clues. There are nine points on the list, although Poirot adds point (10) in Part 2 chapter 14. The list's importance is emphasised when he reads it out in Part 2 chapter 15.

He refers to points (1) and (2) first (in chapter 15) but does not resolve them until he has dealt with points (9) and (7) in chapter 16. Indeed, consistent with his report's convoluted nature, he does not resolve the points in order; and to make matters harder he does not even enumerate points (5) to (8) when addressing them. But readers willing to analyse his report closely can work out that he covers them in essentially the order which follows.

Point (9) is that at 6.30 pm a servant was sent to tell Mrs Boynton that dinner was ready. Poirot suggests that it would have been more natural for one of the family to go and that Nadine, who did perhaps the most waiting on her, did not go because she knew she was dead. That deduction is quite a jump from sending a servant. It was 200 yards to Mrs Boynton's cave and they were all tired that evening. So the 'dispatched servant' clue is not a particularly good one for Poirot's deduction.

Point (7) is that Lennox said that he did not know what time he returned to camp but later admitted changing his mother's wrist-watch to the right time. Poirot's focus is not on whether Lennox actually knew the time but on his replacing of the wristwatch on his mother's wrist. That might have been a cover for Lennox injecting his mother or it might have been seen by Nadine, who thought, when seeing the mark on the wrist, that Lennox had killed her. Those are fair alternative deductions but in fact, either way, the wrist-watch is not a clue to the murder.

Point (1), in chapter 17, is that Mrs Boynton took a drug containing digitalin. (In some editions, the lists in chapters 10 and 15 both refer to *digitalin* but in others the first list says *digitalis* and the second *digitalin* – oddly since Poirot is reading out on the second occasion what he wrote on the first.) He brackets point (1) with point (2), which is that Gerard missed a hypodermic syringe.

The clue lies in the *bracketing* of those two points because Poirot sees them as "quite irreconcilable": since Mrs Boynton was taking a drug containing digitalin, the murderer would surely have put the digitoxin into that medicine, not stolen a hypodermic syringe and injected her. So, Poirot deduces, the murderer was not intimate enough with Mrs Boynton to enter her tent (he means cave) or handle her medicine but was an outsider. This 'syringe' clue is quite clever – though Poirot is wrong to describe the two points as "quite irreconcilable" because reconciling them is what he does.

Carbury says, when looking at the list, that Gerard missed not only a syringe but also the digitoxin. However, Poirot says that the digitoxin is not important in the same way, without ever explaining why. Perhaps he meant that, if the murderer had only taken the digitoxin, this could have been added to the medicine by a family member. But, whatever he meant, the missing digitoxin must surely still be 'significant' because it killed Mrs Boynton.

We also get a red herring relating to the missing syringe, starting in Part 2 chapter 7 when Nadine, a nurse, admits she owns one but says that she left it in Jerusalem. Then in chapter 14 we learn that Miss Pierce saw Carol throw something that glittered into the stream – a metal box with a syringe inside – which Sarah then took from Miss Pierce, saying it was hers. Poirot responds "It completes my case! Everything is now clear and in order".

Quite how Miss Pierce's evidence completes Poirot's case is not at all clear. This second syringe is irrelevant to the murder implemented with *Gerard's* syringe which was returned to him. And there is no suggestion that Poirot had been confused by a side-issue about a missing second syringe. So this is rather unsatisfying. In fact, the second syringe was Nadine's. Raymond took it for his own murder plan and Nadine, unsure where it was, said it was in Jerusalem. It was then taken by Carol after the murder (presumably to protect Raymond) and thrown into the stream before being found by Miss Pierce and claimed by Sarah (presumably also to protect Raymond).

Points (3) and (4), in chapter 18, are that Mrs Boynton took pleasure in keeping her family from enjoying themselves with others and yet, on the afternoon in question, encouraged them to leave her. Like the first pair, the clue comes in their contradictory nature. Why reverse her usual policy? Poirot answers this 'unexpected amiability' clue by explaining that she was clearing the field to interview her new victim.

But, before that, he examines her character, his point (5) being that she is (or was) – editions and lists vary – a mental sadist. In doing so, he refers to the moment when Sarah called her pathetic and she, in her baffled fury, saw a new victim – "a psychological moment". But it is not clear why her psychology is, as he says in Part 2 chapter 18, "the most important thing in this case" unless he means that it was her 'psychology' that made her provide the main clue to Lady Westholme's guilt by saying venomously over Sarah's shoulder "*I never forget. Remember that. I've never forgotten anything – not an action, not a name, not a face …*", which is point (10).

The first thing to say about this '*I never forget*' clue is that the words are in italics and, in clueing *what* is being emphasised, the next sentence says "There was nothing in the words themselves, but the venom with which they were spoken made Sarah retreat a step". So readers may be misled into assuming that the italics just emphasised the venom. But the words are important.

Secondly, as Mrs Boynton spoke, she "looked not at Sarah but oddly over her shoulder. She seemed to address, not Sarah, but some familiar spirit". The word "oddly" should make readers think she was addressing someone else – but they will not yet know who. However, in the next chapter, Sarah fancies that Lady Westholme had been close by – no one else is mentioned – and two chapters later Lady Westholme thinks she saw Sarah talking to Mrs Boynton.

Thirdly, Poirot does not have the '*I never forget*' clue when listing his original points because, when Sarah tells him about the incident in Part 2 chapter 4, it seems that, inexplicably, she did not report Mrs Boynton's words, even though he "cross-examined her closely" and called her account "very significant". It is only in Part 2 chapter 12 that he asks her what exactly Mrs Boynton had said and she tells him, adding that she said it malevolently, not even looking at her. And, before this, she says, for readers who missed the point on the two earlier occasions, that she thought Lady Westholme had probably overheard.

So by Part 2 chapter 12 readers should not need hindsight to spot that Mrs Boynton was probably addressing Lady Westholme. They should also know that she had been in the United States – having met Lord Westholme when he was on a return voyage from there (Part 1 chapter 10) – though we are not told how Poirot knows about this 'return voyage' clue. Since Mrs Boynton had been a prison wardress, one might suppose that she knew of criminal activity by Lady Westholme in the United States. Although that does not of itself mean she is the murderer, the '*I never forget*' clue makes her a suspect and without it there would have been no indication of a motive.

Unfortunately, Poirot over-analyses the clue when presenting his report, saying that the words impressed Sarah because of the loud hoarse tone in which they were uttered. But Sarah did not say that the words were 'loud'. Indeed, Mrs Boynton had spoken in a soft, husky but penetrating voice. Then he says that her words were not a reasonable answer to Sarah and that, if she had said "I never forget impertinence", that would have made sense – "but no – *a face* is what she said". However, Poirot unfairly limits her answer. She had said that she did not forget "*anything*" – of which "*a face*" was just one example in the same way that "*an action*" (such as Sarah's rudeness) was. So her words *were* a reasonable reaction to what Sarah had said.

Of the remaining two points, point (8) is that Gerard and Ginevra had tents next door to each other. He says that Lady Westholme stated "definitely" that the Arab servant had first been into *Ginevra's* tent before approaching Mrs Boynton. But, he says, since Gerard's tent was next door, it is "possible" that the Arab entered *Gerard's* tent to select a suitable drug and a hypodermic syringe before then going up to the victim.

However, his explanation of this 'adjacent tents' clue is not satisfactory because it was Miss Pierce, not Lady Westholme, who mentioned the servant going into Ginevra's tent (Part 2 chapter 5). Since the nub of the clue is that the witness's identification of the wrong tent was the product of her being "very suggestible", it only works if the suggestible witness gives the evidence. So, if it had been Lady Westholme (as Poirot suggests), it would not work.

Moreover, we assume from Poirot's explanations that the servant went into *either* Ginevra's tent *or* Gerard's. But, six paragraphs after revealing that Lady Westholme, dressed as an Arab, went into Gerard's tent, he says that she mistook Gerard's tent and did look *first* into Ginevra's. This, he says, explains Ginevra's story of a sheikh in disguise entering her tent.

Readers will have wondered what to make of Ginevra's comments, not least because Gerard tells Poirot (in Part 2 chapters 3 and 11) that she is escaping into a fantasy world where she is a royal personage in danger, surrounded by enemies. So, is she so mad as to be ignored? Or are there clues in what she says? In Part 2 chapter 12 she tells Poirot that she is in danger with lots of enemies; that Gerard is in love with her because he says her name in his sleep; that the Boyntons are not her real family; and that one of her disguised enemies, sent by "The Sheikh", had looked into her tent.

Believe it or not, there are a couple of clues in what Ginevra says. If one treats *Gerard's* points as genuine delusions and removes them from what *Ginevra* says, this still leaves two of her points – that Gerard said her name in his sleep and that a disguised person looked into her tent. The most astute reader might wonder whether those two points are not therefore delusions – but clues, albeit unusually concealed.

And, in fact they are. The first shows that Ginevra had been into Gerard's tent and seen him lying in his fevered state; but, although Poirot says this is "very significant", it only makes Ginevra, very fleetingly, a suspect. The second, described by Poirot as Ginevra's story of "a sheikh in disguise" (which is not quite what she says) was "significant enough" to show that the Arab servant who looked into Ginevra's tent was *in disguise*. Poirot describes this as one of Lady Westholme's two "slips" but it does not of itself point to her being the disguised person without her other "slip", which derives from the remaining point, number (6), the distance of about 200 yards from the marquee to Mrs Boynton's chair.

The focus of this '200 yards' clue is on what was seen of the Arab servant. Lady Westholme and Miss Pierce said that they could not see his face or hear him because of the distance. However, Lady Westholme had also said that his breeches were very torn and patched and that his puttees were wound untidily. But, says

Poirot, since she could not hear him or see his face, she could not have seen the state of his breeches and puttees – not at 200 yards. That is a fair deduction. It made him wonder *why* she had insisted that the servant wore ragged breeches and untidy puttees.

Could it be that the breeches were not torn and the puttees were non-existent? This drew his attention to her and he concluded that she had pretended to be an Arab by putting on her riding breeches, boots and khaki-coloured coat and making an Arab headdress with a checked duster and a skein of knitting wool.

Readers knew she had riding breeches, boots and a coat (but not that it was khaki-coloured) and a skein of knitting wool and duster (but not that it was checked). However, only the most astute reader would have worked out that she had used these items to dress as an Arab. But in fairness, the author does give a clear description of what a native servant would wear (Part 1 chapter 11) and so a reader wondering about a disguise should know what was needed.

Nevertheless, Poirot still has the problem that Lady Westholme could not have been the Arab servant if she was with Miss Pierce when they saw him. Readers are highly likely to assume, from the description which they both give of the incident in Part 2 chapter 5, that they were together, particularly with Lady Westholme saying "*We* were too far away to hear" and "*We* didn't see his face" and Miss Pierce saying that it happened "… before *we* started out". However, they were not together.

Miss Pierce was alone and would not have known that Lady Westholme had not watched the incident from her tent because, with their tents being on either side of the marquee, they could not have seen *each other*. As Poirot says, this is shown by the fact that Lady Westholme "came to see" if Miss Pierce was awake (she had actually said "strolled along"); and, if she had had to stroll along to check, despite Miss Pierce sitting in the entrance to her tent, similarly Miss Pierce could not have seen Lady Westholme.

This 'strolling' clue is very good, the best in the book, though not perfect because they could still have seen an Arab servant together *after* Lady Westholme had "strolled along". Indeed, perhaps even cleverer than the clueing that they were *not* together is creating the clear impression in Part 2 chapter 5 that they *were* together, without actually saying this.

Looking generally at Poirot's list of significant points, it is not clear how he can identify some as significant as early as Part 2 chapter 10 and yet omit not only the 'dizziness', 'pronoun' and 'opening words' clues but also the mark on Mrs Boynton's wrist, the missing digitoxin, the conflicting statements of Sarah and Raymond about the time of death, the tents being on either side of the marquee and Miss Pierce recalling Poirot's sneeze – all of which could have been listed in an appropriately enigmatic way.

Poirot says that "the only point" where Lady Westholme's plan went "astray" (apart, presumably, from her two "slips") was replacing the syringe; he says that, with Gerard returning so soon, she had to return it during the night. But surely she could have returned it after the murder before leaving the camp with Miss Pierce at 4.15 pm since Gerard did not return until 4.20 pm. And he could not then find his drugs case because "someone had moved it". Failing to return it to its original position after taking the digitoxin seems like another "slip" since Gerard's suspicions led to the investigation.

Finally, there are times where we think we may be getting a clue but it turns out to be insignificant or not a clue at all. First is Cope's story of the pregnant servant fired by Mrs Boynton in Part 1 chapter 12. Although cited twice, it is not mentioned again and just seems to provide another example of her cruelty.

Secondly, in that chapter, as the Boyntons finish lunch, Mrs Boynton drops a spoon with a ringing clatter. This is not mentioned again but in retrospect we wonder if it was a signal from Mrs Boynton for Lady Westholme to stay at camp that afternoon.

Indeed, we are left wondering what arrangements were made between them about going to Petra and meeting that afternoon because, surprisingly, we get no clues about that appointment with death. We don't even know for certain if Lady Westholme went to Petra on Mrs Boynton's "instructions" (as Poirot suggests) or if she did so in order to murder her.

Thirdly, in Part 2 chapter 11 Gerard refers to Miss Pierce wearing chains and beads that clink but no reference is made to this again. In retrospect we guess they are mentioned because Gerard's reference to Lady Westholme's coats, breeches and boots might stand out if there were not also a reference to Miss Pierce's attire.

Last is Poirot's report. Towards the start the room is so silent that a noise in the next room, probably of a shoe being dropped, sounds like a bomb. We wonder whether that sound will be significant but we never learn what it was. We do find out three chapters later that the next room was Lady Westholme's when, as Poirot completes his report, a sound like a shot is heard. We assume that he meant her to overhear his report before taking her own life.

17

Hercule Poirot's Christmas

Solution

Poirot investigates the murder of Simeon Lee, a rich tyrannical patriarch who had originally made his money in diamonds in South Africa. His throat is cut on Christmas Eve while his family are staying with him at Gorston Hall in Middleshire where he lives in a first-floor room as a shrivelled old invalid.

His unhappy wife, Adelaide, had died years before. They had had four sons and one daughter but he had been constantly unfaithful to her. He boasts that he could produce a bodyguard of sons if he looked for the illegitimate ones.

Alfred is the eldest of his four legitimate middle-aged sons. Unlike the others, he lives at Gorston Hall, with his wife Lydia, and manages Simeon's mining machinery works. Harry, an unmarried prodigal son, who had left home after stealing from Simeon, is returning for the first time in 20 years. George, a Member of Parliament, is a skinflint while his younger wife, Magdalene, is extravagant. David, an artist, who considers his father responsible for Adelaide's death, has not been home for 20 years but his wife Hilda persuades him to go at Christmas.

None of the sons have children. But Simeon's daughter, Jennifer, had married a Spaniard, Juan Estravados, and had had a daughter, Pilar, who had been raised in Spain and become a young lady. Both Juan and Jennifer are dead and Simeon, who has never met Pilar, invites her to live at Gorston Hall.

The final guest is Stephen Farr, who arrives unexpectedly on 23 December as the son of Simeon's former business partner in South Africa, Ebenezer Farr, who had died a couple of years before. Simeon insists he should stay, calling him "one of the family", making us wonder if he is an illegitimate son

On Christmas Eve Simeon, ensuring that he is overheard by his family members, tells his solicitor on the telephone that he wants to make a new will after Christmas. That evening at 7.45 pm Superintendent Sugden, collecting for the Police Orphanage, calls on Simeon. He comes down from Simeon's room at 8 pm and is let out by Tressilian, the butler.

After dinner, Alfred and Harry remain in the dining room and Lydia, George, Magdalene, David, Hilda, Pilar and Stephen disperse to other parts of the house. Tressilian is in his pantry and Simeon's male nurse, Horbury, is at the cinema. At 9.15 pm a loud noise is heard: a crashing of china, an overthrowing of furniture, a series of cracks and bumps and then a high wailing scream.

Everyone races to Simeon's room but the door is locked and has to be broken down. They look in. The overturned furniture and splintered china suggest a terrific struggle. But no one is in there except Simeon, lying in front of the fire, in a pool of blood. His jugular vein has been severed and he has bled to death. David says "The mills of God grind slowly" and Lydia says "Who would have thought the old man to have had so much blood in him?".

Meanwhile Superintendent Sugden returns to the house at 9.15 pm. He runs up to the room and sees Pilar pick up something from the floor – a wisp of rubber and a small wooden object – which he asks her to hand to him. But there is no sign of the murder weapon; and some diamonds kept in Simeon's safe are later found to be missing.

Sugden telephones Colonel Johnson, Chief Constable of Middleshire with whom Poirot is staying and they set out for Gorston Hall. There Sugden explains that at about 5 pm Simeon had telephoned and asked him to come and see him at 8 pm, pretending to be collecting for a police charity. He says that he was shown up to Simeon's room and told that his diamonds were missing and that he should return at 9.15 pm, by when Simeon would know if they had been stolen or taken as a joke.

Sugden's investigations had revealed that, of the two windows in the room, one was locked and the other, although open about four inches at the bottom, was fixed there by an anti-burglar screw. Also the wall outside was smooth. So no one could have left that way. Since the only door appeared to have been locked on the inside, with the key seen there by Sugden and Harry, and since the only person in the room was Simeon, readers appear to have been presented, as Johnson spots, with a classic locked room mystery.

However, that mystery is solved almost at once when the key which had been on the inside is examined. There are scratches at the end of the barrel meaning that it was turned from *outside* the door by means of an implement, such as a pair of pliers, which went through the keyhole and gripped the barrel.

When it is established that no one could have left the house without being seen, Poirot says that the murder was "a family affair". He agrees with Sugden that no "stranger" was involved and with Lydia, after Horbury's cinema alibi has been checked, that "It only leaves – the family". However, he later goes on to say, rather tantalisingly, that "It might be a member of the family – and, at the same time, a stranger ..." (Part 5 section III).

The effect of that will be to reinforce the suspicion that Stephen is Simeon's son. Although he is later forced to admit that he is not Ebenezer's son, he claims instead to be called Stephen Grant and that, after meeting Pilar on the train to Gorston Hall, he followed her and pretended to be Stephen Farr whom he had known in

South Africa. But readers know that he is lying because the book's opening section says that he had been making his plans for years. So it is no surprise when he finally admits to being Simeon's son. He says that his mother spoke about Simeon, making him obsessed to see what his father was like. But he had only come to England to see his father, not to kill him.

In fact, the murderer is another illegitimate son – a different "stranger" who is a member of the family – Superintendent Sugden. Poirot says that all his life Sugden had resented the wrong his father did him. Having inherited his pride, patience and revengeful spirit, he decided long ago to kill him. A Superintendent has a good opportunity for getting away with murder and, having entered the Middleshire Police Force, Sugden waited for one.

Poirot says that Simeon never sent for Sugden. Sugden had telephoned Simeon and spoken vaguely about an attempt at robbery. He had said that he would call just before 8 pm and pretend to be collecting for a police charity. Simeon did not know that Sugden was his son. Poirot says that, when Sugden called, he told Simeon a tale of substituted diamonds. It is not clear whether Sugden *knew* that Simeon had some diamonds (or, if so, how) but Simeon opened the safe to show he still had them and Sugden, catching him unawares, cut his throat (we are not told with what).

Then he took the diamonds, piled up tables, chairs and china and twined a very thin rope or cord, which he had brought in coiled round his body, in and out between them. As well as the cord (and the weapon and implement for turning the key), he had, it seems from what Poirot says, brought in four other items.

The first was a long pink bladder (like a balloon) of the sort that were sold at fairs with faces painted on them called 'Dying Pigs'. As the air rushed out of them, they would give an inhuman wail. Sugden blew it up and stopped up its mouth with a wooden peg (his second item) connected to the cord. He must have wedged the bladder carefully in position so that the peg would come out – instead of the bladder moving – when the cord was pulled.

The third item was a bottle of freshly killed animal's blood to which he added his fourth item, sodium citrate, so as to delay the blood clotting. He sprinkled this about and added more to the blood flowing from Simeon's wound. He also made up the fire (which was still blazing an hour and a quarter later) so that the body should keep warm, thus making it seem as if death had occurred later than it had. Then he passed the two ends of the cord out through the slit at the bottom of the window and let them hang down the wall. Somehow he must have known that one window would not be locked at that time.

He then left the room (with the weapon), turning the key from the outside, and hid the diamonds in Lydia's stone sink miniature garden since keeping the diamonds was not part of his plan. If they were found, Poirot says that this would only focus suspicion on the family – presumably, although he does not explain this, because it would eliminate theft by a burglar.

At 9.15 pm Sugden returned and pulled on the cord, dislodging the furniture and china, which crashed down. The peg came out of the bladder (disconnecting from the cord and falling on the floor) and the bladder deflated, causing the scream of the 'Dying Pig'. He then re-wound the cord round his body under his waistcoat before ringing the doorbell. He hoped to retrieve the 'Dying Pig' but Pilar picked it up.

The main feature of the solution is that it is clever for the investigating officer, who is assisted unofficially by Poirot, to be the murderer. At no stage does he really appear to be a suspect. It may be that, when in Part 5 section II he throws back his head and laughs (in the manner of Harry and Stephen) and Poirot says that he may just have seen a ghost, some readers will guess that he is an illegitimate son. Some may even think that he was called in by Simeon to help with the diamonds because Simeon *knew* he was his son. But none of this means he is the murderer, especially since he was outside at 9.15 pm.

His plan of establishing a false time of death with the furniture noise and the dying scream – so making it appear that the murder happened at 9.15 pm rather than before 8 pm – is most ingenious. However, it will have seemed odd to readers, as soon as a terrific struggle is suggested, that that such a frail old man could have put up any struggle, let alone one which overturned a big mahogany chair and table.

It was also risky to assume that pulling a "very thin" cord from outside would reliably cause all the solid furniture and glass to be overturned as well as the peg to come out of the 'Dying Pig' with the desired effect, which makes the murder plan feel unrealistic. Nevertheless, the cord, the 'Dying Pig' and peg – along with the animal's blood, sodium citrate and key-turning implement – are memorably imaginative and clever, although, as Poirot says when examining the body and at the denouement, there was "too much blood" for such a frail, shrivelled, dried up old man.

Sugden had also thought about explaining other points relating to his plan. As for coming to the house at both 7.45 pm and 9.15 pm, he says that the first visit was intended by Simeon to convince the diamond thief that he would call in the police for a second visit at 9.15 pm if restitution were not made. This seems quite clever but Poirot regards it as a weakness because Simeon would have had more leverage over the suspect if he had asked Sugden to stay in the house.

As for the murder happening in a locked room with the key on the inside, Sugden suggests that, although suicide won't do (because there is no weapon in the room), the murderer had tried, by leaving the key on the inside, to make it *look like* suicide. But this is most unpersuasive – not because people do not kill themselves that way[1] but because the murderer can hardly have meant it to look like suicide when, as Poirot says, he had left so much evidence of a struggle and had not left the murder weapon.

Sugden, however, again has answers. The murderer, not expecting a struggle, had no *time* to set the room right with everyone rushing up the stairs; and he didn't leave the weapon because "Criminals usually make mistakes" – which again is unconvincing. He also answers Poirot's concern about Simeon struggling at all by suggesting that the murderer was a woman – though again this doesn't sound convincing with so much solid furniture being overturned.

Despite Sugden's ready (but unpersuasive) answers, one part of his thinking is never clear – which is *why* he left the key on the inside and turned it from the outside. At the denouement Poirot says that he had to turn the key from the outside so that no one could discover the body before 9.15 pm. That, of course, is right. But why leave the key on the *inside* when he knows that, because of the evidence of a struggle, no one will think that the death was suicide?

Why not just lock the door from the outside and dispose of the key? After all, he has no interest in making it look like suicide – he is the very person who says that suicide won't do. Moreover, it would have been "absurd", as Poirot puts it at the denouement, for the murderer to have wasted precious time at 9.15 pm using the special implement, which Johnson says (Part 3 section VII) would not be easy to manage, while everyone is rushing up the stairs in response to the noise. So, the cleverness with the key is an elaboration which seems to give no benefit to Sugden and even undermines the idea of the murder being committed just before 9.15 pm.

More frustrating is the motive. When Poirot says that all his life Sugden had resented the wrong his father did him, he must mean his illegitimacy. But even if Sugden was a proud man, with the Lees' revengeful streak, this seems surprising as a motive for murder – the more so when, according to Poirot, Sugden's mother had, with money which Simeon had given her, doubtless found a husband to stand father to her child. Unfortunately, Sugden gives no better explanation, simply saying "God rot his soul in hell! I'm glad I did it!".

Other motives are also hinted at – but with much less conviction – George's concern about Simeon's intention to reduce his allowance; David's hatred of Simeon; and Simeon's announced intention, whether genuine or not, to make a new will which might affect Alfred, George and David's expectations. Indeed, when Poirot runs over the family's motives and alibis at the denouement, he does not even attribute a motive to Harry. The motives he attributes to the others become weaker as he proceeds. In Lydia's case he even passes over her motive because it is "sufficiently obvious" – what does he mean? Perhaps that she was tired of Alfred dancing attendance on Simeon?

As for alibis, Poirot's strangest comment is again reserved for Lydia who said she had been in the drawing room, as Tressilian confirms (Part 3 section XVI). Poirot, however, suggests at the denouement that the short-sighted Tressilian might not have seen her by the window half concealed by the heavy curtains but only seen the cape of her dress, arranged as if she were standing there. This does not sound plausible. Moreover, Poirot cheats when suggesting that Tressilian thought that Lydia had been half concealed by the heavy curtains. Tressilian had not said that. It was Poirot himself who had seen Lydia standing by the window half hidden by the curtains (Part 5 section III).

This just leaves Pilar, who is not Pilar after all but Conchita Lopez, who had been with Pilar in Spain when she was killed. Conchita knew that Pilar's rich grandfather had sent for her. So, with their faces being alike, she took her passport and went to England to become rich. She herself becomes the object of a highly dubious murder attempt when Sugden balances a cannon ball on her bedroom door so that it crashes down as she enters. Luckily, it misses.

Poirot explains that, when she remarked that she had picked up a pink balloon from Simeon's floor, she was in danger if Sugden had heard her remark. He says it might well have been heard because she "cried out" the remark, "cried aloud" her discovery, her voice was "high and clear" and Sugden heard her "clear, high voice calling out its remark". However, when she actually made the remark (Part 6 section II), she simply "said" it. On one occasion (Part 2 section II) her voice is high and clear but not when making the remark.

Moreover, Sugden's attempt would have been too late anyway to stop Poirot deducing the truth because *he* had heard Pilar's remark. If Sugden knew that Poirot had heard it, his booby trap would not only be highly dubious but senseless. So, maybe one should assume in his favour that he did not know Poirot had heard it, despite Poirot responding to it with a sharp exclamation.

Plot

The plot combines two classic detective story devices. The first is the English house-party murder, which is 'classic' because it is "the quintessentially English murder as far as many readers are concerned".[2] However, it is odd that the story is set at Christmas because, although 'Christmas' is often mentioned (the title in the United States is *Murder for Christmas*), as is the season for peace, goodwill, forgiveness and families, there is no festive spirit at all and no mention of traditional Christmas trappings until Part 6 section II when Pilar indicates what she would have expected of an English Christmas and finds some crackers and the like in a storeroom.

The second classic device is the locked room mystery. This promises much but, within moments of Colonel Johnson describing it as "one of those damned cases you get in detective stories where a man is killed in a locked room by some apparently supernatural agency", it is resolved by the murderer *himself* pointing to the scratches on the key.

Subject to that, the murder is meticulously plotted, with the murderer's identity being a genuine mystery. Even those readers who think that Sugden might possibly be the murderer – not just an illegitimate son – are likely to find the plot mystifying until the end because it is so difficult to work out how or why he might have done it.

The book is divided into seven Parts, each covering one day from 22 to 28 December. Part 1 begins well (with Stephen and Pilar) but after that, starting with Lydia telling Alfred about George's success in his political career (as if Alfred would not know this), the exposition is much too obvious, with family members telling one another facts which they must surely know. As example follows example, readers will feel that the author would have done far better to have provided the family history by way of a narrative than through artificial conversations between family members.

After that, the rest of the story moves steadily but is slowed by a prolonged interviewing of the suspects over 10 of the 17 sections of Part 3. However, the lack of pace takes nothing away from the meticulous plotting and, assuming that one focuses on the ingenuity rather than the realism of the murder plan, the only thing that does jar, apart from the weak motivation and a few errors, is the highly improbable attempt with the cannon ball, which is conceived and executed in so few pages that it could easily have been omitted.

As for the errors, in Part 3 section V Johnson refers to the "Cartwright case" (*Three Act Tragedy*), saying that Poirot came "here" (Middleshire) – an error repeated by Sugden in the next section. In that case Poirot went to Yorkshire, where Johnson was Chief Constable. Johnson is also wrong in suggesting that Poirot came *with* Cartwright because they went to Yorkshire separately.

Then in Part 3 section XVII when Horbury is tricked by Poirot into admitting that he overheard Simeon's telephone call with Sugden just after 5 pm, he says he heard Simeon say "I don't know who to suspect". But, since Simeon's diamonds were *not* missing at that time, he would not have suspected anyone. So, one assumes that the author, pleased with the way in which she has got Poirot to trick Horbury, has lost sight of what he could actually have heard.

Most of the other errors are of a timing nature. One is Tressilian thinking, when seeing Harry in Part 2 Section I, that his features "had all been there three years ago" and yet we are told twice that the prodigal son had been away for nearly 20 years.[3] Another is Sugden referring in Part 5 section I to Horbury getting the wind up "last" night. In fact, that was two nights ago, in Part 3 section III. Then in Part 6 section V he says that Stephen stayed at the King's Arms for *two* days. In fact, Stephen was on the train to Middleshire on the 22nd and came to Gorston Hall on the 23rd. In Part 4 section II we learn that George put through his telephone call to Westeringham at 8.58 pm but in Part 5 section II Sugden says that this happened at 8.59 pm exactly. It is also odd that Sugden rang the doorbell at 7.45 pm when Simeon, who had "made a special point of the time" (Part 3 section VII), had asked him to come at 8 pm.

Finally, we are told in Part 3 section XVII that under Simeon's will half his fortune was to go to Alfred while the other half was "to be divided in equal shares between his remaining children: Harry, George, David and Jennifer". In Part 6 section 1 the solicitor, Mr Charlton, says that, because Jennifer is dead, her portion goes not to Pilar but back into Simeon's estate to be shared by the others. In fact, that was not the case where a gift was made to a number of named beneficiaries, one of whom (Jennifer) had died, leaving a child (Pilar) who was alive when the testator (Simeon) died. The rule there (under section 33 of the Wills Act 1837) was that the deceased beneficiary (Jennifer) was deemed to have died immediately *after* the testator (Simeon) so that her share passed under her will or intestacy (presumably to Pilar) instead of to the others. But, as we later learn, Pilar was dead when Simeon died – so the rule would not actually apply for that reason. In short, Mr Charlton was right that Pilar would not get Jennifer's share – but not because Jennifer was dead but because Pilar was dead.

Clues

In Part 6 section VI Poirot says that the two most valuable clues were Lydia's quotation from *Macbeth* (Act V Scene I) on seeing Simeon's dead body: "Who would have thought the old man to have had so much blood in him?" and Tressilian saying that he had a strange feeling that things seemed to be happening that had happened before.

Looking first at the 'Macbeth quotation' clue, Sugden tells Poirot what Lydia had said but Sugden was not in the room to hear her say it – so how does he know about it? Be that as it may, Poirot indicates at the denouement that his "first glimmer of light" came from there being so much blood. But what was this first "glimmer"? He seems to suggest that he had two thoughts.

The first was that there was "too much" blood. But the quotation did not provide the clue for this because he had already noticed in Part 3 section VII that there was "too much blood" *before* learning what Lydia had said. So, actually, the *excess* of blood, not the quotation, seems to be the nub of the clue. But why is the excess significant? Poirot does not say. Is he thinking that, since not all the blood could have been Simeon's, the murderer had sprinkled extra blood about to give the impression of a struggle? That seems unlikely because he was perplexed by the struggle *anyway*, saying that it was hard to see how any struggle involving the frail old man could result in so much solid furniture being overturned. So his first thought about the 'Macbeth quotation' clue leaves readers with various uncertainties.

However, it is more persuasive than his "second thought", which was that the excess of blood suggested that Simeon's own blood had risen up against him. One presumes that he is referring to his comments in Part 4 section II about David's words on seeing the body – "The mills of God grind slowly" – which are part of an ancient Greek expression that continues "but they grind exceeding small" – meaning that divine retribution may be slow but it is sure. Poirot suggests that, if David killed his father, that might explain the blood-letting, the demand for sacrifice, the wrong (to David's mother) wiped out by expiation. But an excess of blood is an implausible basis for saying that the murder was committed by a blood relation, if this is what Poirot is suggesting.

Looking at the 'Macbeth quotation' clue overall, it is a pity that we are left to make so many presumptions about it when the excess of blood actually provided the story's inspiration – the author having been told by her brother-in-law, James Watts, to whom the book is dedicated, that her murders were becoming too anaemic and that he yearned for a murder with lots of blood.[4]

Poirot says that, in addition to the extra blood, one of the murderer's items was sodium citrate. This is an impressive deduction because nowhere is it clued (no mention is made, for example, of the blood being "fresh, wet, gleaming" at 9.15 pm, as Poirot says at the denouement) but, more frustratingly, Poirot never explains the purpose of this chemical, which retards blood clotting.

As to Sugden's other *howdunnit* items, one was the cord. The cord is not referred to before the denouement and it is only clued, if at all, for the astute reader, by there being an open window. Another item was the weapon – but this provides no clue since, oddly, we never find out what it was or what Sugden did with it. Another item was the key-turning implement, which is obviously a clue to the locked room mystery but not a stimulating one since the scratches explain the mystery almost straightaway.

His final items were the 'Dying Pig' and wooden peg. When Poirot learns that Pilar had picked up "something quite small", he asks Sugden about it. Sugden produces "a little triangular piece of pink rubber and a small wooden peg" and says that the rubber was cut from Simeon's spongebag. So how does Poirot establish that it was a 'Dying Pig'?

He refers to Simeon's dying scream, described by Hilda as "inhuman like a beast" and by Harry as "like killing a pig" (there is also a nice touch in the doctor saying "Throat cut like a pig"). But the key moment comes in Part 6 section II while Pilar and Stephen are playing with balloons. When Stephen's balloon (colour unknown) bursts, Pilar stirs the little wisp of rubber with her toe, saying that this was what she picked up in Simeon's room, only his was pink. Poirot later says that it was not until then that he "saw the truth". So, had he not heard her, he may never have arrived at it. Since it was therefore plainly the 'pink balloon' clue that enabled him to solve the *howdunnit*, his emphasis on the 'Macbeth quotation' clue seems even more surprising.

This brings us to the second of Poirot's two most valuable clues – Tressilian telling him (Part 3 section XVI) of his strange feeling that things seemed to be happening that had happened before – the 'Tressilian repetition' clue. Poirot says that he got that feeling from opening the door to Harry and then the next day (in fact the same day – in Part 2) opening it to Stephen. Since they were "astoundingly alike", opening the door to Stephen was like opening it to Harry. For Tressilian, who had told Poirot (Part 6 section III) that he couldn't see like he used to and mixed people up, it might have been the same man.

In fact Poirot had tested Tressilian's eyesight on Boxing Day when asking him (Part 5 section I) whether the wall calendar with tear-off leaves had been untouched since the murder. Tressilian shuffled across the room until only a foot or two away and said that the calendar had been torn off because it showed the 26th.

Readers, and a puzzled Sugden, wonder if there is something fishy about the calendar but what the author has cleverly concealed, while misdirecting readers towards the dates with the 'calendar' clue, is that, although Poirot never actually says this, he was testing Tressilian's eyesight.

The relevance of Tressilian confusing Harry with Stephen is that, with Harry resembling Simeon so closely, it points to Stephen also being one of his sons – and so to a kind of triangle of resemblance between Simeon, Harry and Stephen. Although this triangle is a red herring because Stephen is merely illegitimate rather than the murderer, it is the basis of the real 'resemblance' clue, which is that in the middle of the triangle there is a fourth person, Sugden, who resembles the other three. That 'resemblance' clue – the triangle with Sugden in its middle – needs careful analysis.

The starting point is the first side of the triangle – the resemblance between the father, Simeon, and his legitimate son, Harry. Even before Poirot's arrival, we know that Simeon has an aquiline nose (Part 1 section VI) and Harry has a high-bridged one (Part 2 section I). Since an aquiline nose has a prominent bridge at its upper part, the author no doubt regarded the terms 'aquiline' and 'high-bridged' as synonymous for the purposes of clueing but wanted to avoid making the resemblance too obvious and so used different terms. Thus also, when their noses are first described, Stephen has a high-bridged one (Part 1 section II) while Sugden has an aquiline one (Part 3 section VI).

On first seeing Harry, Poirot feels he has seen him before – the high-bridged nose, the arrogant poise of the head, the line of the jaw – and he realises that there had been a good resemblance between Simeon and Harry. At that stage he had only seen Simeon's dead body but in Part 5 section IV, when studying a portrait of Simeon as a young man, he agrees with Pilar that Simeon is like Harry might have been ten years before. He mentions the portrait again in Part 6 section VI, saying that the resemblance between Simeon and Harry is quite striking. He mentions the "high-bridged aquiline" nose (the author at last using both terms in the same sentence at the denouement), the long sharp line of the jaw, the backward poise of the head.

He adds that Harry inherited many of Simeon's mannerisms – the habit of throwing back his head and laughing and of drawing his finger along his jaw. However, although there are three occasions before Poirot's arrival when Simeon and Harry stroked their jaws, there is no mention of Simeon throwing back his head even though he cackles, chuckles or laughs over a dozen times before he is killed. And Poirot is not told that Simeon had that habit or stroked his jaw. Further, even though Poirot sees Harry throw back his head and laugh in Part 4 section I, he never sees him stroke his jaw. So the mannerisms (as opposed to the physical similarities) are not legitimate clues for Poirot's confirmation of the resemblance between Simeon and Harry.

The second element of the 'resemblance' clue is the second side of the triangle – the resemblance of Stephen to Harry (and therefore also to Simeon, which is the third side of the triangle). When Poirot says that Harry and Stephen are "astoundingly alike" at the denouement, he says that Stephen has a high-bridged nose, a habit of throwing his head back when he laughs and of stroking his jaw with his forefinger. He adds that, if one looks at Simeon's portrait, one sees not only Harry but Stephen.

Since Poirot sees Harry and Stephen in person, he can see that they each have high-bridged noses. He also sees Stephen's finger caress his jaw in Part 3 section XV. But, although readers are told in Part 2 section V, *prior* to Poirot's arrival, that Stephen laughed throwing his head back, Poirot never sees him display that mannerism. Moreover, the 'Tressilian repetition' clue is not as valuable as he suggests in pointing to Harry and Stephen's resemblance. This is because, when he went to answer the door to

Harry (Part 2 section I) and then to Stephen (Part 2 section IV), he simply saw through the frosted glass the silhouette of a big man in a slouch hat. Although he was worried that everything was happening twice, he had not then actually seen Stephen's face.

Other indications do, however, make it obvious that Harry resembled Stephen. Thus in Part 3 section III Tressilian thinks "Mr Harry was talking enough for twenty – no, not Mr Harry, the South African gentleman". In Part 3 section XV Johnson thinks that the entering figure is Harry but, as Stephen comes in, he sees his error. In Part 4 section I Poirot thinks that the man with Pilar is Stephen but then sees that it is Harry. Finally, at the denouement Sugden says that he had twice mistaken Stephen for Harry, although readers were not previously told about either of those occasions.

Which brings us to the key final element of the 'resemblance' clue – the resemblance of Sugden, the man in the middle of the triangle, to the other three. When Poirot first sees Sugden in Part 3 section VI, he sees a tall man with an aquiline nose, a pugnacious jaw and a flourishing moustache. By then we know that Simeon too had an aquiline nose and that Harry and Stephen had high-bridged noses. However, readers would do well to equate Sugden's pugnacious jaw with Simeon and Harry's jaws having a long sharp line.

Clearer help is given when in Part 3 section XIV Pilar says to Sugden that, as a young man, Simeon must have been "very handsome, like you", so linking Sugden with Simeon and providing a key clue. She adds that Stephen is "very handsome too" – the word 'too' cleverly linking Simeon/Sugden with Stephen. And for those who do not spot Pilar's clever 'handsome' clues, Lydia wonders who is in the garden in Part 6 section I – Sugden or Stephen?

As for Sugden's link with Harry, Poirot relies in Part 6 section VII – as he had done when comparing Stephen to Simeon and

Harry – on the high-bridged nose and, this time legitimately, on the two habits of throwing the head back when laughing and stroking the jaw with his forefinger. He had seen Sugden stroke his jaw four times[5] but the key clue comes when Sugden throws back his head and laughs. Having seen Harry do this in Part 4 section I, Poirot sees Sugden do it in Part 5 section II and says that he may just have seen a ghost. He refers again to this 'ghost' clue at the denouement – the ghost of Simeon.

We know that, when Poirot first saw Harry, he felt he had seen him before. He thought that his resemblance to Simeon caused that feeling. But then, when Sugden threw his head back and laughed, Poirot realised that it was Sugden that Harry reminded him of. Poirot says it was no wonder that Tressilian felt confused when answering the door not to two, but to *three* men who resembled each other – though in fact we were not told that Tressilian was confused when opening the door to Sugden.

Readers will have assumed that an illegitimate son would appear when Simeon tells Pilar (Part 2 section II) that he could produce a bodyguard of sons if he looked for the illegitimate ones and when (Part 3 section II) he swears to the family that he's got a better son somewhere than any of his legitimate ones. But it is not clear how Poirot knows about the first part of this 'boasting' clue (which he mentions at the denouement) since Pilar never told him about it. However, he does know what Simeon said to the family because David tells him in Part 3 section XII. In response, Sugden looks up "suddenly alert" but only an astute reader would spot that this was a small clue to his illegitimacy.

A bigger clue comes in the form of the 'false moustache' clue. Having had Simeon's portrait placed in his bedroom at Gorston Hall, Poirot purchases a false moustache in the village. One would like to think that, with Sugden's moustache having fascinated Poirot when they first met and again in Part 4 section II, readers will spot that he is going to try the false moustache on Simeon's portrait. Indeed, this is what he later tells Sugden he did, adding that "the face that looked at me was yours".

So the 'false moustache' clue becomes yet another of the numerous elements of the 'resemblance' clue, which is impressively constructed across so many different sections of the book and comprises the 'Tressilian repetition' clue, the multiple similarity references (the 'nose', 'poise', 'jaw', 'laugh' and 'handsome' clues) and the 'ghost' and 'boasting' clues.

Of those elements, it is surprising that Poirot selects the 'Tressilian repetition' clue as the most valuable since it is neither the best nor most important. The best clues in the book are probably Pilar's 'handsome' clues about Sugden because, despite their importance, the words "very handsome, like you" and "very handsome too" do not seem like clues; while the key resemblance moment was Sugden throwing his head back and laughing, with Poirot giving us the 'ghost' clue as he realised that Sugden was an illegitimate son.

As for Sugden also being the murderer, the key-turning implement would, as Johnson says, have needed "criminal experience" and Sugden may have had more exposure to criminals than the others (except perhaps Harry). But, on the other hand, Johnson also says that Sugden is "not an *imaginative* chap in any way" (Part 3 section V), which is unfair because the murder plan did not lack imagination. However, the main problem with Sugden being the murderer, is that he was outside the house at 9.15 pm. So, as Poirot tells readers within moments of the 'ghost' clue, the time element is "very important", which seems to be a clue that death must have occurred before 9.15 pm.

At that stage (Boxing Day), however, Poirot does not know how Sugden did it. But he says to Alfred (Part 5 section V) that the facts all point in one direction and that there is just some "irrelevant matter" to be cleared out of the way. Those comments are odd since there is nothing in the three sections after the 'ghost' clue (Part 5 section II, when Poirot realises that Sugden is Simeon's son) enabling him to know *how* he committed the murder (hardly an "irrelevant matter"). So his comments to Alfred seem unjustified.

Indeed, as we have seen, he says that it was not until he got the 'pink balloon' clue (in Part 6 section II) that he "saw the truth" of the *howdunnit* – although he does say a few paragraphs later that he was "not quite sure" until he tried on the moustache. So, which was the key clue – the 'false moustache' clue or the 'pink balloon' clue? He gets the false moustache in Part 6 section I but we don't know if he tries it on before he gets the 'pink balloon' clue in the next section. Whatever the answer, he didn't get either clue until the day after his comments to Alfred, which is another reason why those comments seem unjustified.

Perhaps, by "irrelevant matter", he meant the true identities of Stephen and Pilar. In explaining how he knew that Pilar was an imposter, he refers to the genetic law that two blue-eyed people (Pilar's parents) are unlikely to have a brown-eyed child. We were told three times that Pilar had dark eyes; then separately that Jennifer had blue eyes; and then that Juan had blue eyes.[6] So the 'brown eyes' clue was built up in parts, which is good multiple clueing. Poirot supports his deduction by suggesting that Jennifer was "a most chaste and respectable lady" by which he presumably means that Jennifer would have been faithful to Juan so that Pilar/Conchita could not have been the product of her liaison with another man who had brown eyes.

This story contains an abundance of clues, with two in particular working well. The 'resemblance' clue works so well because there are *two* illegitimate sons, with readers naturally deceived into thinking, after spotting Stephen as illegitimate, that that is the extent of the clue. The 'pink balloon' clue also works well. That is not because it enables Poirot to deduce *how* a false time of death was established – indeed only the most astute reader could have worked out the *howdunnit* from the 'pink balloon' clue. It is because it is a *double* clue, which also relates to the *whodunnit* since, if Pilar had picked up a wisp from a pink balloon, why did Sugden say that it came from a spongebag and why did he fail, highly suspiciously, to mention it until Poirot raised it?

The final clue, which works less well, is the 'Simeon character' clue. In Part 3 section XI Poirot comments that the "whole importance of the case" lay in Simeon's character, adding that, because he was a certain kind of man, he set in motion forces which brought about his death. So what kind of man was he? Poirot knows, at the time of his comment, that the Lees are hot on revenge and do not forget easily. Harry had told him this (Part 3 section X) and it is referred to four times before the denouement. Gradually more characteristics are referred to – his pride, patience and revengeful spirit – and Poirot mentions these when saying that a son may inherit not only his father's features and gestures but also his characteristics.

It is the comment about inheritance that is important because it doesn't matter so much that Simeon was proud, patient and revengeful. What matters is that Sugden inherited those characteristics. But even those who work out that he had inherited them will find it difficult to work out what the 'Simeon character' clue actually tells us. One assumes that Poirot means that, having had an illegitimate son, Simeon had laid the seeds of his own murder by providing a motive (the illegitimacy) for it. But, if so, then, like that motivation itself, the clue is disappointing because it is hard to believe that Sugden would have been motivated by those characteristics to commit murder. After all, Stephen had presumably inherited the same characteristics and yet wasn't motivated to murder Simeon because of his illegitimacy. He just wanted to see the man who was his father.

18

Sad Cypress

Solution

Poirot is engaged by Dr Peter Lord to prove the innocence of the woman he loves, Elinor Carlisle, who is on trial for poisoning attractive 21-year-old Mary Gerrard on 27 July 1939 with morphine hydrochloride.

The morphine was either in the fish paste sandwiches or in the tea which Mary consumed at lunch with Elinor (who made the sandwiches) and District Nurse Jessie Hopkins (who made the tea) at Hunterbury Hall in Maidensford.

The Hall had been owned by Elinor's wealthy aunt, Laura Welman, who had died a month before. Laura had often said that her only family ties were with Elinor and her late husband's nephew, Roddy Welman, to whom Elinor had been engaged. They both understood that they would share her fortune.

However, before Laura's death, Elinor learned from an anonymous letter that someone might be jeopardising their inheritance by sucking up to Laura, who was very ill, after a stroke. That person was the lodgekeeper's daughter at Hunterbury, Mary Gerrard. So, to protect their inheritance, Elinor and Roddy went to Hunterbury but, while they were there, Roddy fell in love with Mary.

Then, following a second stroke, Laura indicated to Elinor on 28 June that she wished to provide for Mary in her will. But she died overnight before doing so. Next morning, Nurse Hopkins, who had stayed overnight to help Laura's resident nurse, Nurse O'Brien, remarked that a tube of morphine tablets was missing from the attaché case which she had left in the hall.

Since Laura died intestate and Elinor was her niece by blood whereas Roddy was her nephew by marriage, Elinor was regarded as Laura's next of kin (under section 46 of the Administration of Estates Act 1925) and entitled to inherit her fortune and Hunterbury Hall. Despite her distress at losing Roddy to Mary, Elinor decided to carry out Laura's wishes by giving £2,000 to Mary, who was then encouraged by Nurse Hopkins to make a will – not in favour of her father but her aunt in New Zealand, Mary Riley, the sister of Mary's late mother, Eliza Gerrard, who had died 14 years before.

By 27 July Elinor had sold Hunterbury and was in Maidensford to sort out things at the Hall. In the village she learned that Mary, whose father had died on 24 July, would be at the Lodge that morning with Hopkins to remove his things. She then bought bread, butter, milk and two pots of fish paste.

After sorting Laura's clothes, she made sandwiches in the pantry and at 1 pm went to the Lodge to invite Mary and Hopkins up to share them. At the Hall, she brought the plate of sandwiches from the pantry into the morning room and handed it to Mary, who took one and proffered the plate to Hopkins before Elinor took a sandwich herself. Hopkins then went out to the pantry to make tea and came in with a tray bearing a teapot, milk and three cups.

Elinor said she wouldn't have any tea. Hopkins pushed the tray towards Mary, who poured two cups. Hopkins drained hers and bustled out to the pantry. After an awkward silence between Elinor and Mary, Elinor picked up the tray, placing the empty sandwich plate on it, and took it out to the pantry, where Hopkins, whose face was a queer colour, remarked on the heat as she wiped it with a handkerchief. Elinor noticed that Hopkins had pricked herself, which she said she had done on a thorn from the rose trellis at the Lodge.

Elinor then asked Hopkins upstairs to advise on the clothes she had sorted. An hour later they went down to the morning room. Mary was asleep, unable to wake. Hopkins said she had been poisoned. She died at 3.30 pm. Death was due to the 'foudroyante' variety of morphia poisoning, a less common form where, instead of an initial period of excitement, deep sleep quickly supervenes.[1]

We know that Elinor was intensely in love with Roddy and couldn't bear the thought of losing him to Mary; that Dr Lord saw "jealous hatred" in Elinor's face as she looked at Mary; that Nurse O'Brien saw "black hate" on Elinor's face as though she'd like to destroy Mary; that Elinor wondered if one could hate anyone as much as Mary and not show it; that the idea of killing Mary came into her head; and that Dr Lord thought her capable of murder: "She might have done it, yes! *I don't care if she did*".

We know that on 27 July she was angry, knowing that she and Roddy could have lived at Hunterbury; that she thought that it would be for the best if Mary were to die; that she refused an offer from Mrs Bishop, who had been Laura's housekeeper at Hunterbury, to help her at the Hall; and that, when purchasing the fish paste, she mentioned cases of ptomaine poisoning to the grocer.

We know that only Elinor, Mary and Hopkins were at the lunch; that the tea, made by Hopkins and poured by Mary, had been drunk by Hopkins as well; that, although Elinor ate the fish paste sandwiches, which she made, the poison could have been in just one sandwich; that Elinor handed the plate to Mary first; and that Mary would have taken the nearest sandwich.

We know from Hopkins that, when Elinor took the tray out to the pantry, she looked guilty and that, when she took Hopkins upstairs, leaving Mary alone for an hour, she delayed as long as possible; and we know that the police found a freshly torn scrap of a label, with (according to Dr Lord) the words "morphia hydrochlor" on it, in a crack in the pantry floor.

We know that Laura died of morphine poisoning; that the tube of morphine tablets, missing after her death, could have been taken by Elinor; that Elinor could have killed Laura to avoid being disinherited in favour of Mary (or perhaps just out of compassion for her condition); and that Mary might have seen her taking the tube, which could be a motive for murdering Mary.

So, overall, the author has comprehensively implicated Elinor in terms of motive, state of mind, opportunity and planning by a series of excellently constructed, interconnecting points. There is the odd loose end: Hopkins' tube could have been taken by Roddy, Dr Lord, O'Brien or even Mary; Roddy thinks it "absurd" and laughable" that Elinor would poison someone; and why, if Elinor were to blame food poisoning (with Mary having eaten bad paste from one pot while she had eaten good paste from the other), would she use morphine whose symptoms are unlike those of food poisoning? But otherwise, as Poirot says: "It is like the pointer at the fair. It swings round, and when it comes to rest it points always at the same name – *Elinor Carlisle*".

So, if Elinor is innocent, who did kill Mary? As for opportunity, the obvious suspect is Hopkins. Also, she was at Hunterbury when Laura died and the morphine tube was hers. Readers may also wonder whether there is anything suspicious in her influencing Mary to write a will or wiping her face in the pantry or having a prick on her wrist. But even though she is the most obvious suspect, it is hard to see how or why she could have done it.

If it's not her, the only other credible alternative is Roddy. He could have learned that Elinor, after inheriting her fortune from Laura, was making a will leaving it to him; he was, it turns out, in England on 27 July; and could have slipped into the pantry, while Elinor was at the Lodge, and tampered with the sandwiches, intending to kill Elinor (so as to inherit under her will), not knowing that they were to be offered to Mary.

However, readers also know that so much has been made of another issue – Mary's parentage – that it must be relevant. Before the end of Part I chapter 1 many readers will have suspected that Gerrard the lodgekeeper was not really Mary's father and this is confirmed in chapter 7.

We also know from Part I that Laura said to Mary: "You're – you're quite like a daughter to me, Mary"; that Laura had been more than friends with Sir Lewis Rycroft, who died in the War in 1917 and whose signed photograph she kept in a big silver frame; that they could not marry because he had a wife in a lunatic asylum; and that Mary's mother, Eliza, had been Laura's maid before marrying Gerrard. So, readers should work out from those clues by the end of Part I that Mary's real parents were Laura and Lewis and that she was given to Eliza to raise with Gerrard, as is finally confirmed in Part II chapter 13.

There Hopkins says to Poirot: "Why should anyone have to know she was a bastard?". In fact Poirot had learned this from her ten chapters earlier (though 'bastard' was not used there) because she had said that Mary was born outside marriage. Although people born outside marriage would be legitimated under section 1 of the Legitimacy Act 1926 if their parents later married each other, Gerrard was not – as Hopkins had also told him then – one of Mary's parents. So she remained illegitimate.

By chapter 13 it seems that Poirot, prompted by O'Brien and Mrs Slattery (Dr Lord's predecessor's housekeeper), has identified Mary's parents and her parentage is confirmed by a letter produced by Hopkins which she says she found at the Lodge after Mary's death. It was written by Eliza and had the superscription "For Mary – to be sent to her after my death". Hopkins says that Gerrard had kept it and so Mary never saw it.

Although the truth is as we had expected, it still takes a very astute reader to identify the significance of Mary being Laura's daughter because the *general* rule under common law at the time was that illegitimate children could not inherit on the intestacy of either parent – which is the opposite of the current law under the Family Law Reform Act 1987. However, by 1939 there existed an exception, under section 9 of the Legitimacy Act 1926.

This essentially said that, where the mother (but not the father) of an illegitimate child died intestate with no surviving legitimate children, the illegitimate child had the same rights on the mother's intestacy as if he or she had been born legitimate. So, with Laura dying intestate and her property therefore going to her next of kin, the person who was her next of kin – described by Elinor's Counsel at the trial as "the crux of the situation" – was not her legitimate niece, Elinor, as was assumed, but her closer blood relation, Mary, who, although illegitimate, could inherit because of section 9. However, with Mary having died as well, the person who was the beneficiary under *her* will, Mary Riley, would be entitled to Laura's fortune.

Mary Riley therefore has a convincing motive. But she seems a distant figure, having been in New Zealand for years, until two witnesses from New Zealand reveal at Elinor's trial that she is in fact Nurse Hopkins.

There we learn that Hopkins could not have pricked herself on the rose at the Lodge (Zephyrine Drouhin) since it is thornless. We also learn that the label scrap found where Elinor made sandwiches was not from a tube of morphine hydrochloride tablets but from a tube of tablets of apomorphine hydrochloride, such a quick and powerful emetic that, if one swallows a lethal dose of morphine and within minutes injects oneself with apomorphine, vomiting will occur and the morphine will be expelled. So that is how Hopkins murdered Mary – poisoning the tea which they both drank and then injecting herself with apomorphine before vomiting and pretending to have been pricked by a rose.

Poirot says that Hopkins did not find Eliza's letter about Mary's parentage at the Lodge because it had not been written to Mary Gerrard but to her (Mary Riley). She had received it in New Zealand. When suspected of murder there, she returned to England, resuming her nursing role in the name of Hopkins, and went to Maidensford where she learned that Laura was very rich. Some chance word may, says Poirot, have revealed that Laura had not made a will. That 'chance word' is weak plotting on such a key point but, having heard it, Hopkins knew that, when Laura asked for her lawyer, she could not delay: Laura must die intestate so that Mary Gerrard would inherit her money.

Mary's murder had already been planned before Laura's, with Elinor as the scapegoat. The anonymous letter, written by Hopkins, was intended to cause Elinor to come and object to Mary's influence over Laura. And, with Roddy unexpectedly falling in love with Mary, this gave the scapegoat a motive. As a nurse, Hopkins could get the morphine to kill Laura and she then spoke of its disappearance to show that Elinor could have obtained it.

Having befriended Mary, she only had to get her to make a will in Mary Riley's favour and await an opportunity, which arose when Elinor asked them for lunch. Of course, she has some real luck. She is lucky to be invited to the Hall with Mary. She is lucky to have morphine, apomorphine and a syringe on her since she was only at the Lodge to help remove Gerrard's things. She is lucky to be asked by Elinor to go upstairs, leaving Mary unaided as she suffers from the morphine. And she is lucky that Mary is dying from the 'foudroyante' variety because, had she suffered from the more common form, her excited behaviour might have attracted Elinor much earlier.

Nevertheless, with the brilliantly inventive use of apomorphine and some luck, the plan works almost perfectly – except for one bit of carelessness. This is not that Hopkins sweated and went a queer colour in the pantry (which was comprehensible enough after vomiting) or that she attributed the prick to a thornless rose (since many people would assume that all roses have thorns) but, rather, that she left a scrap of the apomorphine label on the floor.

However, the main problem is not her carelessness but a major flaw in the plan itself, namely that Elinor might also have drunk the tea. After all, Hopkins did bring in a tray with *three* cups on it plus the teapot and milk; and the morphine was not just in Mary's cup (rather than the teapot) since Hopkins also drank it. What makes the flaw worse is that, after Elinor first declines the tea, Hopkins actually says "persuasively" to Elinor "Are you sure you won't have a cup, Miss Carlisle? Do you good", to which Elinor murmurs "No, thank you".

Some readers may therefore wonder whether Hopkins meant to kill Elinor as well but this makes no sense, not only because killing off her scapegoat would defeat part of the murder plan but also because it would implicate Hopkins herself as the only surviving member of the trio.

So some readers may wonder if they have missed a clue that Elinor did not drink tea and Hopkins knew this. The nearest one gets is Elinor's apparent focus on coffee: as she lays down her shopping (bread, butter, milk and fish paste), she scolds herself for not getting coffee; she then sees that there is a little tea in a canister and thinks "Oh well, it doesn't matter"; she then says that she meant to get coffee but forgot; and then, when Hopkins refers to tea, she says "absently" that there is a little tea in the canister. So, it is fair to say that she comes across as a coffee drinker, who does not really think about tea. However, readers could not deduce that she does not drink tea at all or that Hopkins could risk offering it to her knowing she would decline.

There are two other elements of the plan that are not clear. First is how Hopkins would have murdered Mary and implicated Elinor if she and Mary had not been invited up to the Hall. She only got her opportunity because of both Elinor and Mary happening to be in Maidensford on the same day to sort out things at the Hall and the Lodge. And if, as Poirot suggests, she may have meant to get Elinor and Mary to her cottage, it is not clear how she would then have been able to divert suspicion to Elinor, who presumably would not have purchased the ingredients for, or made, the sandwiches.

Secondly, it is not clear how she would have claimed Laura's fortune. Poirot says she revealed Eliza's letter "just a little sooner than she meant to do!". So perhaps she had originally intended to prove that Mary was Laura's child after Elinor's conviction. But even then, when claiming to be entitled to Mary's estate, she could not risk being recognised as Hopkins and so one is left doubting that she really would have obtained Laura's fortune.

Plot

The title of this book, which was unchanged in the United States, is probably more difficult to fathom than any other Christie title, even though the words "sad cypress" appear before the Prologue in a Shakespeare quotation, which is the first half of a melancholy, death-wish song sung by Feste, the jester, at Duke Orsino's request in *Twelfth Night*, Act II scene IV.[2] It reads:

> Come away, come away, death,
> And in sad cypress let me be laid;
> Fly away, fly away, breath!
> I am slain by a fair cruel maid.
> My shroud of white, stuck all with yew
> O prepare it;
> My part of death no one so true;
> Did share it.

The arresting words are "I am slain by a fair cruel maid". But they are not a clue to Mary's murderer since there is nothing to suggest that

Mary wished to die, or even to Laura's murderer since, although Laura did wish to die because of her helplessness, the song is about dying from unrequited love (Orsino's for Olivia). So "I" must be Elinor, the main character, who has been "slain" by the fair cruel maid, Mary, in the sense that, because of her, she has lost the person she loved so intensely and is likely to be condemned for murder.

She therefore wants to be laid "in sad cypress" – meaning laid in a black coffin made from cypress wood. But, while the song captures her mental torture, it is not clear why the author selects the words "sad cypress" to represent what she wants to convey from the song. The book has no reference to 'coffin' or even to 'cypress'. So perhaps the key word is "sad", with the author emphasising the melancholy nature of the story, which ends, even after Elinor's acquittal, with her removal to a sanatorium.

After the quotation and a short Prologue describing the start of Elinor's trial, the book goes back in Part I to the events of June and July 1939, ending with Mary's death. Part II describes Poirot's engagement and investigation. Part III comprises the rest of the trial, Elinor's acquittal and Poirot's explanations.

The book is as much a romantic novel as it is a detective story and as such it is quite well, if rather obviously, plotted – with the stylish Elinor who loves Roddy intensely but tries to be casual about it; the ordinary Roddy whose world is turned upside down when he falls for Mary; the beautiful Mary, who likes, but does not love, Roddy and proves to be the illegitimate daughter of a cavalry officer and the wealthy Laura; the invalid Laura, who tells Elinor that anyone who has never really loved has never really lived and who asks Dr Lord what's the good of living stretched out as she is; and the comforting Dr Lord, who falls in love with Elinor, wants her acquitted even if she is guilty but who, when it is all over, will never be loved by her like she loved Roddy.

Without Hopkins and her murder plan (and the consequent need for Poirot), the novel could work as a romantic melodrama.

But it is also a good detective story, which works well and is based on three good but simple ideas: that Mary is not only Laura's daughter (which is obviously plotted) but also therefore, as a matter of law, her next of kin; that Hopkins is really Mary Riley; and that apomorphine will cause morphine to be expelled.

However, the very simplicity of those ideas means that, beyond the incrimination of Elinor and placing of clues, there is little plotting to do, either of the murder plan (making the tea-drinking plotting flaw the more surprising) or of a mystifying investigation. And that simplicity also explains the lack of credible alternative suspects to Elinor beyond Hopkins and Roddy. It is really in the comprehensive incrimination of Elinor, which is interwoven most skilfully into the romantic drama, that the plotting is at its best.

Each of the three Parts has its own memorable feature. In Part I, sadly, it is the poor exposition in chapter 1. Despite being childhood friends and engaged to be married, Elinor reminds Roddy that Mary, with whom they played as kids at Hunterbury, is the daughter of the people at the Lodge; and Roddy tells Elinor that she is Laura's brother's child, that he is her husband's nephew, that Laura and her husband bought Hunterbury and that, after he died, she never married again. By the time Roddy has told Elinor how generous Laura has been and Elinor is about to make the same point, readers will feel like screaming out "He knows!" before Roddy even starts nodding.

The memorable feature of Part II, which is about the same length as Part I, is how slow it feels. For the first half chapter readers are engaged with new facts. But, after that, Poirot's investigation seems boring, not just because of a lack of pace and drama but because so little new information is revealed to mystify readers. We do learn that Hopkins was out of Laura's room for five minutes; that Roddy seems to have been abroad from 9 July to 1 August; that Laura was given morphia; that there may be something about Mary that Hopkins doesn't want known; and that Elinor inherited £200,000. But it takes until the end of chapter 10 to disclose that information.

When the author said in a *Sunday Times* interview in February 1966 that the story was "quite ruined" by having Poirot in it, she may have had those chapters in mind. Otherwise Poirot fits into the story rather well, although it is not until chapter 11, when he meets Elinor in prison, and more particularly chapter 12, when he visits Hunterbury, that Part II finally picks up.

Part III, which is only about half the length of the other Parts, is of a very different quality, memorably revealing the solution through the trial evidence, particularly Elinor's defence witnesses, rather than at a denouement presided over by Poirot. Of course, he later explains how he reached the truth but that happens after the verdict and only Dr Lord is present.

One thing does jar, however, which is why, with such a strong case against Hopkins, Elinor nearly pleaded guilty. Perhaps, oddly, she did not know of the plan to call evidence from a rose grower (about the thornless rose), a chemist (about the apomorphine label), two witnesses from New Zealand (about Hopkins' identity) and Poirot (to read Eliza's letter). Nevertheless, the structural device of returning to the trial, before Poirot's investigation seems to be complete, works very well and Part III is a well-constructed success.

There are other nice touches too, such as those resonant of the thornless rose. Thus there are references to the Wars of the Roses; Mary has a "wild-rose unreality", a "rose-flushed skin" and a "wild-rose beauty"; Roddy sends Elinor long-stemmed roses; there is a cross of yellow roses at Laura's funeral; and Hopkins lives in Rose Cottage. But the nice touch which the author probably enjoyed most is Hopkins saying, as early as Part I chapter 1: "I always say there's nothing like a nice cup of tea – a strong cup!". Little do we know then that a nice cup of tea will be the murder weapon.

There are, however, some minor curiosities. The anonymous letter is said to be badly spelt (Part I chapter 1) and misspelt (Part II chapter 6) but it has only one error in over 90 words ("kareful"). Gerrard's Christian name is Ephraim (Part I chapter 1) and Bob (Part II chapter 13). And Poirot says to Elinor (Part II chapter 11) "I shall ask you – nothing. There are things I do not want to know" but yet he had said that arriving at the truth always interested him (Part II chapter 1) and that a detective must ask questions about people's private affairs and feelings (Part II chapter 6).

Clues

The clue that alerts Poirot to Hopkins is the 'thornless rose' clue. It is not until Part II chapter 11 that Elinor tells him that Hopkins had a prick on her wrist which she attributed to a thorn from the rose trellis at the Lodge. When saying this, she does so dreamily, telling him how the roses reminded her of quarrelling with Roddy, which cleverly deflects attention from the prick.

Then, when visiting the Lodge, Poirot touches a rose on the trellis. We are not told that it is thornless but he tells Lord that its name is Zephyrine Drouhin. He adds that, when Elinor mentioned roses, he saw the "promise of daylight" but he explains this, not by clarifying the relevance of the name but referring to what her memories told him of the personalities of Roddy and herself.

Despite this good attempt at concealment, some readers may rightly think that he gave the rose's name for a reason. Of course, only a gardener would know from the name that the rose is thornless and so be able to interpret the clue. But, because Poirot can see that it is thornless, he knows that Hopkins lied, which is important because, as he explains, her lie had been "so seemingly pointless" that it focused his attention on her.

However, it is not clear how any "promise of daylight" can really be justified by Elinor's reference to the roses since there is no reason then, when Poirot has *not yet* seen the rose, to think that it might be thornless. Nevertheless the 'thornless rose' clue is – once Poirot has seen it – a very good one. So, what then caused the prick, if not the rose?

Some readers may wonder if Hopkins injected herself with a protective antidote. However, even they would do very well to deduce that the drug was a quick and powerful emetic, given that in Elinor's trial evidence she had only said that Hopkins "was perspiring and her face was a queer colour" and that the narrative in Part I had just said that Hopkins wiped her face with a handkerchief and remarked on the heat.

Certainly no reader other than one with a chemist's knowledge would know the emetic's name, even with the benefit of the label scrap. We first learn of the 'hydrochlor scrap' clue when Lord describes it as a label with "morphia hydrochlor" on it – the word 'hydrochlor' presumably being part of 'hydrochloride'. The clue, of which there is a pictorial representation in Part III chapter 1, is then carefully considered at the trial.

In fact the scrap does not actually say "morphia hydrochlor". It says "norphin. Hydro" with the 'm' of 'morphin.' looking like an 'n' (though in some editions more of the 'm' is visible) because it was through the middle of the 'm' that the scrap was torn on the left; and with the word 'Hydro' ending with a partial 'o' because this is where the scrap was torn on the right.

The key point is the small 'm' on the scrap. Whether the visible letter is 'm' or 'n', we can see that it is a *small* letter, not a capital. The chemist giving evidence explains that the word 'Morphine' is spelled with a capital 'M' on tubes of morphine hydrochloride; and, although readers would not know that, they could have worked it out for themselves on seeing the word "Hydro" spelled on the label with a capital 'H'. So the word assumed to be Morphine must have been another word with letters prior to the small 'm' (or 'n'). The small 'm' makes the 'hydrochlor scrap' clue an excellent one, the best in a story where the clues are generally of a high order, although its significance would probably only be spotted by the most astute reader.

For readers whose attention is, like Poirot's, focused on Hopkins, there are various things to consider. Her behaviour at the time of the murder does not seem like that of a murderer. She speaks in a cheerful voice with a laugh; she remarks "brightly" about putting the kettle on; and her thoughts while upstairs (about the clothes, Lewis' photograph and O'Brien's letter) are remarkably composed for someone who has just poisoned Mary.

Indeed, from the outset she seems a most unlikely suspect – she is kind (on at least four occasions); homely looking; and seems very supportive of Mary. It is only at the trial, after she has been cross-examined roughly about mislaying the morphine, that she at last says something "viciously".

Nevertheless, we feel that she will have a key role as a member of the Welman family because of her long nose. The first thing we learn about Roddy is that he has a dear face with a long nose, soon after which we are told that Hopkins has a long nose. For readers who do not spot this connection, her long nose is referred to twice again in chapter 2, sections V and VI; then in Part II chapter 1 Roddy's long nose is referred to twice and Lord describes Hopkins as a "Nosey Parker". Laura is also said to have a hawk-like profile in Part I chapter 2 but, since she is not a Welman by blood, readers will rightly assume that this sole reference is just a red herring. However, Hopkins' nose also turns out to be a red herring because it is never referred to again.

As for Hopkins' motive, this does not seem at all apparent. Some readers may wonder if a clue is to be found in her encouraging Mary to make a will and they would be right because the 'Mary's will' clue is the main one to her motive. However, Poirot shows an odd lack of curiosity on learning from Lord that Mary had made a will. Although he refers to it nine chapters later, that is in the context of Elinor's reaction to it. The will therefore hardly seems to be a clue because of Poirot's lack of interest (until the final chapter).

But, if he had asked about it, he would only have learned that it was in Mary Riley's favour. So, interpreting the 'Mary's will' clue depends upon realising that Mary Riley *is* Hopkins. How well, then, is her true identity clued?

First, we know that Mary Gerrard had an aunt called Mary Riley in New Zealand. But, although we also know that Hopkins had only been in Maidensford a couple of years, we do not have any clue that she came over from New Zealand until this is revealed by the witnesses at the trial.

Secondly, Mary said that her aunt in New Zealand was a nurse, adding that nursing was therefore in her blood (though in fact, as the daughter of Laura and Lewis, it was not). Nevertheless, this is a pretty weak basis for assuming that the nurse is Hopkins unless one is already well focused on her. Indeed, Mary's comment was made to Hopkins, not Poirot, and he only knows that the aunt was a nurse because he remembered "a chance remark" made to him in the village, which makes the point weaker still; indeed, one wonders whether the author overlooked how she was going to get Poirot to rely on the 'Mary's will' clue until she got to the final chapter.

Thirdly, Hopkins showed an interest in Mary. But, again, this is pretty weak because it might just have been her kindness or because, as she tells Poirot, there was something romantic about Mary and one can't help taking an interest in people if one knows something about them that nobody else does.

Fourth is the point which, according to Poirot in the final chapter, "gives her away". This is Eliza's letter with the superscription "For Mary – to be sent to her after my death", which Hopkins pretended was intended for Mary Gerrard but which was written to Mary Riley in New Zealand. So, what is within the 'Eliza letter' clue to suggest that it was not written to Mary Gerrard?

Poirot indicates there are two clues within it. First, he says that the "gist" made it plain that Mary Gerrard was not to know the truth. He is presumably referring to the sentence "She [Laura] thought it would be better for Mary not to know the truth". Although one sentence in a letter of about 25 lines hardly constitutes its 'gist', that 'Eliza gist' clue is pretty fair support for his deduction that the letter could not therefore have been written to *her*.

His second clue, the 'Eliza sent' clue, is better. The word in the superscription was *sent* (not *given*); and it is probably fair to say that Eliza would not have written "sent" if it was intended for Mary Gerrard to whom it could simply have been handed.

Actually the letter contains a third, much better clue which Poirot does not mention – the 'third person' clue. The letter consistently refers to Mary Gerrard as if she's a third person – referring to her as the "child" or the "baby" or "her" and even "Mary" (twice). If Mary Gerrard was the intended recipient, then the letter would refer to her as 'you', not as a third person.

Nevertheless the 'Eliza gist' and 'Eliza sent' clues are fairly good ones for indicating that the intended recipient of the 'Eliza letter' clue was not Mary Gerrard – and so was presumably Mary Riley. However, that does not of itself 'give away' that Riley is Hopkins unless one starts by assuming that the letter was received by Riley in New Zealand. If it was, the only way it could then be found among Gerrard's things, as Hopkins had pretended, would be if Riley had put it there, which she could really only have done if she were Hopkins.

As for clues to Laura's death, the timing makes it clear that the murderer did not want Laura making a will. But otherwise, once the cause is confirmed as morphine poisoning, the only clue seems to be Hopkins' missing tube of morphine tablets. But, if she had administered the morphine herself, why, asks Poirot in Part II chapter 6, would she be so "idiotic" as to mention the tube's disappearance (and risk censure for carelessness) when Laura's death certificate had been signed? A good question.

In fact, Hopkins mentioned the disappearance (Part I chapter 4 section II) *before* the certificate was signed by Dr Lord, who did not learn of Laura's death until the next section. So Poirot gets that timing wrong. But he makes up for it in the final chapter with a clever answer to his question. There he, in effect, treats the 'morphine tube' clue as a double clue – not just as a clue to the cause of Laura's death but also as a clue to Hopkins' implication of Elinor since, if she was guilty of Laura's murder, she would only have mentioned the tube's disappearance to show that the scapegoat for *Mary's* murder (Elinor) had a chance of obtaining morphine.

What we also learn about Hopkins is that she had lied. In Part II chapter 12 Poirot gives us the 'five lies' clue, telling Lord that he has been lied to by Roddy, definitely; O'Brien, romantically; Hopkins, stubbornly; Mrs Bishop, venomously – and, as for Lord himself, "Not yet". Readers naturally try to think what lies Poirot has in mind.

First, as to Roddy's definite lie, Poirot based this on three facts: (1) Roddy had said in Part II chapter 6 that he was not in England when Mary died on 27 July (which turns out be a lie) because he went abroad on 9 July, returning on 1 August; (2) Hopkins had said three chapters earlier that Roddy had seen Mary in London; and (3) Mary had left Maidensford for London on 10 July, as Poirot learns in Part II chapter 12.

So, putting these three facts together, how could Roddy have seen Mary in London (fact (2)) and done so after 10 July which was when she had gone to London (fact (3)) but before she died on 27 July if he was abroad between 9 July and 1 August (fact (1))? Poirot deduced that, given those facts, Roddy could not have been abroad for that period and, by then examining his passport, he finds that he was in England from 25 to 27 July.

Poirot's logical deduction is brilliant not only because this 'London' clue is cleverly concealed by being split across three different chapters but also because it is a doubly concealed clue in that it also requires him to spot that fact (2), which does not even mention a date, is part of a clue at all. That is not easy when the text has been written so carefully – with Hopkins remarking that Mary rebuffed Roddy's advances in Maidensford and "when he came to see her in London she said the same". Readers are more likely to be focusing on Roddy being rebuffed than on where it happened.

As a result of the double concealment, this excellent 'London' clue is likely to be spotted only by the most astute textual reader, even though the author is challenging enough to offer us a second chance by getting Hopkins to repeat during her cross-examination that Mary had "said the same to him in London". It is therefore a pity that such a good clue points just to Roddy whose presence in England on 27 July is a red herring.

As to the second of the five lies, Poirot does not identify O'Brien's romantic lie but presumably he means her reference to an old story about "a decent elderly woman with never a breath of scandal about her" (which she confirms is Laura) and "a man who's got a wife in an asylum". Although O'Brien, with her "soft heart for romance", never volunteers what the story is, Poirot never asks and so it is unfair to describe her as lying.

Thirdly, as for Hopkins' stubborn lie, Poirot knows, having seen O'Brien and Mrs Slattery, that Hopkins is aware of Mary's parentage and yet she said in Part II chapter 3 that she didn't know who Mary's father was. She refuses to guess, which is presumably why Poirot describes her as "stubborn". But he later "realised" that she knew something about Mary which she was anxious *should* come out because her every word was, he says, uttered with diametrically the opposite end in view.

Poirot deserves credit here for good instinctive detective work because readers will find no overt clue in the language or manner of Hopkins' reticence in chapter 3 to show that she didn't really want to be reticent at all. Presumably what he has in mind is that Hopkins, by referring to "a mystery romance", "past history", a "tragedy" and "old sins", is trying to tantalise him into persuading her to tell him what she wanted to tell all along.

Fourthly, as to Mrs Bishop's venomous lie, she describes Mary as a "snake in the grass", "Underhand in her Dealings" and "Artful" and claims that she "Wormed her way" into Laura's "Confidence" and was "then Making Up to Mr Roddy". Although Poirot never says what lie he had in mind, he earlier describes Mrs Bishop's impatience with Mary's airs and graces as "venomous".

More interesting about Mrs Bishop's speech is that some words begin with capital letters despite being in mid-sentence, just as more than one third of the words in the anonymous letter similarly begin with capital letters. When she uses the word "Artful" in her discussion with Poirot, readers who remember this word appearing twice in the letter may reckon that she is the author; and two chapters later Poirot has the same idea. But the capital letters and the word "Artful" are, like Mrs Bishop's venom, just red herrings.

Fifthly, as to Dr Lord, it is hard to tell whether in Part II chapter 12 Poirot expected him to lie but he does so at Hunterbury later that chapter when denying that his car was outside the back gate on the fatal day. Then, just after the denial, he and Poirot find a German matchbox in the shrubbery and he suggests that, with Mary having recently returned from Germany, they have "got something now!". But readers know that Poirot is not going to take seriously a German stranger watching Elinor from the shrubbery and then, while she is down at the Lodge, poisoning sandwiches intended for Mary. As he points out, in a good deduction, anyone watching Elinor cutting sandwiches could not have known that they were to be offered to Mary.

Readers will have realised that Lord, in trying to provide an alternative theory to Elinor's guilt, had planted the matchbox *after* Mary's murder. However, that is not the whole story because Poirot *does* believe that someone stood watching in the bushes, namely Lord who, having heard that Elinor was in Maidensford, had gone to the Hall on the chance of seeing her. And he had watched her through the window – just as Werther had (so Poirot indicates) watched Charlotte unseen in Massenet's opera, *Werther* – until she went away.

So his presence in the shrubbery is a red herring, like the German matchbox and his pretence that the car belonged to a stranger. Those red herrings may be rather obvious but others – the style of the anonymous letter, the long noses and, for readers who spot it, Roddy's return to England – keep us guessing much longer. As, of course, do the fish paste and sandwiches, which are referred to as early as the Prologue. Later Poirot and Lord discuss who cut and proffered the sandwiches and how only one person could have been poisoned; and readers may wonder why one paste jar was washed out while another was left half full and perhaps even whether Hopkins ate a sandwich at all because, despite Lord saying that "all three ate them", this is not something we are actually told in the narrative. But the sandwiches turn out to be the major red herring in a story that is rich with them.

19

One, Two, Buckle My Shoe

Solution

Poirot investigates the murder of his dentist, Henry Morley, and two of his patients – Mr Amberiotis, a rich Greek, and Miss Mabelle Sainsbury Seale whose dead body provides Poirot with an "insoluble problem" and what may well be his most complicated puzzle.

Morley is found shot, just below the right temple, in his surgery on the second floor of 58 Queen Charlotte Street at about 1.30 pm on a Wednesday. His appointments earlier that day included:

> 11 am: Hercule Poirot
> 11.30 am: Alistair Blunt
> Fitted in: Miss Sainsbury Seale
> 12 pm: Mr Amberiotis
> 12.30 pm: Miss Kirby

Miss Sainsbury Seale, who had telephoned Morley complaining of toothache, was fitted in after Blunt's appointment, which was a short one. Morley's secretary, Gladys Nevill, who worked in an office off the surgery, was away that day, having received a telegram about an aunt who was ill.

Morley's partner, Reilly, had his surgery on the first floor and his appointments for that day included:

11.30 am: Howard Raikes
12 pm: Reginald Barnes

The only entrance to the house was the front door, answered by the page-boy, Alfred, who took patients up in a lift from the ground floor waiting room when Morley or Reilly buzzed from their surgeries. Some outgoing patients used the lift to go down but many used the stairs, letting themselves out.

After Poirot's appointment, Alfred took up Blunt. As Poirot left the house, he saw a foot protruding from a taxi. On it was a brand-new patent leather shoe with a large buckle. As the lady, Miss Sainsbury Seale, got out, her other shoe caught in the door, wrenching off the buckle. When Morley buzzed for her, Alfred took her up in the lift as Blunt came down and went out.

Soon after, Alfred saw her out and took up Amberiotis, a new patient (unlike her, Poirot, Blunt and Miss Kirby) for whom the buzzer went at 12.05 pm. Amberiotis left at 12.25 pm. The buzzer did not go again. So at 1.15 pm Miss Kirby walked off in a huff. At 1.30 pm Alfred discovered Morley's body. It looked like suicide: a pistol lay by his right hand with only his fingerprints on it.

A motive for suicide surfaces later that day when Amberiotis is found dead at his hotel, the Savoy, as the result of an overdose of adrenaline and procaine (novocaine), the anaesthetic injected by dentists into the gum. Chief Inspector Japp (in his seventh and final Poirot novel) suggests that Morley realised that he had injected the overdose in error and shot himself.

Poirot is not convinced and assesses when Morley could have been murdered. If the murderer was Amberiotis, it was between 12 pm (he means 12.05 pm when the buzzer went) and 12.25 pm. If it was somebody else, it was after 12.25 pm – otherwise Amberiotis would have seen the body. Japp says that it was 12.35 pm at the latest – or Morley would have buzzed for Miss Kirby or said he couldn't see her. So, the time of death must be between 12.05 pm and 12.35 pm.

Poirot also considers who was or could have been in the house then. As well as Morley's sister (Georgina), the cook (Emma), the maid (Agnes) and Alfred (none of whom are realistic suspects) and Amberiotis (who is dead), these are: Reilly; two of his patients, Raikes and Barnes; and Gladys' young man, Frank Carter, who came to the house. Those four are the main suspects.

Although Carter might have disliked Morley for trying to get Gladys to break up with him, two points are soon clear. The first, as Poirot says in the second chapter, is that Morley was only a pawn in the game: "The proper victim was – should have been – Alistair Blunt". He was one of England's richest men and chairman of its greatest bank. When a junior partner, he had married the immensely wealthy banking heiress Rebecca Arnholt, 20 years his senior, and following her death ten years later he dominated her vast banking empire.

Secondly, Morley's murder was not a "private murder" motivated by a cause such as Carter's but a "*public* crime" aimed at Blunt in his "*public* character", as the banker behind the government. Raikes tells Poirot that Blunt's got to go – "he and everything he stands for!" – and Barnes refers to "the organisation that's behind all this", saying "*They're out after Blunt all right*". Although Poirot does not refer to "private murder" until just before the denouement, or to "*public* crime" or "*public* character" until the denouement itself, readers understand from an early stage why Blunt was the target.

Later that day, at about 6.45 pm, after being interviewed by Poirot and Japp, Miss Sainsbury Seale walks out of her hotel, the Glengowrie Court Hotel, and disappears.[1] About ten days later, when she is still missing, Poirot is told a story about her by Jane Olivera, Blunt's great-niece. Jane says that, when she had been with Blunt on a previous visit to the dentist about three months before, a woman approached him and claimed that she had been a great friend of his wife's, which he says she couldn't have been or he would have known.

At last, well over a month after Morley's death, a body believed to be Miss Sainsbury Seale is found in a chest at No. 45 King Leopold Mansions in Battersea. She had arrived at about 7.15 pm on the day she left her hotel and had been there, so the porter says, once before. "Mistletoe Bough up-to-date", remarks Japp.[2] She died of an overdose of medinal, a slightly bitter barbiturate, and after death her face had been battered out of recognition, although this had not concealed her identity since the body was wearing her clothes and buckled shoes and her handbag was in the chest.

Flat No. 45 (later referred to as No. 42) belonged to a Mrs Sylvia Chapman, who hadn't been seen for over a month and whose husband, Albert, was understood to be in the Secret Service. The descriptions of Mrs Chapman and Miss Sainsbury Seale were similar – both women of forty odd, of roughly the same height and build, with greying hair, tinted yellow, blonde or golden. And Mrs Chapman's dentist was also Mr Morley.

Morley's successor, Leatheran, then pronounces, on the evidence in Morley's dental chart, that the dead body is in fact Mrs Chapman. So, where is Miss Sainsbury Seale? When the official search for her ends, Blunt engages Poirot to find her, after inviting him for the weekend at his Exsham estate.

While they are in the garden, a shot is heard and Carter (working there as a gardener) is seen in the grip of Raikes (who is visiting Jane). Raikes claims that Carter shot at Blunt but Carter says that he heard a shot and that the pistol fell at his feet. He claims he was given the gardening job by the "Secret Service" but, with the pistol being a twin to the one that killed Morley, Carter being unable to account for himself from 12.25 pm that day and

Agnes seeing him going towards Morley's surgery at about 12.30 pm, things look black for him.

But at the denouement Poirot tells us who the murderers really are – not Carter, Reilly, Raikes or Barnes but Blunt and his first wife – and he produces some real surprises as he explains how they executed their plan. In particular, it is hard to believe that any reader will have deduced the true identity and role of Miss Sainsbury Seale. And, for the majority, Blunt's guilt will be completely unexpected because it is so well hidden by his public contribution, apparently impeccable character and comprehensive portrayal as the intended victim.

Not once, but many times, says Poirot, was it *forced* on him (like a conjurer *forcing* a card) – as it was forced on readers – that that this was a *public* crime – with Blunt as its focus in his *public* character. Indeed, the misdirection of Poirot, both unwittingly (by Barnes and others) and deliberately (by Blunt), and of readers by the author, is executed with supreme thoroughness.

It is on the Sunday morning at Exsham, as the Catholic Poirot interestingly participates in the traditional morning service in Blunt's village church, that the truth comes to him. He realises, when singing psalm 140, that the idea of a *public* crime could be "a snare laid with cords" and he is in a glorious daze as isolated facts spin wildly round and, like a kaleidoscope, whirl and then settle into a coherent pattern. As we later learn, the crimes were committed for a reason connected with Blunt's *private* life.

About 20 years before, he had married Gerda Grant, a repertory actress. Miss Sainsbury Seale was in the company and knew about them before going to live for years in India. Then Blunt bigamously married Rebecca Arnholt. Gerda knew but she understood: Blunt still loved her but he had the chance to marry into the royalty of wealth. No one else who knew that Blunt was already married seems to have seen any newspaper reports of this important marriage.

When Rebecca died, he and Gerda could have married 'officially' but they didn't; they still enjoyed meeting secretly. She acted as Mrs Albert Chapman (using the proper name of a real secret agent, Q.X.912, to suggest a husband away on intelligence work) and as Helen Montressor, Blunt's cousin.

Then, after nearly 20 years, about three months before Morley's death, Miss Sainsbury Seale, who had returned from India about three months before that on the same boat as Amberiotis, recognised Blunt outside Morley's house, as the husband of her friend Gerda. Overheard by Jane, she told him that she had been a great friend of his wife's. Gerda's name was not mentioned and naturally Jane assumed she was referring to Rebecca.

Blunt did not then regard her as a threat but Amberiotis invited her to lunch at the Savoy. She told him about meeting a friend's husband. Amberiotis, a blackmailer, must have found out that Gerda was alive when Blunt married Rebecca and he contacted Blunt. Blunt couldn't let him ruin his life's work and realised that Miss Sainsbury Seale couldn't be trusted to keep quiet either.

The motive for killing them both, fear of exposure for bigamy, is a convincing private one but Blunt also says "If I was ruined and disgraced – the country, *my* country was hit as well". This *public* motive sounds a little less convincing but the story was originally published in the United States as *The Patriotic Murders* with the public motive in the title.

Gerda then asked Miss Sainsbury Seale to tea at Mrs Chapman's flat. This was the occasion, referred to by the porter, on which she came to the flat. But she never left. The medinal was in the tea. There is no mention of Blunt being there, so Gerda presumably committed this murder. Then Miss Sainsbury Seale's face was battered to make it look as if the body might not be hers – rightly described by Poirot as "a very clever double bluff".

A double bluff involves telling the truth – producing a body that is really Miss Sainsbury Seale – when you want people to think you are bluffing – by disfiguring the face and thus raising a doubt as to whether the body is actually hers. So the face was battered not to *conceal* identity but to *raise a question* about it, which could only be resolved by the dental records of Miss Sainsbury Seale and Mrs Chapman, both held by Morley.

If their dental charts were relabelled, exchanging the names, and if Morley (who could have identified the dead woman from his dental work despite the battered face) was killed so that he couldn't identify her, the swapped charts would be put in as evidence. Of course, this double bluff depends on the charts of the two women being with the same dentist and, as Poirot says, "By coincidence, Mrs Chapman's dentist was Mr Morley". Those charts would show that the body was Mrs Chapman, meaning that the police would not look for her but look again for Miss Sainsbury Seale, whom they could never find.

The murder method, medinal in the tea, is simple. It is the "very clever double bluff" indicating that she is still missing (rather than dead) which adds novelty and great complexity. But one wonders if the double bluff was (as Poirot and Blunt try to convince us) really "necessary", particularly as this involved battering her face and killing Morley. It would not have been "necessary" if she had simply been murdered somewhere other than Mrs Chapman's flat.

Nevertheless, having killed her, Gerda then took her place. Dressed in clothes of the same type and wearing a *new* pair of buckled shoes because Miss Sainsbury Seale's size six buckled shoes were too large for her size five feet, she left the flat, went to the 'real' Miss Sainsbury Seale's hotel in Russell Square, packed, paid the bill and went to the Glengowrie Court Hotel. There she played the part of Miss Sainsbury Seale until the time came, about a week later, to exchange the charts and murder Morley on a day when Blunt, Amberiotis and the 'false' Miss Sainsbury Seale had appointments.

That day Gladys was removed by the telegram pretending her aunt was ill. Blunt went up for his 11.30 am appointment. Reilly entered the surgery at about 11.35 am to ask Morley a question but was there for only a minute. Blunt shot Morley at about 11.45 am. Then he pressed the buzzer, turned on the taps of the basin behind the door and left the room. He timed it so as to descend the stairs just as Alfred was taking the 'false' Miss Sainsbury Seale (whose buckle had been wrenched off in the taxi) to the lift. He went out but, as the lift went up, he slipped inside again and went up the stairs.

Poirot knew (as readers do from the description of his own appointment) what Alfred did when taking up a patient. He knocked on the door, opened it and stood back (so not seeing Morley's body) to let in the 'false' Miss Sainsbury Seale. The running water indicated that Morley was washing his hands but Alfred couldn't have *seen* that. When he had gone, Blunt entered the surgery.

He and the 'false' Miss Sainsbury Seale carried Morley's body into Gladys' office. The charts were exchanged. She went down and left. The buzzer went and Amberiotis was taken up. He had no suspicion that Blunt, now wearing a white linen coat, wasn't a real dentist. Blunt injected Amberiotis, who then left, and the injection had its desired effect hours later. So, Morley's murder was dually motivated by the need to prevent him identifying Miss Sainsbury Seale and to enable Blunt to murder Amberiotis by impersonating him.

Blunt then brought Morley's body out of the office on his own, dragging it on the carpet. He wiped the gun and put it in Morley's hand. He went down and left. The 'false' Miss Sainsbury Seale returned to the Glengowrie Court Hotel where she was later interviewed by Poirot and Japp. That evening she entered King Leopold Mansions where, weeks later, her 'real' body was found.

The day at the dentist's would have required planning about the shooting, the injection and Blunt being seen to leave. But this would have been simple compared with organising the appointment structure. Disappointingly, however, we are not told how Amberiotis became a new patient of Blunt's dentist, how Blunt found out about this or about the timing of the appointment or how he secured the immediately preceding appointment while allowing enough time for the 'false' Miss Sainsbury Seale to be fitted in later.

Readers may also wonder how Blunt acquired sufficient dental knowledge to perform effectively, particularly when injecting into the gum and judging the amount of the overdose. Moreover, the plan was risky because Alfred might have entered the surgery with the 'false' Miss Sainsbury Seale and noticed the body or seen that Morley was not at the basin. And what if Reilly, who had come in at 11.35 am, had done so at about 11.45 am after Morley had been shot?

Otherwise the ingenious plan for the day at the dentist's, based on the clever idea of an unsuspecting victim in a dentist's chair, is highly imaginative and very efficiently structured: Gladys away; Blunt in; Morley dead; Blunt seen out; Gerda in; Blunt back in; records exchanged; Gerda out; Amberiotis in; Amberiotis injected; Amberiotis out; Blunt out; Amberiotis dead. And, as Poirot says, Morley's 'suicide' is explained by his mistake: "The two deaths cancel out".

It should have gone well but, because of Poirot's doubts, Blunt had "a second line of defences" involving a scapegoat, Carter, whom he and Gerda engaged as a gardener at Exsham. There, the "final performance" of the forced *public* card was staged. Poirot says it was "easy" to arrange a loaded pistol among the laurels so that a man clipping them would cause it to go off. However, this doesn't sound at all plausible – and, even if it was, how could one ensure that it would go off when Blunt was there or that Raikes (whom Blunt didn't even know was at Exsham) would be on hand to incriminate Carter?

This "final performance" is disappointing compared with the ingenuity of the main murder plan. It is so comparatively poor that Blunt's pretended commission for Poirot at Exsham deserved to backfire, which it does, not only because Poirot spots the snare while in the village church but also because Carter's arrest leads to Agnes telling Poirot about seeing him going towards Morley's surgery at about 12.30 pm and then to Carter giving Poirot a clue about the timing of the murder which he would never otherwise have been given.

Plot

The title comes from a nursery rhyme first published in London in 1805, in which ten pairs of numbers are followed by short rhyming phrases, which vary in differing versions of the rhyme. The author's version is set out before the first chapter. Each of the ten pairs of numbers/phrases provides a chapter title and she tries to include something relevant to the title in each chapter, with Poirot even quoting from the rhyme a few times. Generally, she is quite successful – although some attempts come across as contrived.

In the chapter "One, two, buckle my shoe" Poirot sees the buckle torn off Miss Sainsbury Seale's shoe. In "Three, four, shut the door", it is as if a door has shut when he hears of Amberiotis' death. In "Five, six, picking up sticks" he takes his stick and goes gathering evidence ("picking up sticks", as he later says). In "Seven, eight, lay them straight" he knows he should set his sticks in order but does not do so. In "Nine, ten, a good fat hen" the hen is not Miss Sainsbury Seale, even though she is referred to as a hen twice, but Jane Olivera's fat mother, Julia, who clacked on, Poirot thought, like a "big, fat hen" (though he means "good fat hen", which he later uses).

In "Eleven, twelve, men must delve" Carter is digging in his role as gardener. In "Thirteen, fourteen, maids are courting" Poirot sees Jane and Raikes courting in Regent's Park. In "Fifteen, sixteen, maids in the kitchen" Poirot interviews Agnes, the maid. In "Seventeen, eighteen, maids in waiting", after exposing Blunt,

Poirot goes to Jane, who is awaiting the outcome. In "Nineteen, twenty, my plate's empty", with the case now solved, there is nothing on Poirot's plate to exercise his grey cells.

In addition to building the story around the nursery rhyme, the author produces a number of plotting twists – of structure, motive, character, location, timing and suspects – designed to misdirect readers away from Blunt's main purpose of eliminating Amberiotis and Miss Sainsbury Seale.

First, as to structure, readers are made to think that Morley's murder is the key one by describing it before the other two and then having it as the main focus of the first third of the book.

Secondly, as to motive, readers are made to think of Blunt as the intended victim, with Morley's death being only an incident – which creates an interesting contradiction with the first plotting twist, since Morley's death therefore appears to be both key and incidental at the same time.

Thirdly, as to character, Blunt comes across as so completely straight that there is never even the whiff of a possibility that he might be the murderer.

Fourthly, as to location, when Jane tells Poirot about Miss Sainsbury Seale's claim to have been a friend of Blunt's wife, Blunt refers to India, where he had been with Rebecca, so misdirecting us away from Miss Sainsbury Seale's acting connection with Gerda towards an Indian connection with Rebecca.

Fifthly, as to timing, we are led to believe that Morley's murder must have happened between 12.05 pm and 12.35 pm when it happened at about 11.45 am.

And sixthly, as to suspects, we are led to believe, by Poirot's reference to the people who were actually in (by which he means *known* to have been in) or who could have been in the house at the time, that there are only four – Reilly, Carter, Raikes and Barnes (although there is in fact a fifth, Morley's 12.30 pm patient, Miss Kirby, who arrived on time, but Poirot shows no interest in her).

Overall, the day at the dentist's, with the comings and goings being carefully timed, is plotted to a very high standard by the *author* – though it is frustrating that we are not told how it was plotted by the *murderers*. And the "insoluble problem" of Miss Sainsbury Seale is brilliantly plotted, with the solution expertly concealed. Even the denouement is structured so that, with pieces of that insoluble problem being explained one by one, we are kept guessing until the final revelation provides a very satisfying solution.

After the body in her clothes is found in Mrs Chapman's flat with the face battered and we learn that, like her, Mrs Chapman hadn't been seen for over a month, we naturally wonder whether they are the same person. If so, was Miss Sainsbury Seale the 'real' person pretending to be Mrs Chapman – or was it the other way round? When the dental records then reveal that the body is Mrs Chapman, not Miss Sainsbury Seale, so that they are probably different people, we wonder how they are connected; whose body is it; where is the one who is alive; what is the significance of the buckled shoes on the body; why was the face battered when this did not conceal the identity of either Miss Sainsbury Seale (because of the clothes and handbag) or Mrs Chapman (because of the dental records); what is the role of Mr Chapman who is said to be in the Secret Service; and how does any of this tie in with the visit to the dentist and the deaths of Morley or Amberiotis?

This complex interconnection of questions means that Poirot faces a puzzle described in the fifth chapter as "the contradictory and impossible problem of Miss Sainsbury Seale. For, if the facts that Hercule Poirot had observed were true facts – then nothing whatever made sense!". This is no exaggeration. The detection of the true identity and involvement of the person who appears to be Miss Sainsbury Seale is plotted so as to provides readers with one of the greatest puzzles in the Christie canon. She is, as Poirot tells Blunt at the denouement, "the beginning and middle and end of the case".

She is the beginning, not so much because Poirot starts his analysis with her at the denouement, telling Blunt that the matter began for him with a shoe, but because the chain of events began three months before when she remembered Blunt after nearly 20 years and accosted him in the street.

She is the middle not so much because her body is discovered shortly before the midway point of the book but because her disappearance, her murder, her identification, her involvement and the apparently insoluble problem caused by her dead body and battered face are central to the mystery.

And she is the end, not only because one cannot reach the solution without explaining her "dual nature" – separating her "dual personality" into two Miss Sainsbury Seales – but also because, when her claim to have been a friend of Blunt's wife is analysed in that separated context, Poirot sees that in making that claim *she* has given him the clue without which he might never have guessed the truth.

Although her dead body provides Poirot with what may well be his most complicated puzzle, the novel is still eminently readable. It is well-paced and engaging with very little padding and it mystifies throughout. And the focus is so much on the mystery of Miss Sainsbury Seale that one isn't troubled by the absence of evidence against the three main suspects other than Carter.

Thus, Raikes is "not really a murderer", as Poirot says as early as the first chapter; Reilly is found by Poirot (we are not told how) at the Shipping Co. counter, going to America, leaving debts and not planning to return, but that is a red herring; and Barnes' main role appears to be to mislead Poirot about the *public* crime more than anyone else because he was in a position to *know* (having been at the Home Office). Barnes also, as we learn at the very end, is himself the real Albert Chapman – so 'Mrs Chapman' could not have been married to agent Q.X.912 – which is an odd twist-in-the-tail because it doesn't advance the solution or any other plot element.

Clues

There are three occasions where Poirot itemises facts in a way that suggests he is giving readers lists of clues.[3] Some are red herrings but there are also genuine clues, with the principal ones (all in the second and third lists) relating to the mystery of Miss Sainsbury Seale – shoe buckles; ten-inch stockings; a damaged face; travelling back on the same boat as Amberiotis; lunching with him at the Savoy; accosting Blunt and claiming an intimacy with his wife; twice visiting King Leopold Mansions where a dead body is found in her clothes with her handbag; and leaving the Glengowrie Court Hotel suddenly.

Before dealing with those, however, five short points about the lists should be made. First, Poirot refers to "Espionage" (first list) and "activities" (second list) in relation to Amberiotis. Those words misdirect us away from blackmail and yet the author plays fair with us by giving us a 'blackmail' clue earlier when listing it among Amberiotis' interests described by Japp.

Second, Poirot refers to the mark on Morley's carpet (first list). This 'carpet mark' clue indicated, so Poirot says, that the body had been dragged along the carpet, suggesting that Morley had been shot, not in the surgery (where a patient would have shot him), but in his office, and so he was shot by one of his household. Barnes thinks that this reasoning is "Neat" but in fact Poirot is wrong on both counts because Morley *was* shot in his *surgery* by a *patient*.

Third, Poirot shows no interest, oddly, in his first list (or for three days) in the 'Gladys telegram' clue. Her aunt lived in the (fictional) Somerset village of Richbourne and the telegram was cleverly handed in at the (fictional) London suburb of Richbarn, which could be mistaken for Richbourne.

Fourth, Poirot refers to Alfred's taste in literature (second list). This is a reference to the (fictional) American detective story he was reading on the fatal morning, called *Death at Eleven Forty-Five*. Of course, this cannot be taken seriously as a clue to the time of the murder but Poirot does describe it as "an omen".

Fifth, after the second list, we are told that Poirot was now "looking at the case *the right way up*". It is not clear if this 'right way up' clue is really intended as a clue but in retrospect it suggests that readers should look the other way up at all they have been told – about Blunt being the target, about what the dental records prove and about Miss Sainsbury Seale not knowing Blunt's wife.

Turning, then, to Miss Sainsbury Seale, Poirot begins his explanations where the matter began for him – with the 'buckled shoes' clue, a comprehensive one, comprising an impressively complex mix of other clues about buckles, shoes and stockings. He starts with the shoe he saw on Miss Sainsbury Seale in the taxi – a *new*, shining patent leather shoe with a large buckle. But later the body in the fur chest wore a *shabby* buckled shoe. This 'shabby shoe' clue is clever since few readers would match the new shoes of the first chapter with the shabby shoes of the fourth.

So, if she had changed out of the new pair into the shabby pair that day, the new shoes should have been in her hotel room. But there were no buckled shoes there, which is very satisfyingly clued by the 'shoe list' clue, where the author lists what shoes were (and therefore what shoes were not) in the room.

However, good as these two clues are, they are at that stage only clues leading to the "insoluble problem" rather than clues for solving it. Here, thought Poirot, was a dead woman in Miss Sainsbury Seale's clothes (except, perhaps, the shoes?) and with her handbag. But why then batter her face to make it unrecognisable? It might be because the body was Mrs Chapman and he had cleverly worked out how to establish this as a result of seeing some cheap, ten-inch stockings in a drawer in Miss Sainsbury Seale's room.

Since the foot protruding from the taxi wore quite an expensive stocking, one assumes he is going to establish whether the body was that of the person who got out of the taxi by looking at the quality of the stockings on it. In fact, that is not his point because, surprisingly, we are not told about the quality of the stockings on the body. His point, rather, is based upon the stockings' size.

He knows that a ten-inch stocking converts into "at least a 6 in shoes" (which is right since even a size six shoe would be tight on someone who wears a ten-inch stocking). He also knows, as readers are told, that Mrs Chapman wore size five shoes. So she had smaller feet than Miss Sainsbury Seale and, if the body was Mrs Chapman, then the shoes on it should be too big. Yet the shoe on the dead woman's foot only came off "with difficulty". So, the body looked as if it *were* Miss Sainsbury Seale after all. But that brought him back to *why* the face was damaged when her identity was proved by the handbag.

The 'damaged face' clue creates a genuinely mystifying puzzle. For Poirot, it is "a tangle". He just does not understand it until his kaleidoscopic moment in church. And one doubts if any reader would have spotted the solution that the damaged face is a clue to the murderers' very clever double bluff.

Although the 'ten-inch stockings' clue again leads to, rather than solves, a mystery, it is another good one because few readers would match a stocking size in the third chapter with a shoe size in the fourth, despite Poirot saying that he thinks Miss Sainsbury Seale is dead "because of a pair of unworn stockings in a drawer". However, his clever deduction based on that clue – that the body was Miss Sainsbury Seale – only works if one assumes that the shoe which he took off the body was a size six and so too big for Mrs Chapman. But, strangely, we are never told the size of the shoe on the body.

At the denouement we learn that it was Miss Sainsbury Seale's body so that the shoe was at least a size six. But when Poirot is checking the fit of the shoe, we don't know whose body it is (the purpose of checking is to find out) so we cannot assume that the foot was at least size six and, since we are not told the size of the shoe, we cannot assume that it was at least size six either.

As far as we know at that stage, the shoe on the foot could have been a size five and so fitted Mrs Chapman. Surely, instead of removing a shoe of unspecified size from a foot of unspecified size, it would have made more sense to have put one of Mrs Chapman's size five shoes, which Poirot had in his hand only moments before, on the foot and see if it fitted (which it would not have done).

Another weakness in Poirot's deduction flows from the evening shoes in Miss Sainsbury Seale's room which were a size smaller than the day ones. At the denouement he explains the 'evening shoes' clue by saying that, because Mrs Chapman's feet were smaller than Miss Sainsbury Seale's, the 'false' Miss Sainsbury Seale bought a smaller pair of evening shoes – so explaining the presence of the smaller shoes and being a clue to the lady in the hotel room having impersonated the 'real' (dead) Miss Sainsbury Seale.

However, in the hotel room Poirot noted that the smaller evening shoes "might be put down to corns or to vanity". So they could have belonged to the 'real' Miss Sainsbury Seale, even though, ordinarily, she wore a larger size. And, if she could fit into size five shoes in the evening, the shoes on the body could be size five shoes and so *not only* have fitted her (perhaps explaining the shoe coming off "with difficulty") *but also* Mrs Chapman (who took that size).

This leaves the 'buckles' clue, the first referred to in Poirot's kaleidoscopic moment. He says that, when he looked at the shoe on the body, the buckle had been sewn on "recently". We were told earlier that it was sewn on "clumsily" but, either way, the impression is that Miss Sainsbury Seale had hurriedly sewn on the buckle that had come off in the taxi. That fits with her not having sewn it when interviewed by Poirot and Japp but having done so by 7.15 pm when seen with buckled shoes at King Leopold Mansions by the porter.

However, the buckled shoes worn by the 'false' Miss Sainsbury Seale in the taxi were the *new* shoes. So why was a buckle clumsily or recently sewn onto the *shabby* shoes worn by the body of the 'real' Miss Sainsbury Seale? No buckle came off *her* shoes. This rather important point seems to have been overlooked because, after Poirot refers to the 'false' Miss Sainsbury Seale's last appearance, re-entering King Leopold Mansions, he never again mentions the shoes or the buckle at the denouement.

A final oddity about the 'buckles' clue is that in the hotel room Poirot wonders if Miss Sainsbury Seale had sewn "the second buckle" on her shoe. However, there is no other reference to a second buckle. Perhaps he meant the buckle on the shoe which he saw *second* as she got out of the taxi.

So, with the puzzle of the damaged face unresolved by the various 'buckled shoes' clues until Poirot's kaleidoscopic moment, he says he was "left now with a psychological problem. What sort of a woman was Mabelle Sainsbury Seale?". But it is not his psychological analysis that provides his "first vague glimmering of the truth". This occurs when he realises that a man would not be suspicious in a dentist's chair. But then, about ten paragraphs later in the ninth chapter, he has his second "first glimmering of the truth" when realising in church that the idea of a *public* crime could be a snare and that, if so, there was "*only one person who could have laid it*".

That person was Blunt because there was a certain "lavishness about the case". Quite a burden is placed on this 'lavishness' clue because, in support of it, Poirot refers to expense or money being no object, and human life being no object or being recklessly disregarded, three times at the denouement.

However, 'lavishness' is a rather intangible clue. What Poirot seems to mean by "reckless disregard" for human life is that the murderers would not regret sacrificing people against whom they sought no independent private satisfaction. If so, that fairly describes Blunt and Gerda's approach to killing Morley and framing Carter (although 'reckless' is not the right word because

Morley and Carter were the subjects of *deliberate* planning). But that type of disregard might also apply to Raikes (not just Blunt and Gerda), who says "What does the death of one miserable dentist matter?".

As for the money element of the 'lavishness' clue, Poirot smells "big money in this business!" in the second chapter. However, Blunt's plans required no real expense beyond the hotel bill at the Glengowrie Court and Poirot's fees for finding Miss Sainsbury Seale. The Battersea flat was already owned by Mrs Chapman, who had gone away before and changed maids pretty often. Moreover, as Barnes says, the "organisation" had a "no expense spared" policy and so could have been as "lavish" as Poirot reckons Blunt had been.

So the 'lavishness' clue is not as good as Poirot thinks but he does recognise that for his "new, strange idea" (Blunt committing a private crime) to be right, it must explain Miss Sainsbury Seale's "dual nature". There seemed to him to be two of them. The first was earnest and conscientious, as borne out by her life in India and her friends' testimony. The second, described twice by Poirot at the denouement, had lunched with a foreign agent, accosted Blunt, almost certainly lied about being a great friend of his wife's, visited two properties where murders had occurred and vanished mysteriously.

He says that her claim to have been a great friend of Blunt's wife was the one incident that fell between the two roles. That is rather opaque. It is not clear why her claim "falls between" the two roles when he has just described it as a feature of the *second* Miss Sainsbury Seale. Nor is it clear why he chooses her claim as the "one incident" falling between the roles when, for example, it was the conscientious Miss Sainsbury Seale (the first one) who actually lunched with a foreign agent (which he ascribes to the second one). So, the 'wife's friend' clue doesn't provide a solid basis for the next step in his thinking.

Nevertheless, treating it as the clue to explain her dual nature, he looks at the matter logically and says that, since the claim was a lie and the conscientious Miss Sainsbury Seale does not lie, the lie must have come from an imposter. But then he looks at the matter "the other way round". He hypothesises brilliantly that the claim had been made by the *real* Miss Sainsbury Seale, not an imposter. If so, then, since she does not lie, the claim must be true. The 'wife's friend' clue therefore shows that she *was* a friend of Blunt's wife.

On that hypothesis, some related clues fall into place – the 'no remarriage' clue (that Blunt, who was jeered for marrying Rebecca for her money and so might have cut loose after her death, had not remarried); the 'scrape' clue (Jane's remark that "it's *queer* the way she tried to scrape an acquaintance with you, Uncle", suggesting that, *because* it was queer, Miss Sainsbury Seale's claim might be true); the 'memory for faces' clue (that she had a good memory for faces, explaining why she was murdered – an irony being that it was the 'false' one who said "I have a *very* good memory for faces"); the 'Indian boat' clue (that she returned on the same boat as Amberiotis); the 'Savoy lunch' clue (that a waiter thought she lunched with him there); and the 'different class' clue (that she and Rebecca were, as Japp says, not in the same class – a clue that the 'wife' she knew was not Rebecca but someone of *her own* class).

Poirot suggests that that type of person would have been an Anglo-Indian, a missionary or an actress, bringing us to the 'actress' clue. Readers may have guessed wrongly that, because Miss Sainsbury Seale had acted, this was a clue to her having acted as Mrs Chapman. In fact the 'real' Miss Sainsbury Seale doesn't do any acting, all of which is done by Gerda as her impersonator.

But impersonation as part of the murder plan is only one element of the 'actress' clue, which is a double clue whose other element is that, *because* she was an actress, she had known Gerda, presumably in Oxford since we get three 'Oxford' clues

– the 'false' Miss Sainsbury Seale having appeared at the Oxford Repertory Theatre; Blunt marrying Rebecca when not long down from Oxford; and Poirot going to Oxford where he obtains the marriage certificate.

Two days before that, he tells Barnes that he had "one very definite piece of luck" – a "fragment of conversation". Since he does not use those words at the denouement, readers may wonder about the 'fragment' clue. But, when he says, referring to Miss Sainsbury Seale's claim, "Otherwise I might never have guessed", it is clear that the 'fragment' and 'wife's friend' clues are the same.

As to the clueing of the motive for Morley's murder, Japp gives us a pointer in the fourth chapter when he says "It's just possible, you know, that he was put out of the way on purpose – so that he couldn't give evidence", a very apposite comment that Poirot fails to pursue with him, despite Morley having told him in the first chapter that he never forgot a patient's face. That 'forget a face' clue is important in indicating that, if he were alive, he might recognise the damaged face from his dental work as Miss Sainsbury Seale's.

Overall, readers may feel that, even if they had interpreted some of the clues listed by Poirot, they would still have found it impossible to solve the puzzle because the plotting is so intricate. The key clue is the 'wife's friend' clue – a simple one (just a lady telling the truth) whose strength lies in the brilliant reverse logic applied to it by Poirot. Readers who understand its significance will be led to Blunt and to part of his motivation but, for the rest of the *who* and the *why*, other clues need to be interpreted, especially those at the heart of the "insoluble problem" of Miss Sainsbury Seale.

Even with those clues, Blunt's performance makes it almost impossible to spot him as a likely murderer. Whenever one might have expected an uneasy or hesitant reaction, he appears relaxed and urbane with an indulgent smile. The best example is his response to Poirot's rhetorical question about where a man would be less suspicious than in a dentist's chair: "Well, that's true, I suppose. I never thought of it like that".

As for the *how* and the *when*, an important clue is provided by Carter who was seen by Agnes going along to Morley's surgery at "getting on for half-past twelve" – which Poirot converts (three times) to the oddly specific time of twenty-six minutes past twelve. Before entering it, Carter had seen a fat gent (Amberiotis) come out and then another gent (whom he did not recognise) come out and go down too. When he went into the room, Morley's hand was cold and there was a hard, black crust of blood around the bullet hole.

This 'dried blood' clue meant that Morley had been dead some time and so the dentist who treated Amberiotis could not have been Morley. It must have been his murderer, namely the other gent seen by Carter (Blunt), who had slipped back into the house, unnoticed by Alfred who was taking the 'false' Miss Sainsbury Seale up in the lift, as we know from his 'Whatsername' clue: "the toff came down and went out as I took Miss Whatsername up in the lift".

The remaining small clues relate to Gerda's conspiracy with Blunt. A few readers may realise that her flat in Battersea would be, as Poirot describes it, "a handy spot", near Blunt's house on Chelsea Embankment. In the flat Poirot remarks about her squirrel coat "First-class skins", a luxury not associated with someone living in a mansion block in Battersea. Japp then says, as Poirot is looking at her bottles of hair application, that she has "probably gone henna red by now" – a good prediction since we later learn that it was a red-haired lady who interviewed Carter for his "Secret Service" job. Also among her cosmetics is some vanishing cream, which the author must have enjoyed listing, especially since Mrs Chapman vanishes before we ever meet her.

Gerda also acts as the lady known as Helen Montressor. Said to be Blunt's second cousin, we get small clues that she might have a closer relationship than that – he didn't like Julia suggesting she shouldn't come for dinner; he was "very kind" in letting her have the cottage on the Exsham estate rent free; and he had made substantial provision for her in his will. In fact the real Helen died seven years before. So 'Helen' was really Gerda, who, much more importantly, also played the part of the lady who is "the beginning and middle and end of the case", Miss Mabelle Sainsbury Seale.

20

Evil Under The Sun

Solution

Poirot investigates the murder of beautiful Arlena Marshall who is, like Poirot, a guest at the Jolly Roger Hotel on Smugglers' Island off the Devon coast. On 25 August she is strangled on the west of the island on the beach at Pixy Cove.

Even after ruling out regular guests, hotel staff and mainland visitors, there are 11 suspects, all hotel guests – her husband, Kenneth; his 16-year-old daughter, Linda, from his first marriage; handsome Patrick Redfern; his pretty but frail wife, Christine; Rosamund Darnley, who loves Kenneth; athletic Emily Brewster; Carrie Gardener, a talkative American; her acquiescent husband, Odell; Horace Blatt, a businessman; Major Barry, an ex-Indian Army bore; and Stephen Lane, a fanatical clergyman.

The "common gossip of the hotel" was Arlena's affair with Patrick. He says he was crazy about her but that she lost interest in a man once she had got him body and soul; and she is described (by Miss Brewster, Lane and Mrs Gardener) in chapters 1, 7 and 10 as *evil*.

On the fatal morning, Poirot helps Arlena, wearing her white backless bathing dress and Chinese hat of jade green cardboard, to launch a float from the bathing beach on the south of the island. She leaves at 10.15 am, paddling clockwise towards Pixy Cove, which can only be accessed from the land side by descending a vertical ladder from the cliff top. Poirot assumes she is meeting Patrick but he then strides down the beach.

Just before 11.30 am Patrick asks if Miss Brewster is going rowing and if he can go with her. She agrees. They set off clockwise. When rounding Pixy Cove, they see a figure on the beach, face down. It looks like Arlena but she does not answer as the boat reaches the beach. He gets to the body first, followed by Miss Brewster, who sees its bronzed limbs and white backless bathing dress and jade green hat. He says she has been strangled. He stays with the body while Miss Brewster, rowing because she cannot face the ladder, goes for the constable at Leathercombe Bay.

The police surgeon advises that the earliest outside limit for Arlena's death is 10.45 am and, since Miss Brewster and Patrick had seen the body from the boat at about 11.40 am, death must have occurred within that time. The strangler cannot have been Patrick since he had been on the beach or with Miss Brewster.

Inspector Colgate suggests two motives – jealousy and money. Poirot is sure that Kenneth knew about Arlena and Patrick and, with his firm in trouble, a £50,000 legacy which she had received from Sir Robert Erskine would be useful. But, despite having both motives, Kenneth has a strong alibi. He was typing in his room from 10.50 am to 11.50 am and he produces three letters, which he could not have prepared earlier since he was answering a letter postmarked that day. Moreover, Rosamund says that she looked in on him at about 11.20 am and that he was typing.

Poirot says that two women guests have a motive. First, the unhappy and jealous Christine, but he thinks she is not passionate enough to strangle anyone and her hands are too small and delicate. And, as Patrick reminds us, she could not have descended the ladder, having no head for heights. Moreover, she met Linda in the hall just before 10.30 am and they went to Gull Cove on the east of the island where she sketched and Linda sunbathed until 11.45 am.

Poirot does not name the second woman and, oddly, Chief Constable Weston and Colgate do not ask. We know that Linda hated Arlena but she is never called a 'woman'; and she was with Christine. So he means Rosamund, aware that she wants to marry Kenneth. At 10.25 am she went to Sunny Ledge on the southwest of the island, where her sunshade was seen by Patrick and Miss Brewster when rowing past, and came back at 11.50 am. She later recalls briefly returning at 11.20 am, when she saw Kenneth typing, but, despite Kenneth saying he saw her in the mirror, it is suspicious that she initially forgot her return.

Miss Brewster might also be motivated by resentment, with Erskine's £50,000 having gone to Arlena instead of the Erskine family into which her cousin had married. But she had been on the beach before rowing with Patrick.

Another angle surfaces when Christine reveals that Arlena had said "You blackmailing brute!" to an unknown man. Blackmail seems likely when only £15,000 is found remaining of Erskine's legacy. Since Arlena might have met the blackmailer at Pixy Cove, the police look in the cave there – Pixy's Cave. They find a box containing heroin, causing Weston to say "The third angle", which is odd since, in addition to Colgate's two motives (jealousy and money), we know by then about Linda's hatred, Brewster's resentment and the blackmail angle. By chapter 11 part 4 Weston is pretty certain that Blatt is the drug smuggler. Poirot agrees but, strangely, this is never actually confirmed.

The Gardeners and Barry are never under serious suspicion. But Lane might be a religious maniac, motivated by the idea that he had to kill the evil Arlena. He had spent over a year in a mental home after resigning his living in Surrey, near which there had been two strangulations. Poirot is not interested in the first victim, Nellie Parsons, but "very interested" in the other, Alice Corrigan.

Alice was found dead in Caesar's Grove by a games mistress, who said she found the body at 4.15 pm. Alice had insured her life in favour of her husband Edward but he had an alibi up to 4.25 pm at a nearby café. So the police decided that the same man killed both Alice and Nellie but they never caught him.

However, the man was not Lane. Nor did he kill Arlena. Nor is her murder explained by inheritance, jealousy, hatred, resentment, blackmail, smuggling or religion, but by self-protection from exposure as a swindler – and by evil.

That *evil* was not in Arlena but in Patrick – an unscrupulous adventurer for whom Arlena, with her passion for men, was easy prey. She was Patrick's victim, not the other way round, and he had already murdered Alice, having married her as Edward Corrigan. He found it easy to induce Arlena to hand him the Erskine money "for investment". He was aided by Christine, who played the "poor little wife" – frail, with her giddiness at heights and white skin. But in fact she had been a games mistress who could climb and run.

The day before the murder, Patrick arranged to meet Arlena at Pixy Cove next morning and, if she heard anyone descending the ladder, she was to slip inside Pixy's Cave. Then the next morning he went out early, descended the ladder and stowed a duplicate of Arlena's green Chinese hat in an appointed place.

Christine went to Linda's room as she was having her morning dip and put her watch forward by 20 minutes. On Linda's return, she arranged the trip to Gull Cove. Then she went to her own room, applied artificial suntan and threw the bottle out of the window where it just missed Miss Brewster who was bathing. She put on a white bathing suit, some beach trousers and a coat with sleeves hiding her newly browned arms and legs and met Linda just before 10.30 am.

At 10.15 am Arlena had left on her float. Just before 11.30 am Patrick went rowing with Miss Brewster. At Gull Cove Christine asked Linda the time, knowing from her concealed watch that it was 11.25 am. Linda said that it was 11.45 am, so giving Christine an alibi until then. Linda went down to the sea and Christine put her watch back to the right time. Then she ran up the cliff to the ladder, removed her pyjamas to reveal her white bathing suit, put them with her sketching box and swarmed down the ladder.

Arlena saw Christine and so ran into Pixy's Cave. Christine got the hat, a red curl pinned under the brim, and lay like a sunbather with her (white) face and neck shielded by the hat and curl. At about 11.40 am Patrick and Miss Brewster saw her figure. He got to it first and declared that Arlena had been strangled.

Once Miss Brewster had rowed off for the constable, Christine sprang up, cut up the hat with scissors which Patrick had brought, stuffed the pieces into her bathing suit and swarmed up the ladder. She put on her beach pyjamas, ran to the hotel and had a bath, washing off the suntan. She took the pieces of the hat and the curl into Linda's room and burned them in her grate, adding a leaf of a calendar to suggest that a *calendar* not a *hat* had been burnt.

Meanwhile Patrick had gone to the cave where Arlena had seen nothing. He called, she came out. He strangled her and lay her body down. He put a piece of Kenneth's pipe by the ladder to implicate him and waited for the police.

Poirot rightly describes the timing as "a work of genius", with the murder being committed *after* the body was supposedly seen and with the murderer having an alibi until then. This ingenuity had been used by Patrick in the Corrigan case, which was why Poirot found in it what he was seeking – a murder committed *after* it was supposed to have happened.

What had really happened there was that Edward (Patrick), with his alibi up to 4.25 pm, had run to Caesar's Grove, killed Alice *after* 4.25 pm and returned to the café. Since the hiker (Christine), who said she had found the body at 4.15 pm, was respectable, with no apparent connection to Edward, and since the body was only examined at 5.45 pm, the time of death was, as with Arlena, accepted.

As for Christine's alibi, Poirot says there was a risk that Linda might notice her watch was wrong – and it is surprising she doesn't after tearing down the stairs to meet Christine at 10.30 am, to be told that it was only 10.25 am. But, Poirot says, that did not matter much because Christine's "real alibi" was the size of her hands (though hand size is not actually an 'alibi').

Poirot also admires Miss Brewster being "carefully chosen" because, with her bad head for heights, she would not ascend the ladder but leave the Cove by boat. However, Patrick's choice was surely limited to whoever went rowing.

One also wonders when and where the Redferns acquired a duplicate Chinese jade green hat. Whatever the answer, they were lucky that Arlena wore the green hat since she could have worn one of her other beach cardboard hats in pale yellow or lacquer red. As for the bathing dress, Poirot says that Christine dressed herself in "a white bathing dress" (as if it was *any* white bathing dress) when Miss Brewster saw "*the* white backless bathing dress" on the body. So, again, when and where did Christine get her duplicate? And what happened to it? We are never told.

Having said that, the murder plan with its pinpoint precision and swapping of Christine and Arlena, is fantastic, if not quite as satisfying as its ingenuity merits because of its dependence on the behaviour of people outside the murderers' control. What if Rosamund had accepted Linda's invitation to go with her and Christine to Gull Cove? And still been there at 11.25 am when Linda said it was 11.45 am? Or if Linda had not gone bathing? What if Miss Brewster had not wanted to row? Or to do so earlier? Or later? Or not wanted Patrick to come? What if Arlena had come out of the cave when Patrick called "Hullo, Arlena" to the body? And what if Miss Brewster had looked at it?

As for motive, Poirot says that men like Patrick usually escape with the booty of unprotected women but, if there is a husband, brother or father about, things can take "an unpleasant turn" for the swindler. He says that once Kenneth found out what had happened to his wife's fortune, Patrick "might expect short shrift" but Patrick was not worried because he would kill her "when he judged it necessary". However, "an unpleasant turn" and "short shrift" do not sound like compelling motives for murder and we are not told why Patrick "judged it necessary" now. Patrick's motive for killing his golden goose when he did is not complete enough to be convincing.

Finally, we come to Christine's attempt to implicate Linda. While in Linda's room altering the watch, she saw a calf-bound volume *A History of Witchcraft, Sorcery and of the Compounding of Untraceable Poisons* (a title created by the author) open at a page describing causing death by moulding a wax figure to represent the victim and then roasting or piercing it. When Linda came in with some candles, Christine guessed her intention (towards Arlena).

Before going to Gull Cove, Linda made a wax figure, maybe adding a snip of Arlena's red hair, and stabbed it with a pin and melted it away by lighting cardboard strips under it. On returning to the hotel, Christine saw the wax and pin in the grate. So she introduced Linda, who believed she had caused her stepmother's death, to sleeping tablets as a speedy way to expiate her crime. Although Linda took six of them, she later recovered.

Plot

There are 13 untitled chapters, each divided into numbered parts. A map of Smugglers' Island (referred to in chapter 2 part 4) identifies the main locations including Pixy Cove, which is mistakenly referred to as Pixy's Cove (like Pixy's Cave) in chapter 4 part 5 and chapter 5 part 2. Some editions have the mainland, which is to the east, at the top but other editions, more naturally, have the north of the island to the top with the eastern mainland to the right.

The backdrop, the holiday season on the south coast, will be engagingly familiar to English readers but what is interesting is that, in a book published in 1941, the author says that 1922 was the year when "the great cult of the Seaside for Holidays" was finally established.

The title is from Ecclesiastes. In chapter 1 part 3, when Miss Brewster says you wouldn't get a body on Smugglers' Island, Poirot responds "there's evil everywhere under the sun", which Reverend Lane says is almost a quotation from Ecclesiastes. In fact it is 'almost a quotation' from five Ecclesiastes verses (4:3; 5:13; 6:1; 9:3; 10:5) – none of which has the exact wording of the title – but the one which Lane must mean, since he quotes more of it, is 9:3, which starts "This is an evil among all things that are done under the sun".

When the 'evil' turns out to be Patrick, not Arlena, one sees how skilfully their true characters have been portrayed in reverse. This deception, along with Patrick's ingenious alibi, is very well plotted and Mrs Gardener later says, referring to her jigsaw puzzle, "But I do think the people who make puzzles are kind of mean. They just go out of their way to deceive you".[1]

She also acts as the initial vehicle for the exposition, which is a bit contrived but comes across pretty naturally in her case because she would say as much as she does, although it has become less so by the time Rosamund completes it with her history of Kenneth. The characterisation is, generally speaking, a success but there is one real oddity when, having been accused, Patrick, "in his high good-humoured Irish voice", replies "Is it daft you are?". Readers will surely be taken aback because nowhere has there been a hint that he is Irish or has an Irish voice and nowhere has he previously used an Irish turn of phrase.

The real strength of the plotting comes in the impressive interweaving of the murder plot with so many suspects, who have so many different motives and alibis. There are also the two sub-plots of the dope smuggling and wax doll; and we are even deceived into thinking there may be other sub-plots involving a blackmailer and a religious maniac, the latter being clever because readers who assume (rightly) that the murderer is not going to be a religious maniac may equally assume (wrongly) that the murders in Surrey are a red herring.

Considerable effort must have gone into the plotting, particularly because, despite its intricacy, the story has a good pace throughout and remains easily readable if one is not trying to interpret the significance of all the clues, alibis and motives. However, if one sets aside the discussions between Poirot and the police about alibis and motives which do not ultimately bear on the main murder plot, the story almost seems to miss out the mystification stage by taking readers from puzzle to solution. This is because, with it appearing that the most realistic suspects just cannot be guilty, there is little discussion to excite readers into deducing how an apparently innocent suspect might have committed the crime. The effect is that, although the identity of the murderer is a mystery and the story most enjoyable, it is not as thought-provoking as it could be, which is a pity given the ingenious murder plan.

With the murder being committed *after* it was supposed to have happened, Poirot says that it was not committed "as is the usual way, *before* it is supposed to have happened". He perhaps had in mind his six earlier novels in which the alibi depended upon the murder happening at a time different from when it actually happened, in five of which the murder was indeed committed *before* it appeared to have been.[2]

In view of the central importance of timing to the murder plan, one wonders about other timing points on the fatal day. A minor problem is caused by the clock. Rosamund says that after looking into Kenneth's room she saw that it was 11.20 am (not 11.15 am, as Poirot later suggests) by the *hall* clock. The *hall* was where Christine and Linda agreed to meet at 10.30 am, and Linda refers to the *hall* at her interview, though Christine says that they agreed to meet in the *lounge*. Poirot refers in chapter 13 to it being

10.25 am by the *lounge* clock and Christine refers to the *lounge* clock in chapter 12 part 3. Eventually one realises that the hall and the lounge must be the same and that there is only one clock.

By 12.45 pm the police (Colgate, Dr Neasden and Constable Hawkes) are at Pixy Cove, which is impressive since the body was discovered at 11.45 am and Miss Brewster had to row to Leathercombe Bay (there was no telephone at the hotel) and find the constable, who had to contact his superiors, who had to get to Leathercombe Bay, then to the island and then down to Pixy Cove. After that, Colgate and Poirot conduct various interviews, one being with Major Barry, who returned at 1.30 pm, "half an hour ago", so the time is then 2 pm. After more interviews and inspecting some guest rooms, they go to Pixy Cove. It is now well after 2 pm and so chapter 9 should not start "For the second time that morning Patrick Redfern was rowing a boat into Pixy Cove".

Clues

There are so many clues in this story that it is hard to know which is the main one until this becomes clear in Poirot's explanations. It seemed to him "from the beginning" that the most likely person to have killed Arlena was Patrick because he was "the type of man" who exploited women like her and "the type of killer" who would take a woman's savings while cutting her throat.

Although it was assumed that she was "the type of woman" who wrecked lives, she did not fatally attract men – it was men who fatally attracted her. She was "the type of woman" for whom men care easily and of whom they as easily tire, "the type of woman" who is invariably defrauded – a predestined prey for men of a certain "type". In Patrick he recognised "that type" at once.

Poirot's repeated reliance on the 'type' clue should be no surprise, in relation to Arlena, because of his earlier comments that "*Because* the victim was the kind of person he or she was, *therefore* was he or she murdered!"; that "the truest and most significant thing" said all morning was Christine's thought that Arlena was "the kind of woman" who might be strangled; and that Arlena "herself is the best, the only clue, to her own death".[3]

Although Poirot saw through the role reversal of Patrick and Arlena because of the 'type' clue, how fairly was it clued for readers? Since it is hard to give clues that someone's personality is the very opposite of the way it is portrayed without giving the game away, the author gives clues, not to the generality of Arlena as a victim, but to two facets that help readers spot that generality.

The first is that Arlena was "the type of woman" who gets defrauded, the clue being a letter from a man, J.N., thanking her for a cheque and saying he wants to give her jewels. Poirot describes the 'J.N. letter' clue as "very important" but readers would do well to interpret this letter from a man who sounds crazy about Arlena in the way that Poirot astutely does, as a clue to a young waster getting money out of her while merely expressing a wish to give her jewels.

The second facet is that Arlena was "the type of woman" for whom men care easily and of whom they as easily tire, the clue being that Lord Codrington, in whose divorce she was cited, refused to marry her. The 'Codrington' clue supports the facet but Kenneth *did* marry her and Erskine left her money – and those facts do not. To counter them, Poirot says that Kenneth found little to sustain his infatuation and that Erskine "had not had time to grow tired of her". But, although Kenneth did not look up as she passed on the beach, there is no clue that Erskine would have tired of her.

Readers may, however, have got a clue that she was a victim from Gardener saying she was "pretty much of a darned fool!", which Poirot thinks "very interesting" – though a better clue, for which he fails to give credit, comes from Barry who says about husbands: "They see a feller sweet on their wife but they don't see that *she's* sweet on *him!*".

As for Patrick, readers would do very well to spot him as an unscrupulous adventurer because the only clue is Poirot telling an apparently jealous and unhappy Christine on the evening before the crime that Patrick loves her – meaning that his true bond is with her and that he wasn't crazy about Arlena.

Although Poirot suspects Patrick, he is faced with his strong alibi. So the second stage of his thinking was to look for other solutions. But none fitted with his "collection of jig-saw puzzle pieces" – clues such as the scissors on the beach, the bottle thrown from a window and the bath that no one would admit taking. So he reconsidered whether there was anything supporting Patrick's guilt. And there was – Arlena's missing money.

He concluded that this had gone to Patrick because Arlena was "the type of woman" to be swindled – but not "the type of woman" to be blackmailed since she was not good at keeping secrets. So we are back on the 'type' clue for his third stage and get quite a good clue that Arlena would be an odd blackmail target when Rosamund says that her conduct was notorious and she never tried to be respectable. Yet, despite the 'notorious conduct' clue, Arlena and her blackmailer had apparently been overheard.

So, if the blackmailer had been invented, why? To explain Arlena's missing money. So, in that fourth stage of his thinking, Poirot realised that Christine – the person who claimed to have heard him – and Patrick were in it together. But, although he had now solved the *whodunnit*, he had not solved the *howdunnit* because of Patrick's alibi up until the *body* was discovered.

But then the word *body* stirred in his mind – *bodies* lying on the beach – *all alike*. Suppose it was not Arlena's body whose face was hidden but that of someone pretending to be dead? Christine, of course. This fifth stage is inspiration, but it is not the fluke it sounds because there had been a discussion in chapter 1, among those on the terrace, about how little difference there was between the sun-tanned bodies lying below them like meat upon a slab.

However, the 'sun-tanned bodies' clue does depend upon Poirot knowing two things which he asserts in chapter 13 – that Patrick alone examined the (Christine's) body and that its face was hidden. But there is no record of him being told either of them.

Nevertheless, he realised the body was Christine's whose white skin explained his 'jig-saw puzzle pieces' clues – the thrown bottle (the artificial suntan); the bath no one would admit taking (to wash it off); and the scissors (used on the hat). Poirot regards these clues as "rendered significant by the fact that no one would admit to them" and yet, although he asked three suspects about the bath, he never actually asked anyone about the bottle or the scissors.[4]

Moreover, the bottle and the bath reduce the suspects to five because the bottle must have been thrown from a window in the east wing where Rosamund, Kenneth, Linda, Patrick and Christine had rooms and the waste water had also come from a bath in that wing. At that time Linda was swimming at Gull Cove while Patrick was at Pixy Cove with the body and yet Christine, Kenneth and Rosamund each denied running the bath, with Rosamund asking if this was "the Sherlock Holmes touch!" – resonant of *Silver Blaze* – with the curiosity of the incident of the midday bath being that no one would admit running it.

Poirot's next question was where Arlena was then. Here he had the 'Gabrielle No 8' clue – the scent used only by Rosamund and Arlena detected in Pixy's Cave. So, which of them was in the cave? It was "certainly not Rosamund", he says, but without giving any reason. Perhaps he believes that she was at Sunny Ledge until 11.50 am, but we are never told definitively whether she was.

The narrative had said that, when Patrick and Miss Brewster looked up, they saw her *sunshade*. Poirot tells her she was seen on Sunny Ledge "or at least your sunshade was seen" but it is not clear why he refers to the 'sunshade' clue in a way that suggests that she *herself* was not seen since by then Miss Brewster has said, surprisingly in view of the narrative, "We saw her there".

Nevertheless, having decided that Arlena was in Pixy's Cave and killed after Patrick had examined Christine's body at 11.45 am, this gave rise to two more problems. First, the time of death had been put at 10.45–11.40 am. This was resolved by the police surgeon having referred *only* to the "earliest outside limit" (words repeated, very fairly for readers, by Weston afterwards); the *latest* outside limit was based on what *Miss Brewster* had said. This 'earliest outside limit' clue is very clever and readers would do well to spot it.

Secondly, Christine had an alibi because she was with Linda from 10.30 am until returning to the hotel at 11.45 am according to Linda's watch. So Poirot had to show that the 'Linda's watch' clue did not help Christine because she could have (a) altered the watch and (b) altered it back.

Altering it back was easy because, as Poirot knew (chapter 6 part 4), Linda entered the sea before Christine left the beach. But, as for altering it initially, he makes two less good points. First, that Christine was alone in Linda's room. Readers know this from the narrative but how does he? Neither Christine nor Linda tells him. He asserts that Christine said in her interview how she went into Linda's room and found her absent, but she did not.

Secondly, that there was "indirect proof" in Linda *being heard to say* she was afraid about being late for meeting Christine but that when she arrived it was only 10.25 am. Linda did indeed tell Rosamund she was afraid about being late but, although she tells Poirot she was afraid, she does not tell him that she *voiced* this concern or that it was only 10.25 am. Nor does Rosamund.

Next Poirot thought that it seemed "a very slick crime" – with "an assurance" about it – making him wonder if Patrick had murdered before. So he asked for details of strangulation cases because, if a past crime closely resembled the present one, "we shall have there a very valuable clue" – which he gets with the 'Alice murder' clue. But his starting point, the 'slickness' clue, is not that convincing because 'slick' is a rather indeterminate adjective, 'slickness' is not necessarily a clue to repetition and the murder is no more 'slick' than in some of Poirot's other cases in which he did not use that word.

Nevertheless readers who spot the resemblance Poirot has in mind – about when the murder really happened (rather than, as Colgate deceptively suggests, a husband (Kenneth) with a cast-iron alibi) – and realise that Edward is Patrick will assume that the woman hiker is Christine. She is otherwise almost impossible to spot as the hiker. It is one thing to look like Arlena by using artificial suntan but quite another to turn from a "hefty" hiker into a "delicate creature" with "dainty" hands and feet. And we are not told that Christine had been a games mistress until Poirot's explanations, only that Rosamund believed she had been a school teacher.

Poirot's final problem with Christine was the ladder, with her saying she had no head for heights. So, suspecting she was lying, he arranged a picnic. There she "sprang lightly from stone to stone" and at a bridge, where Miss Brewster was giddy, "The others had run across the bridge lightly enough" – a clever way of including Christine without naming her.

The 'picnic' clue is important because, if she told one lie, says Poirot, "all the other lies were possible" (meaning "all her other statements were possibly lies") – such as about the blackmail conversation, leaving Gull Cove at 11.45 am and not having a bath. Given the clue's importance, one wonders what Poirot would have done if she had refused to go on the picnic, as seemed likely.

Some readers may spot that during the picnic we get a 'Blatt photograph' clue when Poirot says "I value that group very much" about a photograph taken by Blatt earlier. But they would do very well to guess that the police recognised Patrick and Christine as Edward and the hiker from that photograph.

After Poirot's explanations, Mrs Gardener is excited that her magenta wool had a role. But her wool is of marginal significance, relevant only to whether Kenneth and Rosamund, who 'forgot' about returning to the hotel, might have committed the crime. Rosamund's forgetfulness is so unlikely that readers will have wondered (correctly) if she might just have been bolstering Kenneth's alibi, which he then corroborated by saying he saw her in the mirror. In showing that they both lied, Poirot relies on two clues, with the magenta wool being part of the first one.

When Mr Gardener went up to the hotel to fetch it, he did not see Rosamund (not that readers had been told this), which Poirot says was "rather remarkable" if she left Sunny Ledge at 11.10 am (in fact she said she returned to the hotel at about 11.15 am). But, whatever time it was, the 'unseen Rosamund' clue is not convincing because two guests could easily miss each other if they arrived at the hotel a minute apart.

The second clue is that, although Kenneth's typewriter was on the table under the mirror after the inquest, it had been on the writing table in the corner of the room on the day of the murder; and so he could not have seen Rosamund in the mirror. Only the most astute reader would have noted the typewriter's location in chapter 8 part 1 and that it had been moved by chapter 10 part 5. It is a pity that this excellent 'Kenneth typewriter' clue, probably the best in the book, is deployed only to expose a lie by a couple who are not the murderers.

As for Linda, Poirot describes her interview manner as "significant" without saying how. Then he sees the candle grease and pin in her grate and, after opening the calf-bound volume, says intriguingly "But for the other – is that possible too? No, it is not possible, unless … unless …". We learn later that he realised that she had destroyed a wax figure and was wondering if she had killed the real Arlena too. But she had been with Christine until 11.45 am "unless … unless …" she had said the time was 11.45 am when it was only 11.30 am and then, once Christine had left, had hurried down the ladder, strangled Arlena and returned before the boat came. But she had only destroyed the wax figure.

As well as the grease and pin, Poirot finds other items in Linda's grate and, as these are listed in chapter 8 part 1, readers should realise they are getting what turns out to be the first of three lists of clues. The green cardboard (the pieces of Arlena's hat) and the hair (the false red curl) were burnt by Christine – but Linda may also have burnt cardboard and hair because Poirot says that she "possibly" adorned her figure with Arlena's hair and lit cardboard under it.

The most intriguing item, however, is an unburnt fragment, possibly from a pull-off calendar, bearing a figure 5 and the words "… *noble deeds*". Poirot murmurs *"Do noble deeds, not dream them all day long"* – derived from Charles Kingsley's 'A Farewell' – so presumably those words were on the pull-off page for 25 August as a quotation for that day. Christine added the green calendar page to confuse identification of the green cardboard.

The second list is the collection of objects found on the beach at Pixy Cove in chapter 9 part 1. All are irrelevant except for two items found by the ladder – the scissors which were not out in the previous day's rain and so must have been brought to the beach on the fatal day (described by Poirot as "the one thing" the murderers forgot) and the fragment of "brier" (which should be briar) pipe planted to implicate Kenneth.

The key list, however, is the third one in chapter 11 part 2 where the items are listed so plainly as clues by Poirot, who even uses separate paragraphs for each clue, that one wonders why the author was so unsubtle. Perhaps she was concerned about the level of mystification and seeking a way to get readers to engage in the detection process. The paragraphs are not numbered in the book but it will help analysis to enumerate them here:

1. A morning on the bathing beach some few days before Arlena's death
2. One, two, three, four, five separate remarks uttered on that morning
3. The evening of a bridge game. Poirot, Patrick and Rosamund were at the table. Christine, while dummy, heard a conversation (between Arlena and the blackmailer). Who else had been in the lounge? Who had not?
4. The evening before the crime. Poirot's conversation with Christine and the scene he had witnessed on the way back to the hotel (when he saw Arlena with Patrick and was then joined by Kenneth whose face revealed that he knew about them).
5. Gabrielle No 8
6. A pair of scissors
7. A broken pipe stem
8. A bottle thrown from a window
9. A green calendar
10. A packet of candles
11. A mirror and a typewriter
12. A skein of magenta wool
13. A girl's wristwatch
14. Bathwater rushing down the waste pipe
15. Poirot's own belief in the presence of evil on the island
16. Nellie Parsons and Alice Corrigan

The list includes clues relating not only to Arlena's murder but also Kenneth and Rosamund's alibi and Linda's wax doll. It has no clues relating to the dope smuggling, though there are some: that Blatt nearly drove into a hedge when realising that Poirot was at the hotel and spilt his drink at the mention of Pixy's Cave; that he enjoyed sailing in his yawl with its conspicuous red sails, preferably on his own, unlike his sociability on land; that Poirot thought he would choose Deauville or Biarritz, not Smugglers' Island and there was something not right about him; that he was "uneasy" and "nervous" at his interview; and that he had been making big sums from unexplained sources.

Subject to those omissions, the list looks comprehensive. Even the 'slickness' clue – not been mentioned by then – seems covered by item (16). But in fact, oddly, he omits the Chinese hat; the white bathing dress; the beach pyjamas (though it's not clear how he knows about those); the "very important" letter from J.N.; Blatt's photograph (not been mentioned by then); and the pin, burnt hair and book on witchcraft (despite listing the calendar and candles).

He also gives us two clues in chapter 10, which he does not identify later, with the strange result that we cannot be sure whether they are in the third list. First, in part 4 he says that a "remark" of Mrs Gardener's was "exceedingly helpful" and "illuminating" but never says what it was. It is hard to see how any of her remarks on the bathing beach – item (2) – would help him reach the solution. On the fatal morning she did ask Odell to fetch the wool – item (12) – but 'remark' is an odd word for a request and nothing else she says then becomes an issue in the story. At her interview she said that Rosamund loved Kenneth but that point was not new to Poirot. So her 'remark' is a mystery.

Secondly, in part 7, as Rosamund discusses Arlena's murder with Poirot, she says that, on the day before, anyone could have come on to the island unseen in the rain and mist and spent the night in the cave, to which he responds "You know, there is a good deal in what you have just said". But it is hard to know why, since this was not part of the murder plan (or the smuggling). He already knew from the scent – item (5) – about Arlena or Rosamund being in the cave and that the scissors – item (6) – had not been out in the rain.

As for the clues which *are* in the third list, items (5) to (16) are recognisable in his solution. But items (1) to (4) create issues.

With item (1), it is hard to see what separate clue he got beyond the 'remarks' in item (2). The only candidate in chapter 13 is his comment "Looking on from my place on the beach, I was quite certain that Arlena was Patrick's victim, not the other way round". *If* this (the 'type' clue) is what Poirot intended by item (1), it would be very difficult for readers to spot just from item (1)'s wording.

As for item (2), since he enumerates the five separate remarks ("One, two, three, four, five separate remarks") as if recollecting them one by one, readers assume that he will identify them or that they will be apparent on a re-reading.

However, neither is the case. He may have meant the remarks comprising the 'sun-tanned bodies' clue (because, if not, this clue has been omitted from the list) but all those remarks are made by Poirot himself (except for a repetition by Miss Brewster) and it is unlikely that he would treat his *own* conversational remarks as clues. But, even if he is, what is a 'remark'? When he says "They are not men and women. There is nothing personal about them. They are just bodies!", is that one remark (because it is one speech) or three?

He may have meant the remarks about 'evil' because he says in chapter 13 "It was that day that we spoke of evil – *evil under the sun* as Mr Lane put it" (though Lane didn't use those very words). Again, one assumes that Poirot was not referring to his own remarks and anyway his own belief in the presence of evil is at item (15). But Miss Brewster referred to Arlena as the "personification of evil" and in one speech Lane used the word "evil" in six different sentences and the word "It" (meaning 'Evil') in five more, as well as referring later to Arlena as "evil through and through" and to "the presence of Evil". We don't know which, if any, of these remarks Poirot had in mind.

Other possible candidates for the "five separate remarks" are (i) Christine's remark about her inability to go brown; (ii) Miss Brewster's remarks about (a) Christine's giddiness at heights (wrongly attributed to Christine in chapter 13) and (b) Christine being "a nice little thing", supporting her pretended delicacy; and (iii) Rosamund's remarks about (a) Christine being a school teacher (again wrongly attributed in chapter 13 to Christine, who never says this) and (b) the Codrington divorce. Perhaps Poirot had some of those remarks in mind because, if not, these points have also been omitted from the third list.

It may seem pedantic to have considered item (2) so thoroughly but, if one rates the difficulty of identifying the "five separate remarks" against the ease with which one would expect to do so, item (2) really is one of the author's most frustratingly inaccessible clues.

As to item (3), Poirot never addresses, let alone answers, his questions about who had been in the lounge. And it is odd that he should even pose them if, as he says in chapter 13, the blackmailer story had "never rung true to my mind". As to item (4), although he mentions the Christine conversation in chapter 13, he does not refer to the scene he saw on his way back.

In clueing this story, the author has given readers so many clues that the mind can boggle rather than engage with the detection process. Having said that, there are some good ones – most notably, the excellent 'Kenneth typewriter' clue, the very clever 'earliest outside limit' clue and the quite clever 'J.N. letter' clue. However, readers may well feel that the main clue, the 'type' clue, is too difficult to spot and that there are too many clues where Poirot makes deductions without having the information to justify them or where he fails to explain what he had in mind.

21

Five Little Pigs

Solution

Poirot investigates the 16-year-old murder of a well-known painter, Amyas Crale. His wife, Caroline, had been convicted of the crime and died in prison. Poirot is engaged by their daughter, Carla, who, on reaching age 21, receives a letter left for her by Caroline asserting her innocence.

Amyas, aged nearly 40 and named after Amyas Leigh in Charles Kingsley's *Westward Ho!*, is a full-blooded man who loves life. He has been married for ten years to Caroline who is 34 and, although he dates other women, he always returns to her. But then he meets a beautiful girl aged 20, Elsa Greer, and they fall for each other. He paints her in the garden of his estate in south Devon, Alderbury, where he lives with Caroline, Carla (aged 5), Caroline's 15-year-old half-sister, Angela Warren, and Angela's governess, Cecilia Williams.

The garden, four minutes from the house, is called the Battery because it has battlements set with miniature cannon overlooking the sea. It has a summerhouse containing beer and glasses in case Amyas gets thirsty while painting. Elsa stays at Alderbury twice, posing for him. During the second visit, on 17 September, she tells Caroline that she is marrying him, which he admits is true. Caroline says "I'll kill Amyas before I give him up to *you*".

Next day, with the painting nearly finished, he is poisoned with coniine, the active principle of the spotted hemlock, which causes gradual paralysis, then death. It was in a glass of beer which he drank while painting Elsa.

The suspects, in addition to Caroline, are the five other people at Alderbury that day (ignoring the faithful old servants). They give the novel its title, which comes from the nursery rhyme, 'This Little Pig' (or 'Piggy'):

This little piggy went to market,
This little piggy stayed at home,
This little piggy ate roast beef,
This little piggy had none
And this little piggy cried "wee wee wee" all the way home

All five are still alive and Poirot obtains accounts from each, verbal (Book I) and written (Book II), in the order in which they appear in the rhyme; and he speaks to Caroline's Defence Counsel (Depleach), the junior Prosecuting Counsel (Hogg), the clerk at Caroline's solicitors (Edmunds), the Crale family solicitor (Jonathan) and the senior police officer (Hale).

The first suspect is Philip Blake, a stockbroker who plays the markets. He had become Amyas' best friend when, as boys, he and his elder brother Meredith had come across the creek from their adjoining estate at Handcross Manor. Second is Meredith, a country squire, who still lives at Handcross Manor – a "stay at home sort of chap" – who dabbles in herbs and drugs in his laboratory from which the coniine had been taken.

Third is Elsa, who has been left a cold woman by Amyas' death. She had had three husbands – "they've fed her meat all right". Fourth is Angela's former governess, Cecilia Williams, who exists in a meagre, one-room 'flatlet' with battered furniture – the little pig that had none. Fifth is Angela who, when she was a baby about 15 years before the murder, had a paperweight thrown at her by Caroline (who must have been about 19) in a fit of "adolescent" jealousy or rage. She had lost the sight of an eye and been disfigured and so was entitled to cry "wee-wee". She used to play pranks on Amyas, who wanted her sent off to school but, now aged about 31, she is a distinguished lecturer and writer. Carla was away on the day of the murder, visiting her grandmother.

The evidence which convicted Caroline is very damning: she had ample motive; she was heard to say, in the drawing room and library, that she would kill Amyas rather than give him up to Elsa; she had a temper, having flung a paperweight at Angela years before; she admitted taking the coniine, but with the idea of killing herself, when visiting Meredith's laboratory (with Amyas, Elsa, Philip and Angela) on the afternoon before the murder and only her fingerprints were on the bottle[1]; she had taken it by emptying a jasmine scent bottle from her bag and filling it with coniine and only her fingerprints were on that bottle; she brought an iced beer bottle down to the Battery and poured it into the glass from which Amyas drank before he complained of the foul taste; the coniine was in the dregs of the glass; and, when she found Amyas' body in the Battery after lunch, she was seen by Miss Williams wiping the bottle and pressing Amyas' dead fingers on it; although Miss Williams does not reveal this until Poirot's investigation, it was assumed at the trial that this was what Caroline had done because Amyas' fingers couldn't have held the bottle in the position suggested. Despite all this evidence, Caroline insists it was suicide but she doesn't put up a fight at the trial and writes to Angela afterwards, saying it is "all right" and "One has to pay one's debts".

At the denouement, before exposing the murderer, Poirot reaches various conclusions. Caroline did take the coniine. But she did not poison Amyas because, in wiping the fingerprints from the *bottle* (which had not contained the poison) rather than the *glass* (which had), she showed she did not know *how* he was poisoned.

She insisted on suicide, thinking that Angela had poisoned him because, when she went to get the iced beer from the conservatory, a guilty-looking Angela was there, unscrewing the bottle which Caroline took down to Amyas. She did not want Angela suspected so that she could repay the debt she had owed ever since hurling a paperweight at her. So she wiped the bottle handled by Angela and tried to fit Amyas' fingers round it. But she was wrong because Angela had not put coniine in the bottle. Instead, Angela, upset about Amyas being unfair to her (and having flung a paperweight at him at dinner the evening before, wishing he were dead or would die of leprosy), had looked guilty because she planned to put valerian into the bottle as a prank. And on the fatal morning she took some valerian from the laboratory but before she could put it in the bottle Caroline entered the conservatory. So, neither Caroline nor Angela was guilty.

Poirot then exposes Elsa as the murderer, saying that, in love, she was frighteningly single-minded, with a deep, overmastering passion for Amyas. She assumed that he felt the same for her, that their passion was for life and that he would leave Caroline. He, however, never intended to do so. But he did not undeceive Elsa, who was just another of his women, because he wanted to finish the picture and in the library on the fatal morning he told Caroline that, once he had done so, he would not see Elsa again.

What he (and readers) did not know was that Elsa had overheard his cruel intention to send her packing and return to Caroline. Imagine, says Poirot, her shock to hear the truth, brutally spoken. So, when Amyas then told her it was time to pose, she said she wanted a pullover and went inside, up to Caroline's room to find the coniine, which she had seen her take. Without disturbing Caroline's fingerprints on the jasmine scent bottle, she drew off the fluid into a pipette. She got a pullover and accompanied Amyas to the Battery. She poured him out some beer, poisoned it and he drank it.

After posing, Elsa came up to the house ("this time really to fetch a pullover", as Poirot puts it). Caroline then went to the Battery to tell Amyas that he was being cruel on Elsa, Amyas said (so Poirot assumes, because no witness says so) "It's all settled – I'll send her packing". Elsa reappeared with her pullover and Philip, by the Battery door with Meredith, noticed Amyas stagger.

Amyas complained that the beer in the summerhouse was hot, so Caroline went to fetch some iced beer. When she returned, Amyas drank it and said "Everything tastes foul today" because the taste of Elsa's beer was still in his mouth. Elsa continued to pose, later saying that he complained of pains, stiffness and muscular rheumatism about 40 minutes after drinking Caroline's beer. He continued painting until his limbs failed, helpless, but with his mind still clear. Before Elsa went up to lunch, leaving Amyas painting, she dropped the last few drops of the coniine into the beer glass that had held Caroline's innocent drink, later crushing the pipette to powder on the path.

After finding the dead Amyas, Caroline wiped the bottle and glass in order to pretend, says Depleach in chapter 1, that "she'd never even handled the stuff". But why would she pretend this? Since it was known that she had handled the bottle, why wipe her fingerprints? So readers are faced, almost from the start, with apparently nonsensical behaviour by Caroline, which could only make sense if she wasn't wiping *her own* fingerprints but someone else's. But no one seems to spot this then, not even Poirot.

However, the identity of the murderer is the key issue and Caroline seems like the only person with a realistic motive, especially with Elsa being so in love with Amyas. Hale first describes the motive when referring to Caroline's threat in the drawing room "I'll kill Amyas before I give him up to *you*" – and it is then drummed into readers by being repeated in slightly different ways four more times. But, with Caroline's jealousy motive in mind, it is a small step to regard it as a motive that could apply equally to Elsa and, indeed, it is hard to think of any motive that could apply as well to the other suspects.

There are, however, two ironies about reaching this pretty obvious solution via the jealousy motive. First, nowhere in Poirot's explanations does he indicate what Elsa's motive was. Secondly, jealousy may not be the correct motive after all. In her interview with Poirot she says "So I am vindictive – to anyone who has injured me", meaning that her motive was probably revenge in the form of vindictiveness (directed at Amyas) rather than jealousy in the form of possessiveness (directed at Caroline). It is surprising that neither Poirot nor Elsa resolves this key human aspect of the solution, given that he actually says that his success has been founded on "the eternal *why?* of human behaviour".

Were it not for that frustration and the 'pullover problem' cited below, the solution would be particularly satisfying, not because it is clever or involves the author's usual invention or surprise, but because it is logical and convincing, allowing the reader a satisfied nod towards his own deductive powers because he was right about the *whodunnit*, despite the difficulty of spotting *why* Elsa became vindictive or jealous.

For the *howdunnit*, the murder plan is basic – an impromptu decision by Elsa. But she gets credit for quick thinking about the coniine; for finding it in Caroline's room (Poirot says that women know where other women hide things); for finding a pipette; for drawing some coniine into it without wiping Caroline's fingerprints from the jasmine scent bottle or leaving her own; for knowing (as we are told three times before Poirot's explanations) that Amyas would drink beer in one draught (and so be unable to react to the foul taste); for posing brightly so as to keep him from suspecting; and for dropping the last drops of the coniine into the glass that had held Caroline's innocent drink.

Elsa was lucky, however, that Amyas hardly reacted to her foul-tasting beer, despite knowing that he was the subject of an argument between two jealous, quarrelling women, who had been given a lecture the previous day about poisons. After staggering, even before feeling stiffness and pains, he might have done more than just complain to Elsa, perhaps enabling not only a doctor to come, as Elsa actually suggests, but also her murderous beer to be identified as the cause. His lack of reaction is explained away on the ground that, as is said three times, he hated to admit to illness.

Finally, we come to the 'pullover problem'. Philip says that, after Amyas came out of the library, Elsa went inside to get a pullover (which, Poirot says, is when she obtained the coniine) and that, when she came out, they went down to the Battery. As Poirot says in Book III chapter 3 "She gets a pullover and accompanies him". Then, after posing for a while, she came up to the house, this time, as Poirot puts it in Book III chapter 4, "really to fetch a pullover" and later, "pullover in hand", she came down the path once more. But how could Elsa have accompanied Amyas *with her pullover* on the first occasion if she 'really' went back to the house later to get it? In other words, how could she get her pullover twice?

Plot

This novel, called *Murder in Retrospect* in the United States, is the author's first to investigate a murder committed years before. Its core is Amyas' murder (the main plot) but its solution depends partly upon explaining Caroline's attempt to protect Angela (the main sub-plot), which depends partly on realising why Angela was unscrewing the beer bottle (the minor sub-plot).

So the main characters are Amyas, Elsa, Caroline and Angela, while three little pigs (Philip, Meredith and Miss Williams) are really only relevant in giving evidence about the plots, with the extra feature that Meredith had a laboratory. Although he and Philip are also given unrequited love interests with Elsa and Caroline respectively, those minor storylines are hardly sub-plots and at the denouement Poirot mentions them "only as illustrations".

Poirot first thinks of the rhyme after Depleach has described Philip as a broker who plays the markets and runs to fat and Meredith as a "stay at home sort of chap". Although Meredith fits his role as the second little pig, Philip's playing of the markets is irrelevant and, when Poirot meets him, he focuses instead on "a well-fed pig who had gone to market – and fetched the full market price" but that has no relevance to the story either.[2]

Nor do Elsa's three husbands, even though Depleach's comment "They've fed her meat all right" refers to them. Miss Williams, living near the bone, fits the rhyme well, although her lack of roast beef is also irrelevant. But her main weakness is that she is too minor a character to be an equal suspect or even the subject of one of Poirot's 'illustrations'. As for Angela, Poirot reckons that, despite her scar, there is no suggestion of the little pig who cries "wee-wee", which will surprise readers who might have expected the author to fit the characters to the rhyme.

Nevertheless, the structural device of investigating a murder retrospectively through the verbal and written recollections of five suspects, one of whom must have committed it (if Caroline did not), is very good and provides a most satisfying way of revealing the narrative, with different characters providing different, or slightly different, pieces of the jigsaw.

Hale warns that Poirot will hear five accounts of five separate murders. "That is what I am counting upon", he replies. So, readers will expect to find clues among contradictions or inconsistencies in the accounts. In fact, although the characters do provide information omitted by others, the verbal and written accounts are remarkably consistent as to the main events and they produce a very intricately plotted narrative which comes together very well.

There are, however, a few occasions where characters omit key facts. Thus Hale says that Caroline was heard saying to Elsa in the drawing room "I'll kill Amyas before I give him up to *you*" by both Philip and Miss Williams but neither mentions this important threat. Depleach tells Poirot that Caroline was heard by *two* people threatening Amyas that, if he didn't give Elsa up, she'd kill him; although Elsa claims that such a threat was made in the library, no second witness asserts that. Philip did overhear a vaguer threat which did not mention 'giving Elsa up' ("You and your women! Some day I will kill you"), which Poirot says was also heard by Elsa, but Elsa does not mention hearing that and nor does Hale when reciting what she heard.

However, it is from the narrative as a whole, rather than inconsistencies in it, that Poirot extracts his solution. Not even Elsa's account is inconsistent with anyone else's on key points where she lies since the author cleverly ensures that no one else contradicts her – although there are minor inconsistencies such as whether Caroline put the beer glass down beside Amyas (as Elsa says) or in his hand (Hale) and whether she pretended to think that Amyas had been poisoned (Miss Williams), knifed (Philip), or shot or stabbed (Elsa herself).

In fact the strength of the verbal and written accounts comes not in the varying ways that the suspects describe events but in revealing their personalities, so helping readers to assess their likely guilt. The author also judges nicely the points they might make verbally and their more reflective written approach. Elsa's account is particularly well written because, instead of giving us the usual explanation by a murderer of why and how a murder was committed, she sets out the actions and feelings of someone claiming she *didn't* do it.

The only time when the structure doesn't quite work is with Poirot's five questions, one for each little pig, in Book III chapter 2. Even he admits that Angela's question could wait until chapter 4 (but it's not clear there if it was whether she tampered with the beer or pinched the valerian) but he does ask her two questions in chapter 2 – whether she will bring Caroline's letter to the denouement and whether she had recently read *The Moon and*

Sixpence at the time of the tragedy. His questions for the others also feel disappointing. Although his question to Meredith relates to the missing coniine, his question for Miss Williams relates only to Angela's protection while those for Philip and Elsa relate only to his 'illustrations'.

The unavoidable result of having so many accounts, verbal and written, which are *bound* to overlap to a large extent, is two-fold. First, the book is extremely dense with potentially relevant facts. Sometimes one welcomes some padding in an intellectually demanding story but, since almost every fact is potentially relevant, there is very little extraneous narrative in this one. Secondly, there is considerable repetition. But the repetition never feels boring despite the density. This is because it cements a good understanding of the facts in the reader's mind, because the detail contextualises the key remarks and because one is looking for inconsistencies. If one approaches the story with the aim of solving a puzzle pure and simple, one's attention is maintained.

But the author doesn't just provide a puzzle. She also provides a clever structure with a most engaging way for presenting the narrative; an intricately plotted storyline; a depth of characterisation, through the suspects' accounts, which really brings out their personalities; and a masterly contrast of styles in the five written accounts.

Not only are there allusions to Shakespeare, Milton, Kingsley, Maugham and Plato but also emotional and psychological insights into youth (its ruthlessness and vulnerability); parenting (and healthy neglect); schooling (and the stimulation and discipline of the community); upbringing (and strictness as a defence against envy, discontent and regret): violence (and guarding against it by using violence in language); and understanding (through the benefit of later experience). As for the excellently poignant ending to Poirot's explanations, where he refers to the remarkable "picture of a murderess painted by her victim ... the picture of a girl watching her lover die", this is a class above anything else descriptive the author ever wrote in a detective novel.

Indeed the *combination* of structure, plot, style, characterisation, engagement and insight mean that the story could fairly be regarded as the author's best detective novel from a literary perspective. More than any of her other books, this serious story could genuinely be a worthy student text for academic study. In saying that, however, the emphasis is on the word *novel* rather than *detective* since, as a puzzle, it is not her strongest, in terms of intricacy of murder plan or surprise of solution and it lacks the mystification and inventiveness of a number of her other plots.

Moreover, it omits not only clarification of Elsa's motive but also a definitive conclusion for Caroline taking the coniine. Although there is a good argument, based on her comments to Hale, Meredith and Angela, that she really was thinking of suicide, she had threatened to kill Amyas just before taking it and it is a little unsatisfying not to have this human issue resolved.

One conclusion which Poirot does reach is that Elsa assumed "without asking him" that Amyas was going to leave Caroline. But Elsa *must* have discussed being dragged through the divorce courts with Amyas because, according to Hale, Amyas said to Meredith (though Meredith doesn't mention this himself) "That isn't Elsa's idea at all. *She* isn't going to appear. We shall fix it up in the usual way". Elsa's "idea" was to adopt the then practice of one spouse in an unhappy couple (Amyas) creating legal grounds for divorce by booking into a hotel to commit adultery with a third party (someone other than Elsa), thereby enabling the other spouse (Caroline) to petition.

Hale also says that Meredith was censured by the coroner because coniine comes under Schedule I of the Poisons Acts. The operative Act at the time of the book's publication was the Pharmacy and Poisons Act 1933, which did include coniine, although not in a Schedule but in Part I of a 'Poisons List' prepared pursuant to section 17(2). However, at the time of Meredith's censure (16 years before i.e *before* the 1933 Act), the operative Act was the Poisons and Pharmacy Act 1908. There is only one (unnumbered) Schedule to that Act and, although it refers to "poisonous vegetable alkaloids", it does not refer specifically to coniine.

Clues

This is a story where many of the clues are based upon personality, upon words – what was really said and meant and heard – and upon behaviour – what people really did and saw and even smelled. Unsurprisingly after 16 years, we just have to rely on what we are told about the main tangible clues – the 'coniine bottle' clue; the 'jasmine scent bottle' clue; the 'beer glass' clue; the 'beer bottle' clue; and the 'pipette' clue.

Since Poirot says "It is enough for me to sit back in my chair and *think*", readers may assume that that is what he will do. But in fact he helps Meredith row a boat from Handcross Manor to Alderbury (and back) and climbs a steep path; and, as well as the 'Carla letter' clue in which Caroline asserts her innocence, he gets two other letters – Caroline's letter to Angela (the 'Angela letter' clue) and a letter from Amyas to Elsa (the 'Elsa letter' clue). In the laboratory, which he visits twice before the denouement there, he sees Meredith fling up a window (the 'unfixed window' clue) and smell the jasmine (the 'jasmine' clue) and he sees Amyas' nearly finished painting of Elsa (the 'picture' clue).

The picture was of a girl in dark-blue slacks and a canary-yellow canvas shirt, open at the neck ("and not another thing, I should say!", says Hale), sitting on a grey battlement in full sunlight against a background of violent blue sea. When Poirot sees what Amyas had called his best picture, he realises what a superb artist he had been. The girl was all there could be of life, of youth, of sheer blazing vitality. The face was alive and the eyes, insolent with triumph, were watching Poirot … watching him … telling him something.

In the penultimate chapter, Poirot says that, although we cannot tell how much Amyas' conscious mind knew as he was dying, "his hand and his eye were faithful" and he adds "I should have known when I first saw the picture". Both remarks plainly mean that he thinks that the picture, with its telltale eyes, is giving him a clue. When he sees it, he wonders if the real woman could tell him what the eyes were saying or whether they were saying something she didn't know.

The real woman does admit in the final chapter that she never felt so powerful than when she watched Amyas die. But it is unlikely that, even if the stiffening Amyas realised what she had done, he could have captured her eyes so as to provide a clue that her triumph was not in winning him from Caroline but in watching him die, and more unlikely still if the real woman's eyes were not knowingly saying this. Nevertheless, readers are told that the picture was telling Poirot something and, if it was therefore intended as a clue, it is hard to see how the 'picture' clue could be a clue against anyone other than Elsa.

As to the *whydunnit*, Poirot says that the reason for murder is nearly always found by studying the person murdered (Book I chapter 7). We know that Amyas was always getting mixed up with other women; that he had always returned to Caroline; and that he wanted to finish his picture. But readers need more clues than that to deduce that after finishing he would cruelly send Elsa packing and return to Caroline *this time*.

In fact, however, apart from some really quite difficult clues, all the others suggest that he would be *leaving* Caroline. Thus, remarks by Philip, Meredith and Miss Williams indicate that the relationship with Elsa was "different" and "serious" and other clues suggest that he *would* marry her – his admission that this was true; her 'idea' for his divorce; Caroline's thoughts of suicide; and, especially, the 'Elsa letter' clue, a most telling letter from Amyas (never suggested to be false) in which he says "I'm crazy about you – I can't sleep – I can't eat. Elsa – Elsa – Elsa – I'm yours for ever – yours until death".

So, led down this false path, no reader could have spotted that Elsa was just another of Amyas' women until Philip overhears Caroline cry in the library on the fatal morning "You and your women! I'd like to kill you. Some day I will kill you". Poirot treats her cry as providing two clues.

First, the opening words put Elsa in a class with Amyas' *other* women. This 'You and your women' clue is quite good but very difficult to spot because of Elsa's (untruthful) account of the rest of the conversation in which she claims she overheard Caroline say "Sooner than let you go to that girl *I'll kill you*".

Secondly, says Poirot, Caroline had added that she would kill Amyas because she was revolted by his cruelty *to Elsa* – and so the words were a clue, not to Caroline's intention to kill him, but to *his* intended cruelty. That 'cruelty' clue is supported, so Poirot suggests, by Caroline murmuring after the library scene "It's too cruel!", which he says she did because she was thinking of *Elsa*. But readers would again do extremely well to interpret the 'cruelty' clue as Caroline commenting on Amyas' behaviour towards Elsa, not herself.

There is another difficult clue before the library scene, on the day before the murder. Meredith suggests that Amyas should return to Caroline. Amyas pats him on the back and assures him, *according to Poirot*, that the whole thing is "going to pan out all right" – thus indicating he would return. The problem with this 'all right' clue is that, when Amyas patted Meredith, he did not actually say that. He said it later but at this point he said "you'll admit I was right". Saying "*I*" was right does not have the same import at all as saying that "*the whole thing*" is going to pan out all right because he could just mean that *he* was right about not returning to Caroline.

Another clue comes on the fatal morning after Meredith has realised that some coniine is missing and rows across the creek to discuss this with Philip. They overhear Amyas and Caroline arguing in the Battery, Elsa having gone up to the house to fetch a pullover. Caroline then speaks to the Blakes by the Battery door and, so Poirot suggests, murmurs something about Angela and school so that, by a natural association of ideas, the Blakes judged that Amyas had referred to *Angela* during the argument and said "I'll see to her packing".

Poirot, however, interprets the 'packing' clue as Amyas actually saying about *Elsa* "I'll send her packing" because it would be "absurd" for Amyas to pack for Angela when this was a woman's job. Although this 'packing' clue is a bit contrived, it is quite clever but not as scrupulous as it should be because the Blakes did *not* think that they were talking about Angela and schooling by "a natural association of ideas"; they thought so because, according to both the Blakes, Caroline *expressly said* that that was what they were talking about.

The final clue as to Amyas' intentions is most unusual. In Book III chapter 2 Poirot suggests correctly that at the time of the tragedy Angela had recently read Somerset Maugham's *The Moon and Sixpence*. That 1919 story is about a painting genius who callously discards a model, who had loved him with all her heart, because he had only really wanted her to paint her; he says (chapter 41) "When I'd finished my picture I took no more interest in her".

It seems that Poirot is indicating Amyas' real intentions by '*The Moon and Sixpence*' clue. But it is an odd clue because he never explains the book's significance and it is hard to discern from what Angela says or writes how he knows she had read it. Maybe the answer is to be found in her row with Amyas at dinner when she wished that he would, among other things, die of leprosy – an unusual fate but one that befalls Maugham's painter.

Turning to Elsa, Fogg tells us that "She was honest. Admirably honest". That misleading clue is thankfully mitigated by Poirot's later thought that "She might lie from necessity but never from choice", which is quite important because, apart from questioning Philip's frankness about Caroline, it is the only time he wonders about one of the suspects lying.

We also know that Amyas meant so much to Elsa that she had felt only emptiness since his death; that she thought they were made for each other; and that she had got to have him. But, for readers to deduce that, when she suffered a brutal shock, she would react by murdering him, they need more than that – namely, as Poirot says, not only her assumptions that Amyas had the same deep passion for her, that their passion was for life and that he would leave Caroline for her but also her frightening single-mindedness.

All the same clues suggesting that Amyas and Elsa's relationship was serious and lasting again apply, ensuring that – despite our being led down a false path (offset only by difficult clues) for *Amyas* – the clueing of *Elsa's* assumptions about the relationship is very strong; as is her single-mindedness in various remarks by Depleach, Jonathan, Philip and Miss Williams and Elsa herself. Even being the little pig who ate roast beef makes her the most likely one to get what she wanted.

However, her most probable victim is surely Caroline; as Fogg says, "she might have polished off Caroline, but certainly not Amyas". So there has to be another element explaining *why* she murdered Amyas and a problem is that, of the two candidates for Elsa's motive, her jealousy motive (against Caroline) is much more strongly clued than her vindictiveness motive (against Amyas) because five remarks support it, two from Hale and three from Elsa herself.

Another problem for readers is that it is also hard to spot *why* Elsa would feel jealous or vindictive. Prior to the library scene, she does learn that Amyas told Angela that marrying Elsa was a joke but that remark can be discounted because Elsa just smiles, no doubt presuming that Amyas said it to stop Angela's questions. So the only relevant event is the library scene and readers would do very well to spot what was really said, let alone that Elsa had had a brutal shock, not just because of her untruthful description of the scene but also because, when Philip saw her by the library window, she rose "cool as a cucumber", smiled, said "Isn't it a lovely morning?" and talked to him for five minutes.

Nevertheless she had had a shock, which brings us to her murder plan, the *howdunnit*. Poirot starts by concluding that Caroline took the coniine, despite five people being in the laboratory (he means five *other* people since six were there – although, oddly, Meredith omits Amyas when listing them). She could take it because she was last to leave and Meredith had his back to the room, so could not see what she was doing.

Poirot gets "indirect confirmation" of this from Meredith smelling jasmine through the open laboratory window. He says that the smell could not have come through the window because the murder happened in September and yet jasmine blooms in June and July. So it would have finished flowering, confirming that the smell had come from elsewhere – Caroline's jasmine scent bottle. This 'jasmine' clue is a good one because readers who don't know when jasmine blooms get help from Poirot: when he first visits the laboratory in April, he puts a hand through the window and pulls off a spray of leaves just breaking from their woody stem. So, if the leaves were breaking in April, would the jasmine really be flowering as late as September?

As for Elsa *seeing* Caroline take the coniine, Poirot says that, when Meredith had his back to the room, he was standing in the doorway talking to Elsa, meaning that she would have been *facing* him and so could see Caroline over his shoulder. This 'facing' clue seems quite clever but it has some small weaknesses – first, Meredith never says that he was standing in the doorway; secondly, Elsa would not necessarily have been facing him; and, thirdly, that, if he had been standing there and Elsa had been facing him, she would have done well to have seen over his shoulder what Caroline was doing.

Elsa later finds the coniine in Caroline's room, goes down to the Battery, pours out some beer and poisons it – all very simple – which resonates with Poirot's discussion with Angela about a limited imagination predisposing one to murder. Readers who remember the description of Elsa's house – "Merely 'expense no object', allied to a lack of imagination" – and Philip's comment that she was "lacking in imagination" may wonder if Poirot's discussion with Angela was a clue to Elsa being the murderer.

So far there is nothing that seems "psychologically incorrect" to Poirot. But then we come to the "incongruous" behaviour of Caroline who, despite threatening Amyas in the library, goes down to the Battery, apparently to have a trivial argument about Angela's schooling, and then, when he says that the beer is hot, offers to bring some iced beer. What the 'iced beer' clue reveals is not, as Hale suggests, that Caroline was acting "funny" for someone not on speaking terms with Amyas but, rather, that she *was* on speaking terms (Amyas having said in the library that he would not see Elsa after the picture), which explains her behaviour and is clever of the author.

Then Philip, after being told about Angela's schooling, notices that Amyas staggers, which Poirot says was the first sign of the coniine working, meaning that it had been administered *before* Caroline brought down the iced beer. So, even though Elsa says that Amyas complained of stiffness and pains after drinking Caroline's beer, Caroline cannot have poisoned him in that beer – though a weakness of the 'stagger' clue is that it could simply have been caused, as Philip thought, by Amyas *drinking* (rather than being poisoned).

A better clue that Amyas had already been poisoned is that, according to Hale, he said, after drinking Caroline's iced beer, "Everything tastes foul today". The fact that "Everything" tastes foul is a good, though quite obvious, clue that he had drunk something foul (Elsa's poisoned beer) *before* that iced beer. The issue with the 'foul beer' clue is how Hale knows what Amyas said. He could only have got this from Caroline, who would hardly have implicated the beer she thought Angela had poisoned, or Elsa whose written account says that Amyas remarked that *Caroline's* beer tasted foul, not *everything*.

A similar clue, not mentioned by Poirot, is the 'hot beer' clue – Amyas' complaint to Caroline that the beer down there was hot. Some readers will wonder whether he knew this because he had already had a drink.

However, the main clue that Caroline didn't poison Amyas is Miss Williams' 'wiped bottle' clue – so significant that Poirot says it is "the only thing I need to tell me definitely, once and for all" that Caroline did not kill Amyas. The nub, of course, is that, if Caroline had poisoned Amyas, she would have known that the coniine was in the *glass* – and yet Miss Williams saw her wipe the *bottle*, showing that she (mistakenly) thought it contained poison.

An oddity of the clue is that, unlike Miss Williams (who only mentions the bottle), Depleach refers to Caroline wiping *both* bottle and glass and pressing Amyas' fingers on "them" while Hale also refers to Caroline wiping *both* bottle and glass and then pressing Amyas' fingers on "it" (a confusing use of the singular). If they are right – that Caroline wiped both – that doesn't matter because her innocence does not depend on wiping the fingerprints off the glass; it depends on her wiping the fingerprints, unnecessarily, off the *bottle*.

Despite the apparent brilliance of Poirot's deduction, readers should have remembered that the poison was in the glass and wondered why Caroline wiped the fingerprints from the bottle. Indeed, the police or Caroline's Counsel should have wondered about this. Even more surprising is that Caroline herself, who must have learned that the poison was not in the bottle by no later than the trial, didn't then realise that Angela, who only touched the bottle, could not have killed Amyas. So, although the 'wiped bottle' clue is a good one, it really should have been spotted and interpreted 16 years before.

As to the clueing of the two sub-plots, various clues would have suggested to Caroline that Angela might have killed Amyas – her argument with him (when she threw the paperweight); her guilty look while unscrewing the bottle which, according to Poirot (though readers are not told this until his explanations), she gave to Caroline; and Amyas' remark about the foul beer. Angela might have poisoned the beer either, says Poirot, as a revenge on Amyas – perhaps not meaning to kill him but playing one of her pranks – or for Caroline's sake because she resented Amyas' desertion of her.

As for a revenge prank, this had been clued five times – putting ten slugs in Amyas' bed; putting a slug or something down his back; putting salt into his drink; pinching "cat stuff" to put in his drink (which actually refers to the minor sub-plot, though this is not apparent at the time); and putting a hedgehog in his bed.

As for killing Amyas for Caroline, Poirot regards the paperweights thrown by Caroline and Angela as important, even italicising *paperweight*. The 'paperweight' clue's significance for him is that Angela reminded Caroline of "her own undisciplined violent emotions at Angela's age" (though their ages when throwing them were rather different – 15 and 19), leading her to think, one assumes, that a motivated and guilty looking Angela could kill Amyas.

We also get clues that Caroline was shielding someone – the 'wiped bottle' clue; her claim of suicide; her defeatist attitude at trial; her acquiescence in her fate – and clues that the shielded person was Angela – comments from Jonathan, Meredith, Miss Williams and Angela herself about Caroline not forgiving herself for throwing the paperweight; as well as Caroline's determination to get Angela away from Alderbury; to get her out of England and away from the trial; to get her to school abroad and away from the prison – because she was terrified that Angela might confess.

The clue on which he places greatest emphasis, however, is "*That at no time did Caroline Crale protest her innocence*" (except in the 'Carla letter' clue). Despite his italics, he is wrong because Fogg tells us (twice) that, when accused at the trial, she said "Oh, no – no, I didn't". And her assertion that Amyas committed suicide is also an indirect protestation of innocence.

Poirot is correct, however, in saying that the 'Angela letter' clue written after the trial has no protestation of innocence. That is because Caroline thought Angela was guilty, making a protest to *her* unnecessary. Moreover, by saying "It's all right" four times in the letter and saying "One must pay one's debts", Caroline was trying to stop Angela confessing so that she could repay her debt. An oddity, if the 'Angela letter' clue shows Caroline's wish to repay her debt, is that she should protest her innocence in the 'Carla letter' clue which could, years later, have undermined her wish.

Nevertheless the 'Angela letter' clue provides a good one about Caroline's intentions, the better for being naturally read wrongly as an acceptance by her of her punishment for killing Amyas, with even Poirot reading the letter as a confession at first: "Now, even her own words testified against her".

In fact Caroline was wrong about Angela, who was just pursuing her revenge prank of putting valerian, taken from the laboratory, in Amyas' beer. We get clues that she may have gone across to Handcross Manor that morning – her bathing dress was missing; she could swim across the creek (she did so later with Philip); and Miss Williams thought she had done so. However, when hearing movements in his laboratory, Meredith thought that a cat had probably got in through the window which was open just wide enough to admit one.

So, how do we know that Angela could have got in? The simple answer is that the window was not fixed – the sash moved freely. Meredith never told us that and so Poirot would not have had the 'unfixed window' clue unless he had visited the laboratory and seen Meredith fling up the window.

And how do we know that she took valerian (not coniine)? She told Poirot that she pinched "cat stuff" to put in Amyas' drink; and Meredith had earlier told Poirot that valerian attracted cats. So an astute reader might have worked out that by her 'cat stuff' clue Angela meant valerian. Its smell provides Poirot with a neat but minor clue: after she had taken it, Meredith smelled its unpleasant odour and that is what made him think that a cat had got in.

However, a reader would need to be very astute to link Angela's statement that she pinched "cat stuff" with Meredith's statement that the noise was "probably caused by a cat getting in" so as to deduce that Angela pinched the cat stuff on the fatal morning. It is not that the statements occur at different places or that Angela's 'cat stuff' clue is partly concealed by being twinned with putting a hedgehog in Amyas' bed (both good clueing devices) but rather that there is no indication from Angela when she pinched the cat stuff.

Having done so, she could not put it into the bottle because of Caroline coming into the conservatory. Poirot had spotted this because, when Angela had told him about pinching cat stuff to put in Amyas' drink, she had said "*to put in*", not that she had *done* so. This very subtle 'future tense' clue is highly unlikely to be spotted by readers even though (and this is a point Poirot doesn't make) she contrasts the cat stuff *to put in* Amyas' drink with the hedgehog which she *put* in Amyas' bed.

There are many clues in the story but it never feels that there are too many for such a dense plot. The two which Poirot emphasises most, the 'wiped bottle' and 'Angela letter' clues, are good but they are, along with other good clues such as the 'jasmine' and 'iced beer' clues, not clues to the murderer.

There are some pretty good clues to the murderer but it is almost impossible to spot that Elsa had a brutal shock in view of the way she behaves almost immediately afterwards. It is similarly frustrating that Amyas' real intentions are not consistent enough with the way that his relationship with Elsa is repeatedly clued as different and serious, leaving readers to spot those intentions through various difficult clues.

The strongest clues to the murderer are the motive attributed (mainly by her) to Caroline and the clues which support her assumptions about her relationship with Amyas. But the two most memorable clues, in addition to the 'wiped bottle' clue, are the 'picture' clue and '*The Moon and Sixpence*' clue (respectively revealing Elsa's triumph in watching Amyas die and Amyas' real intentions with regard to Elsa); they are both most unusual because it is hard to believe that they are clues and yet they must be included for a reason.

ENDNOTES

Preface

1 The website of her publishers, HarperCollins, refers to her as "quite simply, the best-selling novelist in history". She has been outsold only by the Bible and Shakespeare. Her books have sold over a billion copies in the English language and another billion in 44 foreign languages. She is "known throughout the world as the Queen of Crime" and has been "translated into more languages than Shakespeare". The website shows that there were new paperback reissues in the UK of about 50 of her detective novels in 2015–2017. She is also the author of the world's longest running play, *The Mousetrap.*

2 Although no author purports to provide comprehensive puzzle analyses:

   a) Dr Gill provides a ten page (p.40–49) 'unjumbling' of the clues and summary of the plot in *The Mysterious Affair at Styles*, which generally speaking is very good, if largely uncritical. She also provides similar commentaries on *Cards on the Table* (p.137–148) – though her focus there is more on character than on puzzle elements – and on the double murder plot in *The Body in the Library* (p.192–196) and its "elegant simplicity and economy" compared with *Styles*.

   b) Professor Cawelti considers the balance between detection and mystification in two works, "one of which is her finest and the other one of her biggest failures" (p.112) – her "finest" being *One Two Buckle My Shoe* (which Morgan also chooses [p.318–319] as her example to explain the genesis of a plot) and the failure being *Third Girl*.

c) Professor Barnard considers "Three Prize Specimens" (p.71): *Hercule Poirot's Christmas* (where he looks at a number of the clues but expressly avoids looking "too closely at the mechanics of the murder" in this story which he regards [p.46] as "good average Christie"); *Five Little Pigs* (where his focus is on the "psychological depth" of the novel springing from its structure, characterisation and style – but it "is also a detective story, and a very good one"; indeed in his view [p.85] "the best Christie of all"); and *A Murder is Announced* (where, although there is reference to verbal and typographical [i.e. textual] clues, the focus is on how memorably the author gets the book moving and on her success at social and domestic commentary).

d) Professor Barnard also says (p.187) that *The ABC Murders* is "analysed at length in Ramsey" but actually Ramsey chooses that book (p.62–67) in order just to discuss "how a detective plot is put together" (p.34).

e) Dr J. C. Bernthal produces a very good 'sketch' (p.173) of the plots in *Sleeping Murder*, *Crooked House* and *They Do it with Mirrors* in chapter 5 of *Queering Agatha Christie* but his focus is on the characters in the context of their families rather than on the puzzle elements.

Chapter 1 - Agatha Christie's Crime Novels

1 Julian Symons gives us a historical perspective on her later works in three books. In *Bloody Murder* he says (p.135, First Edition; p.136, Third Edition) "Her work stayed at its peak until roughly the end of the Second World War" after which there was, subject to some exceptions, "a slow decline". In his chapter in Keating's *Agatha Christie* he says (p.34) that the 1940s "more or less maintained this high level, but after that the decline was steady and near the end it was steep". In his Foreword to Riley

& McAllister he says (p.xv) "It is accepted also that her work showed a decline from the middle fifties onwards that became steep towards the end of her life."

2 Julian Symons in Keating's *Agatha Christie* (p.33) says "If one prefers Poirot it is not only because he is an altogether livelier character, but also because his insights are more rational and less inspirational than Miss Marple's". I interpret this as Symons saying that he *does* prefer Poirot and I find it very surprising that Professor Barnard is able to assert so definitely (p.97) "There is no doubt that most Christie addicts prefer Miss Marple as a detective to Hercule Poirot". I have not seen this generalisation borne out by any of the books I have read about Christie or her detectives, although I can understand Martin Edwards saying (p.155) that Miss Marple's "very ordinariness made her a much more attractive character to many readers than the brilliant egotist Poirot" since he is referring to her as a 'character' rather than as a 'detective'.

3 These adjectives come from various commentators – "rudimentary" from Barnard; "stereotyped" from Barnard, Gill, Bargainnier, Bernthal and others; "cardboard" from Barnard, Robyns, Gill, Bargainnier and Bernthal (referring to Symons); "schoolgirlish" from Robert Graves; "lacking feel" and "vividness", "journeyman" and "simple" from Barnard; and "pedestrian" from Morgan. Perhaps the two most interesting are "schoolgirlish" from the writer Robert Graves in the *New York Times Book Review* of 25 August 1957, referred to in Sanders and Lavallo (p.212) and Thompson (p.382), despite the author having dedicated *Towards Zero* to him in 1944; and "pedestrian" from Morgan (p.260), who goes on to say (p.321) "She could sometimes write extraordinarily badly, her grammar uncertain and her sentences full of tired metaphors". That sentence, perhaps the most critical about Christie's style from someone with no apparent anti-detective story axe to grind, is particularly surprising, given that Morgan was, as her book says, the person invited by Christie's daughter to write the definitive biography and allowed sole access to family papers. The criticism even remains in her 2017 edition (p.321) for which she produced an

updated Foreword. One does not know what she had in mind but, picking a couple of examples from a book chosen at random (*Peril at End House*), she may have been thinking of sentences like "And then I saw at last to what he had been trying to draw my attention" (chapter 1) and "At that moment I bethought me of the strange attitude of the maid, Ellen" (chapter 9).

4 As Laura Thompson insightfully puts it (p.397) "When Agatha is writing at her best, the two separate components of her books – the puzzle and the people – achieve a perfect synthesis."

Chapter 2 - The Puzzle Element

1 Haycraft in *Murder for Pleasure* says (p.228) "Structurally speaking, the first thing to know about the detective story is that it is conceived not forward and developmentally as are most types of fiction, but *backward*. Each tale, whether novel or short story, is conceived solution-foremost in the author's mind, around a definite central or controlling idea." Symons in *Bloody Murder* says (p.182 First Edition, p.191 Third Edition) that the plot of a detective story is "Based on a deception" and that the book is "constructed backwards from this deception". The author's quotation comes from an article by Francis Wyndham in the *Sunday Times* of 27 February 1966, which may well be inaccessible to readers but is quoted by, for example, Professor Bargainnier (p.144).

2 These examples are taken from Osborne (p.45), Morgan (p.121) and Fremlin in Keating's *Agatha Christie* (p.115). Oddly Sanders and Lavallo (p.35) attribute *The News Chronicle* quotation to the *Daily Sketch* while Osborne says that the *Daily Sketch* thought it "the best thriller ever".

3 In Symons' Foreword to Riley & McAllister he says (p.xv) "Her supreme skill was in the construction of plot, and she has never been excelled as a creator of deceptive puzzles." And in Symons' chapter in Keating's *Agatha Christie* he says (p.27) "and it is as a constructor of plots that she stands supreme among modern crime writers." It is odd therefore that he says in *Bloody Murder*

(p.134, First Edition and p.136, Third Revised Edition) that "Her skill was not in the tight construction of plot". I am unable to rationalise the first two statements with the third. I can only say that the first two are obviously right.

Chapter 3 - Poirot's Golden Age Puzzles

1   As Detection Club President, Martin Edwards, suggests in his authoritative and very impressive *The Golden Age of Murder* (p.12), the term 'The Golden Age of Detective Fiction' was first used by John Strachey in *The Saturday Review*, January 1939.

2   1920–1945 is the period given by Curran, *Secret Notebooks* (p.29), which I happily adopt for Christie's work, although, as Martin Edwards says (p.106), opinions vary about how long the Golden Age lasted. Bargainnier (p.4) suggests the period between the two Wars (1918–1939), which Bernthal (p.4) also uses as his "rough timeframe" while Panek starts earlier (1914–1940). Symons' chapters on the Golden Age in *Bloody Murder* (8 and 9) are entitled "the Twenties" and "the Thirties"; and Edwards says (p.106) that it is difficult to argue with Symons defining the Golden Age as the period between the two World Wars, while also pointing out that Christie and her disciples continued to produce new books, and enjoy much success, long after that. He adds (p.403) that Neville Chamberlain's announcement of War (September 1939) also announced "in effect, the end of the Golden Age of detective fiction", although, for those who would argue for a later date, he refers in the opening chapter of his book about the Golden Age (p.6) to 39 members of the Detection Club being elected between 1930 and "the end of the Second World War" (when he could have referred to 1939 since no new members were elected during the War) and near the start of his book he has a list of members elected 1930–1949.

3   There is some uncertainty as to whether *Five Little Pigs* should be regarded as having been published in November 1942 or

January 1943 in the UK. (In the USA it was published in May 1942). The UK copyright is 1942 but the UK reviews appeared in January 1943. In fact, this is all rather academic in relation to Poirot's natural break since *The Hollow* was published at least four years later in September and November 1946 in the USA and the UK respectively.

4   Tuppence Cowley/Beresford (twice); Anne Beddingfeld; Lady Eileen Brent (twice); Jane Marple (twice); Emily Trefusis; Lady Frances Derwent; Bridget Conway; and Vera Claythorne.

1 - *The Mysterious Affair at Styles*

1   Dr Harkup (p.251): This was before research debunked the claims that it acted as one.

2   The *double jeopardy* rule – which barred a person from being tried a second time after he had already been tried and acquitted – was part of the English common law for hundreds of years before the Criminal Justice Act 2003. That Act, resulting mainly from Stephen Lawrence's murder in south-east London in 1993, permitted retrials for serious crimes like murder. In that case Gary Dobson, who had (with two others) been acquitted in 1996, was retried (with a different person) in 2011 and found guilty.

3   Section 18 of the Wills Act 1837. This was even the case when a will – such as the will made by Emily in favour of Alfred on their engagement – was made in favour of the very person whom the testator was to marry (although this was later changed by section 177 of the Law of Property Act 1925). That engagement will in favour of Alfred would have revoked the will made the previous August in favour of John (both those wills are mentioned in chapters 5 and 11) so, although at the trial John's Counsel says that the will in his favour had been revoked by Emily's re-marriage, in fact it would have been revoked by the engagement will.

4   Section 24 of the Statute of Frauds 1677 (Halsbury's Laws, 1st Edition, 1910, Volume XI, *Descent and Distribution*, Part IV para 33, page 16).

2 - *The Murder on the Links*

1   As the first and later editions confirm, this novel is called *The Murder on the Links*, although some commentators omit the first word *The*, as the author does in *An Autobiography* (Parts V and VI).

2   At 12.10 am (chapter 21) or 12.17 am (chapters 5 and 12), the latter presumably being correct since it is spelled out fully in chapter 12 as "seventeen minutes past twelve".

3   Hastings starts the novel with an anecdote about a young writer who, in order to catch an editor's attention, opens his story with the sentence "'Hell!' said the Duchess". This must just be an anecdote since not even Gemma O'Connor's *First Lines* (Wolfhound Press, 1985) identifies a book that begins *'Hell!' said the Duchess*, despite her actually using that title as an alternative one for her book. Although there is a book with the title *Hell! said the Duchess* (by Michael Arlen), it was not published until 1934 and so postdates Hastings' anecdote. Hastings' own narrative has a nicely symmetrical ending ("'Hell!' said the Prince").

4   Namely, after arriving in Merlinville (and meeting Madame Daubreuil); after quarrelling with Jack on 23 May (about marrying Marthe); and on the morning of 7 June (after the tramp dies).

5   Symons in Keating's *Agatha Christie* (1977) accuses the author of "carelessness". He asserts (p.35) that Poirot says that the lead-piping "has been used" to *disfigure* the victim's face (the tramp's face), even though it is described merely as "terribly convulsed". Pendergast (2004) also says that the lead-piping "was used" to disfigure the corpse (p.316). However, Poirot did *not* say that the lead-piping "has been used" or "was used". He said that the lead-piping's purpose was "To disfigure the victim's face so that it would be unrecognisable" (chapter 21); Renauld was killed *before* he could use it for that purpose. So there is no "carelessness". However, Osborne (1982), again referring to "carelessness" (so apparently copying Symons' criticism), not only says (p.27) that the lead-piping "was used" but compounds his error by

describing Renauld's face (chapter 4), which was never going to be disfigured, instead of the tramp's convulsed face (chapter 14).

3 - *The Murder of Roger Ackroyd*

1   In *An Autobiography* (Part IX section Two) the author suggests that Miss Marple arose from the pleasure she had taken in portraying Caroline.

2   The idea of the narrator as villain had been used by the author in a thriller, *The Man in the Brown Suit* (1924), in which extracts from the villain's diary comprised eight of the 36 chapters. Extending the idea from diary extracts to a novel, and in the much more challenging structure of a detective story with a Watson narrator, appears to have come (as indicated in *An Autobiography* and by various commentators) from Christie's brother-in-law, James Watts, and/or Lord Mountbatten, although the book is dedicated to Punkie (Christie's sister, Madge, wife of James Watts). Unfortunately, as Dr Curran points out (*Secret Notebooks* p.44), no notes or outlines exist for the novel.

3   No doubt he means *The Man in the Brown Suit* and *The Murder of Roger Ackroyd*.

4   These include Sheppard saying "To tell the truth" twice in the first five paragraphs of the book (doesn't he normally?); being "considerably upset and worried" at Mrs Ferrars' death and "secretly" agreeing with Caroline (chapter 1); withholding information from Caroline (chapters 1, 3 and 9); reading detective stories (a minor point but made three times – chapters 2, 6 and 11); being "greedy" and investing in a gold mine (chapter 3); being "very uneasy" going into Ackroyd's study (chapter 4); feeling a "momentary throb of anxiety" when remembering Ralph with Mrs Ferrars (chapter 4); being "startled" to see Parker when leaving the study (chapter 4); being "very much startled" by Davis' reference to blackmail (chapter 6); advising Flora not to drag Poirot into the case (chapter 7); being momentarily silenced by Flora when she mentions his visit to the Three Boars and then choosing his words "carefully"

(chapter 7); not telling Poirot everything about Ralph or his "real thought" (chapters 7 and 9); being grumpy about Caroline speaking to Poirot (chapter 10); feeling "rather uneasy" about her helping Poirot (chapter 14); and hating to part with information (chapter 16, and later in 21).

5   We learn in chapter 23 that the young man (from Curtis and Troute – chapter 8) from whom Ackroyd bought the dictaphone represented The Dictaphone Company. "Dictaphone" was the name of the dictating device produced by Alexander Graham Bell's Volta Laboratory, established in 1881. By 1907 the Dictaphone was so successful that it was synonymous for all such devices and that year it became a trade mark of the Columbia Graphophone Company who created a separate company for the Dictaphone in 1923.

6   Given the earlier reference to the 'rules' of detective fiction, one should add that this appears to be a breach of Van Dine's Rule 1 ("The reader must have equal opportunity with the detective for solving the mystery. All clues must be plainly stated and described.") and Knox's Commandment No. 8 ("The detective must not light on any clues which are not instantly produced for the inspection of the reader"). But we do learn of the dictaphone before Sheppard's exposure. However, with the steward's wireless message from the *Orion*, although Poirot receives it before Sheppard's exposure (enabling him to say "I know – now"), we do not know who it is from or what it says until *afterwards*; and nor do we know until then that Sheppard's legacy is a lie. However, those issues are not relevant to the narrator controversy because they are revelations by Poirot, not Sheppard.

7   In Pierre Bayard's ingenious book *Who killed Roger Ackroyd?* he considers (p.61) Sheppard's likely timetable during the afternoon of the murder and concludes (sensibly) that Sheppard only had two hours in which to construct his device. He describes this as "the lightning quick fabrication" of a "sophisticated device", a "complex precision instrument" and "what must have been the "first clock-radio in technological history". His point is to ridicule the prospect of Sheppard doing this within the time. But he overdoes the point. First, the device does not need to

be complex; Poirot even refers to "a simple alarm clock" – so simple that the author, who would not have claimed technical wizardry, could envisage it; in particular, it was not a "clock-radio" but just an alarm to activate an existing recording. Secondly, even if it were more complex, Sheppard was an inventor who was adjusting an alarm clock in his workshop (chapter 20) and so two hours seems ample time for him to do what he had to do.

4 - The Big Four

1   Dr Harkup (p.251).
2   The episodic nature of *The Big Four*, published in January 1927, is explained in *An Autobiography* by Christie (Part VII section Six). Ever since her mother's death on 5 April 1926 she had been unable to write but, with no money coming in following her first husband's demand for a divorce in August (all culminating in her famous disappearance in December), it was vital that she should write another book as soon as possible. Her brother-in-law, Campbell Christie, suggested that the last 12 stories published in *The Sketch* magazine should be run together, so that they would have the appearance of a book, and he helped her with the work. Research reveals that her last publications in *The Sketch* had been her weekly stories, in the series *The Man who was No.4*, which appeared every Wednesday from 2 January to 19 March 1924. *The Big Four* loosely combines those 12 short stories, after appropriate editing, in the order in which they appeared in *The Sketch*. The original titles of the short stories, which were edited into either one or two chapters in the 18-chapter novel in a plainly recognisable way, were *The Unexpected Guest*; *The Adventure of the Dartmoor Bungalow*; *The Lady on the Stairs*; *The Radium Thieves*; *In the House of the Enemy*; *The Yellow Jasmine Mystery*; *The Chess Problem*; *The Baited Trap*; *The Adventure of the Peroxide Blonde*; *The Terrible Catastrophe*; *The Dying Chinaman*; and *The Crag in the Dolomites*.

3 *The Double Clue* was first published on 4 December 1923 in *The Sketch* magazine. It first appeared in book form in the US in a collection called *Double Sin and other Stories* (1961) and in the UK in a collection called *Poirot's Early Cases* (1974).
4 Osborne (p.60) says that "Mrs Christie makes unacknowledged use of a brilliant piece of deduction which she, if not Poirot, ought to have credited to Sherlock Holmes". Presumably Osborne does not mean Sherlock Holmes but G.K. Chesterton's story *The Invisible Man* (1911) in which Father Brown, in explaining the mystery, says "Nobody ever notices postmen somehow".
5 In various editions Poirot misreads from the chess book (or the chess book is wrong) because he says that Black's second move in the Ruy Lopez opening would be "K-QB3" when it should be "Kt-QB3". In other words, it should be the knight moving, not the king.

5 - The Mystery of the Blue Train

1 This train, sometimes called *The Millionaires' Train*, was the French domestic version of the Orient Express.
2 *The Plymouth Express* was first published on 4 April 1923 in *The Sketch* magazine. It first appeared in book form in the US in a collection called *The Under Dog and other Stories* (1951) and in the UK in a collection called *Poirot's Early Cases* (1974). It is referred to in *The Murder on the Links* (chapter 2) published in May 1923.
3 Part VII section Six; Part XI section Three.
4 In fact, the author says in *An Autobiography* (Part IX section Two) that she thinks Miss Marple arose from her portrayal of Caroline Sheppard in *The Murder of Roger Ackroyd*.

6 - Peril at End House

1 We can work out that it is 1931 because Hastings refers in chapter 7 (a Monday) to "the new moon being due in three days' time" (a Thursday) and the only Thursday new moon in (or

within three days of) August between the *Blue Train* mystery (referred to in chapter 1) and 1932 (the year of publication) was on 13 August 1931. Pendergast makes a similar point (p.168) but refers to a "full moon" (which is the opposite of a "new moon") yet still concludes that the year was 1931.

2   Bargainnier (p.160) says that Nick does not enter the discussion about Seton's overdue flight and treats her silence as a clue, which is odd because she enters it four times, including in the US edition.

3   In chapter 4, when Poirot argues that Hastings, who is impressed by Challenger, is too credulous, Hastings refers to his wife as Bella. But readers of *The Murder on the Links* will remember that his wife is Dulcie, Bella's twin sister.

7 - Lord Edgware Dies

1   We are told in chapter 25 that Poirot had left because he was dealing with the strange disappearance of an Ambassador's boots (a case of cocaine smuggling). In fact, that was not a Poirot case but one of Tommy and Tuppence Beresford's cases in *Partners in Crime* (1929).

2   The Gospel according to John, chapter 13, verses 2–5.

3   It thus differs from, for example, the 'fingerprints' clue in *The Murder of Roger Ackroyd* since, unlike that clue, the engraving is deployed to *deceive* readers.

8 - Murder on the Orient Express

1   We are not told when Daisy was killed but Constantine says that the case took place "some years ago" (Part 1 chapter 7) and Masterman was in service for "some years" after the case before joining Ratchett (Part 2 chapter 3). The case brings to mind the real kidnapping in the United States in March 1932 of 20-month-old Charles Lindbergh Jr (son of the well-known aviator), who was found murdered, after payment of $50,000

ransom money, two months later. However, in that case, his parents did not die (but lived for many more years) and the kidnapper (Bruno Hauptmann) was executed in 1936.

2 When Poirot enters Mrs Hubbard's compartment to see the dagger (Part 2 chapter 14), he has to squeeze "his rotundity" past the passengers, which is odd because in the second paragraph of the first chapter of the HarperCollins 2007 edition he is a "small lean man". Odder still is that that he was just a "small man" (not "lean") in the first edition, in the Penguin edition of 1948 and the Fontana edition impressions from 1959 onwards.

3 Part 3 chapter 9 (and Part 1 chapter 5). Notably, although the passengers' luggage was searched, no bloodstained clothing was found, despite the ferocity of some of the blows and the blood on Ratchett's pyjamas which could have got onto the murderers' sleeves. It seems unlikely that the first murderer would not have peeled back Ratchett's bedlinen before stabbing him but maybe that explains it.

4 The connection between Mary and Helena gives us some clues as to when Daisy's murder might have happened. Mary has not seen Helena for over three years (Part 3 chapter 7) but it probably took place longer ago than that because, when Mary last saw Helena (who is now 20 – Part 2 chapter 7), she was probably younger than 16 or 17 because she was then a "little American schoolgirl" (Part 3 chapter 7). However, it is hard to believe that Mary, who is now 26 (Part 2 chapter 11), could have become a governess younger than 18, so Daisy's murder cannot have taken place more than eight years ago. So, perhaps six years ago for Daisy's murder would be fair – with Mary then aged 20 and Helena aged 14.

9 - *Three Act Tragedy*

1 For example, in 1922 the House of Lords in the case of *Rutherford v Richardson* [1923] AC 1 refused to allow Mrs Norman Rutherford to divorce her husband, a homicidal

lunatic in Broadmoor, saying that this was "a harsh and even inhumane result but … the law of England".

2 Dr Alfred Gordon, "Insanity and Divorce", Vol 5 *Journal American Institute of Criminal Law & Criminology* 544 (1915). Insanity became a ground for divorce in 1843 in Pennsylvania but not until 1967 in New York (where the *Rutherford* case was reported in *The New York Times* on 4 Nov 1922).

10 - Death in the Clouds

1 There is an indication in chapter 7 that it is 1935 but, since the flight was on Tuesday 18 September, the year is 1934. At the start of that year there was a French financial scandal caused by Alexandre Stavisky, alluded to by Monsieur Fournier of the Sûreté in chapter 7 and in Giselle's notebook.

2 A good point identified by Dr Curran in *Secret Notebooks* (p.205)

3 The blowpipe does, however, result in Bunson commenting (p.47) "the murder method, a blow gun, is also unique in the Christie annals"; and Cook saying (p.16) "the murder was committed using a lethal dose of snake venom on the end of a thorn, which was shot from a South American Indian blowpipe".

11 - The ABC Murders

1 Ramsey refers (p.64) to the murderer choosing victims whose initials were A.A. and B.B. However, nothing in the novel suggests that the murderer chose victims whose Christian names matched their surnames. And on the inside sleeve of the first edition, it says "Beginning with A, he murders a Mrs Ascher at Andover" (with no reference to the Christian name). It is also interesting that, as indicated by Dr Curran's *Secret Notebooks* (p.169), the author was thinking of using the names Mrs Ames, Janet Blythe and Sir Morton Clarke for the first three murders. So she was plainly not focusing on the Christian names as significant.

2　When Poirot receives the D letter, we are told that 11 September is Wednesday of the following week. So he cannot have received it later than Sunday 8 September. On the day he received it, he had visited Lady Clarke, which he had agreed to do two days before, when meeting the special legion. So that meeting cannot have occurred later than 6 September. It took place "a few days" after Clarke had visited Poirot and so that visit cannot have occurred after, say, 3 September. Clarke had proposed that visit in a letter received the day before, which cannot therefore be after 2 September, making that the latest date on which chapter 17 can really end.

3　Such a statement would be true for many people concerning 2001 when the events of 9/11 occurred.

4　In real life the 1935 St. Leger was won by the favourite, Bahram, owned by The Aga Khan, at only 4/11 – perhaps not surprising since he had already won the 2000 Guineas and The Derby

5　In *Tom Adams' Agatha Christie Cover Story* Julian Symons points out in relation to the Fontana Books cover (p.107) "Clues couldn't be shown, because there are no clues of an ordinary kind in the tale, only deductions". The cover shows *The ABC Alphabetical Railway Guide* for August 1935, with an inset picture of Betty Barnard's corpse on the beach; the belt is not shown.

12 - Murder in Mesopotamia

1　This novel has a murder plan based on the same idea as that in a Poirot short story set in a London house called *The Dream* where the victim is found shot in a room in which no one else was present when he was killed. In that case the victim is also enticed to lean out of a window but he is shot by the murderer who leans out of a window in the room next door. *The Dream* was first published in the US in *The Saturday Evening Post* in October 1937 and in the UK in *The Strand magazine* in February 1938. It first appeared in book form in the US in a collection called *The Regatta Mystery and Other Stories* (1939) and in the UK in a collection called *The Adventure of the Christmas Pudding* (1960).

13 - Cards on the Table

1   The term 'antibiotics' was not even coined until 1942.

14 - Dumb Witness

1   In *Secret Notebooks* Dr Curran analyses an unpublished Hastings short story called *The Incident of the Dog's Ball*. He persuasively concludes (p.459) that it is entirely possible that it was written in 1933 but not offered for publication because it was transformed into *Dumb Witness*.

2   Readers may think that this novel is going to be an extended version of the Poirot short story *How Does Your Garden Grow?* which was first published in the US in the *Ladies Home Journal* in 1932 and in the UK in *The Strand* magazine in August 1935 and first appeared in book form in the US in a collection called *The Regatta Mystery and Other Stories* (1939) and in the UK in a collection called *Poirot's Early Cases* (1974). In that story Poirot also receives a letter seeking discreet assistance from an elderly lady who is poisoned before he arrives at her house and who has left her money to a companion instead of to relatives. But otherwise the story is quite different.

3   In *Secret Notebooks* Dr Curran explains (p.218/458) that the first four chapters were most probably written after Hastings' narrative and then added to help the book's initial publication, a serialisation in the US, presumably by giving the book more of an English village setting. The chapters were then retained in the UK version. That may also explain why the book was her longest to date.

4   In *The Incident of the Dog's Ball* the words appear, not on a jar, but below a picture on the wall above the mantelpiece on which stood a jar in which Bob's ball was kept. As Dr Curran points out in *Secret Notebooks* (p.484), the picture can be seen at Greenway House and may have inspired the author.

15 - Death on the Nile

1 This would have been next June or July (chapters 1 and 26).
2 The words "close against the wound" appear as part of the factual narrative in chapter 12, which is a bit naughty of the author because there was no "wound".
3 This Foreword does not appear in the first edition, being originally written (with Forewords for some other books) for the Penguin paperback edition. It has since appeared in some, but not all, editions
4 In the first edition that chapter is the only one in Part I "Characters in order of their appearance". The other chapters numbered 1 to 30 are in Part II "Egypt". Later editions (such as Penguin, Pan, Fontana, HarperCollins) do not divide the book into Parts but number each chapter consecutively from the start. The more 'modern' chapter numbers are used in this commentary.
5 A cataract is a shallow length of water in which small rocks on the riverbed protrude above the river's surface. Years later, the second of the Nile's six primary Cataracts at Wadi Halfa was submerged by Lake Nasser, the large reservoir created by the Aswan High Dam constructed between 1958 and 1971.

16 - Appointment with Death

1 The common law disqualification which at that time prevented peers from sitting as Members of Parliament never applied to spouses except those who themselves held a hereditary peerage.
2 Dr Gerard actually identifies "four active principles" but in fact he "misidentifies" them according to Professor Gerald (p.161), who corrects him. Dr Harkup explains (p.95) that, of the four compounds listed by Dr Gerard, only digitalin (now known as digoxin) and digitoxin (the two relevant ones in the novel) are still prescribed today, the latter rarely.
3 See, for example, Philmore's *Inquest on Detective Stories* in the magazine *Discovery* (1938) reproduced in Part 6 of Haycraft's *The Art of the Mystery Story* (p.423).

17 - Hercule Poirot's Christmas

1　Internet searches reveal that suicidal throat-cutting is not as rare as one would instinctively expect.

2　The quotation is from Professor Barnard (p.71), although, as he also points out (p.23), it is a device of which the author makes no great use in her other work.

3　Part 2 section I and Part 3 section X.

4　Dr Curran's *Secret Notebooks* indicates (p.318) that the author's original title was *Blood Feast*.

5　Part 3 section VI; Part 4 section II; Part 5 section I; and Part 6 section V.

6　Part 1 section I; Part 2 section II; Part 3 section XIV (Pilar); Part 5 section IV (Jennifer and Juan).

18 - Sad Cypress

1　Confirmed by Dr Harkup (p.192)

2　"Come away, death" means "Come here quickly, death": The Oxford Shakespeare: *Twelfth Night*; Oxford World Classics, Oxford University Press, 2008, p.137, line 50 footnote. Also see line 51 footnote for confirmation that the songwriter wants to be laid in a black coffin of cypress wood.

19 - One Two Buckle My Shoe

1　Japp wonders if they will find her cut up in little pieces like Mrs Ruxton, the victim in a notorious murder case who was dismembered by her common-law husband in 1935.

2　He is referring to the Christmas ghost story about a bride who couldn't get out of a chest in which she had hidden while playing hide and seek and whose body wasn't found for years.

3　First, his sheet of paper in the second part of the third chapter; secondly, during his kaleidoscopic moment in church in the fifth part of the sixth chapter; and, thirdly, while walking in Regent's Park in the second part of the seventh chapter.

20 - Evil under the Sun

1   Readers may think that this novel is going to be an extended version of the Poirot short story *Triangle at Rhodes* from the collection *Murder in the Mews* (1937). In that story Poirot is also on a beach holiday, the two main couples appear to be very similar types to Patrick/Christine and Kenneth/Arlena and the victim is also the Arlena figure. However, the murder plan, the motive and the murdering couple (the Kenneth and Christine figures) are different.

2   The five previous Poirot novels in which the murder was committed *before* it appeared to have been are *The Murder of Roger Ackroyd*, *The Mystery of the Blue Train*, *Appointment with Death*, *Hercule Poirot's Christmas* and *One Two Buckle My Shoe*. The exception is *Murder on the Orient Express*, where the murderers committed the murder *after* the time at which they wanted it thought that the murderer had left the train. In other novels, the murderer was, for example, apparently impersonated, outside or incapacitated, as in *Lord Edgware Dies*, *Murder in Mesopotamia* and *Death on the Nile*.

3   Poirot's comments are from chapter 5 part 4; chapter 6 part 4; and chapter 7 part 5.

4   There is one oddity about the bath. When Poirot is discussing it with Weston towards the end of chapter 8 part 2, there is the line (in the Fontana, Pan and later editions) "No one", he said, "the bath is probably of no importance", which doesn't make sense (because "No one" is not a response to anything just said). However, the first edition starts "No, no," he said, …", which does make sense.

21 - Five Little Pigs

1   During the visit Meredith talked about the spotted hemlock (and pointed out the coniine) as well as the nasty-tasting medical herb valerian (which cats love because it contains actinidine) and afterwards he read out a scene from Plato's

Phaedo describing the death of Socrates, who was sentenced to drink a cup of hemlock in 399 BC.

2   Nor does the inconsistency, well spotted by Pendergast (p.333), that Meredith "preferred watching birds and animals to shooting or hunting them" (Book 1 chapter 4) and yet Poirot was not his "kind of fellow at all. Didn't look as though he'd ever hunted or shot" (Book 1 chapter 7).

Bibliography

Books about Agatha Christie's novels or detective fiction

Bargainnier, Earl F.: *The Gentle Art of Murder – The Detective Fiction of Agatha Christie*; Bowling Green University Popular Press, 1980

Barnard, Robert: *A Talent to Deceive – An Appreciation of Agatha Christie*; William Collins Sons & Co Ltd, 1980; Fontana Paperbacks, 1990

Barzun, Jacques and Hartig Taylor, Wendell: *A Catalogue of Crime*; Harper & Row, Publishers, 1989

Bayard, Pierre: *Who killed Roger Ackroyd?*; English Translation, Fourth Estate, 2000

Bernthal J. C.: *The Ageless Agatha Christie*; McFarland & Company, Inc, Publishers, 2016

Bernthal J. C.: *Queering Agatha Christie*; Palgrave Macmillan, 2016

Brawn, David: *Little Grey Cells: The Quotable Poirot*; HarperCollins Publishers, 2015

Bunson, Matthew: *The Complete Christie*; Pocket Books, 2000

Campbell, Mark: *Agatha Christie*; Pocket Essentials, 2001, revised 2006 and 2015

Cawelti, John G.: *Adventure, Mystery and Romance*; The University of Chicago Press, 1976

Champigny, Robert: *What Will Have Happened*; Indiana University Press, 1977

Christie, Agatha: *An Autobiography;* HarperCollins Publishers, 1977

Cook, Cathy: *The Agatha Christie Miscellany*; The History Press, 2013

Cooper, John & Pike, B. A.: *Detective Fiction The Collector's Guide;* Scolar Press, 1994 Second Edition

Craig, Patricia & Cadogan, Mary: *The Lady Investigates*; St Martin's Press, New York, 1981

Curran, John: *Agatha Christie's Secret Notebooks;* HarperCollins Publishers, 2009

Curran, John: *Agatha Christie's Murder in the Making*; HarperCollins Publishers, 2011

Edwards, Martin: *The Golden Age of Murder*; HarperCollins Publishers, 2015, Paperback 2016

Feinman, Jeffrey: *The Mysterious World of Agatha Christie;* Award Books, 1975

Fido, Martin: *The World of Agatha Christie;* Carlton Books Ltd, 1999

Fitzgibbon, Russell H.: *The Agatha Christie Companion;* Bowling Green State University Popular Press, 1980

Gerald, Michael C.: *The Poisonous Pen of Agatha Christie;* University of Texas Press, 1993

Gill, Gillian: *Agatha Christie – The Woman and her Mysteries*; Robson Books Ltd, 1990

Grossvogel, David I.: *Mystery and its Fictions from Oedipus to Agatha Christie;* The John Hopkins University Press, 1979

Harkup, Kathryn: *A is for Arsenic: The Poisons of Agatha Christie*; Bloomsbury Sigma, 2015

Hart, Anne: *Agatha Christie's Marple;* HarperCollins Publishers, 1997 Edition

Hart, Anne: *Agatha Christie's Poirot;* HarperCollins Publishers, 1997 Edition

Haycraft, Howard: *Murder for Pleasure, The Life and Times of the Detective Story;* Peter Davies, London, 1942

Haycraft, Howard: *The Art of the Mystery Story;* Carroll & Graf Publishers Inc., 1946 with a new introduction in 1992

Keating, H. R. F.: *Murder Must Appetize;* The Lemon Tree Press Ltd, 1975 revised 1981

Keating, H. R. F. (Editor): *Agatha Christie – First Lady of Crime;* Weidenfeld and Nicolson, 1977

Macaskill, Hilary: *Agatha Christie at Home;* Frances Lincoln Ltd, Publishers 2009

Maida, Patricia D. and Spornick, Nicholas B.: *Murder She Wrote – A Study of Agatha Christie's Detective Fiction;* Bowling Green State University Popular Press, 1982

McCaw, Neil: *Adapting Detective Fiction;* Continuum International Publishing Group, 2011

Milne, A. A.: *The Red House Mystery;* Methuen & Co Ltd, first edition 1922, with Introduction added by the author, April 1926

Morgan, Janet: *Agatha Christie, A Biography;* HarperCollins Publishers, 1984; paperback edition, 1997; and with an updated Foreword 2017

Morselt, Ben: *An A-Z of the Novels and Short Stories of Agatha Christie;* Phoenix Publishing Associates Ltd, 1985

Osborne, Charles: *The Life and Crimes of Agatha Christie;* HarperCollins Publishers, 1982 revised and updated 1999

Panek, Leroy Lad: *Watteau's Shepherds, The Detective Novel in Britain 1914-1940*; Bowling Green University Popular Press, 1979

Pendergast, Bruce: *Everyman's Guide to the Mysteries of Agatha Christie;* published on demand in cooperation with Trafford Publishing, 2004

Ramsey, G. C.: *Agatha Christie Mistress of Mystery;* Dodd, Mead & Company, 1967

Riley, Dick & McAllister, Pam: *The Bedside, Bathtub & Armchair Companion to Agatha Christie;* The Continuum International Publishing Group, 1979 Second Edition 2001

Robyns, Gwen: *The Mystery of Agatha Christie;* Doubleday & Company, Inc., 1978

Rodell, Marie F.: *Mystery Fiction Theory and Technique;* Hammond, Hammond & Company, 1954

Ryan, Richard T.: *Agatha Christie Trivia;* Quinlan Press, 1987

Sanders, Dennis & Lovallo, Len: *The Agatha Christie Companion;* W.H. Allen, 1985

Sova, Dawn B.: *Agatha Christie A-Z;* Facts on File, Inc., 1996

Symons, Julian: *Bloody Murder;* Penguin Books Ltd., 1972 and Third Edition 1992

Symons, Julian: *Tom Adams' Agatha Christie Cover Story;* Paper Tiger, 1981

Thompson, Laura: *Agatha Christie An English Mystery;* Headline Review, 2007

Thomson, H. Douglas: *Masters of Mystery – a Study of the Detective Story*; Collins, 1931

Toye, Randall: *The Agatha Christie Who's Who*; Frederick Muller Limited, 1980

Wagoncr, Mary S.: *Agatha Christie;* Twayne Publishers, 1986

Wagstaff, Vanessa & Poole, Stephen: *Agatha Christie A Reader's Companion*; Aurum Press Ltd, 2004

Wells, Carolyn: *Technique of the Mystery Story*; The Home Correspondence School, Springfield, Mass, 1913 and revised edition 1929

Zemboy, James: *The Detective Novels of Agatha Christie: A Reader's Guide*; McFarland & Company Inc, Publishers, 2008, reprinted 2016

Index of Titles

The 21 novels analysed in the commentaries (but see Contents page for their commentary page numbers)

Other Agatha Christie books and stories

A Murder is Announced, 1950: 16, 486

An Autobiography, 1977: 33, 491, 492, 494, 495

And Then There Were None, 1939: 16, 24, 36, 46, 319

By the Pricking of my Thumbs, 1968: 24

Crooked House, 1949: 16, 36, 486

Curtain, 1975: 16, 17, 36

Double Sin and other Stories, 1961: 495

Endless Night, 1967: 16

How Does Your Garden Grow?, 1935 (UK): 500

Mrs McGinty's Dead, 1952: 246

Murder in the Mews, 1937: 503

Partners in Crime, 1929: 496

Poirot's Early Cases, 1974: 495, 500

Postern of Fate, 1973: 24

Sleeping Murder, 1976: 16, 486

Sparkling Cyanide, 1945: 16

The Adventure of the Christmas Pudding, 1960: 499

The Body in the Library, 1942: 16, 23, 24, 301, 485

The Double Clue, 1923: 119, 495

The Dream, 1938 (UK): 499

The Hollow, 1946: 16, 45, 490

The Incident of the Dog's Ball, possibly 1933 but unpublished: 500

The Labours of Hercules, 1947: 25

The Man in the Brown Suit, 1924: 12, 24, 492

The Murder at the Vicarage, 1930: 15, 23, 24

The Plymouth Express, 1923: 495

The Regatta Mystery and Other Stories, 1939: 499, 500

The Seven Dials Mystery, 1929: 24

The Sittaford Mystery, 1931: 24

The Under Dog and other Stories, 1951: 495

They Do It with Mirrors, 1952: 486

Third Girl, 1966: 486

Gill, Gillian, *Agatha Christie – The Woman and her Mysteries*: 485, 487

Gordon, Dr Alfred, *Insanity and Divorce*, 1915: 498

Harkup, Kathryn, *A is for Arsenic: The Poisons of Agatha Christie*: 490, 494, 501, 502

Haycraft, Howard, *Murder for Pleasure, The Life and Times of the Detective Story*: 30, 32, 33, 39, 488

Haycraft, Howard, *The Art of the Mystery Story*: 34, 501

Herbert, A.P., *Holy Deadlock*, 1934: 215

John, *The Gospel*: 496

Keating, H.R.F. (Editor), *Agatha Christie – First Lady of Crime*: 486, 487, 488, 491

Keats, John, *Belle Dame Sans Merci*, 1819: 272

Kingsley, Charles, *Westward Ho!*, 1855: 461

Kingsley, Charles, *A Farewell*, 1856: 455

Knox, Ronald A., Introduction to *The Best Detective Stories of 1928*: 34, 96, 97, 493

MacEwan, Peter F.C.S., *The Art of Dispensing: A Treatise on the Methods and Processes involved in Compounding Medical Prescriptions*, published at the Offices of The Chemist and Druggist, 1888, 1900, 1912: 49, 50

Maida, Patricia D. and Spornick, Nicholas B., *Murder She Wrote – A Study of Agatha Christie's Detective Fiction*: 29

Maugham, Somerset, *The Moon and Sixpence*, 1919: 475, 483

Milne, A.A., *The Red House Mystery*, 1922, 1926: 33

Morgan, Janet, *Agatha Christie, A Biography*: 486, 487, 488

Nesbit, E., *The Railway Children*, 1906: 265, 266

O'Connor, Gemma, *First Lines*, 1985: 491

Osborne, Charles, *The Life and Crimes of Agatha Christie*: 488, 491, 495

Panek, Leroy Lad, *Watteau's Shepherds, The Detective Novel in Britain 1914-1940*: 31, 39, 489

Pendergast, Bruce, *Everyman's Guide to the Mysteries of Agatha Christie*: 491, 496, 504

About the Author

John Goddard read law at Magdalene College, Cambridge. He became a litigation partner at the City law firm Freshfields but is now retired. He lives in Wimbledon with his wife Linda. They have two adult children. And a very chatty cat.

For further information about the author and the book, see **www.stylisheyepress.com**.

Printed by Amazon Italia Logistica S.r.l.
Torrazza Piemonte (TO), Italy